Compendium

Volume Four

to

Commentary

on

The Book of Mormon

Philip M. Hudson

As they learned the principles of the
gospel, the Nephites realized that Sinai is an
attitude and is not a place. Then and now, the
faithful loose the latchets of their shoes when
they witness bushes that burn, but that are
not consumed. Holy sanctuaries, as it
turns out, can be our own creations.
More than that, they can be our
own personalized versions
of God's Rest.

Publishing Services
by BookCrafters, Parker, Colorado.
www.bookcrafters.net

Captain Moroni
delighted in "saving his people
from destruction." (Alma 55:19).
He knew that by obedience, the Lord
would prosper those who trusted
in Him, who loved Him, and
who would abide by His
commandments.

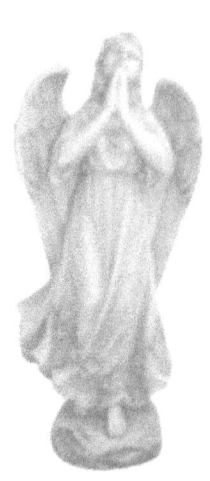

Index
to
Compendia
Volumes 3-7

Every
Nephite family
that was created thru
the power and authority of
God became another of the basic
building blocks of eternity. Today,
the Church of Jesus Christ emphasizes
the worth of the family, and it is held in
the highest esteem. It regards the family as
a definitive expression of individuality,
creativity, and interdependence. But
more than that, it is the tangible
expression of God's glory.
(See Moses 1:39).

Volume 3
Essays

It
must have been
the wish of every of
the Nephite prophets that
the Savior would not send
a famine into the land, but
instead grant that their people
might live in Bethlehem. They
knew that the habitation of the
Lord was as a house of bread
where the faithful could go
to partake of His word,
that was the true
staff of life.

Volume 3 Essays

It
must have been
the wish of every of
the Nephite prophets that
the Savior would not send
a famine into the land, but
instead grant that their people
might live in Bethlehem. They
knew that the habitation of the
Lord was as a house of bread
where the faithful could go
to partake of His word,
that was the true
staff of life.

Volume 4
Essays

Happiness, it
seems, is like a butterfly.
(See 2 Nephi 5:27). The more
we chase it, the more it will elude
us. But if we turn our attention to
selfless acts and service in behalf
of others, it will come and rest
quietly on our shoulder.
(Anonymous).

Volume 5
Essays

When they were just
eight years old, Nephite children
received the ordinance of baptism and
entered in at the strait gate. The way was
narrowly defined and invited their little
ones to be immersed as soon as they had
arrived at the age of accountability,
and then to receive the gift of the
Holy Ghost. For it was by both
water and the Spirit that
they were sanctified
to enjoy God's
gifts.

Volume 6
Essays

In the best
of times, the Nephites
consecrated their behavior
that they might secure both
the blessings and benedictions
of celestial glories, to be destined
to reign as kings and priests, and
queens and priestesses, to become
joint heirs of dominions whose
reach would be bound only
by the holy Order
of the Son of
God.

Volume 7 Essays

"Sometimes, during solitude, the Nephites heard truth spoken with clarity and freshness. Uncolored and untranslated, it spoke from within themselves in a language that was original but inarticulate, heard only with the soul, and they realized they brought it with them, were never taught it, nor could they efficiently teach it to others."
(Hugh B. Brown).

Compendium
Volume 3-7
Scriptures

The Law was not
written with ink, nor on
paper with pen, but within the
hearts of the Nephites. In the best
of times, it unerringly guided their
actions. Without conscious effort on
their part, they held securely to the
rod of iron, for they intuitively
knew it to be true. It had been
stitched into their sinews
by the power of the
Holy Ghost.

Samuel was
a humble servant of the Lord
who preached faith and repentance.
Offering the ordinances of baptism and
the Holy Ghost, he taught the gospel to a society
that was dying of spiritual thirst. There were among
his listeners in Zarahemla a few repentant guilty who
had wandered across the deserts of Idumea. (See Helaman
15:13). They sought the cleansing waters of redemption,
and longed for the healing balm of Gilead promised by
the prophet, who would be a savior on Mount Zion,
who was prepared to reveal to their open hearts
the certain knowledge of the love and
concern of their Father Who
dwelt in heaven.

Righteous Nephites and wicked Lamanites,
as well as everyone else who falls between these two
extremes, will be judged by laws to which they were
accountable during their lives. Their responsibility
before the Judgment Bar, when they are given the
opportunity to explain their behavior, will differ,
depending upon their singular circumstances.
However, the gospel doesn't discriminate, and
every Nephite and Lamanite is alike unto
God. We all enjoy the Light of Christ that
gives us the perspective to see past the
limited horizon of our vision, to act
upon our promptings, and to do
what is right. At the end of
the day, each of us has
to be individually
accountable
to God.

Moroni 10:8 - Gifts of The Spirit

Moroni 10:8 - (The) Manifestation of Spirits

Moroni 10:31 - Zion

Moroni 10:31 - (A) Standard of Excellence

Moroni 10:34 - I Have Fought a Good Fight

The Stick of
Judah has nourished the
Gentiles as manna in the
wilderness during their
journey to Christ, while
the Stick of Joseph is a
gift to the Lamanites,
as the bread of life
to the branch that
has grown up
beyond the
wall.

If you don't find what you are looking for in the Index of Volumes 3 – 7, check out this list of topics with related essay references.

When
the hearts of
the Nephites had been
bruised by the painful
recognition of their sins, it
was easier to negotiate the path
to repentance. Their hearts were
broken and softened and they were
responsive to the quiet whisperings of
the Spirit. They had become teachable,
and their faith had wrought upon them
to convict them of their sins. As soon
as they had descended into the depths
of humility to cast themselves before
the altar of Christ, that they might
trust upon His Atonement, they
were set free from their bondage
to sin. His grace blessed them
with the unfathomable gift
of His unconditional
forgiveness.

When Nephite converts joined
the church of Christ, each one was given
a gift by the Spirit. These were positive, uplifting,
motivational, and enduring. In their fiery crucible that
was the learning laboratory of life, it was their spiritual
gifts that provided them with repetitive opportunities to
vividly role-play being children of God, with the Holy
Ghost acting as their dialogue coach. For their life
lessons to be helpful, they needed to pre-play
and then re-play, and practice over and
over again until they got it right,
until they could do it with
their eyes closed.

Table of Contents

"Scripture consists not in what we read,
but in what we understand."
(St. Hilary).

The Book
of Mormon teaches us
that the Spirit works on us
to break us down with a deep
sorrow for our sins, so that we
become humble and penitent.
Only then will the Atonement
of Christ generate the power
to bind up our wounds
and heal all of our
infirmities.

Author's Note

Introduction

Essays

Of Whom
did the Nephites sing, and to
Whom did they turn when they found
themselves compelled to shout hosanna? To
the Lord of Hosts, their Redeemer. He was their
Shelter, their Refuge, and their Sanctuary.
Their Savior was Jehovah, Christ the Lord.
Surely, they believed, God would save
now, and when they were at their
best, they were determined to
praise Him forevermore,
before His throne.

Observations

Commentary, Compendia, & Observations Index

When we read The Book of Mormon, we
remember that the Spirit of God extends to each
of us the invitation to receive revelation. Upon our
acceptance of that principle, our Father in Heaven will
bless us with both light and knowledge. "No matter
what ability and talent we may possess, all must
come under this rule if they wish to know the
Father and the Son. If knowledge of them
is not obtained thru revelation, it
cannot be obtained at all."
(John Taylor).

Author's Note

These Compendia have taken on a life of their own, expanding into a collection of eight volumes of detailed information about The Book of Mormon that supplement my three volumes of Commentary. In essence, they are a distillation of my feelings that relate to The Book of Mormon. Their content is more visceral that that of the Commentary, and perhaps it more accurately reflects my personal feelings about the monumental themes that run throughout all of scripture. They summarize the more comprehensive body of work in my Commentary and showcase my feelings, in the hope that they might become living documents that not only reflect my present understanding of The Book of Mormon, but also the paradigms that expand with the utilization of new tools of discovery. It's a good bet that there is more to come. As the adage encourages, we need to "Think ourselves empty, read ourselves full, write ourselves clear, pray ourselves hot, and let ourselves go!"

Alma was determined
to warn his neighbors, and
to fulfill the commandments of
the Lord. With all of his heart and as
he received inspiration from the Holy
Ghost, he taught the gospel by precept
and by example, and by his voice,
with gentleness, and also by way
of exhortation when the Spirit
dictated, but always with
love unfeigned.

Introduction

There were very few
chinks in the armor of Mormon's
optimism, and so he must have hoped
that, although his days had been spent
in the midst of conflict, "the mystic chords
of memory, stretching from every battlefield and
patriot grave to every living heart and hearth stone
all over this broad land, would yet again swell the
chorus of the ranks of the Nephite armies, when
again touched, as surely they must be, by
the better angels of their nature."
(Abraham Lincoln).

Cicero wrote: "The first law for the historian is that he shall never dare utter an untruth. The second is that he shall suppress nothing that is true. Moreover, there shall be no suspicion of partiality or of malice in his writing." The accounts in The Book of Mormon written by the prophets Nephi, Jacob, Alma, Mormon, Moroni, and others, and abridged by the prophet-historian Mormon, were true to the mandate given by Cicero. Although, as Washington Irving brooded: "It is the rule that history fades into fable; fact becomes clouded with doubt and controversy; the inscription moulders, and columns, arches, and pyramids are but heaps of sand, and their epitaphs, nothing but characters written in the dust," yet The Book of Mormon stands as a shining example of the divine model.

It "is the witness that testifies to the passing of time. It illuminates reality, vitalizes memory, provides guidance in daily life, and brings us tidings of antiquity." It is the "evidence of time, the light of truth, the life of memory, the directress of life, committed to immortality." (Cicero, "De Oratore," ii, 36). In its pages, "the centuries roll back to the ancient age of gold." (Horace, "Odes," IV, ii, 39).

In one of the beautiful simplicities of the gospel, we are taught that the Plan allows all of us to enjoy the same access to the simplest, and yet most powerful, witness to the truth. In an inarticulate voice softer than the faintest whisper of sweet breath on the cheek, the Holy Ghost gently testifies, or bears witness, of truth. As Moroni 10:5 teaches (in a verse that is often overlooked, in favor of the previous verse): "By the power of the Holy Ghost ye may know the truth of all things."

The Holy Ghost has revealed all that is true, and has illuminated every eternal principle that has guided the minds of men and women since the dawn of history. We constantly benefit from that which He reveals. In the Last Days, when the Spirit is "poured out upon all flesh, and when "young men see visions, and old men dream dreams," (Joel 2:28), it will be the Holy Ghost Who provides the creative drive. The irony is that many will fail to recognize the source of their inspiration. Job did not. He wrote: "For God speaketh once, yea twice, yet man perceiveth it not. In a dream, in a vision of the night, when deep sleep falleth upon men, in slumberings upon the bed; then he openeth the ears of men, and sealeth their instruction." (Job 33:14-16). We cannot help but think of the experience of Joseph Smith in his bedchamber, when we read Job's description of how, at certain times, Heavenly Father chooses to communicate with His children.

All who desire to have a sure personal witnesses must carefully and prayerfully read The Book of Mormon, and then ask in faith if what they have studied is true. They will then receive the testimony of the Holy Ghost to motivate them to seek out the Priesthood and to enter into sacred covenants with God. It will be as it was on the Day of Pentecost, when Peter and others were preaching to a multitude whose hearts and minds were open and receptive to the truth. The words of the Apostles carried the weight of authority, and penetrated the hearts of their listeners to the end that they asked: "Men and brethren, what shall we do? Then Peter said unto them, Repent, and be baptized every one of you in the name of Jesus Christ for the remission of sins, and ye shall receive the gift of the Holy Ghost." (Acts 2:37-38). And on that day, there were about 3,000 souls added to the kingdom of God on earth. (See Commentary Reference to 3 Nephi 15:21-24).

A similar scenario exists today. Since the restoration of the gospel, there has been a Pentecostal outpouring of the Spirit, and those with a sincere desire to understand the will of God bring the same humble petition to the doorstep of the missionaries: "Now that we have heard your message, have put it to the test of prayerful inquiry, and have received a witness of the Spirit, what shall we do?" The response of the servants of the Lord is unequivocal: "You must exercise saving faith that leads to the waters of baptism and to continuing commitment, dedicated discipleship, selfless service, and sustained spirituality."

Shakespeare wrote: "The past is prologue." ("The Tempest," Act 2, Scene 1). The phrase was intended to imply that our

The philosopher
who observed: "When you
came into this world, you cried
and others rejoiced. When you
leave it, others will cry, and
you will rejoice," must
have read The Book
of Mormon.

past is merely a prologue, or an introduction, to the great adventure upon which we will embark if we follow through on our plans. This original interpretation teaches that what has come before on our journey through life doesn't matter in the grand scheme of things, because a new future lies before us, subject to the choices we will yet make. The human condition does not change much over time, which is one reason why the Lord has revealed The Book of Mormon in the Last Days, so that we might profit from the experiences of the Nephites who are distant from us in time and yet are so like us.

Hugh Nibley observed: "Men fool themselves, when they think for a moment that they can read scripture without ever adding something to the text or omitting something from it." Therein lies the power inherent in its study. We glean insight and understanding every time we investigate the word of God. I have learned to love the scriptures, and I often think of St. Hilary, who wrote: "Scripture consists not in what we read, but in what we understand." In these Compendia, I have consistently tried to anchor to the scriptures the ideas swirling around in my head.

Utilization of commentaries and compendia does not replace personal scripture study. The spiritual awakening that accompanies prayerful efforts to understand the mysteries of God through the study of His word cannot be achieved through another person's interpretation. Perhaps, though, my own perspectives on the eternal themes expressed within The Book of Mormon will be helpful to you as you read and seek your own guidance. It is my hope that you will use these compendia only to assist you in your own personal journey to Christ.

Our challenge is to enlist the aid of the Holy Ghost as we undertake that journey. Many years ago, Dallin Oaks wrote: "Latter-day Saints know that learned or authoritative commentaries (and compendia) can help us with scriptural interpretation, but we maintain that they must be used with caution. (They) are not substitutes for the scriptures any more than a good cookbook is a substitute for food. When I refer to "commentaries," I mean everything that interprets scripture, from the comprehensive book-length commentary to the brief interpretation embodied in a lesson or an article, such as this one."

"One trouble with commentaries," he continued, "is that their authors sometimes focus on only one meaning to the exclusion of others. As a result, commentaries, if not used with great care, may illuminate the author's chosen and correct meaning but close our eyes and restrict our horizons to other possible meanings. Sometimes, those other less obvious meanings can be the ones most valuable and useful to us as we seek to obtain answers to our own questions. This is why the teaching of the Holy Ghost is a better guide to scriptural interpretation than is even the best commentary." ("Ensign," 1/1985).

Harold B. Lee taught: "We are convinced that our members are hungry for the gospel undiluted, with its abundant truths and insights. There are those who have seemed to forget that the most powerful weapons the Lord has given us against all that is evil are His own declarations - the plain and simple doctrines of salvation as found in the scriptures." (Regional Representatives Seminar, 10/1/1970).

Bruce R. McConkie explained that "revelation is necessary because ... each pronouncement in the holy scriptures is so written as to reveal little or much, depending on the spiritual capacity of the student." ("A New Witness for The Articles of Faith," p. 71).

And so, as President Oaks continued, "the scriptures are not the ultimate source of knowledge, but what precedes the ultimate source. The ultimate source comes by revelation. We encourage everyone to make careful study of the scriptures and of prophetic teachings ... and to prayerfully seek personal revelation to know their meaning for themselves ... If we seek and accept revelation and inspiration to enlarge our understanding, we will have the mysteries of God unfolded to us by the power of the Holy Ghost."

D&C 42:45
reminds us of the
experience of Alma and
Amulek in Ammonihah. (see
Alma Chapter 14). "Live together in
love, insomuch that thou shalt weep for
the loss of them that die, and more
especially for those that have
not hope of a glorious
resurrection."

Elder McConkie also said: "I sometimes think that one of the best kept secrets of the kingdom is that the scriptures open the door to the receipt of revelation." ("Doctrines of The Restoration," p. 243). And President Oaks reaffirmed: "We do not overstate the point when we say that the scriptures can be a Urim and Thummim to assist each of us to receive personal revelation."

President Oaks enlarged upon the perspective of the young prophet: "Joseph was, by his own admission, no writer. He felt imprisoned by what he called the 'total darkness of paper, pen, and ink." (Joseph Smith to William W. Phelps, 11/27/1832, B.Y.U. Press, 2002, p. 287). He thus considered it 'an awful responsibility to write in the name of the Lord'. (Joseph Smith Papers, 1:367).

He did not suppose that he could receive the revelations perfectly, nor did the Lord ever set that standard. Joseph and his appointed brethren edited the revelations (see D&C 70:1-4) based on (that) same premise ... namely, that he represented the voice of God as he spoke in what he characterized as his own 'crooked, broken, scattered, and imperfect language'. (Joseph Smith to William W. Phelps, 11/27/1832, quoted in "Making Sense of the Doctrine & Covenants, a Guided Tour Through Modern Revelation," Steven Harper. "Personal Writings of Joseph Smith," p. 186-187).

President Oaks concluded his own epistle by stating a simple truth: "Latter-day Saints know that true doctrine comes by revelation from God, and not by worldly wisdom." (See Moses 5:58). He was in good company, for the Apostle Paul wrote that we are not capable of thinking any thing of ourselves; but we look to God for our wisdom. (See 1 Corinthians 3:5).

I could not agree more heartily with these wise words of counsel. As a matter of fact, every time I proofed my compendium (and I did this many times) I found myself scribbling additional notes in the margins and thinking to myself, "Why didn't I see that before?." That is precisely what I hope will be the experience of everyone who takes the time to read my compendia. I trust the process will motivate you to search the scriptures more carefully and to be instructed by the Spirit, as you do so, that you might be led in directions that will prove to be personally illuminating.

I would expect that my older grandchildren who read this compendium will be impacted in ways that are different from my adult children or my contemporaries. I hope that my observations will touch you differently each time you read them. When I am long-gone, perhaps the considerable thought that went into its production will generate a palpable bond that will span the years separating us. Maybe, the gulf that then divides us will not be as great, and our shared energies will pave the way to an eventual joyous reunion.

The substance
of the gospel that is found
in The Book of Mormon is not
so much the sum of "Thou shalt
not" commandments, as it is "Thou
shalt" commandments. Their composite
principles are the consummate compilation
of affirmative actions. When we are converted
to Zion's lifestyle, the relationship between the
commandments and blessings becomes blurred.
Our obedience forges an unbreakable bond with
God and His bounty. It is in the covenants of
the holy priesthood that the real power of
godliness is manifest. Without them, we
could never muster confidence in the
One who is standing at the helm
to help us negotiate dangerous
currents and navigate thru
treacherous shoals on
the vast ocean
of life.

Essays

A consuming fire
and billowing clouds of
smoke (see 2 Nephi 20:17),
as well as deeply penetrating
burnings, an ethereal light, and
a sharp and piercing spirit, are all
symbolic of the presence of the Lord,
and of the glory of God. Frequently,
they depict the splendor of celestial
realms. As Joseph Smith taught:
"God Himself dwells in
eternal fire."

Courage

"If all men had been, and were, and
ever would be like unto Moroni, behold,
the very powers of hell would have been
shaken forever; yea, the devil would
have no power over the hearts of
the children of men."
(Alma 48:7).

The process by which courage is developed is that of testing the mettle of one's convictions. We have no proof until we act on the basis of trust. Then comes the confirmation of the reality, as feelings of self-confidence grow, and our purposeful actions replace tentative overtures. This is why true courage is so intimately tied to righteousness. His way is strait. The test of mortality is, ultimately, eminently fair. The rules are simple, and the rewards are unmistakably plain. Heavenly Father will not cause us to misplace our trust in that which cannot deliver on its promises.

Truly did Paul declare, "God hath not give us the spirit of fear, but of power, and of love, and of a sound mind." (2 Timothy 1:7). Courage is clothed with that power which stems from a grateful heart and that love which only a sound mind is capable of expressing. Thus, courage manifests the desire to do what is right rather than what is expedient. Peter's admonition strikes a consonant chord with those whose actions are consistent with courage: "We ought to obey God rather than men." (Acts 5:29).

As Josiah Gilbert Holland wrote: "God, give us men and women! A time like this demands strong minds, great hearts, true faith, and ready hands. Men and women whom the lust of office does not kill. Men and women whom the spoils of office cannot buy. Men and women who possess opinions and a will. Men and women who have honor; men and women who will not lie. Men and women who can stand before a demagogue and damn his treacherous flatteries without winking. Tall men and women, sun-crowned, who live above the fog in public duty and in private thinking. For while the rabble, with their thumb worn creeds, their large professions and their little deeds, mingle in selfish strife, Lo! Freedom weeps, Wrong rules the land, and Justice sleeps." ("God Give us Men!").

Courage demands availability. Brigham Young once said something to the effect that he never counted the cost of anything. He just found out what the Lord wanted him to do, and he did it. It is this kind of total commitment and dedication that establishes a baseline for courageous action in the kingdom.

All of us are repeatedly faced with times when withdrawals must be made on our spiritual bank accounts. Courageous individuals, however, do not write checks that they cannot cash. They realize that only after deposits have been faithfully made over a period of time, can one rely on the cornucopia of comfort created by the cushion of confidence that flows from consistently courageous behavior.

Courageous individuals never thirst, because they have sent taproots down through deep gospel topsoil to the flowing fountain of living water. Carol Lynn Pearson wrote an insightful poem entitled "Short Roots," with a message that relates to the challenges faced by each of us in our everyday experiences that are tailored by a wise Heavenly Father to meet our individual needs: "The tree at the church next door to me turned up its roots and died. They had tried to brace its leaning, but it lowered and lowered, and then there it lay leaves in grass and matted roots in air, like a loafer on a summer day. "Look there," said the gardener. "Short roots – all the growth went up. Big branches – short roots." "How come?" I asked. "Too much water. This tree never had to hunt for drink." Especially in thirsty times, my memory steps outside and looks at the tree at the church next door to me that turned up its roots and died."

As the courageous quietly carry out their work, the righteousness of their cause will be revealed to them in marvelous simplicity and plainness. Walls of opposition to their progress will crumble and fall away. The Lord will comfort and succor them with the bread of life. As they travel through the harsh environment of mortality, oases will spring up in the deserts of life, and living water will slake their thirst. Their roots will be deeply embedded in the bedrock of eternally valid principles.

Those who are courageous are the architects of their own fate, even as they draw upon a power greater than themselves. Perhaps Victor Hugo heard that majestic clockwork when he wrote: "Be like a bird that pausing in her flight a while on boughs to light, feels them give way beneath her and yet sings, knowing that she hath wings." He who is courageous, is busily engaged "in the armory of thought (where he) fashions the tools with which he builds for himself heavenly mansions of joy and strength and peace ... Man is the master of thought, the shaper of condition, environment, and of destiny." (Spencer W. Kimball).

Angels will attend the courageous: "For I will go before your face," promised the Lord. "I will be on your right hand, and on your left, and my Spirit shall be in your hearts, and mine angels round about you, to bear you up." (D&C 84:88). Once one has received the anointing of courage, one "can never rest until the last enemy is conquered, death destroyed, and truth reigns triumphant." (Parley P. Pratt).

When Joan of Arc was carried to the stake, she was given the opportunity to obtain her freedom by denying her beliefs. Instead, she made this bold statement: "I know this now. Every man gives his life for what he believes. Every woman gives her life for what she believes. Sometimes people believe in little or nothing, and so they give their lives for little or nothing. One life is all we have, and we live it as we believe in living it, and then it is gone. But to surrender what you are and live without belief is more terrible than dying, even more terrible than dying young." (Maxwell Anderson, "Joan of Lorraine," Act 2, Interlude 3). Her character provided the Life Support to stand by her Decisions. Courageously, then, she faced death, ever true to her faith and to her beliefs. Such courage demands consistency with one's convictions. It is this quality of total commitment and dedication that tames the beast within and creates civility.

As a matter of fact, "to sin by silence, when words should be spoken, makes cowards of men." (Abraham Lincoln). Courage can be the moral fiber to face our demons. "It is not the critic who counts, not he who points out where the strong man stumbled or where the doer of deeds could have done them better. The credit belongs to the man who is actually in the arena, whose face is marred by dust and sweat and blood, who tries and comes short again and again, who knows the great enthusiasms, the great devotions and spends himself in a worthy cause; who, at best, if he fails, at least fails while daring greatly, so that his place shall never be with those cold and timid souls who know neither victory nor defeat." (Teddy Roosevelt, speech at the Sorbonne, Paris, 4/23/1910).

Well did Joseph Smith encourage the Saints, when he declared: "Courage, brethren; and on, on to the victory! Let your hearts rejoice, and be exceeding glad." (Joseph Smith, D&C 128:22). The courageous often turn potential stumbling blocks into stepping-stones. Crisis becomes opportunity. Victory is snatched from the jaws of defeat. They know that "change comes like a flash of lightning and a clap of thunder. The people shrink in fear, but after the storm, flowers bloom." ("I Ching"-The Chinese "Book of Change").

As Tom Paine wrote, in each of our lives there are "times that try [our] souls. Yet we have this consolation with us, that the harder the conflict, the more glorious the triumph. What we obtain too cheap, we esteem too lightly; 'tis dearness only that gives everything its value. Heaven knows how to put a proper price upon its goods; and it would be strange, indeed, if ... celestial article(s) ... should not be highly rated." ("The Political Works of Thomas Paine," p. 55).

Our Heavenly Father blesses us with courage so that we may use it to promote goodness and righteousness. Men and women who have been given courage recognize the awesome responsibility its bestowal entails. The last official words of President John F. Kennedy, to have been delivered in Dallas, Texas, November 22, 1963, reflect his appreciation of this responsibility: "We in this country, in this generation, are – by destiny rather than by choice – the watchmen on the walls of world freedom. We ask, therefore, that we may be worthy of our power and responsibility; that we may exercise our strength with wisdom and restraint, and that we may achieve in our time and for all time the ancient vision of peace on earth, good will toward men. That must always be our goal, and the righteousness of our cause must always underlie our strength. For as was written long ago: 'Except the Lord keep the city, the watchman waketh in vain.'" (Psalms 127:1).

Those who are courageous experience fear along with the rest of us. But early on they have recognized that faith is fear that has said its prayers. They are as the Sons of Helaman who "were all young men, and they were exceedingly valiant for courage, and also for strength and activity. But behold, this was not all – they were men who were true at all times in whatsoever thing they were entrusted. Yea, they were men of truth and soberness, for they had been taught to keep the commandments of God and to walk uprightly before him." (Alma 53:20-21).

President Harold B. Lee taught: "You must learn to walk to the edge of the light, and then a few steps into the darkness; then the light will appear and show the way before you." This is the way courage is experienced and developed and strengthened. The courageous have learned that you cannot take darkness into a lighted room. The courageous are surrounded by and enveloped in light. As Helen Keller wrote: "Keep your face to the sunshine, and you cannot see the shadow." The shadow will still exist, but if you are oriented toward the light, it will Is be behind you, out of sight, and out of mind.

Winston Churchill wrote, "Men's and nations' finest hours are those when extraordinary challenge is met with extraordinary response." Courage can be the catalyst that transforms timidity and temerity into powerful presence of mind, which then acts as a platform for assertive action. It is not bravado, but boldness. It is no paper tiger. It is an intense and compellingly positive response to threat. In the fight or flight scenario, it is the launch pad for the anticipated adrenalin rush that carries us beyond the challenge. It is the foundation quality on which is built every other noble characteristic.

Courage can keep us focused on the positive, for there are always two voices operating, "two voices are calling, one coming out from the swamps of selfishness and force, where success means death, and the other from the hilltops of justice and progress, where even failure brings glory. Two lights are seen on your horizon, one, the last fading marsh light of power, and the other the slowly rising sun of human brotherhood. Two ways lie open for you, one leading to an ever lower and lower plane, where are heard the cries of despair and the curses of the poor, where manhood shrivels and possessions rot down the possessor, and the other leading to the highlands of the morning, where are heard the glad shouts of humanity, and where honest effort is rewarded with immortality." (John P. Altgeld).

Courageous individuals, though, are not tormented by confusion. They understand the meaning behind the question Paul asked of the Galatian Saints: "Do I now persuade men, or God?" (Galatians 1:10). They are eager to make commitments, for they have personally witnessed the effects of such action. "Until one is committed there is hesitancy, the chance to draw back, always ineffectiveness. Concerning all acts of initiative, there is one elementary truth, the ignorance of which kills countless ideas and splendid plans: that the moment one definitely commits oneself, then Providence moves too. All sorts of things occur to help one that would never have otherwise occurred. A whole stream of events issues from the decision, raining in one's favor all manner of unforeseen incidents and material assistance, which no man could have dreamed would have come his way." (Tom Hornbein, "Everest – "The West Ridge," Sierra Club, 1966, p. 100).

The courageous have developed the discipline to follow through on the commitments they have made. "You must not compromise your integrity by promising what you will not do," warned President Spencer W. Kimball. "By taking covenants lightly, you will wound your own eternal self." (B.Y.U. Devotional, 9/4/79). They "have integrity like Abraham did, observing with all soberness the solemn contracts [they] have made with God." (Spencer W. Kimball, "The Example of Abraham," Ensign." 6/1975).

Those who fully express themselves in positive and independent action have the courage to be obedient to a Higher Power. "I will go and do the things which the Lord hath commanded," declared Nephi, "for I know that the Lord giveth no commandments unto the children of men, save he shall prepare a way for them that they may accomplish the thing which he commandeth them." (1 Nephi 3:7).

The courageous are often asked to go the second mile. Always, courage has a performance cost, which is often acutely uncomfortable, testing the limits of endurance of both physical and spiritual muscles. It probes them for pliability, measures them for meekness, and searches them for submissiveness, which hones their humility to a higher state of energy. In the process, the courageous develop the ability to endure opposition of all kinds. They welcome the trials of mortality, and view them as pop quizzes in the curriculum of life. They endure to the end, knowing that after the final exam, their grade will simply reflect the summation of a life well spent.

The courageous have developed the power to love unconditionally. "I love everybody," five-year-old Kathryn told her father. "Where did you learn that?" he asked. "In church?" "No," she replied, "when I was up in heaven. Heavenly Father told me that." The courageous have learned that the best way to destroy one's enemies is by making friends out of them. In moments of crisis, the courageous become pro-gospel, rather than anti-enemy. Well did the poet reflect, "He drew a circle that shut me out. Heretic, rebel, a thing to flout. But courage and I had the will to win. We drew a circle that took him in." (Edwin Markham).

This abundance gives them more courage, even the courage to take risks. They break free from the security nets and comfort zones and refuges of safety in which the timid apprehensively squeak out their lives, scurrying from one shadowy refuge to another. Finally, the courageous recognize that emulating the Savior means following Him not only to the I, but to Gethsemane as well. Willingly, then, they surrender their agency to Christ, knowing that it is a necessary and vital step on the path of progress that leads to eternal life.

Covenant Consciousness

"And now, my sons, remember,
remember that it is upon the rock of
our Redeemer, who is Christ, the Son of
God, that ye must build your foundation; that
when the devil shall send forth his might winds;
yea, his shafts in the whirlwind … it shall have no
power over you to drag you down … because
of the rock upon which ye are built, which
is a sure foundation, a foundation
whereon if men build, they
cannot fall." (Helaman
5:12).

In the Last Days, "as many of the Gentiles as will repent (shall become) the covenant people of the Lord; and as many of the Jews as will not repent shall be cast off; for the Lord covenanteth with none save it be with them that repent and believe in his Son, who is the Holy One of Israel." (2 Nephi 30:2). These are known as God's Covenant People.

As we reflect on the covenant consciousness of the church in the Last Days, we realize that the special relationship that God's people have with Him is really not so self-evident. Even Mormon found it necessary to remind the Nephites that they were "of the house of Israel." (Mormon 7:1). After a thousand years, that remnant had forgotten its noble lineage. Sometimes, members of the church today forget that they are either literally or by adoption of the house of Israel and that they too may claim the covenant blessings promised by God so long ago to Abraham and his descendants.

An angel had asked Nephi: "Rememberest thou the covenants of the Father unto the House of Israel?" (1 Nephi 14:8). He was speaking of the Abrahamic Covenant, preserved in The Pearl of Great Price for those in the Last Days. "My name is Jehovah," the Savior had explained to His servant Abraham, "and I know the end from the beginning; therefore, my hand shall be over thee. And I will make of thee a great nation, and I will bless thee above measure, and make thy name great among all nations, and thou shalt be a blessing unto thy seed after thee, that in their hands they shall bear this ministry and Priesthood unto all nations; And I will bless them through thy name; for as many as receive this gospel shall be called after thy name, and shall be accounted thy seed, and shall rise up and bless thee, as their father; And I will bless them that bless thee, and curse them that curse thee; and in thee (that is, in thy Priesthood) and in thy seed (that is, thy Priesthood), for I give unto thee a promise that this right shall continue in thee, and in thy seed after thee (that is to say, the literal seed, or the seed of the body) shall all the families of the earth be blessed, even with the blessings of the gospel, which are the blessings of salvation, even of life eternal." (Abraham 2:8-11).

Later, Jehovah told Abraham's descendants through Jacob: (I will) "scatter thee among all people, from the one end of the earth even unto the other." (Deuteronomy 28:64). This suggests that a very large portion of mankind would ultimately have Israelite blood in order to satisfy the purposes of God.

In Nephi's day, the Ten Tribes had already been lost to the knowledge of the Jews at Jerusalem. (1 Nephi 22:4). About 721 B.C., these tribes of the Kingdom of Israel were led into captivity by the Assyrians. About a year later, according to tradition, they fled toward the north and mysteriously disappeared. Ultimately, after the Babylonian Captivity, all 12 Tribes of Israel were scattered upon the isles of the sea and among all nations.

Nephi's people were among those who lived "after the manner of happiness" by being partakers of the Abrahamic Covenant. (2 Nephi 5:27). The blessings of that Covenant include the priesthood, eternal marriage, and a land of inheritance. Today, "those portions of the Abrahamic Covenant which pertain to personal exaltation and eternal increase are renewed with each member of the House of Israel who enters the order of celestial marriage. Through that order, the participating parties become inheritors of all the blessings of Abraham, Isaac, and Jacob." (Bruce R. McConkie, "Mormon Doctrine," p. 13-14).

Just as the scattering of Israel was foretold, so too was its latter-day gathering. Jeremiah prophesied: "I will gather the remnant of my flock out of all countries whither I have driven them." (Jeremiah 23:3). God is in control of this gathering. In fact, on 4 3, 1836, in the Kirtland Temple, Moses pointedly restored the keys of the gathering of Israel. (See D&C 110:11). One hundred and thirty-nine years later, Spencer W. Kimball declared: "The brighter day has dawned. The gathering is in progress. May the Lord bless us, as we become nursing fathers and mothers unto our (Israelite) brethren and hasten the fulfillment of the great promises made to them." (C.R., 10/1975). The House of Israel is now being gathered as it accepts the restored gospel and serves the God of Abraham, Isaac, and Jacob. (See Deuteronomy 30:1-5).

There are both physical and spiritual elements of the Gathering. First, Israel's spiritual gathering is accomplished as those with the blood of Israel join the church. Converts are Israelites either by blood or by adoption. (See Galatians 3:26-29). Secondly, Israel's physical gathering will occur when she is "gathered home to the lands of (her) inheritance, and (is) established in all (her) lands of promise." (2 Nephi 9:2).

This physical gathering will not be completed until the Second Coming of Christ, but it is already under way, not only among the Jews in Israel, but also among the descendants of Ephraim, who have been gathering since 1830 by virtue of their membership in The Church of Jesus Christ of Latter-day Saints. Zenos prophesied that "when that day cometh" that Israel no longer turns her heart aside from the Master, "then will he remember the covenants which he made to their fathers. Yea, then will he remember the isles of the sea; yea, and all the people who are of the house of Israel." (1 Nephi 19:15-16). In essence, Zenos promised that Israel would be gathered from the four quarters of the earth.

At that day, "all the earth shall see the salvation of the Lord, saith the prophet; every nation, kindred, tongue and people shall be blessed." (1 Nephi 19:17). The members and missionaries of The Church of Jesus Christ of Latter-day Saints will bring the message of salvation to a world in desperate need, and by priesthood authority and ordinance will provide the covenant blessings of Abraham to all nations.

The church was restored so that Israel might receive the gospel and enter into the covenants of salvation and exaltation, be taught how to build temples and learn how to use them, be clothed in the garments of the holy priesthood, be given power and authority among the nations, be prepared to take the gospel into the world, and be sanctified so that she might be holy when she meets the Savior. The Gathering of Israel is unfolding to prepare her for a celestial glory.

Today, "every stake on earth is the gathering place for the lost sheep of Israel who live in its area. Scattered Israel in every nation is called to gather to the fold of Christ, to the stakes of Zion, as such are established in their nations." (Bruce R. McConkie, "Ensign," 5/1977, p. 118). Long ago, Isaiah prophesied that, in the Last Days, the Lord would establish "an ensign for the nations." (2 Nephi 21:12). This "ensign" is The Church of Jesus Christ of Latter-day Saints. As the Lord said to Joseph Smith, "I have sent mine everlasting covenant into the world, to be a light to the world, and to be a standard for my people, and for the Gentiles to seek to it, and to be a messenger before my face to prepare the way before me." (D&C 45:9).

In the church and kingdom of God,
our hands-on training teaches us that if we plan our
work, and then work our plan, we will enjoy success in our
endeavors. We know that proper prior planning prevents poor
priesthood performance. We dream big, and by establishing
deadlines, we create realistic goals. We know by our own
experience that work without vision is drudgery, and
vision without work is dreamery, but work with
vision is destiny. We know these things to be
true because of our experience, and as the
inevitable result of undeviating
commitment to the cause
of truth.

Covenants

"Ye need not imagine in your
hearts that the words which have been
spoken are vain, for behold, the Lord
will remember his covenant which
he hath made unto his people
of the house of Israel."
(3 Nephi 29:3).

Technically, members of the church do not have a lock on covenants, per se. I say tomāto. You say tomăto. I say potăto. You say potăto. Broadly speaking, a covenant is a historical term for a treaty or other agreement. It is a legal term, particularly restricting the use of property; for example, Conditions, Covenants, and Restrictions or CC&Rs. Loan covenants define the conditions relating to financial instruments. The U.N. uses the term, as in its International Covenant Council on Civil and Political Rights. The P.L.O. uses the term, as in the Palestinian National Covenant of 1964, which outlined the aims of the Palestine Liberation Organization. So does the I.R.A., as in the Ulster Covenant of 1912, which protested against British home-rule. Covenants also define a series of solemn agreements believed by many to exist between God and Israel. The foundation of the Torah is the belief that God chose the Children of Israel, and made His covenant with them.

The Latter-day Saint concept of religious "covenants" goes back to Abraham, and even to Adam and Eve in the Garden of Eden, and concerns the agreements we make with God. Abraham was righteous and refused to worship his father's idols. In recognition of this, the Lord made a covenant with him and his descendants.

That covenant is defined in the scriptures, in Abraham 2:11 & in Genesis 17:4-8. In it, God promised Abraham that he would have numberless descendants who would be entitled to receive the gospel, the priesthood, and the ordinances of exaltation. God would establish the same covenant with all the generations of Abraham's children. They would ultimately carry the gospel to the nations of the earth and through them, would extend the blessings of God to all mankind. The Abrahamic Covenant is of such power and force that its conditions bless all of Heavenly Father's children with the opportunity to participate in and receive the blessings of the Plan of Salvation.

We do not need to be the literal descendants of Abraham to qualify to participate in this covenant. Literal descendants of Abraham are not the only people whom God calls His covenant people. Speaking to Abraham, God said, "As many as receive this gospel shall be called after thy name, and shall be accounted thy seed and shall rise up and bless thee, as their father." (Abraham 2:10). Thus, two groups of people are included in the covenant madewith Abraham: (1) Abraham's righteous literal descendants and (2) those adopted into his lineage by accepting and living the gospel of Jesus Christ. (See 2 Nephi 30:2). It is precisely because of its importance to the Abrahamic Covenant, that a person's lineage is declared during the administration of a patriarchal blessing.

Today, members of His church make a number of covenants with the Lord. There are baptismal covenants, sacramental covenants, The Oath and Covenant of the Priesthood, and several temple covenants. If God did not make these covenants with His children, if there were no law given, if men could sin with impunity, "what could justice do, or mercy either, for they would have no claim upon the creature? ...The works of justice would be destroyed, and God would cease to be God." (Alma 42:21-22).

Latter-day Saints view religious covenants in a way that is uniquely personal and peculiar to their beliefs. They believe that covenants are received only by revelation from God, and are binding contracts, and since He is a party to every gospel covenant, they must necessarily come through revelation. No person can, therefore, enter into such covenants without direct revelation from God. In their minds, it follows that the only ones who can make covenants with God are members of The Church of Jesus Christ, who believe in latter-day revelation. (See the Seventh Article of Faith).

Latter-day Saints go to a great deal of effort to make covenants with God, because they believe that covenants are integral to the Plan of Salvation that has been designed to bring to pass our immortality, exaltation, and eternal life. They feel that covenants are particularly powerful because they reveal something about the attributes of God Himself. Latter-day Saints believe that covenants describe the parenting style of God. He is our Father, and He is perfect in every way. He could give us everything He has, but what He is, we must earn for ourselves, as we struggle to overcome adversity and gain self-mastery. Covenants bridge the gulf between mortality and eternity, by helping us, more than any other thing, to focus our efforts to become as He is.

If it were not possible to become as God is, Latter-day Saints believe that religious covenants would be unnecessary. This provides insight into why the world doesn't immediately understand why Latter-day Saints make covenants with God, particularly in the temple, but it suggests the direction that our teaching should follow. As Joseph Smith observed: "Reading the experience of others, or the revelation given to them, can never give us a comprehensive view of our condition and true relation to God. Knowledge of these things can only be obtained by experience through the ordinances of God set forth for this purpose." (H.C., 6:50).

As a result of my exposure to the teachings of the church, beginning with a short film ("Man's Search for Happiness") at Flushing Meadows, New York, during the 1964 World's Fair, I learned that the covenants we make with God reflect His attributes. For example, God is moral, so He gives us the Covenant of Chastity. He has charity, so He commands us to love Him and each other. God is disciplined, so He gives us the Law of Obedience. Because He is a righteous steward, He gives us the Law of Consecration. Because He loves His less fortunate children, He gives us the Law of the Fast. Because His is a perfected, resurrected body, He gives us the Word of Wisdom. Because He is omniscient, He gives us the commandment to seek knowledge. In consequence of the Gift of His Son, He gives us the Law of Sacrifice. Because He rested from His labors on the seventh day, He gives us the Law of the Sabbath.

I learned that our covenant relationship with God releases the power within us to receive specific blessings. We receive the right to enjoy continual guidance from the Holy Ghost. Worthy men receive the right to hold and exercise the priesthood. Women receive the rights, privileges, blessings, and responsibilities relating to femininity. They also receive the right to exercise authority, under special circumstances in the temple. Families receive the blessings of the priesthood relating to eternal life in the celestial kingdom.

I learned that the covenants we make with God have the power to put us beyond the reach of the adversary. Obedience gives us the priesthood and spiritual power necessary to overcome evil and obtain exaltation. The Prophet Joseph Smith explained: "Salvation consists of a man's being placed beyond the power of his enemies, meaning the enemies of his progression, such as dishonesty, greediness, lying, immorality, and other vices." (Sermon delivered at Nauvoo temple site on May 21, 1843. Source: Joseph Smith Diary).

Those who make covenants have been promised: "The gates of hell shall not prevail against you; yea, and the Lord God will disperse the powers of darkness from before you, and cause the heavens to shake for thy good, and His name's glory." (D&C 21:6). The gates of hell mark the entrance to the Spirit Prison of the Unjust, where the disobedient are allowed to go to work out their own salvation and to await the day of their redemption, and their deliverance from the iron grip of Satan. (See D&C 76:73, 138:8 & 28, Isaiah 61:1, 1 Peter 3:19, & Moses 7:57).

After joining the church, I quickly learned about my responsibilities relating to the covenant relationship I had established with God. I learned about my duty to keep His commandments. I learned about my duty to be a missionary and how I fit in with the promise that had been given to Abraham, that through his descendants the gospel would be taken to all the earth.

I am continually learning more about the fulness of the gospel, which is The New and Everlasting Covenant, including the covenants I made at my baptism, at my ordination to the Melchizedek Priesthood, and that I renew during the administration of the Sacrament, and in the temple. The Lord calls the covenant everlasting because it is ordained and ratified by His everlasting authority. He assures us that the foundations of the covenant, meaning the blessings associated with obedience, will never be changed. He has given this same covenant to Adam, Enoch, Noah, Abraham, and other prophets, during each dispensation of the gospel. The words may change slightly, but the intent and purpose, and the blessings related to obedience, do not. The Lord calls the covenant "new" because each time the gospel is restored after being taken from the earth due to apostasy, it is new to the people who receive it. (See Jeremiah 31:31-34 & Ezekiel 37:26).

As I have matured in the church, I have learned about the "contract provisions" of the New and Everlasting Covenant. Initially, I agreed to repent, be baptized, to receive the Holy Ghost, and then I was taught about the endowment, and the covenant of marriage in the temple. With spiritual and priesthood power, I have determined to follow and obey Christ to the end of my life. Heavenly Father has promised me, in turn, that I will receive the blessing of exaltation in His celestial kingdom. (See D&C 132:20-24). The scope of that promise is hard for me to understand. I do know that the commandments are for my benefit, and that through faith I may share in the blessings and beauties of heaven and earth. I may look forward, once again, to living in His presence, to partake of His love, compassion, power, greatness, knowledge, wisdom, glory, and dominions.

I have learned that my Father in Heaven established His Covenant to release me from my bondage to sin, and to set me free to completely take advantage of all the features of the Plan of Salvation, and particularly of its keystone, the Atonement of Christ. Without His Covenant in my behalf, I realize that the Plan would be frustrated. I am thrilled to know that covenants have set me free from the iron bands of death. I believe the words of King Benjamin, who said: "There is no other name given whereby salvation cometh, therefore, I would that ye should take upon you the name of Christ, all you that have entered into the covenant with God." (Mosiah 5:8).

The covenants I have made with God have set me free to reach my potential, and I rejoice that I have been born again. Truly, did Benjamin declare that those who enter into the Covenant "are born of him." (Mosiah 5:7). I understand that I am a "Born Again Christian," who has joined the ranks of others who are in a covenant relationship with the Lord. (See Mosiah 27:25, Alma 5:14, & 7:14, Mosiah 15:10-11, Alma 22:15 & 36:24).

As the Lord revealed to Joseph Smith, so have I learned that the "greater priesthood administereth the gospel and holdeth the key of the mysteries of the kingdom, even the key of the knowledge of God. Therefore, in the ordinances thereof, the power of godliness is manifest. And without the ordinances thereof, and the authority of the priesthood, the power of godliness is not manifest unto men in the flesh." (D&C 84:19-21).

(The) Creation of The World

"If there be no Christ, there be
no God; and if there be no God, we
are not, for there could have been no
creation. But there is a God, and he
is Christ, and he cometh in the
fulness of his own time."
(2 Nephi 11:7).

How does an airplane stay in the air? How does a television set process its signal? How do plants grow? How does the Internet work? Why do we need to breathe? Rather than understanding these things completely, most of us comprehend only general concepts without the detail that comes through scholarship. The same rules apply when considering revealed truth about the creation. The Lord has given us only the portion that our mortal minds can grasp and that we need to know in our quest for salvation. Details may come later, when we are more mature in the gospel and have a greater capacity to understand. For now, we are given revealed truth on a need-to-know basis.

6,000 years after the Fall of Adam, we have yet to formulate the scientific hypothesis that might provide a context for the Creation. True wisdom and knowledge of these things can only be gained through the Spirit of God. When Moses was blessed with this discerning spirit, his mind expanded with spiritual comprehension, and he was able to behold the earth in its most minute fashion and appreciate the grand design of the Lord's creations.

Even with the world's most powerful optical instruments, we have only taken a peek at what Moses beheld in the spirit. Speaking of the mind and soul-expanding power of spiritual comprehension, Joseph Smith said: "Could you gaze into heaven five minutes, you would know more than you would by reading all that ever was written on the subject." ("Teachings," p. 156). Thus, if we wish to fully understand the Creation, we must prepare ourselves as did Moses.

Scientific study, though worthwhile, can only provide a drop in the bucket of information that is available through the source of all truth. As Sir Isaac Newton famously declared: "I do not know what I may appear to the world, but to myself I seem to have been only like a boy playing on the seashore, and diverting myself in now and then finding a prettier shell, or a smoother pebble than ordinary, whilst the great ocean of truth lay all undiscovered before me."

How wonderful it would be to stand on the shoulders of giants and see as Moses did. He beheld a vision of God's creations and was commanded to write an account of the organization of the earth. "But only an account of this earth, and the inhabitants thereof, give I unto you," declared Jehovah. (Moses 1:35). It would be fascinating to know more about His awe-inspiring creations throughout the universe and to understand how they fit into the gospel plan.

Apparently, to fulfil our purpose on earth, this knowledge is unnecessary. The scriptures remain virtually silent on the subject of the other creations of God. Our focus should be on the scriptures and revelations the Lord has given us and not on unfathomable mysteries that have not yet been revealed. What has been given to us is a comprehension of that portion of the Lord's eternal word that we must believe and understand for the Fall and Atonement to become our stepping-stones to the stars. This is all we are obligated to know.

Although an account of the Creation is included in the book of Genesis, its importance is explained only in latter-day revelation. When we ponder the Creation in the context of the Plan of Salvation, we realize that its purpose was to provide a place where we could come to obtain physical bodies and be tested or proven to see if we would obey Him after we left His presence, if so, we would receive eternal life.

As the Gods explained: "We will go down, for there is space there, and we will take of these materials, and we will make an earth whereon these may dwell. And we will prove them herewith, to see if they will do all things whatsoever the Lord their God shall command them." (Abraham 3:24-25). "Herewith" means "with this earth." In other words, the Lord created the earth as a learning laboratory with room and to spare to accommodate all His children, a place where each of His children would be tried and tested after being infused with positive energy, and proven in tailor-made and uniquely individual ways, in order to develop character. "For behold," said the Lord affirmatively, "this is my work and my glory - to bring to pass the immortality and eternal life of man." (Moses 1:39).

Wilford Woodruff explained: "The Lord Almighty created the earth that we might come here and exercise our agency. The probation we are called upon to pass through is intended to elevate us so that we can dwell in the presence of God our Father." ("The Discourses of Wilford Woodruff," p. 8). Six times in the brief account of the Creation in Genesis, God declared that His work was 'good.' (Genesis 1:4, 10, 12, 21, 25, 31). It was so good, in fact, that earth life can prepare us for eternal life. "The stars fade away, the sun himself grow dim with age, and nature sink in years; But thou shalt flourish in immortal youth, unhurt amidst the war of elements, the wreck of matter, and the crash of worlds." (Joseph Addison, "Cato" Act 5, Scene 1).

Dancing With the Stars

"The scriptures are laid before thee, yea,
and all things denote there is a God; yea
even the earth, and all things that are upon
the face of it, yea, and its motion, yea, and
also all the planets which move in their
regular form do witness that there
is a Supreme Creator."
(Alma 30:44).

"The Great Silence" is the contradiction between the astronomically high estimates of the probability of extraterrestrial life and its corresponding lack of evidence. After all, we ask ourselves: Hasn't humanity reached the point where it should be "Dancing with The Stars?" Shouldn't we be holding up the Mirror Ball Trophy with our extra-terrestrial quickstep partners? The universe is around 13.7 billion years old and contains something on the order of 70 sextillion (7 x 1022) stars, many of which undoubtedly have planets, so somewhere, sometime, life should have evolved into societies of technologically advanced species who have either intentionally or inadvertently broadcast news of their existence across the far reaches of space. Yet, back in 1950, the physicist Enrico Fermi wondered aloud why no such evidence has been detected. His question ("Where is everybody?") has come to be known as "The Fermi Paradox." It is also known as "Silentium Universi." Basically, the paradox is a conflict between scale and probability on the one hand, and the aforementioned lack of confirming evidence on the other.

The "scale" involved is mind-boggling. There are an estimated 200 to 400 billion stars in the Milky Way Galaxy alone. Somewhere out there should be intelligent life capable of having made its presence known. Think of the electromagnetic signals from earth - for example, all those broadcasts of "Sesame Street" - that have been traveling at the speed of light outward through space since the early years of the Twentieth Century.

The second foundation of the Fermi Paradox, which is probability, is the assumption that extraterrestrials would have developed the ability to overcome scarcity and colonize new habitat, and ultimately to possess the technology to explore neighboring star systems. But after having had so much time (13.7 billion years) in which to do so, no terrestrial evidence of alien life seems to now exist, thereby creating a conflict begging for resolution.

It may be that life is precious and is found relatively infrequently in the cosmos. Perhaps we are unique, after all. Hamlet may have been right when he exclaimed: "What a piece of work is a man, how noble in reason, how infinite in faculties, in form and moving how express and admirable, in action how like an angel, in apprehension how like a god! The beauty of the world, the paragon of animals." (Shakespeare, "Hamlet," Act 2, Scene 3).

It may be that our best efforts to reach out and touch someone, anyone, might be corrupted by an "Observer Effect" that significantly alters the state of the elusive objects of our investigation and makes their detection and measurement more difficult. Perhaps the very devices we have constructed to search for the evidence of alien life have tainted the data that would have otherwise confirmed its existence.

It may be that our neighbors in the infinite reaches of space and time are defined by bounds and conditions that make their detection with our five physical senses impossible. William W. Phelps mused: If only we "could hie to Kolob in the twinkling of an eye, and then continue onward with that same speed to fly, do you think that (we) could ever, through all eternity, find out the generation where Gods began to be, or see the grand beginning, where space did not extend, or view the last creation, where Gods and matter end? Methinks the Spirit whispers, 'No man has found pure space, nor seen the outside curtains where nothing has a place.' The works of God continue, and worlds and lives abound. Improvement and progression have one eternal round. There is no end to matter; there is no end to space; there is no end to spirit; there is no end to race." ("If You Could Hie to Kolob").

Our arguable "nobility" notwithstanding, after 4 billion years of evolutionary development, it is still up in the air whether "intelligent" life on earth will make it past a Type 0 civilization. (See the definition below of Types 0, 1, 2, and 3 civilizations). Perhaps other cultures have embraced, as we have, the insane policy of Mutually Assured Destruction, (MAD), that has inexorably led to their ultimate annihilation. Perhaps the control of exponentially expanding technology ultimately proves to be impossible by those moving too quickly along its path of hopeful progress toward Type 1 planetary stability. Perhaps alien civilizations too often seal their fate by inadvertently opening a Pandora's Box of uncontrollable knowledge, thereby sowing the seeds of their own ruin.

Perhaps technology harbors a fatal flaw and nurtures a hidden Achilles Heel. As Type 0 societies evolve, though they may envision a technological shield of protection, they may instead inadvertently pursue the creation of a dispassionate "Sky Net." Our own terrestrial storytellers have already described how such a coldly logical machine could one day take on a deadly "life" of its own to bite the hand that had created it. (See the movie: "Terminator 3: Rise of The Machines").

Perhaps intelligent life in the universe has a very difficult time moving beyond our own "Type 0" civilization described by Michio Kaku, with all the petty jealousies, regional conflicts, social and economic inequalities, and sectarian violence that have plagued us for millennia. Dr. Kaku has conceptualized "Type 1" planetary civilizations, right out of "Buck Rogers" and "Type 2" stellar civilizations, like "Star Trek - The Next Generation." He also envisions "Type 3" galactic civilizations on the order of The Empire, in the movie Star Wars.

Dr. Kaku believes that "in about 100 years our Type 0 civilization will become planetary (a Type 1 civilization). We'll be able to harness all the energy output of earth. We'll play with the weather. The danger period is now (Type 0), because we still have the savagery. We still have the passions. We have sectarian, fundamentalist ideas swirling about, and we also have nuclear, chemical, and biological weapons capable of wiping out life on earth."

He sees two mutually exclusive trends developing, the one toward a multi-cultural, scientific, tolerant, nurturing, interactive, and interdependent society, with easy access to educational opportunity, meaningful employment, and the satisfaction of temporal needs. The Internet, Facebook, and other social media, rock and roll, fashion, sports, the European Union, NAFTA, and even English as a planetary language are evidence that we are inching in that direction. We are witnessing the genesis of a Type 1 economy and a Type 1 culture. However, we also see its opposite in economic inequality and poverty, organized crime and secret societies, political corruption and terrorism, violence against minorities, cultural myopia, drug and alcohol abuse, sectarian conflicts, and religious fundamentalism, that are all self-destructive reactions against a Type 1 civilization. Whether we make it beyond Type 0 or not is still undecided.

Dr. Kaku continues: "Now, in outer space, we look for signs of intelligent life. So far we find none. Civilizations like Type 1 should be commonplace in the galaxy. Some people assume, therefore, that Type 0 civilizations are rather common, but only a few of them make it to Type 1 because that society for the first time in its history has the ability to commit planetary suicide. Maybe that is the reason why we don't see evidence of alien life. Maybe they never made it. Maybe one day when we have starships and visit their worlds we'll see atmospheres that are irradiated because they had nuclear war, or atmospheres too hot to sustain life because they had a runaway greenhouse effect. Maybe when we explore the galaxy we'll see the corpses of Type 0 civilizations that never quite made it to Type 1."

At the cosmic speed limit, (the speed at which light travels, or about 6 trillion miles per year), it would take only 120,000 years, (the blink of an eye on a cosmological scale), for a probe or vessel from a Type 2 or 3 civilization to traverse the Milky Way. Our own solar system is a relative newcomer on our 13.2-billion-year-old galactic stage, yet we have no indication that life forms have stopped by earth at any time during its own 4.6-billion-year history, to leave their calling cards. Perhaps they have, and we are asking the wrong questions, or are looking in the wrong places for the unique signatures that have indelibly marked their passing.

However, unless alien physicists have worked out the details to permit travel at warp speed, where space itself is distorted to shorten the distance between points A and B, the physical evidence of life elsewhere in the galaxy, let alone in the universe, may not exist. Still, there are promising launch platforms, right in our own vicinity, for space-faring visitors. For example, the Alpha Centauri System, (our nearest stellar neighbor), is only 4.2 light years away, almost within shouting distance, about 25.62 trillion miles from earth. A potentially habitable planet, named Proxima Centauri, has been discovered orbiting Alpha Centauri.

In 1977, the United States of America created the cosmic equivalent of the slogan "Kilroy was here" when it sent Voyager 1 out into space like a bottle in a deep and boundless intergalactic ocean. After forty-seven years (2024), it has traveled 14.5 billion miles at a constant velocity of 36,387 miles per hour, or just over 10 miles per second. At this rate, it will take Voyager 1 about 14,000 years to travel one light year. (Learn about Voyager 1 in real time at Voyager.jpl.nasa.gov/mission/status/, or go to Voyager.jpl.nasa.gov/where). Light, traveling at 186,200 miles per second, takes over 22 hours to reach the probe that has now passed the Termination Shock of the solar wind and has entered interstellar space. In about 40,000 years, Voyager 1 will be as close as it's going to get (about 1.6 light years) to another star: (AC+79 3888 in the Ophiuchus Constellation). Its Golden Record and pictograms describe life on earth. Electroplated upon the exterior of the probe is an ingenious "atomic clock," a sample of uranium-238 with a half-life of 4.468 billion years. If Voyager 1 has enough specific orbital energy to leave the Milky Way, in 1,288,000,000 years it will enter intergalactic space. It is possible that, one day in the distant future, within the boundaries of a galaxy far, far away, a civilization may stumble upon Voyager 1 and determine its age by calculating the decay of the isotope, and also vector its location of origin. "Twentieth Century" humans would be to them as a voice crying from the dust, for our sun would have long since become a red giant after running out of its hydrogen fuel. Although the earth and its life forms will be destroyed in that process about 5 billion years from now, Voyager would nevertheless remain our enduring legacy, representing a small token of our fleeting influence on the intergalactic stage.

If Voyager were headed in the direction of Proxima Centauri, which happens to be the closest of 51 stars within 16 light years of earth, it would only take 80,376 years to reach it. The earth is about 28,000 light years from the center of the Milky Way Galaxy, which itself is around 120,000 light years in diameter. Its closest major neighbor is the spiral galaxy Andromeda, composed of over a trillion stars 2.6 million light years from earth. These large numbers suggest that intergalactic two-way communication, let alone travel, might just take too much time to complete, even if "ridiculous" or "ludicrous" speed, depicted in the motion picture "Space Balls," were possible.

So where is everybody? Let's forget our intergalactic second cousins, (we always considered them a strange bunch, anyway) and just concentrate on our more immediate family who might be living in the neighborhood. In our own Milky Way, astronomers have found evidence of 160 billion of one particularly promising type of red dwarf star, 40% of which (64 billion) are thought to have planets, supposed "M Class" planets, similar to earth. If conditions on only one in a thousand of those 64 billion has actually germinated life, there could be 64 million planets with thriving life forms. If only one in a thousand of those 64 million has life similar to our own, there could be 64,000 "sister" planets out there in the night sky, embedded within the fuzzy wash of the Milky Way's light. On many of these, alien cosmologists might even now be gazing up in the chill of the evening, wondering if they too are alone in the universe, and their wives might be wondering if they are going to be late for dinner again.

Myths from around the world give the Milky Way its name and explain its origin. The Greeks believed it was created when suckling Heracles dribbled the breast milk of Hera, wife of Zeus, across the night sky. It was also described as the trail to Mount Olympus, the home of the Gods, and as the path of ruin made by the chariot of the Sun God Helios. In Sanskrit, the Milky Way was called Akash Ganga (Ganges of the Heavens), and was considered sacred. Hindu cosmology explains the galaxy as an ocean of milk churned by the gods for a thousand years in order to release Amrita, the nectar of immortal life.

Using our aforementioned calculations relating to the probability of life in the Milky Way Galaxy as a baseline, we may extrapolate that within the 200 to 400 billion galaxies in the known universe there could be as many as 25,600,000 trillion (2.56 x 1019) "earths" with life just like our own. That mind-boggling number pales in comparison to the endless possibilities within a multiverse, or parallel universes that together might comprise everything that exists and can exist; the entirety of knowable and unknowable space, time, matter, and energy. But that is the subject of another ambitious essay.

Perhaps we have found no proof of extraterrestrial life because we have an over-developed anthropocentric viewpoint. Perhaps we look too closely for evidence of the kinds of activities we would perform, without realizing that extraterrestrial life might behave in entirely different ways that make perfect sense to them, but are completely "alien" to our nature, inclination, experience, or means of detection.

Then there is the distinct possibility that the evolution of life on alien worlds has taken a very different path than that on earth. To use an example with which we are all familiar, if a comet had not struck earth 70 million years ago, thus effectively ending the cretaceous period with its exponential proliferation of dinosaurs, we might even now look and think like our velociraptor distant cousins. Perhaps alien life is so unlike Homo Sapiens that the gulf separating our species is just too great to bridge with comprehensible communication.

Early in 2012, NASA's planet-hunting Kepler spacecraft confirmed the discovery of the first alien world that lies within the habitable zone of its host star, where temperatures would allow liquid H2O to exist. New finds bring the space telescope's total haul during its first 16 months of operation to 2,326 planets. The exciting thing about this particular planet, though, is that it is a potentially habitable alien world orbiting a star very much like our own sun.

"As of January 2015, Kepler and its follow-up observations had found exoplanets in about 440 stellar systems. In November 2013, astronomers estimated, based on Kepler space mission data, that there could be as many as 40 billion rocky, earth-size exoplanets orbiting in the habitable zones of Sun-like stars and red dwarfs within the Milky Way. The nearest such planet may be 3.7 parsecs away, according to the scientists."– Wikipedia).

Using the High Accuracy Radial Velocity Planet Searcher (HARPS) spectrograph at the European Southern Observatory in Chile, astronomers have found within the Milky Way nine more similar planets only slightly larger than earth. The investigators estimate that about 100 such planets lie in the immediate neighborhood of the sun. The "new observations with HARPS suggest that about 40 percent of all red dwarf stars have an 'earth' orbiting in the habitable zone." (Space: on MSNBC.com on 3/28/2012)

It seems plausible that over billions of years, intelligent life should have flourished on at least some of these "M Class" ("Earth Similarity") planets that likely permeate our galaxy. Technological accomplishments of humans over the past 50 years, or 5 years, or even the last 5 minutes, beg the question: "Where is everybody? If intelligent life is out there, why have we detected no evidence of its existence? At the very least, why hasn't its presence revealed itself through the distribution of electromagnetic signals that should be the unmistakable signature of a technologically advanced civilization?

Perhaps we are looking through a very small keyhole into what may be the wrong microscopic portion of the night sky. When we gaze up into its vast expanse, the visible stars (about 6,000 of them) are nearly all in the Milky Way. Aside from the Large and Small Magellanic Clouds, Andromeda and Triangulum are among fewer than half a dozen discernable galaxies. Centaurus A is the furthest, at a distance from earth of 13.7 million light years. Maybe the evidence of alien life is not only hidden from our optic nerves and occipital lobes, but is also beyond the reach of our most sophisticated instruments, as well.

Perhaps First Contact has not yet been made because members of the United Federation of Planets unerringly adhere to The Prime Directive, Starfleet's General Order #1, the most prominent guiding principle in the fictional universe of "Star Trek: The Next Generation." Interestingly, the Prime Directive, which dictates that there can be no interference with the internal development of pre-warp civilizations, is consistent with the historical real-world concept of Westphalian sovereignty.

The rationale behind the Prime Directive, which is that civilizations with advanced technologies should not alter, modify, revise, amend, adjust, improve, develop, expand, or change in any way the natural development of emerging societies, wherever they may be found, even if the aid is well-intentioned or kept secret, is that to do so might radically influence its natural evolution. This could be detrimental to its society or to its celestial neighbors within the sphere of its expanding power, or it could be beneficial, but the effect would most certainly not be neutral. In any case, the culture's natural progression, and that of others with whom it might come in contact, would be artificially influenced in ways that would be difficult to anticipate and impossible to control. Regardless of the outcome, there would be no turning back.

So, perhaps aliens have been observing our behavior for some time, but have exercised God-like prudence and restraint when they have been tempted to reveal their presence. Perhaps they are keenly aware of our sense of urgency, but maintain the disciplined reserve that allows us to take the necessary baby steps that might one day lead us to interplanetary familiarity. Perhaps they ascribe to the philosophy of "milk before meat," and before they make their presence known they have determined to see how our transition from a "Type 0" to a "Type 1" civilization fares. Perhaps their patience reflects a more accurate timeline for growth and development than our hasty and imprudent demands for playdates would dictate.

On the other hand, perhaps alien ambassadors are among us even now in the disguise of the greatest minds of the 20th and 21st centuries, conducting tutorials in disciplines that range from astrophysics to zoology, and everything in between. After First Contact had been made in "Close Encounters of The Third Kind," a terrestrial scientist at

Devil's Tower was heard to exclaim: "Einstein was right!" To which a colleague replied: "Hell, Einstein was probably one of them!" "Truth is stranger than fiction, but it is because fiction is obliged to stick to possibilities, while truth isn't." (Mark Twain).

Perhaps aliens are among us now, but utilize "cloaking devices" that allow their observation posts to remain hidden from our view until we have independently developed not only the Type 2 technology, but also the maturity, to move with responsibility among the stars in the untresspassed sanctity of space. Cloaking technologies with which we are already familiar include radar absorbing materials, optical camouflage, and minimization of electromagnetic emissions (in the infrared portion of the spectrum) through cooling. Cloaking technologies with which we are only beginning to familiarize ourselves include the utilization of "Metamaterials," artificial substances engineered to have properties that may not be found in nature. These have been theorized to allow EM radiation to pass right through cloaked objects.

Perhaps the natural inquisitiveness of extraterrestrials has been tempered by their appreciation of simple math and sobering terrestrial statistics. In the United States, over a span of 40 years, the annual budget for The National Aeronautical and Space Administration (NASA) has been just under $10 billion (1958-2011), while the budget for the Department of Defense (called "The War Department" until 1947) in just one of those years was $680 billion (2010), or 54% of all federal spending, and the budget for the Department of Homeland Security was $43 billion (2011). Perhaps extraterrestrials have noted with alarm that the "World Nuclear Club" spends $1 trillion each year to maintain its arsenals, in contrast to the annual U.S. Budget for the International Space Station, which is a paltry $2.1 billion.

Perhaps we have a flawed anthropomorphic assumption about the attitudes of other intelligent species. Perhaps quite simply, a self-imposed "radio silence" is in effect because they just want to be left alone. Perhaps masters of the universe (Type 3 civilizations) have overcome the ego-centric desire to affirm their prominence in the profane, self-destructive, self-important, and self-aggrandizing ways with which we are all-too familiar. Perhaps as they have become increasingly self-actualized and have honed their capacity to reach their potential, they have effectively extinguished the self-defeating need to draw attention to themselves. Perhaps their unconscious shyness is a highly evolved defense mechanism.

Perhaps their reticence has been carefully cultivated through genetic selection as a self-deprecating personality trait. Perhaps they have achieved a "star power" that transcends the craving for media attention, admiration, adulation, and adoration. Perhaps their silence is a galactic, self-effacing understatement. Perhaps their P.I.N. is such a jealously guarded secret that they view extra-terrestrial knowledge of their existence as the ultimate form of identity theft. Perhaps they have finally learned how to control the invasive harassment by the paparazzi and the exploitation upon which our supermarket tabloids voraciously feed. Perhaps they relish their anonymity and cherish their privacy. Perhaps to hide from prying eyes, they have developed the technological equivalent of the dark glasses worn by our own cultural icons to disguise their identities.

Perhaps alien geneticists have manipulated the genome of their species in order to temper the fires attendant to their transition from Type 0 to Type 1, 2, or 3 cultures. But, in the process, perhaps their zeal to "go where no-one has gone before" has been selectively bred out of them, as well. Perhaps they are more comfortable just staying home "for the evening," hunkered down in overstuffed easy chairs with good books to enjoy. Perhaps they have discovered that greener pastures lie on their own side of the fence, and they have finally found the elusive inner peace that had been right in front of their noses all the while. Perhaps their tranquility has come at the expense of the primal sense of wanderlust with which we are familiar. Perhaps the excitement that gets our juices flowing and pushes the boundaries of our experience has been suppressed or even extinguished. Perhaps when they "MapQuest" or "Google" their travel itineraries, they delete without interest earthly attractions that garner our own attention, like the world's largest ball of twine (measuring 41.5 feet in diameter) in Branson, Missouri.

That scenario notwithstanding, there is always the possibility that aliens don't need to pack their bags, gas up the family mini-van, and experience the thrill of the wind in their faces on the open interstellar or intergalactic road. Perhaps they travel at the speed of thought, rather than at the speed of light. (See the movies "Total Recall" and "K-Pax"). Perhaps they dismiss the temporal and spatial limitations with which we are familiar with a cursory wave of the hand that initiates energy bursts deep within the cerebral cortical grey matter of their highly developed brains. As omniscient Q told Captain Picard: "The universe has been my backyard." ("Star-Trek: The Next Generation." "Deja Q"). In another episode he exulted: "We are going to have fun! I'll take you to places no human could ever hope to See" ("Qpid").

Perhaps in the evolution of intelligent life, electromagnetic waves are no longer generated because alien communication technologies have become more sophisticated than our crude instruments that emit radiation (at a range between 3 kilohertz and 300 gigahertz, and corresponding wavelengths from 1 millimeter to 100 kilometers). Perhaps William W. Phelps was right, when he declared: "No man has found pure space, nor seen the outside curtains where nothing has a place," even though "the works of God continue, and worlds and lives abound" across the vast reaches of the universe. ("If You Could Hie to Kolob").

Perhaps Type 3 civilizations move about freely in a space-time continuum with which we are unfamiliar. Perhaps they are just as comfortable navigating tesseracts, (4-dimensional hypercubes), as we are the three spatially dimensional boundaries of up-down, front-back, and side-to-side. (See the movie "Interstellar"). As "One among them that was like unto God" said, before the earth was formed: "We will go down, for there is space there," thus making a clear distinction between their limitless natural habitation and our confined world of every day that is defined by one temporal and three spatial realities. (Abraham 3:24).

Perhaps we are not only looking in the wrong places, but we are also looking at the wrong time, as well. Perhaps for them, its arrow moves not just in one (forward) direction, but in two (forward and backward) directions. If aliens have learned to manipulate time as well as space, they may have already established lively communication with our past or our future, rather than with our present. Perhaps as they have fine-tuned the orientation of their messages, they have been intentionally programmed to reach us at more opportune times when we have been, or will be, better prepared or equipped to receive them. (See the movie: "Interstellar").

The concept of "ancient aliens" popularized by The History Channel and books by Erich von Daniken ("Chariots of The Gods," "Twilight of The Gods," and "Signs of The Gods") suggests that within historical texts, archaeology, myths, and legends, there is evidence of past human-extraterrestrial contact. Millions believe, or would like to believe, that the monolith found on the moon (see the movie: "2001: A Spacy Odyssey") was created millions of years ago by an alien race known as "The Firstborn," whose intention was to assist in the evolution of the human race. It may be that in the year 2513, a monolith will yet be found in Olduvai Gorge, Africa, buried in ancient rock. If so, it may be the first hard evidence of humankind's prehistoric evolutionary predecessors. (See "Marvel Comics").

Should there prove to be monoliths in the real world, a face-to-face encounter with our alien counterparts may already be in the works. In anticipation of such a discovery, perhaps we should now be making a determined effort to scatter invitations throughout the galaxy, announcing to alien races that we have proposed an interstellar orientation meeting at a specific point in normal space and time, that lies in our future. If a Type 2 or a Type 3 alien civilization has mastered time-travel, it should be a simple thing for them to make a dramatic entrance at just the appropriate moment, no matter when the summons may have been received. Our contemporary efforts could then be better directed toward finalizing preparations to receive our invited guests at the aforementioned venue, rather than being engaged in spinning our wheels without gaining any traction by searching for random R.S.V.P.s from aliens who might not wish to be such interstellar party-crashers.

Steven Hawking observed: "The quantum theory of gravity has opened up a new possibility, in which there is no boundary to space-time and no need to specify behavior at the boundary. There are no singularities at which the laws of science break down and no edge of space-time at which one has to appeal to some new law to set new boundary conditions for space-time. One could say: 'The boundary condition of the universe is that it has no boundary.'" ("A Brief History of Time: From the Big Bang to Black Holes," p. 136). From our perspective in space-time, aliens from a distant future might even now be getting ready for the festivities.

Or perhaps aliens communicate at energy levels like those described by String Theory, that are mathematically complex and observationally obtuse. For example, the "Everett Many-Worlds Interpretation" of quantum mechanics, proposed in 1956, states that all the possibilities described by quantum theory simultaneously occur in a multiverse composed of independent parallel universes that are forever hidden from our view by the laws of physics.

Even if our timing is right, and there is a surfeit of alien Type 1, 2, and 3 civilizations, perhaps we are not looking in the right places, and they have been trying in vain to communicate all along, but have been doing so within the elusive dark matter that has recently been postulated to fill 73% of what has heretofore been described as "empty space."

Perhaps since the moment of Creation, there have been points in space-time that are "without form, and void, and (there continues to be) darkness (here and there, then and now) upon the face of the deep." (Genesis 1:2). Perhaps in these places "worlds and lives abound (while) improvement and progression have one eternal round." Perhaps in the far reaches of the universe, "there is no end to (dark) matter, there is no end to space, there is no end to spirit, (and) there is no end to (alien) race." (William W. Phelps, "If You Could Hie to Kolob").

Perhaps our efforts to detect signs of extra-terrestrial intelligence have been ignorantly adjusted so that they are attuned to the wrong scale. For example, if environmentally-responsible and economically-conscious aliens have chosen to scatter sophisticated and recyclable non-biological "nano-probes" throughout the Milky Way, thereby avoiding the label of galactic litterbugs, and dodging the need for EPA equivalent Super-Fund cleanup, we may not have detected them because our primitive sensors haven't been upgraded to High Definition, or because we haven't yet invented the appropriately sensitive "Smart Card" to be inserted into our instruments. Perhaps we have been looking on a terrestrial order of magnitude for the unique signatures of alien life, while our efforts would have been better served by scanning the celestial section of cosmically calibrated classified ads for their calling cards.

What if evidence of alien life, or even evidence of its attempts at communication, is represented by terrestrial patterns of complex biological information vigorously interacting on subtle sub-cellular levels? After all, it's only been 59 earth-years since Watson and Crick unraveled the mystery of D.N.A. In order to reduce its footprint on the environment, alien life may long ago have become atomic or even sub-atomic, and we're simply not noticing its influence because it's flying well beneath our radar. Perhaps as we continue to investigate the human genome, we will find embedded within its vast matrix of TACG (thymine, adenine, cytosine, and guanine) the blueprint of a galactic family history. As the dog Frank in the movie "Men in Black" observed: "You humans are always looking for the spectacular. Look for something very small, like a jewel."

Carl Sagan has suggested that our natural senses may allow us to look at only one of "an infinite hierarchy of universes, so that an elementary particle, such as an electron, in our universe, would, if penetrated, reveal itself to be an entire closed universe. Within it, organized into the local equivalent of galaxies and smaller structures, there may be an immense number of other, much tinier elementary particles, which are themselves universes at the next level, and so on forever, an infinite downward regression of endless universes within universes. And upward as well. Our familiar universe of galaxies and stars, planets, and people, would be a single elementary particle in the next universe up, the first step of another infinite progression."

"This is the only idea I know," he said, "that surpasses the endless number of infinitely old cycling universes in Hindu cosmology. What would those other universes be like? Would they be built on different laws of physics? Would they have stars and galaxies, and worlds, or something quite different? Might they be compatible with some unimaginably different form of life? To enter them, poised at the edge of forever, we would jump off" into a reality that could be more revealing than any we had ever before experienced. ("Cosmos," p. 262-267). If we were to look more carefully, we might discover that alien cartographers have already provided us with the gift of a hidden map intended to nudge us through a "Stargate" that leads to the heavens. (See the movie "Stargate SG1"). Perhaps "we can hear their message even now, as our heads buzz with a hum that won't go away." Perhaps "our stairway lies on the whispering wind," and we will ascend on a double helix to a new Aquarian Age. (Led Zeppelin, "Stairway to Heaven"). Perhaps there is "a secret something" that whispers, "You're a stranger here." Perhaps our own ancestors have "wandered from a more exalted sphere" and have imprinted incontrovertible evidence of their epic journey within the chemistry of life itself. (Eliza R. Snow, "O My Father").

If so, then perhaps alien intelligence is more impressive than we could have ever imagined, because it has already subtly communicated with us by planting the seeds of evolution into our DNA, thereby leaving an indelible and enduring stamp. Perhaps the protein-rich primordial broth agitated by the volcanic and seismic contractions and contortions of our early earth was really a bubbling alphabet soup created by intelligent design to spell out innovation, progress, strategy, and success. Perhaps the evidence has been right before our noses all along. Perhaps a superior intelligence had something to do with the creative process of our growth and development, but worked through genetics to provide the push we needed to achieve greatness. (The Discovery Institute defines "intelligent design" as "'certain features of the universe and of living things that are best explained by an intelligent cause, not an undirected process such as natural selection.") Think of it. The immensely popular cookbook "The Joy of Cooking" could not have been created without an author. Its existence presupposes a chef in the kitchen. The galactic equivalent of a perfect soufflé (on its page 137) may be just the hard evidence of extra-terrestrial intelligence that we have been looking for all along.

Along similar lines, perhaps interstellar space has been infused with a culture medium brewed by extra-terrestrial biologists. We may just now be beginning to discern its presence as quorum sensing, the intuitive decision-making process used by decentralized groups (that could be either millimeters or light years apart) to coordinate behavior. Pervasive and complex chemical communication could be the indelible signature of an alien influence not only on human behavior, but also on that of all other carbon-based life forms (mammals, fish, birds, and insects, to name a few). The biotechnology of quorum sensing could be the lifeblood of all the species on earth. Instinctive as well as sentient behavior could trace their common origins to a cosmic point of singularity, the equivalent of an intergalactic exclamation point. Quantum mechanics could be the evidence of our rudimentary efforts to explain this phenomenon.

Perhaps if we could somehow unravel the mysteries surrounding the complex matrix of life teeming in air, on land, and within the deepest oceans, there would lie before us, like an open book, the tangible evidence of a continuity of existence that has no temporal or spatial boundary. "May the Force be with you," is an expression with which we are familiar, even though its origins are popularly traceable to imaginary extraterrestrials. (See the movie: "Star Wars"). Maybe, if we tempered our appetite for the wholesale destruction of entire species and ecosystems, we would notice a majestic clockwork at work, and sense its celestial calibration. Perhaps we would then discern the quiet ticking away of the precious minutes of a day that is waning, and proactively intervene to avoid the gathering darkness that is looming on the eastern horizon. Perhaps we could then discipline ourselves to recognize a harmonic pulse, to better feel the surge of a spiritual essence rhythmically beating throughout nature, in perfect cadence across the cosmos, and we would be better prepared to more fully participate in and more positively influence the circle of life that is grandly defined and expansively circumscribed by nothing short of the universe itself.

It could be that evidence of alien life has been around us all the while, but we have been too preoccupied to notice. Perhaps we have not been able to see the forest for the trees. Perhaps we need to stand back and take a collective deep breath in order to see more clearly that "there is no end to virtue; there is no end to might; there is no end to wisdom, (and) there is no end to light. There is no end to union; there is no end to youth; there is no end to priesthood; (and) there is no end to truth. There is no end to glory; there is no end to love (and in fact) there is no end to being" itself in the limitless expanse of the universe. (William W. Phelps, "If You Could Hie to Kolob").

Perhaps the neurochemical reactions that lie at the foundation of the ideas that pop into our heads are the hard evidence we seek of alien life, since these thoughts often seem to have lives of their own that outlive their so-called "creators." Perhaps our déjà vu moments are electromagnetic anomalies, the mirrored reflections of forces that lie just beyond our comprehension, but are chronologically correct. Maybe this is why inspiration comes, from time to time, as a whisper from the dust "with clarity and freshness, uncolored and untranslated, (speaking) from within (ourselves) in a language original but inarticulate, heard only with the soul." (Hugh B. Brown).

Perhaps the "codex" of Type 3 civilizations is represented by the Periodic Table, the tabular display of the building blocks of life composed of the 118 naturally occurring chemical elements organized on the basis of their properties. In fact, when we look at the "molecules that make up our bodies, we find that they are traceable to the crucibles that were once the centers of high-mass stars that exploded into the galaxy, seeding pristine gas clouds with the chemistry of life. We are all connected to each other biologically, to the earth chemically, and to the rest of the universe atomically." (Neil deGrasse Tyson). Perhaps unconsciously, we have been part of an interconnected universe all along.

At the very least, when we ask: "Where is everybody?" our comprehension is catalyzed to embrace expanding self-awareness. When we ask: "What is the origin of the universe?" or "Why do its disparate elements behave as they do?" or "What is its ultimate destiny?" what we are really asking is "Where did we come from, and where are we going?" Perhaps it is the seething background radiation from the Big Bang itself that makes our blood hot to the touch. Perhaps the faint whisper of barely discernible communication from the stars lies not only within the constant cosmic background radiation temperature of precisely 2.725 degrees Kelvin, but also within the steady maintenance of our own body temperature at exactly 37.0 degrees Celsius.

Or it may be that extraterrestrials have evolved beyond life that is based on the biological functions that warm our blood, to embrace a reality that lies outside the boundaries of our narrow definitions. V'Ger (Voyager), reprogrammed by alien mechanical entities, may one day be sent back to earth to establish two-way communication in a universally understood binary language, in an effort to reconnect with its creator. (See the movie: "Star Trek, The Motion Picture").

Perhaps the genesis of our own terrestrial lives can be found elsewhere, and can be traced to an alien cosmic laboratory, where it was nurtured in a secret garden, later to be transplanted onto the fertile soil of a primordial earth that had been carefully cultivated by its creator to be pristine in its setting. If so, the hard evidence of extra-terrestrial life may be independently confirmed each time we see our reflection in the mirror, or share with our friends the photographs of our children and grandchildren. Maybe the most enduring illustration of alien / terrestrial interaction lie in our visual image of storks dropping bundled-up newborn human babies down chimneys in Medieval Europe.

Where is everybody? There is within each of us the innate yearning to know that we are not alone in the universe. The Search for Extra-terrestrial Intelligence, (S.E.T.I.) is a worthy endeavor because it represents our determination to raise our sights to the possibility of an expanded view of life. Our efforts represent our desire to be up and moving on the pathway to personal re-discovery and self-actualization. Our blood is stirred when we recall the words of Captain James Tiberius Kirk, who declared: "Space is the final frontier," for he personified our yearning to imitate the daring and bravado of sea captains of old, who precariously ventured forth in fragile vessels on uncharted oceans to accomplish missions of noble purpose. (See the movie: "Star Trek").

Without the evidence that that there are others in the far reaches of space who are navigating the ocean of life, and who are going through trials similar to ours, where will our own sanctuaries be when the wind blows, and the rain beats down? To what sheltered harbor will we flee when tempests toss us about and our lives are in turmoil? When we are thrown to and fro as flotsam and jetsam, never coming to a knowledge of what is real, to what source will we look for the stability we so desperately seek, or for the answers to the questions that continually trouble our spirits? When we raise our sights to the possibility of an expanded view of life on an interstellar scale, and consider the remarkable potential it would have to catalyze greatness, we are up and moving on the pathway to personal re-discovery in the larger arena of higher-dimensional awareness.

Nevertheless, we must concede the possibility that our desire to contact extra-terrestrials could be dangerous. As Q warned Captain Jean Luc Picard: "You judge yourselves against the pitiful adversaries you've encountered so far - the Romulans and the Klingons. They're nothing compared to what's waiting. Picard, you are about to move into areas of the galaxy containing wonders more incredible than you can possibly imagine, and terrors to freeze your soul." ("Star Trek: The Next Generation," "Q Who?"). Later in the same episode, after a particularly traumatic encounter with the recently discovered malevolent Borg, Q warned Picard: "If you can't take a little bloody nose, maybe you ought to go back home and crawl under your bed. It's not safe out here. Its wondrous, with treasures to satiate desires both subtle and gross. But it's not for the timid."

It is also possible that we are inadvertently sending the wrong messages, and alien life has chosen to ignore us because of its basic goodness and instinct for self-preservation, when measured against our primitive incivility. Our electromagnetic signatures could be perceived as threatening or simply obscene. Think of all those episodes of "Miami Vice," the movies "Apocalypse Now" and "Full Metal Jacket," not to mention "War of The Worlds," "Aliens," "Predator," and Internet porn. These electronic emissions could be interpreted by our neighbors as caustic noise pollution on an interstellar magnitude of scale.

To counteract the potentially negative influence or misrepresentation of even a minority of our transmissions, on February 4, 2008, at 7:00 p.m. E.S.T., NASA beamed an interstellar dispatch, the Beatles song "Across the Universe," into deep space, sending a message of peace to any extraterrestrials who happen to be in the vicinity of Polaris, also called the North Star, in 2439. (Polaris is 431 light years distant from earth). The transmission coincided with the celebration of the 40th anniversary of the song's recording, the 45th anniversary of the Deep Space Network, an international antenna array that supports missions to explore the universe, and the 50th anniversary of NASA. "Words are flowing out like endless rain (and) slither wildly as they slip away across the universe. Waves of joy are drifting through my opened mind, possessing and caressing me. Images of broken light, which dance before me like a million eyes ... call me on and on across the universe. Thoughts meander like a restless wind. They tumble blindly as they make their way across the universe. Sounds of laughter (and) shades of life are ringing through my opened ears, inciting and inviting me. Limitless undying love, which shines around me like a million suns ... calls me on and on across the universe."

The lyrics, set to music, may represent our best effort to establish a positive connection with extra-terrestrial life. Such a bond would set in motion and catalyze an infinite expansion of the appreciation and understanding of our temporal and spatial realities that would, in turn, liberate us from fear, doubt, apprehension of danger, the turmoil of the world, and the vagaries of men. Casting off the self-limiting conditions that have heretofore blinded us to a larger view of life, we would expect to enjoy a more settled conviction of the truths of an infinitely expanding reality. We would experience the liberating peace that follows obedience to newly discovered, but spiritually coherent, celestial guideposts and principles.

When we have our own personal epiphanies, and believe that we are not alone in the universe (whether or not we have found hard evidence), we will have begun a journey that will carry us beyond every conceivable event horizon to more intense and reflective self-awareness, deeper and more abiding humility, and incomprehensively more profound and enduring faith. Our reinvigorated confidence will intensify our capacity for mind-expanding higher-level thinking and propel us on our way to Type 1 planetary stability, and beyond.

So, when our inquiry ("Where is everybody?") is rephrased and we ask: "Where did we come from? Why are we here? Where are we going?" the power of creation itself is unleashed in our behalf and we experience the exhilaration of a personally tailored "Big Bang" moment. It is as if we are present in the V.I.P. viewing section at the moment of creation itself. Our power "to become" is released from the oppressive bondage of ignorance and from self-defeating behaviors spawned by arrogance. The genesis of the universe falls into a comprehensible perspective and creates a context and continuity that allows our reality to expand to mind-boggling proportion.

Where is everybody? If we lift our eyes and strain to see beyond our limited horizons, we will intuitively know the answer to that question, and we just might find ourselves cast off into a stream of expanding self-awareness and carried along in quickening currents that take us on a fantastic journey to a far country. We might even come to the point where we begin to appreciate that "the universe is a machine for the making of gods." (Henri Bergson). As Q told Captain Picard: "Con permiso, Capitán. The hall is rented, the orchestra engaged. It's now time to see if you can dance." ("Q Who?"). Whether or not E.T. is calling, today we are one day closer than we were twenty-four hours ago to the discovery of what it really means to be "Dancing with the Stars."

(The) Desert Shall Rejoice
(D&C 57)

"Thus saith the Lord
God: Behold, I will lift up mine hand
to the Gentiles, and set up my standard to
the people; and they shall bring thy sons in their
arms, and thy daughters shall be carried upon their
shoulders. And kings shall be thy nursing fathers,
and their queens thy nursing mothers; they shall
bow down to thee with their face toward the earth,
and lick up the dust of thy feet; and thou
shalt know that I am the Lord."
(1 Nephi 21:22-23).

In the Last Days, said Isaiah, "more are the children of the desolate than the children of the married wife." (Isaiah 54:1). In other words, there shall be a great gathering of Israel from among the Gentile nations, and those who then enter the Fold shall outnumber those who had previously found their way into the church or who were bound by covenant to Christ. Consequently, the Lord commanded Joseph Smith on more than one occasion to "seek to bring forth and establish my Zion." (D&C 6:6, 11:6, 12:6, & 14:6).

To that end, Isaiah had urged: "Enlarge the place of thy tent, and let them stretch forth the curtains of thy habitations; spare not, lengthen thy cords and strengthen thy stakes." (Isaiah 54:2). That is to say, make room for the Children of the Covenant, who will flock to the gospel standard as the gathering of Israel gains momentum. The Lord reaffirmed in the Last Days that "Zion must increase in beauty, and in holiness; her borders must be enlarged; her stakes must be strengthened; yea, verily I say unto you, Zion must arise and put on her beautiful garments" that had been washed clean in the redeeming blood of Christ. (D&C 82:14). Later, He told Joseph Smith that the Saints should remain in Zion "until the day cometh when there is found no more room for them; and then I have other places which I will appoint unto them, and they shall be called stakes, for the curtains or the strength of Zion." (D&C 101:21).

The building of Zion and the establishment of the City of New Jerusalem has been a subject of great interest to members of the church during the years since its organization. But in 1831, the question on the minds of the Saints was: "Where is the city to be located?" The Lord had explained to Joseph Smith in September 1830 only that "no man knoweth where the city of Zion shall be built, but it shall be given hereafter. Behold, I say unto you that it shall be on the borders by the Lamanites." (D&C 28:9).

"Following instructions given in D&C 52 that was recorded on June 7, 1831, Joseph and several elders journeyed to Missouri, preaching as they went. On July 21 of that year, he received D&C 57, in which the Lord explained that Zion would be built in Independence, Jackson County, Missouri." (D&C Class Member Study Guide, p. 11).

This revelation was received in Zion, which is now a suburb of Kansas City, Missouri. "In contemplating the state of the Lamanites and the lack of civilization, refinement, and religion among the people generally, the Prophet (had) exclaimed in yearning prayer: 'When will the wilderness blossom as the rose?'" (Superscript). Four months earlier, he had learned that "before the great day of the Lord shall come, Jacob shall flourish in the wilderness, and the Lamanites shall blossom as the rose." (D&C 49:24). Through his biblical scholarship, he was familiar with the scripture that declared: "The wilderness and the solitary place shall be glad for (Latter Day Israel); and the desert shall rejoice, and blossom as the rose." (Isaiah 35:1).

Four months later, in November 1831, the Lord would reveal: "In the barren deserts there shall come forth pools of living water; and the parched ground shall no longer be a thirsty land." (D&C 133:29). In 1838, at Far West, Missouri, the Lord would promise Joseph: "Therefore, will I not make solitary places to bud and to blossom, and to bring forth in abundance?" (D&C 117:7). He would prosper His people, and Israel would "blossom and bud, and fill the face of the world with the blessings of salvation" through the administration of the Abrahamic Covenant. (Isaiah 27:6). "When will Zion be built up in her glory?" the Prophet had asked. (Superscript). The Lord told Joseph only that "Zion shall flourish upon the hills and rejoice upon the mountains, and shall be assembled together unto the place which I have appointed." (D&C 49:25). Long ago, the Psalmist asked the same enduring question: "Who shall ascend into the hill of the Lord? Or who shall stand in his holy place?" The self-evident answer: "He that hath clean hands, and a pure heart; who hath not lifted up his soul unto vanity, nor sworn deceitfully. He shall receive the blessing from the Lord, and righteousness from the God of his salvation." (Psalms 24:3-5). Covenant Israel "shall flourish like the palm tree: he shall grow like a cedar in Lebanon. Those that be planted in the house of the Lord shall flourish in the courts of our God." (Psalms 92:12-13). Palms often thrive in what appear to be desert wastes. It is only on closer inspection that oases of underlying currents of life sustaining water are noticed, that bring nourishment to the roots of the thirsty trees.

In September 1831, the Lord assured the young Prophet that "the glory of the Lord shall be upon (Zion), and she shall be an ensign unto the people, and there shall come unto her out of every nation under heaven. And the day shall come when the nations of the earth shall tremble because of her, and shall fear because of her terrible ones." (D&C 64:41-43).

Zion is the world's most tangible reflection of Christ Who is its Standard of Righteousness. He said: "Behold I am the light; I have set an example for you." (3 Nephi 18:16). He is the Light we are to hold up and the Example we are to follow. When He said: "Let your light so shine before this people that they may see your good works and glorify your Father who is in heaven," He meant that He should be reflected in all that we do, so that when others see our good works, their thoughts will naturally turn to Christ. He deserves the credit, and His most pious disciples are not worthy to unloose the latches of His shoes. (See Luke 3:16).

The Prophet knew that the House of The Lord could be a homing beacon, and so he wondered: "Where will thy Temple stand, unto which all nations shall come in the last days?" (Superscript). At Fayette, New York, the Lord had promised, "I will give unto you my law; and (in Ohio) you shall be endowed with power from on high." (D&C 38:31). Malachi had also prophesied: "The Lord whom ye seek shall suddenly come to his temple, even the messenger of the covenant." (Malachi 3:1). The prophecy was at least partially fulfilled when the Lord came to the temple at Kirtland, on 4/3, 1836. But from the first days of the Restoration, Joseph Smith knew that if he and the body of Saints were to assist in the establishment of Zion and help to prepare the earth for the millennial reign of Christ, they would need to be endowed with spiritual and priesthood power found only in the ordinances of the gospel that are administered in the temple.

Mormon's description of Jesus as the Holy Child of God the Father in Moroni 8:3 suggests the intimacy between parents and children, and gives us a glimpse of just how strong the relationship is between our Father and His offspring. Our goal, after all, is to discover the very personal levels of the experiences of the Savior, for when He speaks of "knowing Him," He is referring to a special sense of the word. It is not enough that we know about Him, by reading the Gospels, or by listening to others speak of Him. We must know Him through the common bonds and feeling.

Melvin J. Ballard related an experience that might be shared by all those who have received in their hearts the Messenger of the Covenant. He said: "I found myself one evening in the dreams of the night in the sacred building, the temple. After a season of prayer and rejoicing, I was informed that I should have the privilege of entering into one of those rooms, to meet a glorious Personage, and, as I entered the door, I saw, seated on a raised platform, the most glorious Being my eyes have ever beheld or that I ever conceived existed in all the eternal worlds. A I approached to be introduced, he arose and stepped towards me with extended arms and he smiled as he softly spoke my name. If I shall live to be a million years old, I shall never forget that smile. He took me in his arms and kissed me, pressed me to his bosom and blessed me, until the marrow of my bones seemed to melt. When he had finished, I fell at his feet, and as I bathed them with my tears and kisses, I saw the prints of the nails in the feet of the Redeemer of the world. The feeling that I had in the presence of Him who hath all things in his hands, to have his love, his affection and his blessing was such that if I ever can receive that of which I had but a foretaste, I would give all I am, all that I ever hope to be, to feel what I then felt." ("Sermons and Missionary Experiences of Melvin Joseph Ballard," p. 156).

The Lord whom we all seek can be found in His House. This prophecy continues to be fulfilled as temples of the Lord are constructed throughout the earth. Of the Kirtland Temple, Jesus Christ said: "I have accepted this house, and my name shall be here; and I will manifest myself to my people in mercy in this house." (D&C 110:7). This has been true of every temple subsequently built by the church. In the Lord's House, He may be found Who binds us to eternity through the covenants of the priesthood.

Without the temple, civilization is an empty shell and a structure of custom and convenience only. Those who constructed the Tower of Babel did so in order to establish a binding place of heaven and earth where it was hoped that celestial contact could be established. In fact, that profane ziggurat was a vain and corrupt counterfeit of the temple, where alone we can get our bearings on the eternities. The confounding of languages that took place after the destruction of the tower was so that one could not understand another's verbal communication. Its objective was to teach man to rely on the universal language of the Spirit and gain fluency in that supernal means of communication.

In our own day, those who build sanctuaries to be used just one day each week restrict their worship to the time spent while in church. But we cannot draw near to God either spiritually or physically by constructing elaborate edifices for Sunday-only worship. We feel a kinship with God by redefining our nature.

If we resist the character-shaping forces that would lead us to the awakening of our divine potential, or if we "undertake to cover our sins, or to gratify our pride, (or) our vain ambition … behold the heavens withdraw themselves, (and) the Spirit of the Lord is grieved." (D&C 121:37). Speaking of those who are faithful and habitual patrons of the Temple, Hugh Nibley wrote: "Here is a band of mortals who are actually engaged in doing something which has not their own comfort, convenience, or profit as its object. Here, at last, is a phenomenon that commands respect in our day and could safely be put forth among the few valid arguments we now have to induce Deity to spare the human race; thousands of men and women putting themselves out for no ulterior motive. The Temple, as its very name proclaims, is a place where we take our bearings on the universe." ("On The Timely and Timeless," p. xxvii). When we qualify to enjoy the blessings of the Atonement, we are freed from the bondage created by unresolved sin When we have received the blessing of the temple, our characteristics are simply the result of a spiritual transformation that comes about as we live in obedience to the Celestial Law of the Lord. In this way, a Zion society is created, conceived in Royal Courts on High, fashioned out of our ardor and conviction, and preserved through the ordinances in which we participate in the temple.

In the early days of the Restoration, by and large the converts were extraordinarily devoted to Christ. After entering the Fold, it was often as it had been among the Nephites during the time of the post-resurrection ministry of the Lord, when "many of them saw and heard unspeakable things, which are not lawful to be written. And they taught, and did minister one to another; and they had all things common among them, every man dealing justly, one with another. And it came to pass that they did do all things even as Jesus had commanded them." (3 Nephi 26:18-20).

Without really comprehending what was happening, they were being transformed into a Zion society, "for this is Zion - THE PURE IN HEART." (D&C 97:21). They "were called the church of Christ." (3 Nephi 26:21). What a great example they became for later Saints! As we attempt to embrace the gospel and emulate the Master, we remember His wise counsel: "Ye know the things that ye must do in my church; for the works which ye have seen me do that shall ye also do." (3 Nephi 27:21).

The endowment of spiritual and priesthood power that the Saints would receive in the anticipated temple would be critical to their spiritual welfare. Satan knows the Lord's servants as marked men and women. Therefore, they need a solid foundation of doctrinal understanding, a firm and abiding testimony of the principles of the gospel, of the Plan of Salvation, and of the Savior, a blessing and setting apart by file leaders, the special protection of the ordinances of the Melchizedek Priesthood, the companionship of the Spirit, and the continual prayers of the faithful. Adult members of the church also require the endowment of spiritual power received only in the Lord's House. The ordinances of the temple strengthen them against the influences of the world. "Without the ordinances thereof, and the authority of the priesthood," declared the Savior to Joseph Smith, "the power of godliness is not manifest unto men in the flesh." (D&C 84:21).

Joseph F. Smith wrote of the endowment: "We enter into covenants with the Lord that we will keep ourselves pure and unspotted from the world. We have agreed before God, angels, and witnesses, in sacred places, that we will not commit adultery, will not lie, that we will not steal or bear false witness against our neighbors, or take advantage of the weak, that we will help and sustain our fellow men in the right, and take such a course as will prove most effectual in helping the weak to overcome their weaknesses and bring themselves into subjection to the requirements of heaven. We cannot neglect, slight, or depart from the spirit, meaning, intent and purpose of these covenants and agreements that we have entered into with our Father in Heaven, without shearing ourselves of our glory, strength, right and title to His blessings, and to the gifts and manifestations of His Spirit." ("Improvement Era," 8/1906, p. 813). It would be difficult to more clearly compose a statement explaining the need for establishing a covenant relationship with God. It would be nigh impossible to visualize a more appropriate place in which to do so than the House of The Lord. Therefore, the Lord has given His people a continuing responsibility: "Organize yourselves; prepare every needful thing; and establish a house, even a house of prayer, a house of fasting, a house of faith, a house of learning, a house of glory, a house of order, a house of God." (D&C 88:119).

"For thus saith the Lord God: (Joseph Smith) have I inspired to move the cause of Zion in mighty power for good, and his diligence I know, and his prayers I have heard." (D&C 21:7). Even though conditions in the world would degenerate and peace would be taken from the earth, those in Zion would enjoy the safety and security that only righteousness can guarantee, and there would be such an outpouring of the Spirit that the time would come when the earth would be "full of the knowledge of the Lord, as the waters cover the sea." (Isaiah 11:9).

B.H. Roberts had a great testimony of the prophet, and knew that here was a man who could lead his people to safety and security in Zion. "Having gone word by word and line by line through his writings, and having read everything he could find on his life, he found Joseph Smith to be possessed of a deeper and richer comprehension of (the gathering to Zion) than anyone he had read in the Christian tradition since the apostles." He knew that Joseph Smith was an instrument of the Lord in moving forward its cause. "This conviction never diminished. Joseph Smith told the truth. Joseph Smith was a prism of the Lord Jesus Christ." (Truman Madsen, "Defender of The Faith," p. 93).

A primary reason for our consecration of time, talents, and means is to raise holy sanctuaries so that, as the Lord explained: "My covenant people may be gathered in one in that day when I shall come to my temple. And this I do for the salvation of my people." (D&C 42:6). The opportunities for sanctification by the Spirit are never greater than when we enjoy the blessing of the temple. The temple is that most magnificent of earthly constructions, where alone pure knowledge flows as the dews of Carmel. In the Dispensation of The Fulness of Times, the House of the Lord will continue to be a dominant feature of the church and kingdom, and is a tangible confirmation of the fulfillment of prophecy, of the restoration of priesthood keys of authority, and of God's concern and love.

"Subsequently, (the Prophet) received this revelation." (Superscript to Section 57). On January 5, 1831, the Lord had told Joseph Smith: "Thou art called to labor in my vineyard, and to buildup my church, and to bring forth Zion." (D&C 39:13). The Saints knew that anciently "the Lord (had) called his people Zion, because they were of one heart and one mind, and dwelt in righteousness." (Moses 7:18). Joseph Smith had learned when studying the Bible that the power or strength of Zion is to "break mountains, to divide the seas, to dry up waters, to tur them out of their course; to put at defiance the armies of nations, to divide the earth, to break every band, to stand in the presence of God." (J.S.T. Genesis 14:30-31). No wonder the Saints sought Zion with such zeal.

Now, the Lord finally revealed: "Missouri ... is the land which I have appointed and consecrated for the gathering of the saints." (V. 1). On September 26, 1830, the Lord told Joseph Smith: "Wherefore the decree hath gone forth from the Father that (the Saints) shall be gathered in unto one place upon the face of this land, to prepare their hearts and be prepared in all things against the day when tribulation and desolation are sent forth upon the wicked." (D&C 29:8). For "the time will come that war will be poured out upon all nations." (D&C 87:2).

To save His people and in fulfillment of prophecy, on 4/3, 1836, in the Kirtland Temple, the Lord directed Moses to restore the keys of the gathering of both Covenant and Blood Israel. One hundred and thirty-nine years later, Spencer W. Kimball declared: "The brighter day has dawned. The gathering is in progress. May the Lord bless us, as we become nursing fathers and mothers unto our (Israelite) brethren and hasten the fulfillment of the great promises made to them." (C.R., 10/1975).

The Lord has not forgotten Israel, although she has repeatedly forsaken Him. "For can a woman forget her sucking child, that she should not have compassion on the son of her womb?" (1 Nephi 21:15). Israel shall yet inherit her former lands in great glory. "For thy waste and thy desolate places, and the land of thy destruction, shall even now be too narrow by reason of the inhabitants; and they that swallowed thee up shall be far away." (1 Nephi 21:19). In 1830, there were fewer than seven thousand Jews living in the Holy Land. In 1980, there were over three million. In 1830, only one in five hundred persons living in the Holy Land was a Jew. In 1980, one in five was a Jew. The prophecies are being fulfilled.

As the end approaches, the Gentile nations of the earth shall assist in the gathering of Israel. "Thus saith the Lord God: Behold, I will lift up mine hand to the Gentiles, and set up my standard to the people; and they shall bring thy sons in their arms, and thy daughters shall be carried upon their shoulders." (Isaiah 49:22). The ensign to which the people would look is the gospel standard. As the Lord told Joseph Smith: "And even so I have sent mine everlasting covenant into the world, to be a light to the world, and to be a standard for my people, and for the Gentiles to seek to it, and to be a messenger before my face to prepare the way before me." (D&C 45:9).

So thoroughly and convincingly will the Lord touch the hearts of the Gentile nations, that He promised Israel through Isaiah that "kings shall be thy nursing fathers, and their queens thy nursing mothers; they shall bow down to thee with their face towards the earth, and lick up the dust of thy feet; and thou shalt know that I am the Lord." (Isaiah 49:23). As we witness the governments of the earth bowing down in humility and assisting the efforts of Israel to gather to the land of her inheritance, we are seeing signs that the Lord is God.

At the same time, those who have persecuted and oppressed Israel shall be punished. "For the mighty God shall deliver his covenant people (and) I will contend with them that contend with thee, and I will save thy children." (J.S.T. Isaiah 49:25). "And I will feed them that oppress thee with their own flesh; and they shall be drunken with their own blood, as with sweet wine; and all flesh shall know that I, the Lord, am thy Saviour and thy Redeemer, the Mighty One of Jacob." (Isaiah 49:26).

For the righteous, though, a way of deliverance has been prepared. "A prophet shall the Lord your God raise up," said Moses. "This prophet of whom Moses spake was the Holy One of Israel." (1 Nephi 22:20-21). Because of His ministry, the righteous will not be confounded. Because they will listen to His counsel, which has been given by revelation to His Prophets, and which is also found in the scriptures, they will not be destroyed. For their own safety, though, they will need to gather in the wards, stakes, and missions of the church. For "the time cometh speedily that the righteous must be led up as calves of the stall." (1 Nephi 22:24).

In fact, the gathering of the Saints to the Stakes of Zion is "for a defense, and for a refuge from the storm, and from wrath when it shall be poured out without mixture upon the whole earth." (D&C 115:6). Ezra Taft Benson taught that our stake ecclesiastical units have "at least four purposes. One is to unify and perfect the members who live in those boundaries, by extending to them the church programs, the ordinances, and gospel instruction. (Secondly), the members of stakes are to be models, or standards, of righteousness. (Third), stakes are to be a defense. They do this as stake members unify under their local priesthood officers and consecrate themselves to do their duty and keep their covenants. (Fourth), stakes are a refuge from the storm to be poured out over the earth." ("Ensign," 1/1991, p. 2-5).

The elect are gathered to the church, "even as many as will believe in me," said the Lord, "and hearken unto my voice." (D&C 33:6). It is our mission to preach the gospel throughout the world in fulfillment of the promises of the Abrahamic Covenant, because those through whose veins runs the blood of Israel (the elect) need the foundation covenants. David B. Haight once said that we do not preach the gospel so that people can enjoy better lives. We do it so that they can be saved in the Celestial Kingdom of God.

The Lord said: "No power shall stay my hand." (D&C 38:33). The endowment will empower His missionary army with the spiritual strength to meet any challenge. "Then shall ye, who are a remnant of the house of Jacob, go forth among them; and ye shall be in the midst of them who shall be many; and ye shall be among them as a lion among the beasts of the forest, and as a young lion among the flocks of sheep, who, if he goeth through both treadeth down and teareth in pieces, and none can deliver." (3 Nephi 20:16). Thus, will His missionaries march through Spiritual Babylon in the Last Days, "fair as the moon, clear as the sun, and terrible as an army with banners." (Song of Solomon 6:10). "The nations of the earth shall tremble because of (Zion), and shall fear because of her terrible ones." (D&C 64:43). "And they shall stand afar off and tremble. And all nations shall be afraid because of the terror of the Lord, and the power of his might." (D&C 45:74-75).

In February 1831, Joseph Smith had been instructed that the missionaries should preach the gospel "until the time (should) come when it (would) be revealed … when the city of the New Jerusalem (should) be prepared." (D&C 42:9). Without modern revelation, we would be in complete ignorance concerning the New Jerusalem. Elsewhere in these revelations, the Lord stated that "Mount Zion … shall be the city of New Jerusalem." (D&C 84:2). This can be taken literally, or the mountain of the Lord's house can be thought of as both allegorical and figurative, referring to a high place of God, a place of revelation, and certainly to the temple of the Lord.

Isaiah made a distinction when he said: "For out of Zion shall go forth the law, and the word of the Lord from Jerusalem." (Isaiah 2:3). "The Lord shall roar out of Zion, and utter his voice from Jerusalem," declared the Prophet Joel. (Joel 3:16). The Lord further clarified the difference between the New and Old Cities of Jerusalem, when He warned: "Let them, therefore, who are among the Gentiles flee unto Zion. And let them who be of Judah flee unto Jerusalem, unto the Mountains of the Lord's house." (D&C 133:12-13).

In vivid terms, the Doctrine & Covenants identifies the New Jerusalem as "a land of peace, a city of refuge, a place of safety for the saints of the Most High God. And the glory of the Lord shall be there, and the terror of the Lord also shall be there, insomuch that the wicked will not come unto it, and it shall be called Zion. And it shall come to pass among the wicked, that every man that will not take his sword against his neighbor must needs flee unto Zion for safety. And there shall be gathered unto it out of every nation under heaven; and it shall be the only people that shall not be at war one with another. And it shall be said among the wicked: Let us not go up to battle against Zion, for the inhabitants of Zion are terrible; wherefore we cannot stand. And it shall come to pass that the righteous shall be gathered out from among all nations, and shall come to Zion, singing with songs of everlasting joy." (D&C 45:65-71).

On February 9, 1831, the Lord had told Joseph Smith: "And ye shall hereafter receive church covenants, such as shall be sufficient to establish you." (D&C 42:67). Later, He said: "A commandment I give unto you, to prepare and organize yourselves by a bond or everlasting covenant that cannot be broken." (D&C 78:11). Because of the ministry of Joseph Smith and others, faith has increased to the point that the Covenant that God made with Abraham has now been re-established all over the world. It has become possible for the fulness of the gospel to be "proclaimed by the weak and the simple unto the ends of the world, and before kings and rulers." (D&C 1:23). The strength of the gospel is its theology, circumscribed by the Abrahamic Covenant, which will bear up under the careful scrutiny of even the most critical minds on earth.

In this revelation, Joseph Smith was told unequivocally: "This is the land of promise, and the place for the city of Zion." (V. 2). That city is the New Jerusalem, and "the kingdom of Zion is in very deed the kingdom of our God and his Christ." (D&C 105:32). The prophet Ether had seen in vision, "the Jerusalem from whence Lehi should come, (and that) after it should be destroyed it should be built up again, a holy city unto the Lord; wherefore, it could not be a new Jerusalem for it had been in a time of old." He also saw that "a New Jerusalem should be built up upon this land" of America. (Ether 13:5-6). Here, the remnant of the house of Joseph would "build up a holy city unto the Lord, like unto the Jerusalem of old." (Ether 13:8). In this millennial New Jerusalem will reside those "whose garments are white through the blood of the Lamb; and they are they who are numbered among the remnant of the seed of Joseph who were of the house of Israel. And then also cometh the Jerusalem of old; and the inhabitants thereof, blessed are they, for they have (also) been washed in the blood of the Lamb; and they are they who were scattered and gathered in from the four quarters of the earth, and from the north countries, and are partakers of the fulfilling of the covenant which God made with their father, Abraham." (Ether 13:10-11).

As well as a place, Zion is an attitude that focuses our thoughts, words, and deeds on the Law of the Gospel, brotherhood, stewardship, equality, agency, accountability, consecration, charity, and selflessness. "How carefully most men creep into nameless graves," observed Phillips Brooks, "while now and again one or two forget themselves into immortality." Zion requires this higher level of thinking and acting inasmuch as expands our view beyond the limited horizon of our natural sight. Zion requires vision. As Helen Keller observed from her unique perspective: "Why cannot the soul discard the poor lenses of the body, and peer through the telescope of truth into the infinite reaches of immortality?" ("My Religion," p. 76).

When Joan of Arc was led to the stake, she was given the opportunity to obtain her freedom by denying what she believed. Instead, she said: "I know this now. Every man gives his life for what he believes. Every woman gives her life for what she believes. Sometimes people believe in little or nothing, and yet they give their lives for little or nothing. One life is all we have, and we live it as we believe in living it, and then it is gone. But to surrender what you are and live without belief is more terrible than dying, even more terrible than dying young." (Maxwell Anderson, "Joan of Lorraine," Act 2, Interlude 3). The inhabitants of Zion experience the same burning zeal.

Boyd K Packer said of this dedicated commitment to uncompromising obedience to eternal law: "That which God will never take by force, He will accept when freely given. And he will then return to you freedom that you can hardly dream of; the freedom to feel and to know, the freedom to do and the freedom to be, at least a thousand-fold more than we offer him. Strangely enough, the key to freedom is obedience." ("B.Y.U. Address," 12/1971). The key to a Zion centered mind set is the adjustment of our internal attitudes reflected in the phenomenon of being born again. Once again, we are reminded of the wisdom of Helen Keller, who said that the real tragedy in life is not being born without sight, but living in the shadows without vision.

"We are from the Philippines," a young woman said. "It is a beautiful country besieged by unfortunate violence. It is during these challenging times of war that we cling to the gospel and its truth and light. The most glorious addition to our poor country has been the beautiful temple which stands tall and bright in the midst of the city of Manila. It has been a symbol of hope and strength for our growing congregation of Latter-day Saints.

In 1989 the violence became particularly bad. With bombers flying overhead and sharpshooters firing at any moving object, people, young and old, weak and strong, military and civilian began flocking to the grounds of the temple. For four days, we stayed on the temple grounds, and watched as planes dropped bombs all around us. The statue of the Angel Moroni standing tall and bright above the temple was a clear target for any trained fighter pilot. But four days went by and not one bomb touched the beautiful temple, and not one person standing on those temple grounds was injured. It was as if we were surrounded by an army of angels. We felt the protective hand of our Heavenly Father." (Retold by Sister Joanna Hudson, a young missionary).

We are all in the midst of a raging war. Life on earth subjects us to violence, crime, and other dangers everyday. We find ourselves trying to ward off the bombardment of evil, all too often feeling frustrated and helpless. In our schools, at work, and sometimes in our very own homes we face challenges that test our strength to endure. But as Nephi said, we "must press forward with a steadfastness in Christ, having a perfect brightness of hope, and a love of God and of all men." (2 Nephi 31:20). What a great thought! If we remain strong and unfaltering, we can all stand in holy places and be not moved. We can enjoy the safety and security of Zion.

Neal A. Maxwell assured us: "When in situations of stress we wonder if there is any more to give. We can be comforted to know that God, who knows our capacity perfectly, placed us here to succeed. No one was foreordained to fail or to be wicked." ("Ensign." 2/1979). It just isn't in the Plan. We all chose to come to earth to prove ourselves worthy of citizenship with the Saints in the household of faith. We were not placed here by accident. Elder Maxwell went on to say: "When we have been weighed and found wanting, let us remember that we were measured before and were found equal to our tasks. Therefore, let us continue, but with a more determined discipleship. When we feel overwhelmed, let us recall the assurance that God will not press upon us more than we can bear. For the faithful, our finest hours are sometimes during or just following our darkest hours." When Zion is tested, she puts on her strength and shows her true colors.

"The place which is now called Independence is the center place, and a spot for the temple is lying westward, upon a lot which is not far from the courthouse." (V. 3). In the years since the Lord delivered this revelation to Joseph Smith, significant changes have taken place both in the church and in the world. From its temporary headquarters in Salt Lake City, Utah, the gospel is being taken to every nation, kindred, tongue, and people, and prophetic vision is being validated. The stone cut out of the mountain is rolling over the whole earth, and cannot be stopped. (See Daniel 2:34). What a thrill it is for members of the restored church of Jesus Christ to march in the ranks of Christian soldiers who take the battle for truth directly into the camp of the willfully or ignorantly disobedient.

"The land should be purchased by the saints, and also every tract lying westward ... that they may obtain it for an everlasting inheritance." (V. 4-5). In association with His instruction regarding missionary work, the Lord had revealed on June 7, 1831, that "the land of Missouri ... is the land of your inheritance." (D&C 52:42). It seems natural that He would provide this specific instruction to those who were to be fishers of men. After all, the commission of the missionaries is to gather the elect from the world and bring them to Zion. Now, they would be able to include this new revelation regarding the location of Zion as part of their message to those receptive to the truth. The spirit of gathering would become a strong motivator to action.

The inheritance spoken of by the Lord is a great blessing to the Saints, because "we live in a day and in a world full of doubts and confusion, where people do not know what to believe, where tensions are high, where the pace is frantic and progress in terms of righteousness is not a popular goal. Violence and crudity are everyday patterns all around us. What a blessing it is to know there is a haven, a place of rest from the turmoil of the world. The prophets and the Savior have called upon us to (establish Zion), where life has purpose and direction, and where priesthood power is possible." ("Gospel Doctrine Manual," p. 79).

The Lord has told His people: "I hold forth and deign (or condescend) to give unto you greater riches, even a land of promise, a land flowing with milk and honey, upon which there shall be no curse when the Lord cometh. And I will give it unto you for the land of your inheritance, if you seek it with all your hearts." (D&C 38:18-19). When it is transformed to its terrestrial state, the curse on the earth will be lifted. Therefore, Zion must be prepared to receive her King, for at that time only the righteous will remain on the earth. These are they who will have tried the virtue of the word of God in the crucible of adversity.

One reason why all profane government will be destroyed before the Second Coming of the Lord is that its concept of welfare is defined by a detached, disinterested, and ineffectual paternalism, in contrast to the active, meaningful brotherhood that characterizes the inhabitants of Zion. Hugh Nibley spoke of the "Mahan Principle," that he defined as "the great secret of converting life into property." ("Approaching Zion"). There is, we discover in every government action, an economic baseline that ignores the worth of souls. At the present time, the Lord counters this Satanic twisting of the principle of consecration with the Law of Tithing. Beginning in 1838, even though they were in the most straitened circumstances, He declared to the Church: "And this shall be the beginning of the tithing of my people." (D&C 119:3). Since its introduction, this Law has remained a foundation principle. Tithing is paid with faith more than it is with currency, and in obedience the Saints are blessed beyond measure. On the other hand, when government has immense powers to siphon off the productivity of its citizens, and when taxpayers involuntarily contribute to the support of programs they cannot morally support, the roots of evil become entrenched.

We could learn from the lesson illustrated in The Book of Mormon, when the rulers "were supported in their laziness, and in their idolatry, and in their whoredoms, by the taxes which King Noah had put upon the people; thus did the people labor exceedingly to support iniquity. Yea, and they also became idolatrous because they were deceived by the vain and flattering words of the kings and priests." (Mosiah 11:6-7). In the Zion society envisioned for the Latter-day Saints, the celestial character trait of consecration would be woven into every fiber of their being.

To His disciples in the Holy Land, the Savior had cautioned: "Take heed that ye do not your alms before men to be seen of them; otherwise ye have no reward of your Father which is in heaven." (Matthew 6:1). Such individuals have not yet been ignited by the flame of faith. They are not yet white-hot sparks struck off the divine anvil of God. Their spirits do not yet generate enough intrinsic energy to power the City of Light.

In Zion, he that would be master is the servant of all. Ralph Waldo Emerson lamented: "Once we had wooden chalices and golden priests. Now we have golden chalices and wooden priests." ("Lectures & Biographical Sketches," p. 229). As Alvin R. Dyer cautioned: "We must not be caught in the bind of building a church and killing the articles of its faith, or permitting form to triumph over spirit. The church and kingdom of God is built by the ardor and conviction of its members. We must be alert to the expansion of its assets at the cost of lost conviction. When buildings or institutions grow bigger and bigger, let us be fearful lest the Spirit will thin out." ("A Foundation for Education").

The Lord has not forgotten His Chosen People. To them, He promised: "This shall be my covenant with you, ye shall have (Zion) for the land of your inheritance, and for the inheritance of your children forever, while the earth shall stand, and ye shall possess it again in eternity," when the earth finally receives its celestial stature, "no more to pass away." (D&C 38:20). When the Son of God comes to receive His millennial kingdom, He will come in glory. "Come unto Christ," urged Jacob, "and partake of the goodness of God, that (you) might enter into his rest." (Jacob 1:7). For God's Rest "is the fulness of His glory." (D&C 84:24). In this sense, Jesus came to the earth in His glory, that is, as a lamb without spot or blemish, worthy at all times throughout His mortal life of the inner peace that is born of righteousness. "The glory of God," after all, "is light and truth." (D&C 93:36). Our progression involves the grand principle that we may be "glorified in truth (until we know) all things." (D&C 93:26). This is the spirit of Zion. It was the possibility of the fulfillment of these promises through a partnership with God that drove the Saints through years of hardship in the hope that they might establish Zion.

"Keep all the commandments and covenants by which ye are bound," said the Lord, "and I will cause the heavens to shake for your good, and Satan shall tremble and Zion shall rejoice upon the hills and flourish." (D&C 35:24). The wicked will be as Belshazzar of old, "whose thoughts troubled him so that the joints of his loins were loosed, and his knees smote one against another." (Daniel 5:6). But those who dwell safely within the boundaries of the Lord's inheritance are promised a safe haven from the insecurity and uncertainty of a worldly lifestyle.

Nephi said that those who are of the "kingdom of the devil" are the ones who should fear. They are "all churches which are built up to get gain, and all those who are built up to become popular in the eyes of the world, and those who seek the lusts of the flesh, and the things of the world, and to do all manner of iniquity; yea, in fine, all those who belong to the kingdom of the devil are they who need fear, and tremble, and quake." (1 Nephi 22:23). These institutions that represent the devil's kingdom stand in stark contrast to the government of Heavenly Father.

The Church of Jesus Christ of Latter-day Saints represents itself as the Lord's church on the earth. He owns it, for He organized it and gave Himself for it. It is the sacred depository of His truth and is His instrument for the perfecting of the Saints as well as for the work of the ministry. It is Christ's church in all these respects, but it is an institution that belongs to the Saints. It is their refuge from the confusion and religious doubt of the world, their instructor in principle, doctrine, and righteousness, and their guide in matters of faith and morals. They have a conjoint ownership in it with Jesus Christ, which is recognized in the latter part of the title: The Church of Jesus Christ of Latter-day Saints.

"And now concerning the gathering - Let the bishop and the agent make preparations for those families which have been commanded to come to this land, as soon as possible, and plant them in their inheritance." (V. 15). In March 1831, at Kirtland, Ohio, the Lord had told Joseph Smith that these leaders would "be appointed to purchase the lands, and to make a commencement to lay the foundation of the city; and then shall ye begin to be gathered with your families." (D&C 48:6). "For thou shalt devote all thy service in Zion; and in this thou shalt have strength." (D&C 24:7). When we free ourselves from the bondage of personal agendas, we are guided by a greater sense of our stewardship responsibilities. As King Benjamin declared: "When ye are in the service of your fellow beings," he said, "ye are only in the service of your God." (Mosiah 2:17).

The Creator does not generally intervene personally in our affairs, nor is He typically served directly. The Savior set the pattern when He declared: "Inasmuch as ye have done it unto one of the least of these my brethren, ye have done it unto me." (Matthew 25:40). We all should focus on what C.S. Lewis called "acts of quiet Christianity," those charitable acts of service for which there is no thought of recognition, recompense, or reciprocation.

The Lord has established the pattern for all to follow: "Keep my commandments, and seek to bring forth and establish the cause of Zion." (D&C 11:6). While selfishness results in contention, apostasy, affliction, and persecution, the service of the faithful brings peace, plenty, and unity. Righteous stewards concentrate on the quality of their service, and not on their position or recognition within the church. The only authority the brethren of the priesthood are given is the power to bless the lives of others. God notices and watches over us. But it is usually through the priesthood or those who act under its direction that He meets our needs. "Therefore, it is vital that we serve each other. The abundant life is achieved as we magnify our view of life and expand our view of others and our own possibilities. Thus, the more we follow the teachings of the Master, the more enlarged our perspective becomes. We see many more possibilities for service that we would have seen without this magnification. There is great security in spirituality, and we cannot have spirituality without service." (Spencer W. Kimball, "Ensign," 10/1985).

"And Israel shall be saved in mine own due time; and by the keys which I have given shall they be led, and no more be confounded at all." (D&C 35:25). Quoting Isaiah, the Savior declared: "And then shall be brought to pass that which is written:" Awake, awake, put on thy strength, O Zion; put on thy beautiful garments, O Jerusalem, the holy city." (Isaiah 52:1). The Doctrine & Covenants provides the explanation to this scripture: "What is meant by the command in Isaiah, 52nd chapter, 1st verse, which saith: Put on thy strength, O Zion - and what people had Isaiah reference to? He had reference to those whom God should call in the last days, who should hold the power of priesthood to bring again Zion, and the redemption of Israel; and to put on her strength is to put on the authority of the priesthood, which she, Zion, has a right to by lineage; also, to return to that power which she had lost." (D&C 113:7-8).

Brigham Young taught that the power God gives us "is designed to test us and enable us to show to ourselves, our fellows, and all the heavens just how we would act if entrusted with God's power." (Hugh Nibley, "Subduing the Earth," p. 89-90). When we have been unwavering, and have passed our individually tailored tests with high marks, we are made "mighty in word and in deed, in faith and in works." (Helaman 10:5). Under those conditions, we are given the power of God because we can be trusted to do exactly as God would do in similar circumstances.

Joseph Smith clearly taught that the exercise of priesthood power is based solely upon the principles of righteousness. If, in its capacity, we "undertake to cover our sins, or to gratify our pride, our vain ambition, or to exercise control or dominion or compulsion upon the souls of the children of men, in any degree of unrighteousness," its authority is taken from us. (D&C 121:34-37).

"You are, and always will be, independent in that stage of development to which your voluntary decisions and divine powers have led," taught Truman Madsen. "There are limits all along the way to what you can be and do. But you are not a billiard ball. No power in the universe can coerce your complete assent or dissent. This thesis on capacity translates Bergson's metaphor into breath-taking fact: 'The universe is a machine for the making of gods.'" ("Eternal Man," p. 18).

Zion represents what man has been unable to accomplish for two millennia - the Gathering of Israel and the establishment of a utopian society. Bruce R. McConkie believed that it would specifically be under the direction of the First Presidency of The Church of Jesus Christ of Latter-day Saints that this would come to pass. (See "A New Witness for Christ," p. 572). When the Kirtland Temple was dedicated, the prayer offered by Joseph Smith included a plea that "the children of Judah (might) begin to return" to the lands which God had given to their father Abraham. (D&C 109:63).

Soon thereafter, Moses appeared in that temple and committed to Joseph Smith "the keys of the gathering of Israel from the four parts of the earth, and the leading of the ten tribes from the land of the north." (D&C 110:11). Later, by direction of the Prophet, Orson Hyde traveled to the Holy Land and stood on the Mount of Olives, overlooking the Old City of Jerusalem. From that vantage point, he offered a prayer, dedicating that land for the return of the Jews.

With the blessing and power of the priesthood of God vested in the First Presidency and Quorum of The Twelve, Israel shall "loose (herself) from the bands of (her) neck." (Isaiah 52:2). In his explanation of this verse, Joseph Smith said: "We are to understand that the scattered remnants are exhorted to return to the Lord from whence they have fallen; which if they do, the promise of the Lord is that he will speak to them, or give them revelation. The bands of her neck are the curses of God upon her, or the remnants of Israel in their scattered condition among the Gentiles." (D&C 113:10).

Obedience to the principles of the gospel allows us to wipe the slate clean. As we grow in grace, we enjoy in greater abundance the gifts and power of God by which we may be brought to perfection. Even the Savior "received not of the fulness at first, but continued from grace to grace, until he received a fulness." (D&C 93:12). "And it came to pass that Jesus grew up with his brethren, and waxed strong, and waited upon the Lord for the time of his ministry to come. And he served under his father, and he spake not as other men, neither could he be taught, for he needed not that any man should teach him. And after many years, the hour of his ministry grew nigh." (J.S.T. Matthew 3:22-25). The conditions for receiving the gifts of God in a Zion setting are submission to His will and obedience to His commandments, for we are incapable of perfection through our own efforts. A greater endowment beyond own capabilities is required if we are to take up residence in the Celestial City. Blessed with that endowment, however, we are even now able to enjoy a beautiful spirit in our meetings that are "conducted by the church after the manner of the workings of the Spirit, and by the power of the Holy Ghost; for as the power of the Holy Ghost (leads us) whether to preach, or to exhort, or to pray, or to supplicate, or to sing, even so it (is) done." (Moroni 6:9).

After all, "the great objective of all our work is to build character and build faith in the lives of those whom we serve." (Spencer W. Kimball, C.R., 4/1948). The keys that were restored through the Prophet Joseph Smith allowed his successors to continue the process of sanctification. To put it in terms we can understand, the Lord said: "I am the same which (has) taken the Zion of Enoch into mine own bosom." (D&C 38:4). To be "in the bosom" is a Hebrew idiom derived from the fact that anciently, a man's clothing consisted of flowing robes with a sash, forming a space where precious possessions, and even small children, were carried. The expression implies a very close and favored relationship.

For the early Latter-day Saints, Zion was the City of Light, the Celestial City of God, far removed from the mud and overcast skies, the hardship and persecution, and the sickness and death so familiar to them in their telestial surroundings. Joseph F. Smith said: "If we would carry out that which the Lord revealed, it would only be a matter of a very short time until this people would be in the same condition as were the people of the City of Enoch." (C.R., 4/1921). "And it came to pass (in Enoch's day) that he built a city that was called the city of Holiness, even Zion." (J.S.T. Genesis 7:25). "And Enoch and all his people walked with God, and he dwelt in the midst of Zion; and it came to pass that Zion was not, for God received it up into his own bosom; and from thence went forth the saying, Zion is Fled." (Moses 7:69).

In the summer of 1831, Joseph Smith was immersed in the translation of the Bible. Through his efforts, he gained both doctrinal and historical understanding relating to Zion. This came to him in promptings that motivated him to revise, amend, clarify, and add to that body of literature, particularly to the early chapters of the book of Genesis. He also received many revelations that have been incorporated into The Doctrine & Covenants that shed light on Zion, revealing its nature and characteristics, and making its establishment a realistic opportunity. The Lord's promise was unfolded before the Latter-day Saints as both a challenge and a goal: "And righteousness and truth will I cause to sweep the earth as with a flood, to gather out mine own elect from the four quarters of the earth, unto a place which I shall prepare; an holy city, that my people may gird up their loins, and be looking forth for the time of my coming, for there shall be my tabernacle, and it shall be called Zion, a New Jerusalem. And the Lord said unto Enoch, Then shalt thou and all thy city meet them there; and we will receive them into our bosom; and they shall see us, and we will fall upon their necks, and they shall fall upon our necks, and we will kiss each other; And there shall be mine abode, and it shall be Zion, which shall come forth out of all the creations which I have made; and for the space of a thousand years shall the earth rest." (J.S.T. Genesis 7:70-72).

How satisfying it will be for the Latter-day Saints to "come out of the world, to leave the loneliness and estrangement of a fallen creation and enter the realm of divine experience, to forsake the orphanage of spiritual alienation, and be received into the family and household of the Lord Jesus Christ. They will have left the ranks of the nameless to take upon them the blessed name of Jesus Christ. They are Christians. Through their Master, they will become, in time, joint heirs to all that the Father has." (Robert L. Millet, et. al, "Doctrinal Commentary on The Book of Mormon," 4:202).

In the Last Days, said
Isaiah, "more are the children of the
desolate than the children of the married wife."
(Isaiah 54:1). In other words, there shall be a great
gathering from among the nations of the Gentiles,
and those who then enter the Fold shall outnumber
those who had previously found their way into the
Church or who were bound by covenant to Christ.
Consequently, on more than one occasion, the
Lord commanded Joseph Smith to "seek to
bring forth and establish my Zion."
(D&C 6:6).

Diversity

"Behold, there were divers
ways that he did manifest
things unto the children of
men, which were good."
(Moroni 7:24).

God is the Author of the greatest diversity on the planet earth. In fact, He created diversity when He divided the light from the darkness, the waters from the firmament, the heaven from the earth, the earth from the sea, the day from the night, and when he created all manner of living things, each to go forth and multiply after its own kind. The Nephites and the Lamanites are examples of diversity in The Book of Mormon. But God's quintessential act of creative diversity was when "male and female created he them." (Genesis 1:27). He may have even created Mars and Venus specifically to be the habitation of men and women, respectively.

He expanded on His recurring theme of diversity when he established the twelve tribes of Israel, when He drew a distinction between Israel and gentile nations, when He established His covenant with Abraham, Isaac, and Jacob, when He separated the Levites from the other tribes of Israel, and when He highlighted the differences between Blood Israel, Land Israel, and Covenant Israel.

Paul addressed diversity when he wrote about spiritual gifts. "Now there are diversities of gifts," and "diversities of operations" is how he phrased it. (1 Corinthians 12:4 & 6, See D&C 46:16). He also alluded to diversity when he wrote: "The body is not one member, but many." (1 Corinthians 12:14).

As a result of God's creative efforts, there are about 8.7 million species on our planet (give or take a million); about 6.5 million on land, and 2.2 million in the oceans. ("The Census of Marine Life"). The scattering of people after the Tower of Babel created diversity within the human race. (See 1 Corinthians 12:28). Today, there are roughly 6,500 languages in the world, contributing to even more diversity. (However, about 2,000 of those have fewer than 1,000 speakers. The most popular language in the world is Mandarin Chinese, with about 1.25 billion speakers).

All we need to do is look around us to realize that God's creations are the expression of diversity. The scriptures affirm that He "is no respecter of persons." (Acts 10:34). "He denieth none that come unto him, black and white, bond and free, male and female; and he remembereth the heathen; and all are alike unto God, both Jew and Gentile." (2 Nephi 26:33). Interestingly, even with diversity, "all are alike unto God."

If we take a close look at the human genome, we will see that our closest living relatives (chimpanzees) share 96 percent of our DNA. The number of genetic differences between humans and chimps is ten times smaller than that between mice and rats. However, the 4% difference between human and chimpanzee DNA makes all the difference. Once again, even with genetic homogeneity, it is our diversity that trumps conformity. Our individual gene expression makes possible Beethoven's Moonlight Sonata, da Vinci's The Last Supper, and Einstein's Theory of Relativity, as well as stick figure finger paintings from the pre-school co-op down the street.

Just as our diversity builds strength, so do uniformity and conformity weaken our adaptive capacity as a species. Genetic diversity leads to resilient strains that resist disease. When you stop to think about it, this is one reason why converts are such an asset to the church. They introduce new genetic material that expands the genome of the members and gives it elasticity. When these strains are nourished by gospel soil, the tender shoots of our collective testimonies are protected from the withering sun of the heat of day. The whole of the church is greater than the sum of its parts, because its pliancy that is the result of diversity allows it to continually transform in to new and refreshing expressions.

Diversity is like a gyroscope that steadies our course as we negotiate rough seas. It also blesses us with an adaptive capacity to resist chafing irritation from both the acute infection of anxiety and the chronic inflammation of complacency. The classic signs of physical inflammation are redness, pain, heat, swelling, and loss of function. But we also have transmissible influences in our lives that combine to contribute to the loss of our identity. Diversity gives us a competitive edge in the unforgiving arena of survival of the fittest. God may have been on to something when He created diversity, because it seems to strengthen our common identity as His children. E pluribus unim. or One out of many.

Even the family, the basic cohesive unit of solidarity, teaches us about diversity. In my own life, each of our seven children has a distinct personality. One, for example, is more of a nurturer, another is an empathizer, and another tends to be a doer. One is definitely a peacemaker, another is a facilitator, another is a natural organizer, and another is a determined provider. One reason our family gets along so well is because we build consensus as we draw upon each other's strengths, which are qualities that we might not individually possess in abundance or recognize in ourselves. We have a common purpose, and naturally gravitate toward unity and harmony, even as we approach solutions to problems from different perspectives. Our diversity gives our family a resilience it might not have otherwise enjoyed, it quickens our family gatherings, and guarantees that there will never be a dull moment when we are together.

The young men and women who have joined our family through marriage have learned to hang on for a wild ride. Our family has been determined to put the fun back in dysfunctional. Our conversations are peppered with a variety of opinions that are the spice of life. Our senses are stimulated with new ideas that light up our temporal and frontal lobes with creative expression. Our interests and activities reflect our zest for life.

Diversity has given our family the opportunity to learn to be tolerant, to be patient and long-suffering, to be forgiving, to be appreciative, and to express gratitude and show unconditional acceptance. Our familial diversity has exposed us to opportunities that might not have been ours under different circumstances. It has allowed us to venture into uncharted territory and to have experiences that can only be described as stimulating and refreshing. We have proven the Lord's assurance, first given to Joseph Smith: "All these things shall give thee experience, and shall be for thy good." (D&C 122:7).

Our diversity has evolved into a tool that has allowed us to stimulate our imaginations, and to brush with bold strokes as we create sweeping swaths of color across a very large canvas. Embracing our diversity has allowed us to venture into uncharted territory, where we have been blessed with refreshing, unconventional, and unorthodox experiences that have significantly contributed to our personal progress. Our diversity has allowed our home to become a learning laboratory. As the children have matured in years, that workshop has, by extension, expanded seven-fold. We've had a few minor explosions along the way, but so far we haven't burned down the house. But if we do, you can be sure that it is our diversity that will stimulate us to quickly improvise new ways to roast marshmallows, and then to build an even better home with exciting esthetic and technical innovations.

The diversity in our family is refreshingly apparent when we bear our testimonies, offer prayers, give service, teach lessons, express feelings, deal with challenges, approach our callings, spend our free time, exercise our agency, raise our children, apply our talents, teach each other, embrace change, and prepare for the future.

We are grateful for our diversity. It has served a purpose by illuminating our common autobiographical thread that leads back to our Father in Heaven. We recognize that in His kingdom there are many mansions, with enough room in the household for Greeks and Romans, Jews and Gentiles, Nephites and Lamanites, the rich as well as the poor, and for those who might be black or white, and bond or free. There may even be room for hetero and homosexuals, believers and infidels, and saints and sinners.

Here's to diversity, "to those who are different, to those who didn't always get A's, to those who have ears twice the size of their peers, and noses that go on for days. Here's to those who are different, the ones they call crazy or dumb; the ones who don't fit, with the guts and the grit, who dance to a different drum. Here's to those who are different, to those with a mischievous streak. For when they have grown, as history has shown, it's their differences that have made them unique." (Anonymous).

God is the Author of the greatest
diversity on the planet earth. In fact, He created diversity
when He divided the light from the darkness, the waters from
the firmament, the heaven from the earth, the earth from the sea,
the day from the night, and when he created all manner of living
things, each to go forth and multiply after its own kind. His
quintessential act of creative diversity was when "male
and female created he them." (Genesis 1:27). He
may have even created Mars and Venus
specifically to be the habitation
of men and women,
respectively.

(The Meaning of) Doctrine

"This is the
way; and there is none
other way nor name given
under heaven whereby many can
be saved in the kingdom of God. And
now, behold, this is the doctrine of Christ,
and the only and true doctrine of the Father,
and of the Son, and of the Holy Ghost,
which is one God, without end."
(2 Nephi 21:31).

"Many Latter-day Saints, from the Presidents of the church and members of the Quorum of the Twelve down to individual members who may write books or articles, have expressed their own opinions on doctrinal matters. Nevertheless, until such opinions are presented to the church in general conference and sustained by vote of the conference, they are neither binding nor the official doctrine of the church. Critics of LDS doctrine seldom recognize this vital distinction. Rather, if any Latter-day Saint, especially one of the leading Brethren, ever said a thing, these critics take it to represent "Mormonism," regardless of whether any other Latter-day Saint ever said it or believed it. Often the Latter-day Saints themselves are guilty of this same error and search through the Journal of Discourses as if it were some sort of Mormon Talmud, looking for 'new' doctrines not found in the standard works and not taught in the church today." (Stephen Robinson, "Are Mormons Christian?" p. 15).

President Henry B. Eyring said: "We must be cautious and careful not to go beyond teaching true doctrine." This requires that we be sensitive to the whisperings of The Holy Ghost. "His confirmation is invited by our avoiding speculation or personal interpretation. One of the surest ways to avoid even getting near false doctrine is to choose to be simple in our teaching. Safety is gained by that simplicity, and little is lost." (CR 4 2009).

Jeffrey Holland addressed a similar theme in General Conference: "The scriptures are not the ultimate source of knowledge for Latter-day Saints, he said." The living God is the ultimate source, and His teaching comes as vibrant revelation. This doctrine is central to the message of the Restoration. "God is engaged in our lives," said Elder Holland, and "continues to speak His word and reveal His truth." This basic belief by faithful Latter-day Saints demands that we maintain an open canon of scripture. (CR 4/ 2008). "Canon" scripture is a set of religious writings regarded as authentic and definitive.

Elder Dallin Oaks said much the same thing about scripture, in an article in the January 1995 Ensign. "For us, the scriptures are not the ultimate source of knowledge, but what precedes the ultimate source, (which is) revelation. Because of our belief in continuing revelation, we Latter-day Saints maintain that the canon (the authoritative body) of scriptures is open (and) continuing revelation is crucial."

Both Elders Holland and Oaks mentioned an "open canon" in the sense that we believe God gives man additions to the existing body of scripture through His prophet. Elder B.H. Roberts explained: "The church has confined the sources of doctrine by which it is willing to be bound before the world to the things that God has revealed and which the church has officially accepted, and those alone. These would include the Bible, The Book of Mormon, the Doctrine and Covenants, (and) the Pearl of Great Price; these have been repeatedly accepted and endorsed by the church in General Conference assembled, and are the only sources of absolute appeal for our doctrine." (B.H. Roberts)

This has been the pattern and the practice of the church since its organization. In General Conference of the church, the membership votes on the proposed new "revelation." After its ratification, it is added to the existing body of scripture. For example, this is how the Doctrine and Covenants has evolved over the past 175 years, and how Sections 137 and 138 were more recently added to that book of canon scripture.

But we also believe that the canon is open in the sense that God is free to clarify His existing doctrine. This is a bit more complicated to understand, because it is our belief that revelation is either public (coming through prophets, seers, and revelators) or private, coming to individual students of the scriptures, and this illumination depends upon their spiritual capacity. Hugh Nibley observed: "Men fool themselves when they think for a moment that they can read the scripture without ever adding something to the text, or omitting something from it. For in the wise words of St. Hilary, 'Scripture consists not in what one reads, but in what one understands.' Consequently, in the reading of the scripture we must always have an interpreter" (The World and the Prophets, 3:202). The interpreter of which Brother Nibley speaks is the Holy Ghost.

Elder Dallin Oaks taught: "Latter-day Saints know that learned or authoritative commentaries can help us with scriptural interpretation, but we maintain that they must be used with caution. Commentaries are not a substitute for the scriptures any more than a good cookbook is a substitute for food. When I refer to "commentaries," I refer to everything that interprets scripture, from the comprehensive book-length commentary to the brief interpretation embodied in a lesson or an article, such as this one." (Underlining mine).

"One trouble with commentaries," he continued, "is that their authors sometimes focus on only one meaning, to the exclusion of others. As a result, commentaries, if not used with great care, may illuminate the author's chosen and correct meaning but close our eyes and restrict our horizons to other possible meanings. Sometimes those other less obvious meanings can be the ones most valuable and useful to us as we seek to understand our own dispensation and to obtain answers to our own questions. This is why the teaching of the Holy Ghost is a better guide to scriptural interpretation than even the best commentary."

It seems there was great prophetic wisdom in the counsel of President Spencer W. Kimball, who told the members of the church that he was "convinced that each of us, at some time in our lives, must discover the scriptures for ourselves." The process invites personal revelation. If we depend only upon our own reasoning or the scholarship or commentaries of others, including the manuals of instruction provided by the Curriculum Department of the church, we will never obtain the understanding that can come only by revelation. If we "harden our hearts" in any degree to the influences of the Spirit, we will receive "the lesser portion of the word, until (we) know nothing concerning his mysteries" which are the saving principles of the gospel. (Alma 12:11).

(The) Door Swings Both Ways

"If ye forgive men their
trespass, your Heavenly Father will
also forgive you. But if ye forgive not
men their trespasses, neither will your
father forgive your trespasses."
(3 Nephi 13:14-15).

"God so loved the world that He gave his Only Begotten Son, that whosoever believeth in Him should not perish, but have everlasting life." (John 3:16). He is involved in our lives in the most intensely personal way possible, for He sent His Firstborn Son to be our Savior. When we are at one with Him, we are quickened, filled with joy, and are at peace. We are able to declare, as did Joseph Smith: "I have a conscience void of offense towards God, and towards all men." (D&C 135:5).

The Savior died to loose the bands of death that bind us. In Gethsemane, he accepted our weaknesses in order to know "how to succor his people according to their infirmities." (Alma 7:12). The crucified Christ is the primary focus of Christianity today, but if we fail to understand the Mortal Messiah, we receive only a one-dimensional view that ignores the wonderful symmetry of His humanity and divinity.

His example teaches us that in spite of our own hardships we may look to Him for understanding as we develop empathy to put our own trials into perspective. He taught us to be patient even in the face of challenges whose portion seems unfair, whose difficulty seems unreasonable, and whose proportions seem insurmountable. In addition to forgiveness for our sins, one of the blessings of repentance is that we will receive the strength to endure suffering that is not of our own making. "If we can bear our afflictions with understanding, faith, and courage, we shall be strengthened and comforted and spared the torment which accompanies the mistaken idea that all suffering comes as a chastisement for transgression." (Marion G. Romney, C.R., 10/1964).

Latter-day Saints tend to emphasize the Savior's suffering in Gethsemane as the pivotal experience circumscribing His sacrifice, but it was really a many-faceted drama played out on different stages. It began even before the creation of the earth, for the scriptures identify Jesus Christ as "the Lamb slain from the foundation of the world." (Revelation 13:8). It will only end when the Redeemer has interceded for the last repentant sinner.

Alma said of the Savior's ministry: "And he shall go forth, suffering pains and afflictions and temptations of every kind; and this that the word might be fulfilled which saith he will take upon him the pains and the sicknesses of his people." (Alma 7:11). It seems that the work in which He was engaged followed a natural progression and gradually built to a crescendo until His preparation was complete and every necessary detail relating to the Atonement had been worked out. Early in His ministry, Jesus said, "My time is not yet come." (John 7:6). But later, when all had been accomplished, He confirmed, "My time is at hand." (Matthew 26:18). Gethsemane, Calvary, and the empty tomb validate His thorough preparation. Ours generally need some more work. We may be perfect in our repentance, but need to hone our capacity to forgive others.

As we struggle to deal with the trespasses of others, it is well to remember that we are all unprofitable servants. That is because we can do nothing that puts God in our debt. The Sacrifice of His Son is completely beyond our ability to pay. But He does not ask us to settle our account with Him; He only asks that we keep the commandments. These include perfect repentance leading to forgiveness, and perfect forgiveness of others leading to peace of mind. The marvel of His love is that the more we try to do this, the more He blesses us. Therefore, we become even more deeply indebted to Him and remain so forever. When, ultimately, we are redeemed by the precious blood of Jesus Christ, it is by His grace alone that we enjoy salvation. We are as the dust of the earth and are as nothing in comparison to our debt to God. In this sense, Brigham Young declared: "There is no man who ever made a sacrifice on this earth for the kingdom of heaven except the Savior. I would not give the ashes of a rye straw for that man who feels that he is making a sacrifice for God. We are doing this for our own happiness, welfare, and exaltation, and for nobody else's. What we do, we do for the salvation of the inhabitants of the earth, not for the salvation of the heavens, the angels, or God." (J.D., 16:114).

Learning to forgive another can be a lifetime process and drawn-out struggle. God knew this might be the case, so He said: "I will give unto the children of men line upon line, precept upon precept, here a little and there a little; and blessed are those who hearken unto my precepts." The experience may feel like Gethsemane, but the reward will be wisdom and increased capacity, understanding, knowledge, insight, and perception. Our experiences with others are designed to try us and prove us (D&C 98:12), and they give us "consolation by holding forth that which is to come, confirming our hope!" (D&C 128:31).

As we go through life, "enduring to the end" includes intimate mastery of two principles: repentance for our own sins and forgiveness of others. The Savior obtained forgiveness for the sins of mankind only after the most excruciating suffering on His part. Is it, then, too much for Him to ask us to forgive each other, even though it might be staggeringly painful to do so? He recognized that unless this frequently overlooked dimension of forgiveness is a part of our daily lives, the Plan of Redemption will fail, and our souls will be lost.

The depth and breadth of our forgiveness, then, is a celestial barometer that measures the way we deal with the high blood pressure of self-inflicted pain and the telestial trauma seemingly exacted by others. Its quality is a cosmic compass, pointing us toward eternal life. It is a stethoscope, measuring the vital capacity of our prideful hearts that must be broken in contrition in order to exhibit the steady sinus rhythm that confirms perfect harmony with the proven principles of perfection. Our forgiveness acts as a pacemaker measuring out therapeutic doses of doctrinal energy. If we are to have a stable heart rate and avoid the angina of anguish we must be absolutely and unconditionally forgiving. If we want to one day live comfortably with our Heavenly Father in His I, we must first put a few nitroglycerin tablets of tenderness under our tongues to temper the urge to use them as weapons to lash out at others who may have offended us. Taking an 81 mg. tablet of the aspirin of acceptance of others will assuage our annoyance with them and reconcile us to those whom we feel may have taken advantage of us. The Lord commanded Joseph Smith: "I, the Lord, will forgive whom I will forgive, but of you it is required to forgive all men." (D&C 64:10). Brigham Young put it a little more bluntly, when echoing Confucius, he reminded the Saints: "He who takes offense when none was intended is a fool, and he who takes offense when one was intended is usually a fool." We are only fully repentant when we endure to the end in righteousness by being strictly obedient to the principle of forgiveness, and that door swings both ways.

Dry Humor in The Book of Mormon

"A merry heart doeth
good, like a medicine." (Proverbs 17:22).
Humor can ease tension, relieve uncomfortable
or embarrassing situations, change attitudes, and
generate love and understanding. It adds sparkle
to life. A properly developed sense of humor is
sensitive to the feelings of others, and is
flavored with kindness and
understanding.

"I, Nephi, being exceedingly young, nevertheless being large in stature, (whatever that has got to do with what he is about to say) and also having great desires to know of the mysteries of God, wherefore, I did cry unto the Lord." (1 Nephi 2:16).

"The course of the Lord is one eternal round" (of golf)? (1 Nephi 10:19). This reminds us of the reference to tennis in the Book of Genesis, where we learn that Joseph served in Pharaoh's court.

"Now I, Chemish, write what few things I write, in the same book with my brother; for behold, I saw the last which he wrote, that he wrote it with his own hand; and he wrote it in the day that he delivered them unto me." (Omni 1:9). In other words, don't expect much, here.

"And it came to pass that after the space of two years that Abinadi came among them in disguise, that they knew him not, and began to prophesy among them," thereby, immediately blowing his cover. (Mosiah 12:1).

Zeezrom, who was "expert in the devices of the devil" when it came to trickery, debated Amulek on the most important question in the history of the universe: The existence of God. As his opening salvo, the lawyer asks: "Will ye answer the questions which I shall put unto you?" To which Amulek responds: "Yea." Then, of all the questions he could draw from his formidable arsenal, Zeezrom basically dropped the following bombshell (which, as it turned out, was a dud): "I will pay you if you deny the existence of God." Couldn't he possibly have done better than that? (Alma 11:21-22).

"And it came to pass that king Lamoni inquired of his servants, saying: Where is this man that has such great power? And they said unto him: Behold, he is feeding thy horses" (Alma 18:8-9) and probably mucking the stalls, as well.

This one speaks for itself: "Go in and see my husband, for he has been laid upon his bed for the space of two days and two nights; and some say that he is not dead, but others say that he is dead and that he stinketh, and that he ought to be placed in the sepulchre; but as for myself, to me he doth not stink." (Alma 19:5)

"Now the joy of Ammon was so great even that he was full; yea, he was swallowed up in the joy of his God, even to the exhausting of his strength … Now the joy of Alma in meeting his brethren was truly great, and also the joy of Aaron, of Omner, and Himni; but behold their joy was not that to exceed their strength." (Alma 27:17 & 19). It was great, but not nearly on a par with Ammon's joy.

"As he went forth among the people, yea, among a people who had separated themselves from the Nephites and called themselves Zoramites, being led by a man whose name was Zoram - and as he went forth amongst them, behold, he was run upon and trodden down, even until he was dead." (Alma 30:59). It sounds like the driver backed up his horse and cart over him a few times, just to make sure the deed was done.

"If ye could be healed by merely casting about your eyes that ye might be healed, would ye not behold quickly, or would ye rather harden your hearts in unbelief, and be slothful, that ye would not cast about your eyes, that ye might perish?" (Alma 33:21).

"Whomsoever of the Amalickiahites that would not enter into a covenant to support the cause of freedom, that they might maintain a free government, he caused to be put to death; and there were but few who denied the covenant of freedom. "Duh! (Alma 46:35).

"They were thus cautious that no poison should be administered among them; for if their wine would poison a Lamanite it would also poison a Nephite." (Alma 55:32). Sounds about right. That's how poison works.

"And it came to pass that when Coriantumr had leaned upon his sword, that he rested a little, he smote off the head of Shiz. And it came to pass that after he had smitten off the head of Shiz, that Shiz raised up on his hands and fell; and after that he had struggled for breath, he died." (Ether 15:30-31). The moral of this story is that it's hard to breathe after your head has been chopped off.

"A merry heart doeth good, like a medicine." (Proverbs 17:22). Humor can ease tension, relieve uncomfortable or embarrassing situations, change attitudes, generate love and understanding, and add sparkle to life. A properly developed sense of humor is sensitive to others' feelings and is flavored with kindness and understanding.

(The) Dust of The Earth

"Our lives are fairy tales waiting
to be written by the hand of God."
(Hans Christian Andersen).

"I ask, can ye say
aught of yourselves? I answer
you, Nay. Ye cannot say that ye are
even as much as the dust of the earth;
yet ye were created of the dust of the
earth; but behold, it belongeth
to him who created you."
(Mosiah 2:25).

"We are created as much from the dust of eternity as we are from the dust of the earth." (Joseph Wirthlin, C.R., 4/2006). In contrast to the coarse, crude, profane, and vulgar materials of the earth, there are at our core, immortal elements that have come to us from our former home. These are untainted, uncontaminated, and undefiled. When they are woven into the tapestry of our mortal cloth, the injunction to care for our bodies as if they were temples of God takes on a new meaning whose undertone conveys an immediate sense of urgency.

These foundation elements facilitate a miraculous transformation of our tabernacles of clay, not of maturation, but rather of generation. They quicken within us the embryos of deity, and "our birth," the portal opening onto mortality, becomes "but a sleep, and a forgetting. The soul that rises with us, our life's star, hath had elsewhere its setting, and cometh from afar. Not in entire forgetfulness, and not in utter nakedness, but trailing clouds of glory do we come, from God who is our Home." (William Wordsworth). When we return to our former home, we will be reacquainted with a generous measure of the glory we formerly enjoyed, as we reclaim our royal birthright.

Even now, we are as "children coming down like gentle rain through darkened skies, with glory trailing from (our) feet as (we) go, and endless promise in (our) eyes. We are the "young ones growing tall, growing strong, like silver trees against the storm, who will not bend with the wind or the change, but stand to fight the world alone. (We) are the few, the warriors saved for Saturday, to come the last day of the world. (We) are they, of Saturday. (We) are the strong, the warriors rising in (our) might to win the battle raging in the hearts of men, on Saturday. Strangers from a realm of light, who have forgotten all; (even) the memory of (our) former life and the purpose of (our) call. And so, (we) must learn why (we're) here, and who (we) really are." (Doug Stewart, "Saturday's Warrior").

Peter Pan said: "All we need is trust, and a little bit of pixie dust, and we can fly!" (J.M. Barrie). With that magical formula, each of us may "be like a bird, that pausing in her flight a while on boughs to light, feels them give way beneath her, and yet sings, knowing that she hath wings." (Victor Hugo). Ultimately, we will be borne home as on the wings of eagles.

(The) Duty of The Priest

"The priest's duty is to preach, teach,
expound, exhort, and baptize, and
administer the sacrament."
(D&C 20:46)

"Mosiah granted unto Alma
that he might establish churches
throughout all the land of Zarahemla;
and gave him power to ordain priests and
teachers over every church. Now this was done
because there were so many people that they
could not all be governed by one teacher;
neither could they all hear the word
of God in one assembly."
(Mosiah 25:19-20).

There is logic and symmetry in the order in which these responsibilities are identified. Perhaps these can be best illustrated by describing the process by which a gospel principle is presented for consideration, contemplation, comprehension, and commitment, to the end that the development of character leads to a covenant relationship with God. Take, for example, the principle of self-reliance.

Preach: To introduce a principle, truth, or concept. A great way to get the ball rolling is by quoting a relevant scripture such as: "Behold, this is the preparation wherewith I prepare you, and the foundation ... which I give unto you. That the church may stand independent above all other creatures beneath the celestial world." (D&C 78:13-14).

Preaching may require no more than the citation of an appropriate scripture. Like a footing of concrete poured in a rough-dug trench, the introduction need not be profound to achieve the desired result. Its purpose is not to end the discussion or to establish closure, but rather to create a foundation for elaboration that naturally follows.

Teach: To bring into focus and to illustrate in a meaningful way. What better tried-and-true, proven way to do this than by utilizing a story? Take, for example, the following illustration of self-reliance, related by Howard W. Hunter: "It was on a summer day, early in the morning. I was standing near the window. The curtains obstructed me from two little creatures out on the lawn. One was a large bird and the other a little bird, obviously just out of the nest. I saw the larger bird hop out on the lawn, then thump his feet and cock his head. He drew a big fat worm out of the lawn, and came hopping back. The little bird opened its bill wide, but the big bird swallowed the worm. There was squawking in protest. The big bird flew away, and I didn't see it again, but I watched the little bird. After a while it hopped out on the lawn, thumped its feet, cocked its head, and pulled a big worm out of the lawn." ("B.Y.U. Fireside Address," 1/2/1992).

Stories cultivate fertile fields of common emotion and experience. After preaching a principle, the point can easily be lost on us if a connection has not been established. Teaching goes far beyond introduction (preaching) because of the creation of this emotional rapport. Perhaps this is why the Lord explained that without the Spirit to facilitate the connection, we simply cannot teach effectively.

Even though teaching may enhance communication, it is not the final word. As Paul wrote: "When for the time ye ought to be teachers, ye have need that one teach you again which be the first principles of the oracles of God; and are become such as have need of milk, and not of strong meat." (Hebrews 5:12). In other words, after introducing new concepts by preaching, we should next teach basic tenets in order to strengthen developing belief systems. This will prepare our listeners prepared for weightier matters of the law, so that we may expound upon the principles that have been introduced by preaching and brought into focus with teaching.

Expound: To enlarge upon the principle and to expand the understanding of the listener. When we expound upon a subject that has been properly introduced and reinforced, its relevance and application are unfolded to our view. If our desire is to communicate beyond the mere cognition level to the level of a deeper understanding, we may expound upon the subject by choosing from a wide range of teaching techniques: rapport and example, analogy, questions, personal experience, literary devices, cause and consequence, testimony, admonition, and challenge, to name a few.

The best communication that is oriented toward learning is structured so that the message is received in a hierarchy based first on understanding, next on acceptance, then on commitment, and finally on recommitment. Preaching is related to understanding, teaching to acceptance, and expounding to commitment. (Exhortation is equivalent to re-commitment that can be appreciated best by those who are accustomed to making gospel covenants administered by the priesthood).

The following story expounds upon the principle of self-reliance as it powerfully brings us to the point of commitment to both the principle and its application. A member of a successful Mount Everest expedition was asked how members of the climbing party who would make the summit attempt were chosen. He replied that in the "death zone" at 25,000 feet there are three factors that bear down on every climber. First, there is the unrelenting cold. It penetrates to the very core to such an extent that one has to fight an almost overriding urge to stop climbing.

Second, is the sickness that accompanies strong exertion at high altitude. When a climber feels sick, he wants to stop climbing. Third, is fatigue that causes distance to be measured not measured in miles, or yards, or feet, but in the mental and physical discipline required to put one foot in front of the other. Every muscle screams out the message to stop climbing! In reality, then, no one else chooses who will be on the team to reach the top. Rather, each individual climber chooses for himself.

Exhort: To help the listener to want to incorporate the principle into his or her own life; to encourage ownership; to validate the worth of the principle through personal witness or testimony. Exhortation dramatically brings us to the moment in time when the rubber hits the road. Exhortation creates worth or value and causes the relevance of the principle to seem larger than life. Joshua declared before the Israelites: "Choose ye this day whom ye will serve … but as for me and my house, we will serve the Lord." (Joshua 24:15). So might we also draw a line in the sand and take our stand, based on the exhortations of our teachers.

When our preaching, teaching, and expounding have generated a commitment to belief in a true principle, there is always the chance that resolve may falter. Thus, the effective teacher always offers exhortation to keep the faith. Choice is at the heart of the matter. "There are many called, but few are chosen," wrote Joseph Smith from Liberty Jail. "And why are they not chosen? Because their hearts are set so much upon the things of this world, and aspire to the honors of men, that they do not learn this one lesson." (D&C 121:34-35). The lesson is that passive acceptance of principles that govern lifestyle is not enough to weather the storms that will come,

When belief systems are raked by the winds of adversity, compromise, doubt, rationalization, and temptation, or with the allure of complacency, ease, indifference, or laziness. If we were given to exhortation regarding the principle of self-reliance, we might recite the stirring words of Josiah Gilbert Holland, who wrote: "God, give us men and women! A time like this demands strong minds, great hearts, truth, faith, and ready hands. Men and women whom the lust of office does not kill. Men and women whom the spoils of office cannot buy. Men and women who possess opinions and a will. Men and women who have honor. Men and women who will not lie! Men and women who can stand before a demagogue and damn his treacherous flatterings without winking! Tall men and women, sun-crowned, who live above the fog in public duty and in private thinking. For while the rabble, with their thumb-worn creeds, their large professions and their little deeds, mingle in selfish strife, lo! Freedom weeps, Wrong rules the land, and Justice sleeps." ("God, Give us Men!").

Exhortation at its very best is the catalyst of commitment initiating a flood of light that is difficult to ignore, although it may not always be recognized. "I said to the man who stood at the gate of the year, 'Give me a light, that I may tread safely into the unknown.' And he replied, 'Go out into the darkness, and put your hand in the hand of God. That shall be to you better than a light, and safer than the known way.'" (Minnie Haskins, "A Dialogue Between a Man, and The Keeper of The Gate of The Year").

This reagent generates a warm glow that is the feelings of satisfaction and even of joy. "The best education," wrote Edward Everett Hale, "is to be perpetually thrilled with life." One reason exhortation is critical is because it practically guarantees a rooted, prepared, spiritually sensitive, and eager convert who is ready to take up the torch, no matter the cost, and to carry on in the footsteps of his mentor.

Finally comes peace of conscience that is no less than "the consciousness of victory over self, and of communion with the infinite." (David O. McKay, C.R., 10/1969). Exhortation is best when it admonishes us to live in harmony with the principles of the gospel.

Baptize: The gospel Plan is better than any worldly program that elicits conformity. There are many ways to lose our zeal, but there is a rule that is the foundation for purposeful living, and the order of counsel is significant. When a true principle has become rooted in our hearts, we must take care to watch our thoughts, words, and deeds, because as the architects of our own fate, even a slight deviation from the blueprint can have disastrous consequences.

What has baptism got to do with self reliance or with a hierarchy of communication skills in general? Only that baptism is outward evidence of a personal commitment and is the public manifestation of a covenant relationship made with God. It is the ultimate expression of self-reliance, because it is a voluntary surrender of free will to a higher power akin to a "Gethsemane" experience. It is an expression of "Thy will," and not my will, "be done." (Matthew 6:10).

Baptism also provides a way to avoid premature burnout through overzealous effort. Those who are in a covenant relationship with God "walk the walk, and talk the talk." But if we want to be Christ-centered, we need to use common sense in all our endeavors. King Benjamin's practical advice was: "See that all these things are done in wisdom and order; for it is not requisite that a man should run faster than he has strength." (Mosiah 4:27). Without wisdom and patience, overzealous efforts lead to error. Being sensitive to our baptismal covenant helps us to develop perspective, maintain momentum, turn stumbling blocks into stepping-stones, and overcome adversity that would otherwise diminish and tarnish the inherent sparkle of our spirituality.

The uncircumcised in heart lack the depth enjoyed by those who have been born again. Baptism can enhance our self-reliance even as it fosters the mutual support that is part of the gospel Plan. No other religion stresses so much the meaning and worth of the individual as does the restored gospel. Interdependence is the ultimate value, and the church is the instrument for its development. The family is the highest expression within the church of individuality, is the foundation for happiness on earth, and is the basic building block of life in the eternities. This is one of the hardest things for the unconverted to fathom, but those who come up out of the waters of baptism understand its wisdom, because it is experiential.

Administer the Sacrament: "Selfishness is simply self-destruction in slow motion," whereas the Sacrament represents the spiritual transformation from self-centered behavior to a Christ-centered life. (Neal A. Maxwell, "Ensign," 5/1999, p. 23). The Sacrament facilitates the internalization of truth and principle, creating an environment within which disciples may endure to the end, not in wickedness, but in righteousness.

The ordinance of the Sacrament is a weekly renewal of the baptismal covenant whose power lies in its ability to help us to remember the Savior and to follow Him. Our "witness" before God is a promise to take upon ourselves His name, remember Him, and keep His commandments. His part of the bargain is to put in a good word with us to the Holy Ghost so that He may help us to do our duty. As baptized members of the church, we are blessed with the greater light of the Holy Ghost because we have a responsibility to be true to our baptismal covenants.

God glories in the possibility that His children who obey Him and endure to the end might become like him. His work is to nurture our progression until we merit immortality and eternal life. We formally initiate the process at the waters of baptism, in a covenant of salvation. When we are confirmed members of the church, we receive the gift of the companionship of the Holy Ghost in a covenant of justification.

Throughout our mortal lives, as we endure to the end in righteousness, the Sacrament that is a covenant of sanctification, comforts us, and leads us toward our eternal destiny in the Kingdom of God. We qualify for that blessing because of our obedience to the laws and ordinances received in the temple where we make covenants of exaltation.

If, by the grace of God, we are able to be perfect in our obedience to the principles of the gospel and we do not deny His power, then, said the Savior, we are "sanctified in Christ by the grace of God, through the shedding of the blood of Christ, which is in the covenant of the Father unto the remission of (our) sins, that (we) become holy, without spot." (Moroni 10:33). It would be difficult to state more succinctly, yet more powerfully, the essence of the gospel of Jesus Christ.

If we open our hearts and follow the path that leads to the Sacrament Table by preaching the word, teaching according to priesthood principles, expounding upon these principles, followed by exhortation to life-long commitment, we can become holy, without spot.

In summary, then, the priests are to preach the gospel, which involves introducing principles, truths, and concepts pertaining to the Plan of Salvation. After this introduction, they are to teach the principles, or bring them into sharp focus, and illustrate them in a meaningful way. Then ,the priests are to expound, or enlarge upon the principles, in order to expand understanding and facilitate their adoption. Next, they are to offer exhortation by illuminating the principles in such a way that their integration is facilitated; to encourage ownership; through personal witness or testimony, to validate the worth of the principle.

When the commitment level is appropriate, the priest stands ready with authority to baptize. This ordinance is outward evidence of a personal commitment to obedience, and is the public manifestation of the desire to establish a covenant relationship made with God. Baptism is the ultimate expression of self-reliance, because it is a voluntary surrender of agency to a higher power. The waters of baptism are refreshing, uplifting, inviting, engaging, and invigorating to the penitent, the humble, the meek, the poor in spirit, and the pure in heart.

To those who have enjoyed the rejuvenation of baptism, and who have been washed clean in the element of Spirit represented by its waters, the Priests may administer the sacrament, which is an ordinance that allows the Saints to regularly recommit themselves to internalize every truth and every principle necessary to enjoy eternal life through God's grace in His kingdom.

"The priest's
duty is to preach,
teach, expound, exhort,
and baptize, and administer
the sacrament." (D&C 20:46).
There is logic and symmetry
in the order in which these
responsibilities are
identified.

Education

"To be learned is
good, if they hearken unto
the counsels of God."
(2 Nephi 9:29).

We don't need to be enrolled in school in order to continue our studies. The best education, after all, is to be perpetually thrilled with life, and that kind of enthusiasm should continue 365 days a year. As the dictionary defines it, enthusiasm is to be "possessed by God, to have celestial inspiration." If we really are "white hot sparks struck off the divine anvil of God," as B. H. Roberts suggested, then we will live to learn, learn to love, and love to live.

James Madison said that "knowledge will forever govern ignorance, and a people who mean to be their own governors must arm themselves with the power which knowledge gives." Universal formal education in Madison's day was only a dream, but there were many self-educated men who, nevertheless, made their mark on society. As a matter of fact, Elbert Hubbard declared that every man should "have a college education in order that he might see how little the things is really worth!"

Echoing his thoughts, John W. Garner, President of The Carnegie Foundation, declared: "A society that scorns excellence in plumbing because plumbing is a humble activity, and tolerates shoddiness in philosophy because philosophy is an exalted activity, will have neither good plumbing nor good philosophy. Neither its pipes nor its theories will hold water."

We don't need impressive credentials to do a job well. We just need to roll up our sleeves and get to work. Teddy Roosevelt reminded us: "It is not the critic who counts, not he who points out where the strong man stumbled nor where the doer of deeds could have done them better. The credit belongs to the man who is actually in the arena, whose face is marred by dust and sweat and blood, who tries and comes up short again and again, who knows the great enthusiasms, the great devotions, and spends himself in a worthy cause who, at best if he fails, at least fails while daring greatly so that his place shall never be with those cold and timid souls who know neither victory nor defeat." (4/23/1910, Sorbonne, Paris, France).

The Savior said that "men should be anxiously engaged in a good cause, and do many things of their own free will, and bring to pass much righteousness; For the power is in them, wherein they are agents unto themselves … But he that doeth not anything until he is commanded, and receiveth a commandment with doubtful heart, and keepeth it with slothfulness, the same is damned." (D&C 58:27-29). Damnation is the failure to continue to progress on the path leading to the Celestial Kingdom of God. It is to hide the talent we were given. it is the failure to reach our potential. it is the knowledge that we did not fulfil the measure of our creation. it is to be content with mediocrity. It is a victory for the devil, because it thwarts the very Plan of Salvation for mankind.

God respects agency, and has placed within each breast the power to work tirelessly to achieve the goal of eternal life. True education, from a gospel perspective, isn't how much you have committed to memory, or even how much you know. It's being able to differentiate between what you do know and what you don't. it's knowing where to go to find out what you need to know; and it's knowing how to use the information you then receive. it is the ability to use your God-given talents, and expand the scope of their application. We are, after all, the architects of our own fate, left by a wise Father to "work out [our] salvation with fear and trembling" before the Lord. (Philippians 2:12).

Of all the creations of God, we are the only ones who have the capacity of willful disobedience to natural law. We are the recipients of the great blessing of agency, or independence of action. Squirrels gather nuts, bees produce honey, birds fly south for the winter, beavers build dams, salmon return to the streams of their birth to spawn, but we are given the freedom to choose our own destiny or to surrender it into the hands of another.

As Truman Madsen wrote, "You are, and always will be, independent in that stage of development to which your voluntary decisions and divine powers have led. There are limits all along the way to what you can be and do. But you are not a billiard ball. No power in the universe can coerce your complete assent or dissent. This thesis on capacity translates Bergson's metaphor into breathtaking fact: 'The universe is a machine for the making of gods.'" ("Eternal Man," p. 18, from "Two Sources of Morality & Religion").

But with agency comes great responsibility to make good choices. Every decision carries with it risks that cannot be avoided. We must live with the consequences of our actions. A woman was out for a drive in the country, and the road she was following degenerated into gravel, then washboard, and finally a mud-filled, pothole strewn track. She stopped the car in front of two deep clefts in the earth that stretched before her on to the horizon. Beside the track was a sign that read: "Choose your ruts carefully. You'll be in then for the next twenty miles."

"You may know me. I'm your constant companion. I'm your greatest helper; I'm your heaviest burden. I will push you onward or drag you down to failure. I am at your command. Half the tasks you do might as well be turned over to me. I'm able to do them quickly, and I'm able to do them the same every time if that's what you want. I'm easily managed; all you have to do is be firm with me. Show me exactly how you want it done; after a few lessons I'll do it automatically. I'm the servant of all great men and women, and the servant of failures, too. But I work with all the precision of a marvelous computer. You may run me for profit, or you may run me to ruin; it really makes no difference to me. Work with me. Be easy with me and I will destroy you. Be firm with me and I'll put the world at your feet. Who am I? I'm Habit!" (Anonymous).

The following adages make a lot of sense, when viewed from an educational perspective. "What you get by reaching your destination is not nearly as important as what you become by reaching your destination." "Many people are unhappy because they trade what they want most for what they want now." "Our character gets us off our status quo, our commitment gets us moving, and our discipline keeps us on track." "In the gospel, we are not so much committed to improving our standard of living, as we are our quality of life. When that improves, so does our standard of living." "Your yearning power is much more than your earning power." "There is plenty of room at the top, but not enough to sit down." "You can't purchase an education. You buy it on the installment plan and make payments every day."

Education is not an end in itself, but is a treasure to be used for the good of mankind. Truth, beauty, and virtue are the fruits of a quality education, and are confirmed by their application in practical life. They exist to make our lives better, so that we might live more abundantly. When we are able to tap into the source of all knowledge, our education moves to a new and dynamic level, and we glimpse vistas of incomprehensible dimension. As President David O. McKay was fond of saying, "Spirituality," the best education, "is the consciousness of victory over self, and of communion with the infinite."

The
best education
is to be perpetually
thrilled with life, and
that kind of enthusiasm
should continue every day
of the year. As the dictionary
has defined it, our enthusiasm
is to be "Possessed by God, or to
have celestial inspiration." If we
are "white hot sparks struck off
God's divine anvil" as B. H.
Roberts suggested, then
we will live to learn,
learn to love, and
love to live.

(The Best) Education
Is To Be Perpetually Thrilled by Life

*"A mind once stretched by a new idea never
reverts to its original dimension."
(Oliver Wendell Holmes).*

*"For it shall come to pass
in that day that the churches which
are built up … the one shall say unto the
other: Behold, I, I am the Lord's; and the others
shall say: I, I am the Lord's; and thus shall every
one say that hath built up churches and not unto the
Lord. And they shall contend one with another, and
their priests shall contend one with another, and
they shall teach with their learning, and deny
the Holy Ghost." (2 Nephi 28:3-4).*

Most young people in the United States spend twelve years gaining what some people call "an education." But for some, the process is sporadic at best. Often it is put on hold, or worse, it stops altogether. All of us remember in elementary school going back in September and writing an essay entitled: "How I spent my summer." So, the real questions may be: "Does education continue even when we are not in school? Does education cease during our undisciplined free time? Does Eternal Progression relate to education? Does the Latter-day Saint tradition relating to education have a foundation in gospel principles? Is improvement through education a key to successful living?"

A zest for living may be one of the best indicators of physical and spiritual symmetry. When we are perpetually thrilled with life, we are enthusiastic. Enthusiasm is derived from root words that mean: "God is with you," or "Possessed by God," or "Celestial inspiration." Truly, if we live to learn, and learn to love, we'll love to live.

A young woman enrolled in college. When she was shown the curriculum, she asked, "Isn't there a shorter course?" Her advisor responded, "Oh yes. It just depends on what you want to make of yourself. When God makes an oak tree, He takes a hundred years, but when he throws together a squash, he does it in three months."

Whatever we do, we should do it well, and not shirk our responsibilities or leave our destiny to the whims of fate. "We all know about those four people named Everybody, Somebody, Anybody, and Nobody. There was an important job to be done and Everybody was sure that Somebody would do it. Anybody could have done it, but Nobody did it. Somebody got angry about it because it was Everybody's job. Everybody whined that Anybody could have done it, and Nobody realized that Somebody could have stepped in. It ended up that Everybody blamed Somebody when Nobody did what Anybody could have done." (Anonymous).

"Suppose that we state as a tenet of wisdom that knowledge is not for delight of the mind nor an end in itself, but, rather, is a packet of treasure to hold and employ for the good of mankind. A torch or a candle is barren of meaning except it gives light to men as they climb, and theses and tomes are but impotent jumble unless they are tools in the building of time. We scholars toil on with the zeal of a miner for nuggets and nuggets and one nugget more. But scholars are needed to study the uses of all the great mass of data and lore. And truly our tireless and endless persuasions need yoking with man's daily problems and strife. For truth and beauty and virtue have value confirmed by their uses in practical life." (Anonymous). As John W. Garner, President of The Carnegie Foundation said: "The society which scorns excellence in plumbing because plumbing is a humble activity, and tolerates shoddiness in philosophy because philosophy is an exalted activity, will have neither good plumbing nor good philosophy. Neither its pipes nor its theories will hold water."

An education isn't how much we have committed to memory, or even how much we know. It's being able to differentiate between what we do know and what we don't. It's knowing where to go to find out what we need to know; and it's knowing how to use the information we receive. It's seeing our knowledge properly put to practical pur4poses, benefiting not only our lives, but also the lives of our neighbors. It's being excited to share our newfound knowledge with others. It's being a mentor, and seeing our vision infuse and energize others with more energy and an even greater perspective. As Sir Isaac Newton said: "If I have seen a little farther than others, it's because I have stood on the shoulders of giants."

An education is viewing ourselves as disciples. With education, as we learn to channel our powers through obedience to eternal principles, we secure our freedom, and our choices expand exponentially. Education repetitively reinforces patterns of behavior that indelibly imprint a blueprint for success. "You may know me," said the personality trait. "I'm your constant companion. I'm your greatest helper; I'm your heaviest burden. I will push you onward or drag you down to failure. I am at your command. Half the tasks you do might as well be turned over to me. I'm able to do them quickly, and I'm able to do them the same every time if that's what you want. I'm easily managed; all you have to do is be firm with me. Show me exactly how you want it done; after a few lessons I'll do it automatically. I'm the servant of all great men and women, and the servant of failures, too. But I work with all the precision of a marvelous computer. You may run me for profit, or you may run me to ruin; it really makes no difference to me. Work with me. Be easy with me and I will destroy you. Be firm with me and I'll put the world at your feet. Who am I? I'm Habit!" (Anonymous)

What if we committed ourselves to a perpetual program of self-improvement and looked on "graduation" as a commencement or the beginning of a wonderful journey? Our formal education prepares us how to think, how to process information, and how to act. Then, if we approach lifelong education with an appreciation of the dynamic influence it can have, and of its ability to focus our energy and steady our course, we can use it as a perpetual motion machine to reach for the stars. "Of all the communities available to us," said Albert Einstein, "there is not one I would want to devote myself to, except for the society of the true searchers, which has very few living members at any time." If we were to view each challenge as an opportunity for growth and understanding, we would find ourselves richer for the experience. Helen Keller "asked a friend who had just returned from a long walk in the woods what she had observed. 'Nothing in particular,' she replied. How was that possible, I asked myself? I, who cannot hear or see, find hundreds of things to interest me through mere touch. I feel the delicate symmetry of a leaf. I pass my hands lovingly about the rough shaggy bark of a pine. Occasionally, if I am very fortunate, I place my hand gently on a small tree and feel the happy quiver of a bird in full song." ("The Atlantic Monthly").

The graduate school of hard knocks reinforces what our spiritual kindergarten should have already taught us. Wickedness never was happiness. Don't try to re-invent the wheel by ignoring divine tutorial training and going it alone. The Plan that Heavenly Father has devised is perfect in every detail. We should never yield to the temptation to trade the celestial sureties He promises for the telestial toys that are the trinkets of the tempter. Any detours and disappointments that we experience along the way are in reality the strait and narrow path to the Savior. It is all part of the fantastic education we receive while on our brief missions in mortality.

The Book of Mormon addresses themes
of self-denial, meekness, and charity, and it
asks that we surrender to the greater good our desire
for self-actualization, self-renewal, self-determination,
self-fulfillment, self-aggrandizement, and self-control.
It asks us to concentrate our efforts on behaviors that
honor God's design, rather than patronizing the
twisted temporal theories of emotional or
spiritual well-being that lack
an upward thrust.

Enduring to The End

"I am the law, and the light.
Look unto me, and endure to the
end, and ye shall live; for unto
him that endureth to the end
will I give eternal life."
(3 Nephi 15:9).

When we are on the path leading to eternal life, it is important to move forward with purpose. It is not enough to have been baptized and to have received the Holy Ghost. We must not camp out on the path and remain in a passive or vegetative state. The dictionary is the only place where success comes before work. Hence, the Savior's observation: "Many will say to me in that day: Lord, Lord, have we not prophesied in thy name, and in thy name have cast out devils, and in thy name done many wonderful works?" (3 Nephi 14:22). This verse applies particularly to members of the church who have held the priesthood. A problem is created when confusion arises between priesthood authority and power. The one comes by the laying on of hands, and the other through righteousness. Sometimes, when those who hold the priesthood are asked to officiate in the ordinances, they do so without the supporting power of Christ. Their acts are only valid because of their ordination and because of the sustaining faith of those for whom they minister. Thus, the Savior's recurring admonition: "Be ye clean that bear the vessels of the Lord." (3 Nephi 20:41).

The verse also suggests that there will be many at the Judgment Bar of Christ who will continue to press a point that is stubbornly advocated on earth. Namely, they will argue that there are many paths leading to the Kingdom that are equally acceptable to God. They will ask if it matters so much whether they were Methodist, or Quaker, or Lutheran. They will claim that as long as they accepted Christ, invoked his Holy Name, and gave Him the credit for whatever accomplishment resulted, their sincere efforts were surely not in vain.

But the position of the Savior is clear. At the Bar of Justice, He will declare the simple fact: "I will profess unto them: I never knew you." (Matthew 7:23). What a contrast this will be to those who come to the Lord with their sheaves of good works. (See Psalms 126:6). These will be as Job, who was known by the Lord Who said of him: "There is none like him in the earth, a perfect and an upright man, one that feareth God, and escheweth evil." (Job 1:8).

Interestingly, the J.S.T. renders the verse in Matthew: "Ye never knew me." (J.S.T. Matthew 7:33). This translation is more in harmony with the following verse that ties discipleship to performance. "Therefore, whoso heareth these sayings of mine and doeth them, I will liken him unto a wise man." The key is spiritual consistency. Brigham Young once said something to the effect that he never counted the cost of anything. He just found out what the Lord wanted him to do, and he did it

It must be remembered, though, that the Lord rewards the simple faith of those who press forward with what light they have received. Their efforts will be acknowledged. For example, in the springtime of the year 1820, a young boy approached God in a quiet grove of trees in western New York State. He was not yet a member of The Church of Jesus Christ nor did he have a clear understanding of God. Nevertheless, his humble prayer was answered with spectacular results. That drama is replayed hundreds of thousands of times each year as the Holy Ghost visits those who earnestly seek the truth.

For members of the church, though, the expectations of the Savior are much higher. "For of him unto whom much is given much is required; and he who sins against the greater light shall receive the greater condemnation." (D&C 82:3). Since we will be judged by the law we received while on the earth, we will vary in our responsibility to account for our deeds. The gospel endows us with the power of an eternal perspective to see beyond the limited horizon of our vision. Without it, we are likely to confuse our dreams with reality, and suffer a defeat of cosmic proportion when, coming back down to earth, those dreams are surrendered to the narrow reality of carnality, sensuality, and worldliness.

"Life is a sheet of paper white, where each of us may write a line or two, and then comes night. Greatly begin. If thou hast time but for a line, make that sublime. Not failure, but low aim is crime." (James Russell Lowell). Bruce R. McConkie was asked, "How can we reach the Celestial Kingdom." His answer was "Set your course, and move along it."

We acknowledge the leadership of Jesus Christ and emulate His example. He sets the course, and we follow the established guidelines. He gives the commands, and we yield to His will. He requires obedience, and we accept the rewards for determined discipleship, as well as the consequences for willful neglect of our responsibilities. What makes the Plan fair is continual feedback from the Holy Ghost. We accepted the risks attendant to mortality because we believed in the Plan, and we knew He would never leave us. When we leave Him, though, we are vulnerable. When we feel His Presence or that of His servants in our lives, and when our foundation is grounded on the bedrock of the gospel, we can be sure of our ultimate success, because it was ordained in the heavens before the world was. After all, it is the Great Plan of Redemption and the key to our salvation.

Entropy in The Physical and Eternal Worlds

Without opposition
to the Plan of Salvation,
without entropy, "righteousness
could not be brought to pass, neither
wickedness, neither holiness nor
misery, neither good nor bad."
(2 Nephi 2:11).

"In everyday language, entropy is the law that tells us things wear out. Buildings fall down and crumble away; living things grow old and die. These changes are linked to the passage of time, marking a distinction between the past and the future. They correspond to an increase in the amount of disorder in the Universe. This disorder is measured in terms of entropy. The flow of time from the past to the future means that the entropy of the Universe must always increase" in accordance with the Second Law of Thermodynamics. ("Steven Hawking, A Life in Science," p. 142).

This law is one of many that govern the physical universe in which we live. But if we were to pass through the veil separating us from the eternal world, the laws that had been left behind might no longer apply. Order, instead of disorder, might prevail by other laws of physics peculiar to eternity and in some way superior to temporal laws.

As the poet wrote: "Oh, this world has more of coming and of going than I can bear. I guess it's eternity I want, where all things are, and always will be. Where I can hold my loves a little looser. Where, finally, we realize Time is the only thing that really dies." (Carol Lynn Pearson). In fact, it is "in the dark recesses of memory, in unbidden suggestions, in trains of thought unwittingly pursued, in multiplied waves and currents all at once flashing and rushing, in dreams that cannot be laid to rest, in the force of instinct, in the obscure, but certain, intuitions of the spiritual life, (that) we have glimpses of a great tide of life ebbing and flowing, rippling and roiling and beating about where we cannot see it." (E.S. Dallas).

We are fortunate, indeed, if we have shared the experience of the aviator who ecstatically wrote: "Oh, I have slipped the surly bonds of earth and danced the skies on laughter-silvered wings. Sunward I've climbed, and joined the tumbling mirth of sun-split clouds, and done a hundred things you have not dreamed of. [I've] wheeled and soared and swung high in the sunlit silence. Hovering there, I've chased the shouting wind along, and flung my eager craft through footless halls of air. Up, up the long, delirious, burning blue I've topped the windswept heights with easy grace, where never lark, or even eagle flew. And, while with silent, lifting mind I've trod the high untrespassed sanctity of space, I put out my hand, and touched the face of God." (John G. Magee, Jr., "High Flight").

Time itself may be an artificial and relative dimension in which man, an eternal being, cannot be completely comfortable. it is transitory by definition, and it is only our perspective that makes it seem that we move through it. it just may be the other way around. For youth, it never seems to pass quickly enough. Perhaps the young, so recently removed from the eternal world, are impatient to return to that more natural environment. in any event, as we approach the event horizon between mortality and immortality, the perception of the passage of time changes again; it seems to speed up.

In the last scene of the last episode of Star Trek, The Next Generation, Captain Jean Luc Picard mused: "Someone once said that time is a predator that stalks us all our lives. I prefer to think of it as a companion that accompanies us on the journey, reminding us to cherish every moment." In fact, growing old may be strictly a unique quality of mortality, a built-in mechanism that affords us an opportunity to gauge the approach of our reunion with our Heavenly Father.

He sees with eternal perspective, which is arguably more "real." Before His view is yesterday, today, and forever, in one eternal round. He is "the Great I AM, Alpha and Omega, the beginning and the end, the same which looked upon the wide expanse of eternity, and all the seraphic hosts of heaven, before the world was made." (D&C 38:1-2). Elder Neal A. Maxwell wrote that we are given glimpses of His eternal world, as, for example, "when a baby is born, and as we wait with those who are dying. We brush against the veil, as goodbyes and greetings are said almost within earshot of each other. in such moments, this resonance with realities on the other side of the veil is so obvious that it can be explained in only one way.

Even now," argued Elder Maxwell, "time is clearly not our natural dimension. Thus, it is that we are never really at home in time. Alternately, we find ourselves impatiently wishing to hasten the passage of time or to hold back the dawn. We can do neither, of course. Whereas the bird is at home in the air, we are clearly not at home in time, because we belong to eternity. Time, as much as any one thing, whispers to us that we are strangers here. if time were natural to us, why is it that we have so many clocks and wear wristwatches?" ("BYU Speeches of The Year," 1979).

Eternity may be an open system in spacetime that cannot be defined by borders. if so, then entropy would not increase in eternity, as the Second Law of Thermodynamics would otherwise require. Only in our physical universe (a closed system) would everything move toward disorder and less structure.

In our own fragile environment, it takes a great deal of effort to create order, and very little to allow chaos to reign. in fact, if we do not consciously focus on the creation of structure and order, and exert effort to progress, everything tends to fall apart. For example, a monumental sculpture in marble may be destroyed with one inadvertent stroke of a hammer on a chisel. A thousand-year-old redwood tree can burn to the ground in hours. The city of Babylon took hundreds of years to build, but it is today only a dusty memory. Even the effort it takes to organize words into coherent sentences or paragraphs can be erased with one keystroke, or one swipe of a magnet over a computer disk.

Entropy rules the behavioral sciences as well. it explains why friendship can be devastated by a careless action or word, and how a life of moderation can be forfeit by one thoughtless act of indulgence in a moment of weakness. One glass of liquor can ruin a lifestyle of temperance, and a single act of passion can negate the constructive efforts of a lifetime of chaste behavior. Testimony that has taken years to build can be destroyed through carelessness or inattention.

Entropy is a physical law whereas the Law of Eternal Progression belongs to the eternities. Hence, the concept of eternal progression is encompassed by celestial laws that can be foreign to the rational mind. As Paul explained to the Corinthian Saints: "The natural man receiveth not the things of the Spirit of God: for they are foolishness unto him: neither can he know them, because they are spiritually discerned." (1 Corinthians 2:14).

Even though they may seem to be at odds, or to be contraries, inasmuch as they come from opposite ends of the spectrum, the two laws must ultimately be in balance with each other. in fact, it was ordained in heaven, and "must needs be, that there is an opposition in all things." (2 Nephi 2:11). Jesus Christ had a perfect understanding of the laws of physics before His creation of our universe. For God, who dwells in eternity, the Law of Eternal Progression is paramount, but it is as much defined by its opposite in the physical universe as it is by itself.

Since Satan operates more by subtraction than by addition, his program of deceit, deception, and fraud that tears down individuals and relationships seems to prosper because of entropy. From God's perspective, however, in circumstances that involve the exercise of agency, entropy may simply represent the manifestation of the natural consequence of inappropriate behavior. if this is so, its effects will be inevitable unless the Author of Salvation and the Maker and Fashioner of the Universe intervenes. As Paul explained to the Hebrews, "ye have in heaven a better and an enduring substance." (Hebrews 10:34).

The promise for those who rely upon the Merits of Christ is that "the gates of hell shall not prevail against them." (D&C 10:69). in other words, the laws of the physical universe (entropy) will not doom them to inevitable destruction. The gate may be strait, and the way narrow, but those who accept Christ as their guide will find it within their reach to travel the path of eternal progress. On the other hand, "broad is the gate, and wide the way that leadeth to the deaths, and many there are that go in thereat," because they do not receive Christ, nor do they abide His law. (D&C 132:25). When individuals choose to ignore celestial law, they have tacitly chosen a course leading to destruction, that is the natural consequence of the operation of the immutable laws of physics that govern our material universe.

However, if there were no opposition, conflict, or contrary between entropy and eternal progression, "righteousness could not be brought to pass, neither wickedness, neither holiness nor misery, neither good nor bad." (2 Nephi 2:11). Therefore, the two laws co-exist in an atmosphere of mutual acknowledgment and accommodation. They set the stage for the exercise of moral agency and necessitate the implementation of other equally important and co-existing laws: Justice and Mercy. Mercy, in particular, exists to mitigate the otherwise inevitable effects of entropy in this world and facilitate the journey of progress both in time and eternity.

The scriptures suggest that there is an eternal equivalent to the Unified Field Theory of physics, a law that encompasses all the laws of both worlds, for as Lehi taught "all things must needs be a compound in one." (2 Nephi 2:11). in other words, even though there are physical laws of nature upon which progress and development naturally hinge, ultimately, they will all harmonize in a unified, cohesive, and coherent way through the intercession of the Mediator of the Covenant and the Savior of the world, and creation will make perfect sense. His act of Atonement brings together in harmony the work of both the Spoiler and the Creator and is the ultimate reconciliation between heaven and hell. Because of the Atonement, "there is a resurrection, therefore the grave hath no victory, and the sting of death is swallowed up in Christ. He is the light and the life of the world; yea, a light that is endless, that can never be darkened; yea, and also a life which is endless, that there can be no more death." (Mosiah 16:9).

Only through living gospel principles can the disorder and destruction that result from transgression, and which are the natural physical consequences of entropy, be reversed. While the contrary of obedience nurtures the development of personality traits that are consistent with God's nature and the philosophy of eternal progression, sin is harmful because it destroys the capacity of individuals to develop the character traits of Heavenly Father. Disorder takes the disobedient further and further from the influence of the Holy Ghost. To counteract the consequences of sin, the worst example of entropy, "the days of the children of men were prolonged, according to the will of God, that they might repent while in the flesh; wherefore, their state became a state of probation, and their time was lengthened, according to the commandments which the Lord God gave unto the children of men. For he gave commandment that all men must repent; for he showed unto all men that they were lost," because of the entropy that naturally followed Adam and Eve's introduction into the telestial world. (2 Nephi 2:21).

After the Fall, Satan came among their posterity, flushed with excitement because he knew how difficult it would be for them to counteract the natural tendency toward disorder. Many of them did love Satan more than they loved God, and from that time forth, they began to manifest the behavioral consequences of entropy. That is to say, they were "carnal, sensual, and devilish." (Moses 5:13). Without the intervention of other laws, these consequences pointed them toward inevitable and ultimate destruction.

The Lord had confidence, though, in the ability of Adam's posterity to live a celestial law, and so He "called upon men by the Holy Ghost everywhere and commanded them that they should repent. And as many as believed in the Son, and repented of their sins, should be saved" from the destructive effects of entropy. (Moses 5:15). By following the counsel of the Savior, they could bring their character into a state of harmony with the Law of Eternal Progression, eventually becoming "heirs of God, and joint heirs with Christ." (Romans 8:17). Opposition would work to their benefit.

It may come as a surprise to some to realize that the purpose of the ministry of the Savior was to create divisions among the people. The scriptures teach that at the end of the physical world, "before him shall be gathered all nations: and he shall separate them one from another, as a shepherd divideth his sheep from the goats. And he shall set the sheep on his right hand, but the goats on the left." (Matthew 25:32-33).

Entropy seizes on these divisions. The Lord explained to His disciples: "Think not that I am come to send peace on earth: I came not to send peace, but a sword. For I came to set a man at variance against his father, and the daughter in law against her mother-in-law. And a man's foes shall be they of his own household." (Matthew 10:34-36). Therefore, He counseled: "If thy right hand offend thee, cut it off, and cast it from thee: for it is profitable for thee that one of thy members should perish, and not that thy whole body should be cast into hell." (Matthew 5:30). As long as we live in the telestial world, we must be vigilant to distance ourselves from any stain upon our character that makes us vulnerable to the effects of entropy. in this sense, we are commanded to "forsake the world" (D&C 53:2), to keep ourselves "unspotted from the world" (D&C 59:9), and to "overcome the world." (D&C 63:47). Because He honors both the law of entropy and the law of eternal progression, God "will not spare any that remain in Babylon." (D&C 64:24). He cannot do so because entropy will increase in the universe as long as men make choices that separate themselves from the influence of celestial law. "Wherefore, if ye believe me," He declared, "ye will labor while it is called today." (D&C 64:25). In effect, "you will exercise agency in order to make good choices that mitigate the effects of entropy and maximize the effects of obedience to the law of eternal progression."

By living a celestial law, we may have the Spirit to open our eyes, "so as to see and understand the things of God, even those things which were from the beginning before the world was." (D&C 76:12-13). We will see things more clearly when we escape the negative limitations of our mortal clay, that now focus our attention on carnality, sensuality, and the devilish nature that denies the power of the Atonement. Too often, we are "like unto a man beholding his natural face in a glass." (James 1:23). We satisfy ourselves with a glimpse of salvation in a mirror, without ever beholding the real thing.

When we finally do see things as they really are, with a clarity that comes more from the heart than from the physical senses, perhaps we will understand how Helen Keller could have had such vision. She wrote not from the vantage point of severe physical impairment, but rather with profound spiritual enlightenment: "I believe that no good shall be lost, and that all man has willed or hoped or dreamed of good shall exist forever. I believe in the immortality of the soul because I have within me immortal longings. I believe that the state we enter after death is wrought of our own motives, thoughts, and deeds. I believe that my home there will be beautiful with colour, music, and speech of flowers and faces I love. Without this faith, there would be little meaning in my life. I should be a mere pillar of darkness in the dark. Observes in the full enjoyment of their bodily senses pity me, but it is because they do not see the golden chamber in my life where I dwell delighted; for dark as my path may seem to them, I carry a magic light in my heart. Faith, the spiritual strong searchlight, illuminates the way, and although sinister doubts lurk in the shadow, I walk unafraid towards the Enchanted Wood where the foliage is always green, where joy abides, where nightingales nest and sing, and where life and death are one in the presence of the Lord." ("Midstream").

The Savior uses the very laws of the physical universe to help Him to accomplish His mission. Natural digression in the temporal world from order to disorder suits his purposes as long as the disorder created jars mankind out of its collective complacency. This disorder upsets the status quo, gets people thinking, and prods them to expend their energy purposefully. Sentient beings are able to put their agency to work constructively. The Lord declared through His prophet John: "I know thy works, that thou art neither cold nor hot. I would thou wert cold or hot." He might have been saying that their works qualified them to be neither the victims of fate nor the beneficiaries of the blessings that follow obedience. He continued: "So then because thou art lukewarm, and neither cold nor hot, I will spue thee out of my mouth." (Revelation 3:15-16). As Brigham Young so often taught, "The first principle that ought to occupy the attention of all mankind and which is the mainspring of all action, is the principle of improvement." ("Discourses of Brigham Young," p. 87).

Progress becomes the recompense for perseverance, salvation is the reward for surmounting obstacles, and the hope of eternal life is the blessing for enduring opposition. By experience, we learn that gospel principles that relate to the eternities can supersede physical laws that relate only to the temporal universe. Those who enter into the covenants are figuratively and quite literally, "born of him." (Mosiah 5:7). They become new creatures in Christ, oriented more to the laws of the eternal world and the commandments of the Master than to the limitations imposed by the physical world. (See 2 Corinthians 5:17). Their experience is inexplicable, and yet undeniable. "Whatsoever is born of God overcometh the (laws governing the physical) world." (1 John 5:3).

Thus, President Spencer W. Kimball's counsel to the Saints rings with a sense of real urgency. He told the Saints: "So much depends upon our willingness to make up our minds, collectively and individually, that present levels of performance are not acceptable, either to ourselves or to the Lord. in saying that, I am not calling for flashy, temporary differences in our performance levels, but for a quiet resolve to lengthen our stride." ("Church News," 3/22/1975).

When President Kimball exhorted members of the church to lengthen their stride, he knew that the exertion would cause discomfort, as it tested the limits of endurance. But in doing so, spiritual muscles would be stretched. Christ urged the man in bondage to do the same thing, to go the second mile, doubling his stride. "The second mile is a gift of spiritual independence that removes the veil of insensitivity from a destiny." (Richard L. Gunn, "A Search for Sensitivity and Spirit," p. 197). This independence is exhilarating when it dawns on us that we are spiritual beings having mortal experiences and we recognize the soul-expanding implications of that truth.

Nevertheless, for as long as we live in this world, when we commit to a lifestyle of obedience to the laws of the gospel, other laws governing the physical universe that may not seem to be oriented toward eternal life must still be honored. The Savior said: "If any man will come after me, let him deny himself, and take up his cross, and follow me. For whosoever will save his life shall lose it: and whosoever will lose his life for my sake shall find it." (Matthew 16:24-

25). Submission to one law (seemingly destructive) creates the opportunity to be obedient to another law (clearly constructive) with a potential to assist us to reach even greater heights that could not otherwise be attained. Thus, the Savior's ominous warning: "If a man come to me, and hate not his father, and mother, and wife and children, and brethren, and sisters, yea, and his own life also, he cannot be my disciple." (Luke 14:26-27).

Spiritual maturity gives us the confidence to sacrifice all temporal things, to understand that such a sacrifice is necessary to overcome the physical world, and to muster the discipline to allow the law of eternal progression to supersede the law of entropy in our lives. As Paul acknowledged: "When I was a child, I spake as a child, I understood as a child, I thought as a child. But when I became a man, I put away childish things." (1 Corinthians 13:11).

The Lord appreciates how hard it is for mortals to forsake the supposed security and comfort of the world. Even Paul admitted, "For now we see through a glass, darkly." (1 Corinthians 13:12). Therefore, the Lord has revealed a basic truth, that "when we obtain any blessing from God, it is by obedience to that law upon which it is predicated." (D&C 130:21). "For all who will have a blessing at my hands," He said, "shall abide the law which was appointed for that blessing, and the conditions thereof, as were instituted from before the foundation of the world." (D&C 132:5). Paul urged the Galatians to "be not deceived. God is not mocked: for whatsoever a man soweth, that shall he also reap. For he that soweth to his flesh shall of the flesh reap corruption; but he that soweth to the Spirit shall of the Spirit reap life everlasting." (Galatians 6:7-8). Even though we toil with blood, sweat, and tears to obtain temporal treasures, sacrificing even those things that are near and dear to us, at the last day entropy still equals physical destruction, while the reward of steady obedience to the laws of the gospel is the opportunity to progress eternally.

Since most of us have not yet made the transition to be the architects of our own fate, the disciples of Christ are commanded: "Give your language to exhortation continually." (D&C 23:7). "Let us not weary in well doing," wrote Paul. (Galatians 6:9). Because the law of entropy is so powerful in the physical universe, those who are born again still require constant and repetitive encouragement in their quest to progress eternally. Progression is a pathway, and not a point, and Brigham Young believed that "all organized existence is in progress either to an endless advancement in eternal perfections, or back to dissolution. There is no period in all the eternities," he declared, "wherein organized existence will become stationary, that it cannot advance in knowledge, wisdom, power, and glory." (J.D., 1:349).

Truly, "if any man be in Christ, he is a new creature: old things are passed away; behold, all things are become new." (2 Corinthians 5:17). By means of the ministry and Atonement of His Son, Heavenly Father's Plan of Salvation has bridged the gap between the temporal and eternal universes. Paul repetitively described this as a process of reconciliation. Ultimately, he wrote, "all things are of God, who hath reconciled us to himself by Jesus Christ, and hath given to us the ministry of reconciliation. To wit, that God was in Christ, reconciling the world unto himself, not imputing their trespasses unto them; and hath committed unto us the word of reconciliation." (2 Corinthians 5:18-19).

Modern scientists take the rational view, and in their quest to increase their understanding, have discovered laws of physics that fit the observable universe back to a point just after its Creation. Under different circumstances that fall outside the parameters of the observable universe, however, they admit that other laws might apply. This leaves the door ajar for theologians who testify that just such a scenario exists.

As it is, until Albert Einstein worked out the principles of the general theory of relativity, physics was dominated by the classical thinking of Sir Isaac Newton. The mathematical equations he devised described a universe that was ordered, logical, and static, in which time and space were absolutes. Einstein's equations, on the other hand, suggested that gravity dynamically interacts with both time and space. Others built upon his work, and devised quantum theory, which explains how everything else in the physical world works. These two theories are the twin pillars of modern science. The Holy Grail is a Unified Field Theory, which would combine all the equations of physics into one neat package that would describe the universe in a comprehensive and complete way.

Newton's equations described a majestic clockwork that followed a predetermined, predictable path. Unfortunately for philosophers and theologians alike, it did not really allow for free will. Heisenberg's "uncertainty principle" has effectively taken care of that problem. It states, in effect, that there is uncertainty that can measure by physical means such things as basic as space and time, and perhaps even human foibles. In such an "uncertain" world there is plenty of latitude for individual expression.

Newton recognized his woeful inadequacies, writing late in his life: "I do not know what I may appear to the world, but to myself I seem to have been only like a boy playing on the seashore, and diverting myself now and then in finding a smoother pebble, or a prettier shell than ordinary, while the great ocean of truth lay all undiscovered before me." ("The Ascent of Man," p. 236).

He understood that the mind of man is generally locked on telestial targets, and that even so-called higher-level thinking is too often mere vanity. "For my thoughts are not your thoughts," chided the Lord. "Neither are your ways my ways ... For as the heavens are higher than the earth, so are my ways higher than your ways, and my thoughts than your thoughts." (Isaiah 55:8-9).

Long ago, a Psalm written by David warned: "Except the Lord keep the city, the watchman waketh but in vain." (Psalms 127:1). Man will never understand the physical sciences so completely that he will become Master of the Universe. He can never, in any significant way, alter the course of events while he remains in the physical world. He would do well to leave these things in the hands of God. Wisely did the Psalmist counsel: "Be still, and know that I am God." (Psalms 46:10).

In the meantime, though, none of us must ever be found asleep at our posts. We cannot allow ourselves to be swept along by entropy to the precipice of destruction. The offices in the priesthood, for example, are not given as sedatives, but rather as stimulants to increase our capacity for activity and service. It is a simple formula: the Lord will strengthen and bless those who repent and keep the commandments, but not necessarily with telestial toys that might lead the faithful on detours leading away from the strait and narrow path. Nor will He strengthen us by making our way easy, lest we be pacified into a false sense of carnal security.

Instead, He will fortify us in subtle ways. He will see that we have opportunities to be anxiously engaged in good causes. He will give us the capacity to think, so that, on our own initiative, we might avoid conceptual cul-de-sacs. He will help us to work out our salvation with fear and trembling before the Lord. He will cause us to move out of our comfort zones into the stimulating environment of service, and even onto the uncomfortable road that leads to Gethsemane. Socrates said: "Know thyself," Cicero admonished, "Control thyself," and Jesus taught by the greatest example of all, saying "Give thyself" completely and without reservation.

The Savior exhorted his disciples to drink copiously and unceasingly from the fountain of truth. He understood the difference between celestial sureties that are represented by eternal progression, and telestial tendencies that are represented by entropy. "Great and marvelous are the works of the Lord," Jacob exclaimed. "How unsearchable are the depths of the mysteries of him; and it is impossible that man should find out all his ways. And no man knoweth of his ways save it be revealed unto him; wherefore, brethren, despise not the revelations of God." (Jacob 4:8).

Joseph Smith taught: "Reading the experience of others, or the revelation given to them, can never give us a comprehensive view of our condition and true relation to God. Knowledge of these things can only be obtained by experience through the ordinances of God set forth for that purpose. Could you gaze into heaven five minutes, you would know more than you would by reading all that has ever been written on the subject." (H.C., 6:50)

"O the vainness, and the frailties, and the foolishness of men! When the are learned, they think they are wise, and they hearken not unto the counsel of God, for they set it aside, supposing they know of themselves, wherefore, their wisdom is foolishness and it profiteth them not. And they shall perish. But to be learned is good if they hearken unto the counsels of God." (2 Nephi 9:28-29). As Paul cautioned the Colossian Saints: "Beware lest any man spoil you through philosophy and vain deceit, after the tradition of men, after the rudiments of the world, and not after Christ." (Colossians 2:8).

In these Last Days, we have again been blessed with the wise counsel of prophets of God. Joseph Smith taught true doctrine. One of his greatest strengths was his knowledge of the physical world, and his understanding of the eternal world, and one of his greatest contributions was his explanation of the relationship between the two. He clarified our understanding of heaven and made it seem within our grasp to improve ourselves in both time, when we are still influenced by the law of entropy, and in eternity, when we have progressed to benefit fully from the law of eternal progression to reach our divine potential.

Environmental Concerns
(An Eternal Perspective)

"The rocks of the earth
must rend; and because
of the groanings of the earth,
many of the kings of the isles
of the sea shall be wrought upon
by the Spirit of God, to exclaim:
the God of nature suffers."
(1 Nephi 19:12).

In the scriptures, we are taught that God created, or more properly organized, the heaven, and the earth." (Moses 2:1). He did this within the matrix of an eternal principle, that of work, so that in the great scheme of continual progression, His creations are inextricably bound to their environment in a symbiotic relationship.

Life has a function inseparably connected with the biosphere we call the earth. Tiny corals, in time, cause great island masses to be formed. The sediment layers from ancient lake bottoms wind up as the stratified cliff sides of present-day mountain ranges. Beavers dam streams with timber from the forest, slowing the floods of spring, and creating ponds for water life. These eventually turn into meadows, and then into woodlands.

Earthworms constantly enrich the soil in which they live. The vulture is nature's garbage can, and he never goes on strike. Ants devour what the vulture misses. Birds excrete guano rich in nitrogen that is essential for life. Plants excrete oxygen necessary for animal life, and animals excrete carbon dioxide without which photosynthesis is impossible. The ecosystems of animal and plant life function perfectly as a unified whole, in harmony with the physical world. In the manifestations of nature, the hand of God, our Creator, is visible to us all. (See D&C 88:42).

We who have agency as a gift from God often disregard the laws that govern nature, despite the fact that God has entrusted us with a stewardship responsibility to care for the earth. That law operates in accordance with the other laws of the gospel and is in perfect harmony with them. The day will come, when Christ will ask us to give an accounting to determine if we have nurtured the biosystems of the earth, and allowed them to fulfil the measure of their creation. (Luke 16:2).

The difficulty lies in the fact that after the Fall, the sons and daughters of men began to live a telestial law of carnality, sensuality, and worldliness. In this sense, the consequences of Adam's transgression negatively affected the earth. This has eternal consequences, because our physical surroundings are subject to law just as we are, for the earth has a living soul and is also on a path of progression leading to celestialization. (See Moses 3:5-9, Abraham

5:3-5, D&C 29:30-35, 2 Nephi 2:22, & the Tenth Article of Faith). Thus, it is sensitive to the physical demands placed upon it by those who sometimes abuses their stewardship responsibility.

The world today underappreciates the intimate relationship existing between plant and animal life, and the earth itself. Yet God is truly the God of nature (1 Nephi 19:12), and the so-called primitive peoples of the earth, living in concert with nature, have often intuitively recognized this fact. Indigenous peoples have often made waterfalls, monoliths, or mountains their gods. For example, the mountain known as Rainier in the state of Washington (elevation 14,410 feet) was called by the Native Americans Tahoma, "the mountain that was God." Tibetans call Mount Everest "Chomolungma," or "The Goddess Mother of the World." The Black Hills of South Dakota were considered sacred land by the Sioux Indians, as was Devil's Tower, Wyoming.

Because of modern man's seeming inability to consistently exercise their stewardship in righteousness, their tendency to refuse to acknowledge the hand of God in all things, and their disobedience of eternal principles of the gospel, there are physical manifestations of nature that could be interpreted as God's displeasure with the disobedient. What could be more ominous than the declaration from the Lord, who said "I ... am angry with the wicked; I am holding my spirit from the inhabitants of the earth."? (D&C 63:32).

The matter of withdrawal of the Spirit should be of concern to everyone, because but for this Spirit, in whom 'we live, and move, and have our being' (Acts 17:28), the universe would again revert to chaos.

Myriad life forms and physical manifestations of the Creation have been given coherence and unity by the influence of the Spirit. Without it, disorder reigns. An example of its withdrawal was at the time of the Flood. Many chaotic conditions of our dispensation must be the result of the partial withdrawal of the Spirit, for the Lord has said "with famine, and plague, and earthquake, and the thunder of heaven, and the fierce and vivid lightning also, shall the inhabitants of the earth be made to feel the wrath, and indignation, and chastening hand of an Almighty God, until the consumption decreed hath made a full end of all nations." (D&C 87:6).

It is our challenge to bring the unique Latter-day Saint eternal perspective to the forum of the discussion of ecology and its related subjects. The world needs to understand that an all-knowing God has created the earth, and that He has placed us upon it. It needs to understand the subtle difference between subduing and destroying the earth. It needs to understand that there is a code of eternal principles whereby we may exercise our stewardship in righteousness, within the context of a unified ecosystem that operates in perfect symmetry with those principles. It needs to understand that this code is called the Plan of Salvation.

Especially, we need to publish the fact that God, Who knows the end from the beginning, has said through His prophets that we are that we might have joy. (See 2 Nephi 2:25). Conditions in the world will deteriorate only insofar as we stray from God and place our trust and faith in false ideologies that will ultimately betray our inherent weaknesses. The world will avoid the inevitable consequences of disobedience only if it hearkens to the voice of the prophets and lives in harmony with the unifying influence of the gospel of Jesus Christ.

Establishing the Word

"Those who shall be destroyed
shall speak unto them out of the
ground and their speech shall be low
out of the dust and their voice shall be as
one that hath a familiar spirit; for the Lord
God will give unto him power, that he may
whisper concerning them, even as it were
out of the ground; and their speech
shall whisper out of the dust."
(2 Nephi 26:16).

It is hard to say just how old the writings in the Bible are, but scholars generally agree that oral traditions were passed down over the millennia, until they were first written down by Moses. Scripture affirms that "the Lord spake unto Moses, saying: Behold, I reveal unto you concerning this heaven, and this earth; write the words which I speak." (Moses 2:1).

In a sense, Latter-day Saints know better, for scripture translated by Joseph Smith and given to the world in the Last Days reveals that "a book of remembrance was kept ... in the language of Adam, for it was given unto as many as called upon God to write by the spirit of inspiration; and by them their children were taught to read and write, having a language which was pure and undefiled ... This was the book of the generations of Adam." (Moses 6:5-6, 8).

As Pharaoh from the Thirteenth Dynasty (around 1,700 B.C.) said: "My heart yearned to behold the most ancient books of Atum (Adam). Open them before me for diligent searching, that I may know God as he really is." (Hugh Nibley, "Genesis of the Written Word," in "Nibley on The Timely and Timeless," p. 104). Enoch continued in the pattern of the ancient patriarchs, and confirmed that Adam kept "a book of remembrance." (Moses 6:46). Abraham, as well, kept "a record of the fathers, even the patriarchs (and) a knowledge of the beginning of the creation." He recorded that he would "endeavor to write some of these things upon (that) record, for the benefit of (his) posterity." (Abraham 1:31). Jacob indirectly indicated that many in ancient Israel recorded their testimonies, when he wrote that "none of the prophets have written, nor prophesied, save they have spoken concerning ... Christ." (Jacob 7:11).

In fact, the Semitic alphabet itself may have been devised for the express purpose of recording scripture. If so, when we read the scriptures, we are witnessing forms of the original symbols in which the message was first conveyed by God. In this light, we are bound to approach the scriptures with a new-found reverence and respect. The bottom line is clear: The Bible did not begin in some uncertain origin, or without authority, but rather, it was given to us by inspiration from the very beginning to show us the way of salvation.

From the time of Ezra after the Babylonian Captivity (587 B.C.), a collection of official Hebrew literature began to be kept by the prophets. Latter-day Saints have a special knowledge of at least one such collection, that was collectively called "the Plates of Brass." (1 Nephi 4:16). But Israel hardly embraced these writings. Jeremiah, for example, prophesied "against Israel, and against Judah." He wrote: O Lord ... I am in derision daily. Every one mocketh me. For since I spake, I cried out; I cried violence and spoil; because the word of the Lord was made a reproach unto me, and a derision, daily. Then I said, I will not make mention of him, nor speak any more in his name. But this word was in mine heart as a burning fire shut up in my bones, and I was weary with forbearing, and I could not stay." (Jeremiah 20:7-9). He was in the good company of his contemporary, Lehi, who was mocked by the Jews "because of the things which he testified of them; for he truly testified of their wickedness and their abominations; and he testified that the things which he saw and heard, and also the things which he read in the book, manifested plainly of the coming of a Messiah, and also the redemption of the world. And when the Jews heard these things they were angry with him; yea, even as with the prophets of old, whom they had cast out, and stoned, and slain; and they also sought his life, that they might take it away. (1 Nephi 1:19-20).

As the Word was preserved, it was compiled and arranged in a variety of ways. Today, it is organized as the Pentateuch, the five books of Moses, as a compilation of historical books, and of writings such as Psalms, Proverbs, Job, and Esther. The organization of the Old Testament is not chronological, but follows a pattern based on subject matter such as law, history, poetry, and prophecy. The word was preserved on papyrus, clay tablets, and writing boards that when hinged together became a folding book. Hence, Ezekiel wrote: "Take thee one stick, and write upon it, For Judah, and for the children of Israel his companions: then take another stick, and write upon it, For Joseph, the stick of Ephraim, and for all the house of Israel his companions. And join them one to another into one stick; and they shall become one in thine hand." (Ezekiel 37:16-17).

Leather was used, as were plates of metal. "There is an interesting account in Idrisi (1,226 A.D.) of the opening of the tomb of Mycerinus, in the third of the three great pyramids. The writer reports that al that was found in the tomb was a blue sarcophagus containing 'the decayed remains of a man, but no treasure, excepting some golden tablets inscribed with characters of a language which nobody could understand.' The tablets were used to pay the workmen. We leave the reader to speculate on what might have been written on those plates of gold which one of the greatest of Pharaohs apparently regarded as the greatest treasure with which he could be buried." (Nibley, "Lehi in The Desert," p. 120).

However the writings were preserved, Israel considered them to be of great importance. Those of Moses were safeguarded in the Ark of the Covenant, a sacred chest 45 inches long, 27 inches wide, and 27 inches high. "Take this book of the law, and put it in the side of the ark of the covenant of the Lord your God, that it may be there a witness." (Deuteronomy 31:26). The story is told of one such chronicler, who cautioned: "My son, be careful in thy work, for it is heavenly work, lest thou err in omitting or in adding one jot (the smallest letter in the Hebrew alphabet) and so cause the destruction of the whole world." (Geddes MacGregor, "The Bible in the Making," p. 48).

In the Last Days, what had been lost has been restored by modern day prophets. The Book of Mormon was translated by Joseph Smith in just six weeks, between April 7, 1829, and the first week of June 1829. The translation was unlike that of any other text, because it was accomplished "through the mercy (and) power of God." (D&C 1:29). This is as specific an explanation as is found regarding just how Joseph Smith translated the plates. During his lifetime, he tended to let the record speak for itself. it was appropriate that he do so, because when one understands that it is an inspired translation, the reader is drawn to the book itself, and without distraction can put to the test the challenge left by Moroni: "And when ye shall receive these things, I would exhort you that ye would ask God, the Eternal Father, in the name of Christ, if these things are not true; and if ye shall ask with a sincere heart, with real intent, having faith in Christ, he will manifest the truth of it unto you, by the power of the Holy Ghost." (Moroni 10:4).

Jesus Christ Himself testified that The Book of Mormon is true. "He translated the book, even that part which I have commanded him, and as your Lord and your God liveth it is true." (D&C 17:6, See D&C 19:26). it is interesting that the Savior used an ancient Hebrew oath in His witness. As Paul said, "because he could swear by no greater, he sware by himself." (Hebrews 6:13).

One of the most daunting challenges of modern-day translation of ancient records is to preserve the nuance and language of the original authors while making the narrative understandable to the modern mind. After all, when "a book of remembrance was (first) kept, (it was) in the language of Adam," or in the Adamic tongue. (Moses 6:5). Then came Hebrew, then from the Fourth Century B.C., Aramaic, then the Greek Septuagint, then Latin, and so it goes.

In 250 B.C., Ptolemy of Egypt desired to accumulate all the books of the known world into a library in Alexandria. Incidentally, the Christian Roman emperor Theodosius the Great, in the interests of the church, destroyed around 700,000 volumes in the Library of Alexandria, around 300 A.D. As we ponder this wanton act of spiritual sabotage, we remember that "writing was not devised by men as a tool to help them in their everyday affairs: successful businessmen have been illiterates, and there is ample evidence that writing was adapted to commercial uses only after such uses were found for it. If you bring together all the written records of man's past, you will discover that the overwhelming mass of material is religious in nature, and that the primary purpose to which writing has been put through the ages has not been for business records and correspondence, in which writing is employed awkwardly and without enthusiasm, but for keeping a remembrance of God's dealings with men. The specific purpose of writing, as the Egyptians put it, is to record the divine words. (Hugh Nibley). If we can take anything positive from that senseless destruction of historical and religious records, it might be that we have at least been given a greater opportunity to walk by faith.

But back to the Septuagint. Six elders of every tribe, 72 in all, translated the scriptures into Greek in the third century B.C., reportedly in 72 days. It was called the Septuagint, or "The Version of the Seventy." This book was the one used by the first Christians following the mortal ministry of Christ. Written in the international language of Greece, it facilitated the teaching of the gospel throughout the known world.

The Septuagint creates a remarkable opportunity to determine the authenticity of The Book of Mormon as an inspired record. 2 Nephi 12:16, a translation of Isaiah 2:16, declares: "Yea, and the day of the Lord shall come upon all the cedars of Lebanon ... and upon all the ships of the sea, and upon all the ships of Tarshish." This verse is quite significant because the phrase "and upon all the ships of the sea" is found in The Book of Mormon, but not in the K.J.T. Book of Isaiah. it is, however, found in the ancient Greek, or Septuagint, version of Isaiah.

Joseph Smith did not know any Greek at the time he translated The Book of Mormon, and there is no record that the Septuagint was available for his comparative study at the Palmyra Public Library. Until the discovery of the Dead Sea Scrolls, scholars searching for original copies of the books of the Old Testament were unable to find any older than the 9th century A.D. Part of the reason for this is that as copies were made, the originals were burned or buried. But the Dead Sea Scrolls, it was discovered, contain all of Isaiah, including the aforementioned original translation of Isaiah 2:16. The only logical conclusion is that The Book of Mormon rendering of this verse from Isaiah is a direct quotation from a text at least as ancient as the Septuagint. In fact, this Book of Mormon quotation from 2 Nephi 12 may be attributed to the Plates of Brass, which is a text hundreds of years older than the Septuagint. It is only one of innumerable small coincidences that confirm the historicity and divine authenticity of The Book of Mormon record.

When we read the scriptures, we are witnessing forms of the original symbols in which the message was conveyed by God. Thus, we are bound to approach the scriptures with a new-found reverence and respect. It is our testimony that "in the beginning was the Word ... and the Word was God ... And the Word was made flesh, and dwelt among us." (John

1:1, 14). Joseph Smith was counseled: "These words are not of men nor of man, but of me; wherefore, you shall testify they are of me and not of man; For it is my voice which speaketh them unto you; for they are given by my Spirit unto you; and by my power you can read them one to another; and save it were by my power, you could not have them. Wherefore, you can testify that you have heard my voice, and know my words." (D&C 18:34-36).

The Savior rebuked the Sadducees: "Ye do err, not knowing the scriptures." (Matthew 22:29). In the Last Days, even with the Reformation and the so-called Age of Enlightenment, there can be no revelation when there is no student. Of the rulers who possessed the word in His day, but did not keep the commandments, the Lord said: "The scribes and the Pharisees sit in Moses' seat: all therefore whatsoever they bid you observe, that observe and do; but do not ye after their works: for they say, and do not." (Matthew 23:2-3).

Rather be like the travelers on the road to Emmaus, who said: "Did not our heart burn within us … while he opened to us the scriptures?" (Luke 24:32). We have an opportunity to know the scriptures in a way that is unparalleled in the history of the world. In 1974, L. Tom Perry was sustained as a member of the Council of Twelve Apostles, and he took his place next to Bruce R. McConkie. in their weekly meetings in the temple, one or another of the Apostles would often quote from the scriptures, and whenever assistance was needed to complete the verse, the speaker would ask, 'Bruce, can you help me?' Invariably, Elder McConkie would complete not only the verse in question, from memory, but he would also go on for several more verses. Elder Perry reports that in the eleven years that he sat next to Elder McConkie, he never had the occasion to respond to a request, 'Tom, would you please help me with this verse?'

Another Apostle, John Widtsoe, promised that if we would develop the habit of reading the scriptures for 15 minutes a day, that in 5 years we would know more about the gospel than any 100 persons in the church who were selected at random. "Now it is high time to awake out of sleep: for now is our salvation nearer than when we believed." (Romans 13:11).

(Our) Eternal Nature

"The soul shall be restored
to the body, and the body to the
soul; yea, and every limb and joint
shall be restored to its body; yea, even
a hair of the head shall not be lost; but all
things shall be restored to their proper and
perfect frame. And now, my son, this is
the restoration of which has been spoken
by the mouths of the prophets."
(Alma 40:23-24).

The Cryonics Society of California is an organization whose creed is "Death, like old age, can now be regarded as a disease; a very serious disease, to be sure; indeed, generally fatal, but not necessarily incurable." To that end, a service is provided wherein the body of a deceased person is immersed in liquid nitrogen (at - 320 degrees F), and then stored in anticipation of the day when a cure may be found for the processes that caused the death of the individual. (A less expensive alternative preserves just the head of the person).

Contrast this desperate philosophy with the teachings of the gospel regarding the immortality of the soul. Listen to the fresh perspective of the poet who wrote: "Oh, this world has more of coming and of going than I can bear. I guess it's eternity I want, where all things are, and always will be. Where I can hold my loves a little looser. Where, finally, we realize Time is the only thing that really dies." (Carol Lynn Pearson). Here and now, time is really the substance of the issue. it seems to be human nature to want to hold on to it dearly, and the prospect of death is terrifying to many, for the body abruptly becomes completely inanimate and time, at least from our perspective, grinds to a halt.

Someone once said that time is a predator that stalks us all our lives. I prefer to think of it as a companion that accompanies us on the journey, reminding us to cherish every moment." So said Captain Jean Luc Picard, in the last episode, the last scene of "Star Trek, The Next Generation."

Faithful individuals have learned to use their agency to manipulate time so that they can not only make the most of their gift of mortality, but also insure their happiness and continued progression in eternity through the grace of God. Thus, they give careful attention to the way in which they spend their time, and also the care with which they make time, the diligence with which they find time, the joy with which they give time, and the discipline they exhibit in taking time. This process allows thoughtful, active individuals to create more time for accomplishment in their already busy lives! Only foolish people who have lost their focus on things of real worth would treat time so disdainfully that they would flagrantly waste time, steal time, or actually kill time. And it is vain and desperate to grasp at the slim chance of cheating both time and justice by suspending animation in a stainless-steel tank at -320 degrees F.

The Spirit quickens all life, and long before sentient beings have reached the age of accountability, they have begun to exercise their freedom to act. This ability to choose how we utilize our time is sometimes called "Free Agency." But it is never free. Agency actually carries a very high price. Some use their freedom of choice to build lean-tos, while others construct temples. On what foundation should we build? We are, after all, "fellowcitizens with the Saints, and of the household of God; and are built upon the foundation of the apostles and prophets, Jesus Christ himself being the chief cornerstone: In whom all the building fitly framed together groweth unto an holy temple in the Lord." (Ephesians 2:18-19).

"Life is a sheet of paper white where each of us may write a line or two, and then comes night. Greatly begin. if thou hast time but for a line, make that sublime. Not failure, but low aim is crime." (James Russell Lowell). The following story illustrates the point: "A young man enrolled at Oberlin College. When the president showed him what he would have to study, the student said: "Isn't there an easier way? Isn't there a shorter course?" The president said: "Oh yes. it just depends on what you want to make of yourself. When the Lord starts out to make an oak tree, he takes a hundred years, but if he wants to make a squash, he does it in six months." (LeGrand Richards, "1975 Speeches of The Year," p. 52). The scriptures ordain that man might have the privilege to live to the life of a great oak. (See D&C 101:30, & Isaiah 65:22). But however brief or long our lives may be, whatever the circumstances of our mortal experience, we can be certain that, if our allotted time is well-spent, "whatever principle of intelligence we (have) attain(ed) unto in this life, it will rise with us in the resurrection." (D&C 130:18).

With our gifts of time, talents, agency, and spiritual gifts we may constantly add to the stature of our eternal selves, even as we struggle with the challenges of mortality. We do not need liquid nitrogen as a hedge against the specter of the void of an eternal night. Rather, we have the assurance of our Savior, Who said: "If ye are faithful, ye shall be laden with many sheaves, and crowned with honor, and glory, and immortality, and eternal life." (D&C 75:5).

Many people, not understanding why they have challenges, and feeling acutely uncomfortable in their surroundings, try to avoid the experience altogether by using mind-altering drugs, or engaging in other self-destructive behaviors. Some are so poorly disciplined that they abuse the gift of mortality to the point that life ends prematurely for them. Only weak-willed individual, though, need to settle for life in a "second-class hotel." While we are here, the freedom of choice that we have been given permits us to use our time constructively, as we earn our Heavenly Father's trust. He believes in us and knows we can succeed, and has provided us with endowment enough to accomplish every needful thing.

This life, after all, is the time to prepare to meet God. "What a piece of work is man! How noble in reason, how infinite in faculty, in form and moving how express and admirable, in action how like an angel, in apprehension how like a god - the beauty of the world, the paragon of animals!" (Shakespeare, "Hamlet," Act 2, Scene 2).

Eternal Progression in a Dynamic Universe

"All men's souls are immortal, but the souls
of the righteous are immortal and divine."
(Socrates).

"Then are ye in this strait
and narrow path which leads to
eternal life; yea, ye have entered in
by the gate; ye have done according to
the commandments of the Father and the
Son; and ye have received the Holy Ghost,
which witnesses of the Father and the Son,
unto the fulfilling of the promise which
he hath made, that if ye entered in
by the way ye should receive."
(2 Nephi 31:17-18).

Abinadi declared that "the time shall come when all shall see the salvation of the Lord; when every nation, kindred, tongue, and people shall see eye to eye and shall confess before God that his judgments are just." (Alma 16:1, see Patrick Kearon, C.R., 4/2024). From their understanding of the scriptures, Latter-day Saints believe that this shall take place as a result of the universality of the resurrection just before, during, and at the end of the Millennium.

Salvation is, after all, a gift of God given to all mankind. For "the way is prepared from the fall of man, and salvation is free." (2 Nephi 2:4). We are redeemed from the Fall and have overcome physical death because of the resurrection of Christ. "O how great the plan of our God!' exclaimed Jacob. For "all men become incorruptible, and immortal, and they are living souls." (2 Nephi 9:14). In this sense, God denies "none that come unto him, black and white; bond and free, male and female; and he remembereth the heathen; and all are alike unto God, both Jew and Gentile." (2 Nephi 26:33).

Exaltation, however, is a gift of God reserved for the obedient. "He that overcometh shall inherit all things, and I will be his God, and he shall be my son," said the Lord to John the Revelator. (Revelation 21:7). "We are the children of God," wrote Paul to the Romans. "And if children, then ... heirs of God, and joint-heirs with Christ." (Romans 8:16-17). As such, we may "receive a crown of glory that fadeth not away." (1 Peter 5:4). This quality of glory is of a different nature than salvation. Exaltation represents eternal life in the Celestial Kingdom of God. Those who are blessed to live there have conformed their nature to that of their Father in Heaven. They have completely internalized the admonition of the Son of God, Who said: "Be ye therefore perfect, even as your Father which is in heaven is perfect." (Matthew 5:48).

For many, redemption will occur only when the demands of justice have finally executed the required consequences for the violation of eternal law, after which they will be released from bondage in the Spirit Prison of the Unjust. (See D&C 76:73, 138:8 & 28, Isaiah 61:1, 1 Peter 3:19, & Moses 7:57). Or, it may occur at a post-mortal time when those formerly disobedient children of our Heavenly Father have improved their nature until it conforms to the laws of the Celestial Kingdom, and they are able and qualified to receive the grace of God and a fullness of joy in the eternities to come.

Nevertheless, there are certain points of doctrine that simply are not clear. To his son, Alma once declared: "Now these mysteries are not yet fully made known unto me; therefore, I shall forbear." (Alma 37:11). He felt that it was better to keep his opinion to himself, rather than to speculate without the foundation of revelation. Sometimes, it is better to remain silent and be thought a fool, than to speak, and remove all doubt. Still, a measured appraisal of the avenues open to the post-mortal children of our Heavenly Father seems indicated, in light of the latitude afforded by the relevant scriptures.

Joseph Fielding Smith, Jr. agreed with Abinadi that "the time will come when every knee will bow and every tongue confess that Jesus is the Christ," and yet he felt that "the vast majority of mankind will go into the telestial kingdom eternally." ("Doctrines of Salvation," 2:30-31). It may be that the time when we may elect to live a celestial law has passed when we leave mortality and are judged and assigned to a lesser kingdom of glory. According to this scenario, we could thereafter progress only within the limitations of whichever kingdom we were in. Our progression would not be to the extent that it would ever lead us to live a celestial law. To put it another way, we would have lost the ability to exercise our capacity to become as God is because we had neglected to take advantage of the opportunity of a lifetime during the lifetime of the opportunity.

It does seem certain that if we wish to obtain exaltation and eternal life in the Celestial Kingdom, we must do more than simply acknowledge that Jesus Christ is Lord. The critical point of conversion, beyond which lie the encircling flames of fire in the Celestial Kingdom of God, rests in making a conscious decision to accept not only Jesus Christ, but also obedience to the principles of His gospel.

A simple yet uncommitted recognition of Jesus will not qualify us for the Celestial Kingdom. Christians of convenience lack the fire ignited by the demands of discipleship. Many honorable people who accept Jesus will still go to the Terrestrial Kingdom. According to the scriptures, these are they who "received not the gospel, neither the testimony of Jesus, neither the prophets, neither the everlasting covenant. Last of all, these are all they who will not be gathered with the saints, to be caught up unto The Church of the Firstborn, and received into the cloud." (D&C 76:101-102).

Only those who passionately embrace the gospel with its ordinances and covenants, and who then partake of God's divine nature, may go to the highest degree of glory and live in His presence. "These are they who are priests and kings, who have received of his fullness, and of his glory; and are priests of the Most High, after the order of Melchizedek, which was after the order of Enoch, which was after the order of the Only Begotten Son. Wherefore, as it is written, they are (as the) gods, even the sons of God." (D&C 76:56-58, cf. John 10:34).

This distinction becomes vitally important to those billions of souls whose improvement, at least from a superficial or shallow telestial perspective, would seem to halt at the Last Judgment because of poor decisions made in mortality. However, our faith in the divine Plan of the Father is founded on the marvelous principle that its implementation was designed to bring His children back into His presence after they had achieved spiritual maturity. (See Moses 1:39).

In fact, the Plan was so magnificent that upon its implementation, when the "foundation of the earth" was laid, all of the children of God, "the morning stars, sang together, and all the sons of God shouted for joy." (Job 38:7-8). It is inconceivable that a Plan of such transcendent perfection was intentionally and purposefully created to save only a small percentage of Heavenly Father's children in His Celestial Kingdom.

The question thus becomes: "Are our actions during mortality so significant that they will determine our status forever?" Before the Fall, Adam lived in the Garden of Eden in a morally static, vegetative state. It seems Satanic to argue that, for all practical purposes, most of his posterity will do so again, in a telestial existence stretching out in mind-numbing monotony throughout all eternity. After all, it was the devil, and not our Elder Brother Jesus Christ, who sought "that all men might be miserable like unto himself." (2 Nephi 2:27). It is inconceivable that Satan would be declared the ultimate numerical winner in the conflict that commenced in heaven so long ago, and at least temporarily, separated the children of God into ideologically opposing camps.

It is more palatable to consider the possibility that we may add to our glory to such a degree that we can eternally progress not only within a kingdom, but also from one degree of glory to another. In essence, this posture dictates that when we have outgrown the apartment that once satisfied our needs, it will be possible to move on to a domicile that more adequately suits our then current circumstances. The definitive answer to this question remains unsettled in the church. The position of the First Presidency has always been one of neutrality. "The church has never announced a definite doctrine upon this point. Some of the Brethren have held the view that it (is) possible in the course of progression to advance from one glory to another, involving the principle of eternal progression; others of the Brethren have taken an opposite view." (Joseph Anderson, Secretary to The First Presidency, Letter to Ward Magleby, 3/5/1952).

The 70+ year-old statement by Joseph Anderson quoted above recognizes that, even today, there are faithful members of the church who believe that it may still be possible to progress, after the Final Judgment, from one degree of glory to another. D&C 76:112 has repetitively been quoted as one evidence that progression between degrees of glory is not possible: "And they (referring to those who inherit telestial glory) shall be servants of the Most High; but where God and Christ dwell they cannot come, worlds without end."

But this verse does not talk about progression from one degree to another but only states that individuals with telestial characteristics cannot come where God and Christ dwell. This passage refers to qualities of general classes of people rather than to those of individuals, and it does not say what might happen to those who are able to change their nature. In other words, those with the described characteristics obviously cannot come where Christ is. But if they are able to make behavioral lifestyle changes, if they can change their nature so that as they mature their character more fully reflects that of their Father, perhaps they will then be permitted to enjoy His hearth and home.

Those who inherit telestial glory are described as heirs of salvation through the ministration of angels who shall be servants of the Most High. (D&C 76:88 & 112). But the Lord revealed to Moses that His whole focus of attention, His very work and glory expressed in His mission statement, is to bring about both the immortality and the eternal life of His children. (Moses 1:28-29).

Misunderstanding has also arisen from a casual reading of D&C 76:73-74: "These are they who are of the terrestrial ... Behold, these are they who died without law; and also they who are the spirits of men kept in prison, whom the Son visited, and preached the gospel unto them, that they might be judged according to men in the flesh; Who received not the testimony of Jesus in the flesh, but afterwards received it."

Some misinterpret these verses, erroneously concluding that those who accept the gospel after leaving this life will be eligible only for a terrestrial degree of glory. If that were true, then much, if not most, of the vicarious work for the dead that is performed in the temple would be ineffectual in accomplishing the end for which it was designed.

The difficulty arises out of a failure to recognize the aforementioned distinction between the acceptance of Jesus Christ and acceptance of His gospel with all its ordinances and covenants that are administered by the holy priesthood. Those "who shall come forth in the resurrection of the just (are) they who" accept the fulness of the gospel, who "received the testimony of Jesus, and believed on his name and were baptized ... that by keeping the commandments they might be washed and cleansed from all their sins, and receive the Holy Spirit by the laying on of the hands of him who is ordained and sealed unto this power; And those who overcome by faith, and are sealed by the Holy Spirit of promise ... are they who are the church of the Firstborn." (D&C 76:51-54).

Another way of looking at this issue is to accept the premise that hell is a reformatory designed to improve the quality of our moral nature. In this sense, it is a penitentiary where faith can still convict us of our sins. Perhaps its purpose is to help disobedient spirits recognize that Christ is the Mediator of the Covenant through His infinite and eternal Atonement. D&C 76 teaches that the gospel was taught to the spirits kept in that prison. If, while there, they have been able to exercise their agency and accept only Christ, but not the fulness of His gospel, they will then inherit glory in the Terrestrial Kingdom.

However, those in the Spirit Prison who accept the fulness of the gospel and have the necessary ordinances of exaltation performed in their behalf in the temple, will be heirs of the Celestial Kingdom of glory. "These shall dwell in the presence of God and his Christ forever and ever." (D&C 76:62). And "the presence of the Lord shall be as the melting fire that burneth, and as the fire which causeth the waters to boil." (D&C 133:41). Those of His children who have matured in spirituality and have grown to the stature of their Father shall approach His dwelling place, and shall see "the transcendent beauty of the gate through which the heirs of that kingdom will enter, which (is) like unto circling flames of fire; Also the blazing throne of God, wherein (shall be) seated the Father and the Son." And the "beautiful streets of that kingdom, (shall have) the appearance of being paved with gold." (D&C 137:2-4).

It was mercifully foreordained that the prisoners thronging the pit should in due time be visited (see Isaiah 24:21-22) and be offered means of amelioration. (See Isaiah 42:7). Even David rapturously sang : 'Thou wilt not leave my soul in hell.' (Psalms 16:10). True, the scriptures speak of endless punishment, and depict everlasting burnings, eternal damnation, and the sufferings incident to unquenchable fire, as features of the Judgment reserved for the wicked. But none of these awful possibilities are anywhere in scripture declared to be the unending fate of the individual sinner." (James E. Talmage).

Elder Talmage went on to say: "Blessing or punishment ordained of God is eternal, for He is eternal, and eternal are all His ways. His is a system of endless and eternal punishment, for it will always exist as the place or condition provided for the rebellious and disobedient, but the penalty will terminate when through repentance and excipiation the necessary reform has been effected and the uttermost farthing paid.

Even to hell there is an exit as well as an entrance; and when the sentence has been served, commuted perhaps by repentance and its attendant works, the prison doors shall open and the penitent captive be afforded opportunity to comply with the law which he aforetime violated. But the prison remains, and the eternal decree prescribing punishment for the offender stands unrepealed. So it is even with the penal institutions established by man." ("The Vitality of Mormonism," p. 264-265).

J. Reuben Clark, Jr. reasoned: "I am not a strict constructionist, believing that we seal our eternal progress by what we do here. It is my belief that God will save all His children that He can; and while, if we live unrighteously here, we shall not go to the other side in the same status, so to speak, as those who live righteously; nevertheless, the unrighteous will have their chance, and in the eons of the eternities that are to follow, they, too, may climb to the destinies to which they who are righteous and serve God, have climbed." ("Church News," 3/23/1960).

Perhaps God will leave his unrighteous and disobedient children in the Spirit Prison of The Unjust only long enough for them to recognize the error of their ways, and to motivate them to make behavioral changes that are consistent with the teachings of the gospel of Jesus Christ. With a full recognition of their violation of law, such individuals might be required to pay directly for the sins committed in mortality that had fallen outside the merciful sphere of influence of the Atonement of the Savior. Such a punishment would be eternally and endlessly in harmony with the Law of Justice. (See D&C 76:73, 138:8 & 28, Isaiah 61:1, 1 Peter 3:19, & Moses 7:57).

Our Father in Heaven wants us to accept His Firstborn Son and His gospel so that we may avoid the "weeping and gnashing of teeth" that accompany the recognition that our "days of probation are past; (when we) have procrastinated the day of (our) salvation until it is everlastingly too late, and (our) destruction is made sure." (J.S.M. 1:54, see Helaman 13:38).

When we seek "all the days of (our) lives for that which (we) cannot obtain, and … have sought for happiness in doing iniquity, which thing is contrary to the nature of that righteousness which is in our great and Eternal Head," we must nevertheless ultimately face the consequences. (Helaman 13:38). It is then, in the most difficult circumstances of repentance imaginable, when the uttermost farthing is paid, that the necessary reform can take place.

How much better it would have been to have listened to the prophets. "And in the days of your poverty ye shall cry unto the Lord; and in vain shall ye cry, for your desolation is already come upon you, and your destruction is made sure; and then shall ye weep and howl in that day, saith the Lord of Hosts. And then shall ye lament, and say: O that I had repented, and had not killed the prophets, and stoned them, and cast them out. Yea, in that day ye shall say: O that we had repented in the day that the word of the Lord came unto us." (Helaman 13:32-36).

Such a scenario is in harmony with Brigham Young's belief that "all organized existence is in progress either to an endless advancement in eternal perfections, or back to dissolution. There is no period in all the eternities," he believed, "wherein organized existence will become stationary, that it cannot advance in knowledge, wisdom, power, and glory." (J.D., 1:349).

Joseph Smith declared to an assembly of the Saints: "I could explain a hundred-fold more than I ever have of the glories of the kingdoms manifested to me in vision, were I permitted, and were the people prepared to receive them." (H.C., v. 5, p. 402). After all is said and done, when all the leaders of the church have been quoted and the scriptures cited, the fact remains that we have not been given the revelations that answer the questions relating to progression between kingdoms of glory. But intuitively we want to believe that it is possible.

We
can't comprehend
the sacred language
of the Spirit that is spoken
in The Book of Mormon until
we have paid the price. We may
choose to dismiss its whisperings
as nothing more than a breeze that
causes a gentle rustle of the leaves
in the forest that is our conscience.
It may sound pleasant to our ears,
but its quiet counsel will remain
maddeningly elusive, until we
have done all that we can to
merit the companionship of
the gifts of the light of
Christ, and the Holy
Ghost.

(Our) Eternal Nature

"The soul shall be restored
to the body, and the body to the
soul; yea, and every limb and joint
shall be restored to its body; yea, even
a hair of the head shall not be lost; but all
things shall be restored to their proper and
perfect frame. And now, my son, this is
the restoration of which has been spoken
by the mouths of the prophets."
(Alma 40:23-24).

The Cryonics Society of California is an organization whose creed is "Death, like old age, can now be regarded as a disease; a very serious disease, to be sure; indeed, generally fatal, but not necessarily incurable." To that end, a service is provided wherein the body of a deceased person is immersed in liquid nitrogen (at - 320 degrees F), and then stored in anticipation of the day when a cure may be found for the processes that caused the death of the individual. (A less expensive alternative preserves just the head of the person).

Contrast this desperate philosophy with the teachings of the gospel regarding the immortality of the soul. Listen to the fresh perspective of the poet who wrote: "Oh, this world has more of coming and of going than I can bear. I guess it's eternity I want, where all things are, and always will be. Where I can hold my loves a little looser. Where, finally, we realize Time is the only thing that really dies." (Carol Lynn Pearson). Here and now, time is really the substance of the issue. it seems to be human nature to want to hold on to it dearly, and the prospect of death is terrifying to many, for the body abruptly becomes completely inanimate and time, at least from our perspective, grinds to a halt.

Someone once said that time is a predator that stalks us all our lives. I prefer to think of it as a companion that accompanies us on the journey, reminding us to cherish every moment." So said Captain Jean Luc Picard, in the last episode, the last scene of "Star Trek, The Next Generation."

Faithful individuals have learned to use their agency to manipulate time so that they can not only make the most of their gift of mortality, but also insure their happiness and continued progression in eternity through the grace of God. Thus, they give careful attention to the way in which they spend their time, and also the care with which they make time, the diligence with which they find time, the joy with which they give time, and the discipline they exhibit in taking time. This process allows thoughtful, active individuals to create more time for accomplishment in their already busy lives! Only foolish people who have lost their focus on things of real worth would treat time so disdainfully that they would flagrantly waste time, steal time, or actually kill time. And it is vain and desperate to grasp at the slim chance of cheating both time and justice by suspending animation in a stainless-steel tank at -320 degrees F.

The Spirit quickens all life, and long before sentient beings have reached the age of accountability, they have begun to exercise their freedom to act. This ability to choose how we utilize our time is sometimes called "Free Agency." But it is never free. Agency actually carries a very high price. Some use their freedom of choice to build lean-tos, while others construct temples. On what foundation should we build? We are, after all, "fellowcitizens with the Saints, and of the household of God; and are built upon the foundation of the apostles and prophets, Jesus Christ himself being the chief cornerstone: In whom all the building fitly framed together groweth unto an holy temple in the Lord." (Ephesians 2:18-19).

"Life is a sheet of paper white where each of us may write a line or two, and then comes night. Greatly begin. if thou hast time but for a line, make that sublime. Not failure, but low aim is crime." (James Russell Lowell). The following story illustrates the point: "A young man enrolled at Oberlin College. When the president showed him what he would have to study, the student said: "Isn't there an easier way? Isn't there a shorter course?" The president said: "Oh yes. it just depends on what you want to make of yourself. When the Lord starts out to make an oak tree, he takes a hundred years, but if he wants to make a squash, he does it in six months." (LeGrand Richards, "1975 Speeches of The Year," p. 52). The scriptures ordain that man might have the privilege to live to the life of a great oak. (See D&C 101:30, & Isaiah 65:22). But however brief or long our lives may be, whatever the circumstances of our mortal experience, we can be certain that, if our allotted time is well-spent, "whatever principle of intelligence we (have) attain(ed) unto in this life, it will rise with us in the resurrection." (D&C 130:18).

With our gifts of time, talents, agency, and spiritual gifts we may constantly add to the stature of our eternal selves, even as we struggle with the challenges of mortality. We do not need liquid nitrogen as a hedge against the specter of the void of an eternal night. Rather, we have the assurance of our Savior, Who said: "If ye are faithful, ye shall be laden with many sheaves, and crowned with honor, and glory, and immortality, and eternal life." (D&C 75:5).

Many people, not understanding why they have challenges, and feeling acutely uncomfortable in their surroundings, try to avoid the experience altogether by using mind-altering drugs, or engaging in other self-destructive behaviors. Some are so poorly disciplined that they abuse the gift of mortality to the point that life ends prematurely for them. Only weak-willed individual, though, need to settle for life in a "second-class hotel." While we are here, the freedom of choice that we have been given permits us to use our time constructively, as we earn our Heavenly Father's trust. He believes in us and knows we can succeed, and has provided us with endowment enough to accomplish every needful thing.

This life, after all, is the time to prepare to meet God. "What a piece of work is man! How noble in reason, how infinite in faculty, in form and moving how express and admirable, in action how like an angel, in apprehension how like a god - the beauty of the world, the paragon of animals!" (Shakespeare, "Hamlet," Act 2, Scene 2).

Eternal Progression in a Dynamic Universe

*"All men's souls are immortal, but the souls
of the righteous are immortal and divine."*

Graphic
"Then are ye in this strait
and narrow path which leads to
eternal life; yea, ye have entered in
by the gate; ye have done according to
the commandments of the Father and the
Son; and ye have received the Holy Ghost,
which witnesses of the Father and the Son,
unto the fulfilling of the promise which
he hath made, that if ye entered in
by the way ye should receive."
(2 Nephi 31:17-18).

Abinadi declared that "the time shall come when all shall see the salvation of the Lord; when every nation, kindred, tongue, and people shall see eye to eye and shall confess before God that his judgments are just." (Alma 16:1, see Patrick Kearon, C.R., 4/2024). From their understanding of the scriptures, Latter-day Saints believe that this shall take place as a result of the universality of the resurrection just before, during, and at the end of the Millennium.

Salvation is, after all, a gift of God given to all mankind. For "the way is prepared from the fall of man, and salvation is free." (2 Nephi 2:4). We are redeemed from the Fall and have overcome physical death because of the resurrection of Christ. "O how great the plan of our God!' exclaimed Jacob. For "all men become incorruptible, and immortal, and they are living souls." (2 Nephi 9:14). In this sense, God denies "none that come unto him, black and white; bond and free, male and female; and he remembereth the heathen; and all are alike unto God, both Jew and Gentile." (2 Nephi 26:33).

Exaltation, however, is a gift of God reserved for the obedient. "He that overcometh shall inherit all things, and I will be his God, and he shall be my son," said the Lord to John the Revelator. (Revelation 21:7). "We are the children of God," wrote Paul to the Romans. "And if children, then ... heirs of God, and joint-heirs with Christ." (Romans 8:16-17). As such, we may "receive a crown of glory that fadeth not away." (1 Peter 5:4). This quality of glory is of a different nature than salvation. Exaltation represents eternal life in the Celestial Kingdom of God. Those who are blessed to live there have conformed their nature to that of their Father in Heaven. They have completely internalized the admonition of the Son of God, Who said: "Be ye therefore perfect, even as your Father which is in heaven is perfect." (Matthew 5:48).

For many, redemption will occur only when the demands of justice have finally executed the required consequences for the violation of eternal law, after which they will be released from bondage in the Spirit Prison of the Unjust. (See D&C 76:73, 138:8 & 28, Isaiah 61:1, 1 Peter 3:19, & Moses 7:57). Or, it may occur at a post-mortal time when those formerly disobedient children of our Heavenly Father have improved their nature until it conforms to the laws of the Celestial Kingdom, and they are able and qualified to receive the grace of God and a fullness of joy in the eternities to come.

Nevertheless, there are certain points of doctrine that simply are not clear. To his son, Alma once declared: "Now these mysteries are not yet fully made known unto me; therefore, I shall forbear." (Alma 37:11). He felt that it was better to keep his opinion to himself, rather than to speculate without the foundation of revelation. Sometimes, it is better to remain silent and be thought a fool, than to speak, and remove all doubt. Still, a measured appraisal of the avenues open to the post-mortal children of our Heavenly Father seems indicated, in light of the latitude afforded by the relevant scriptures.

Joseph Fielding Smith, Jr. agreed with Abinadi that "the time will come when every knee will bow and every tongue confess that Jesus is the Christ," and yet he felt that "the vast majority of mankind will go into the telestial kingdom eternally." ("Doctrines of Salvation," 2:30-31). It may be that the time when we may elect to live a celestial law has passed when we leave mortality and are judged and assigned to a lesser kingdom of glory. According to this scenario, we could thereafter progress only within the limitations of whichever kingdom we were in. Our progression would not be to the extent that it would ever lead us to live a celestial law. To put it another way, we would have lost the ability to exercise our capacity to become as God is because we had neglected to take advantage of the opportunity of a lifetime during the lifetime of the opportunity.

It does seem certain that if we wish to obtain exaltation and eternal life in the Celestial Kingdom, we must do more than simply acknowledge that Jesus Christ is Lord. The critical point of conversion, beyond which lie the encircling flames of fire in the Celestial Kingdom of God, rests in making a conscious decision to accept not only Jesus Christ, but also obedience to the principles of His gospel.

A simple yet uncommitted recognition of Jesus will not qualify us for the Celestial Kingdom. Christians of convenience lack the fire ignited by the demands of discipleship. Many honorable people who accept Jesus will still go to the Terrestrial Kingdom. According to the scriptures, these are they who "received not the gospel, neither the testimony of Jesus, neither the prophets, neither the everlasting covenant. Last of all, these are all they who will not be gathered with the saints, to be caught up unto The Church of the Firstborn, and received into the cloud." (D&C 76:101-102).

Only those who passionately embrace the gospel with its ordinances and covenants, and who then partake of God's divine nature, may go to the highest degree of glory and live in His presence. "These are they who are priests and kings, who have received of his fullness, and of his glory; and are priests of the Most High, after the order of Melchizedek, which was after the order of Enoch, which was after the order of the Only Begotten Son. Wherefore, as it is written, they are (as the) gods, even the sons of God." (D&C 76:56-58, cf. John 10:34).

This distinction becomes vitally important to those billions of souls whose improvement, at least from a superficial or shallow telestial perspective, would seem to halt at the Last Judgment because of poor decisions made in mortality.

However, our faith in the divine Plan of the Father is founded on the marvelous principle that its implementation was designed to bring His children back into His presence after they had achieved spiritual maturity. (See Moses 1:39).

In fact, the Plan was so magnificent that upon its implementation, when the "foundation of the earth" was laid, all of the children of God, "the morning stars, sang together, and all the sons of God shouted for joy." (Job 38:7-8). It is inconceivable that a Plan of such transcendent perfection was intentionally and purposefully created to save only a small percentage of Heavenly Father's children in His Celestial Kingdom.

The question thus becomes: "Are our actions during mortality so significant that they will determine our status forever?" Before the Fall, Adam lived in the Garden of Eden in a morally static, vegetative state. It seems Satanic to argue that, for all practical purposes, most of his posterity will do so again, in a telestial existence stretching out in mind-numbing monotony throughout all eternity. After all, it was the devil, and not our Elder Brother Jesus Christ, who sought "that all men might be miserable like unto himself." (2 Nephi 2:27). It is inconceivable that Satan would be declared the ultimate numerical winner in the conflict that commenced in heaven so long ago, and at least temporarily, separated the children of God into ideologically opposing camps.

It is more palatable to consider the possibility that we may add to our glory to such a degree that we can eternally progress not only within a kingdom, but also from one degree of glory to another. In essence, this posture dictates that when we have outgrown the apartment that once satisfied our needs, it will be possible to move on to a domicile that more adequately suits our then current circumstances. The definitive answer to this question remains unsettled in the church. The position of the First Presidency has always been one of neutrality. "The church has never announced a definite doctrine upon this point. Some of the Brethren have held the view that it (is) possible in the course of progression to advance from one glory to another, involving the principle of eternal progression; others of the Brethren have taken an opposite view." (Joseph Anderson, Secretary to The First Presidency, Letter to Ward Magleby, 3/5/1952).

The 70+ year-old statement by Joseph Anderson quoted above recognizes that, even today, there are faithful members of the church who believe that it may still be possible to progress, after the Final Judgment, from one degree of glory to another. D&C 76:112 has repetitively been quoted as one evidence that progression between degrees of glory is not possible: "And they (referring to those who inherit telestial glory) shall be servants of the Most High; but where God and Christ dwell they cannot come, worlds without end."

But this verse does not talk about progression from one degree to another but only states that individuals with telestial characteristics cannot come where God and Christ dwell. This passage refers to qualities of general classes of people rather than to those of individuals, and it does not say what might happen to those who are able to change their nature. In other words, those with the described characteristics obviously cannot come where Christ is. But if they are able to make behavioral lifestyle changes, if they can change their nature so that as they mature their character more fully reflects that of their Father, perhaps they will then be permitted to enjoy His hearth and home.

Those who inherit telestial glory are described as heirs of salvation through the ministration of angels who shall be servants of the Most High. (D&C 76:88 & 112). But the Lord revealed to Moses that His whole focus of attention, His very work and glory expressed in His mission statement, is to bring about both the immortality and the eternal life of His children. (Moses 1:28-29).

Misunderstanding has also arisen from a casual reading of D&C 76:73-74: "These are they who are of the terrestrial ... Behold, these are they who died without law; and also they who are the spirits of men kept in prison, whom the Son visited, and preached the gospel unto them, that they might be judged according to men in the flesh; Who received not the testimony of Jesus in the flesh, but afterwards received it."

Some misinterpret these verses, erroneously concluding that those who accept the gospel after leaving this life will be eligible only for a terrestrial degree of glory. If that were true, then much, if not most, of the vicarious work for the dead that is performed in the temple would be ineffectual in accomplishing the end for which it was designed.

The difficulty arises out of a failure to recognize the aforementioned distinction between the acceptance of Jesus Christ and acceptance of His gospel with all its ordinances and covenants that are administered by the holy priesthood. Those "who shall come forth in the resurrection of the just (are) they who" accept the fulness of the gospel, who "received the testimony of Jesus, and believed on his name and were baptized … that by keeping the commandments they might be washed and cleansed from all their sins, and receive the Holy Spirit by the laying on of the hands of him who is ordained and sealed unto this power; And those who overcome by faith, and are sealed by the Holy Spirit of promise … are they who are the church of the Firstborn." (D&C 76:51-54).

Another way of looking at this issue is to accept the premise that hell is a reformatory designed to improve the quality of our moral nature. In this sense, it is a penitentiary where faith can still convict us of our sins. Perhaps its purpose is to help disobedient spirits recognize that Christ is the Mediator of the Covenant through His infinite and eternal Atonement. D&C 76 teaches that the gospel was taught to the spirits kept in that prison. If, while there, they have been able to exercise their agency and accept only Christ, but not the fulness of His gospel, they will then inherit glory in the Terrestrial Kingdom.

However, those in the Spirit Prison who accept the fulness of the gospel and have the necessary ordinances of exaltation performed in their behalf in the temple, will be heirs of the Celestial Kingdom of glory. "These shall dwell in the presence of God and his Christ forever and ever." (D&C 76:62). And "the presence of the Lord shall be as the melting fire that burneth, and as the fire which causeth the waters to boil." (D&C 133:41). Those of His children who have matured in spirituality and have grown to the stature of their Father shall approach His dwelling place, and shall see "the transcendent beauty of the gate through which the heirs of that kingdom will enter, which (is) like unto circling flames of fire; Also the blazing throne of God, wherein (shall be) seated the Father and the Son." And the "beautiful streets of that kingdom, (shall have) the appearance of being paved with gold." (D&C 137:2-4).

It was mercifully foreordained that the prisoners thronging the pit should in due time be visited (see Isaiah 24:21-22) and be offered means of amelioration. (See Isaiah 42:7). Even David rapturously sang : 'Thou wilt not leave my soul in hell.' (Psalms 16:10). True, the scriptures speak of endless punishment, and depict everlasting burnings, eternal damnation, and the sufferings incident to unquenchable fire, as features of the Judgment reserved for the wicked. But none of these awful possibilities are anywhere in scripture declared to be the unending fate of the individual sinner." (James E. Talmage).

Elder Talmage went on to say: "Blessing or punishment ordained of God is eternal, for He is eternal, and eternal are all His ways. His is a system of endless and eternal punishment, for it will always exist as the place or condition provided for the rebellious and disobedient, but the penalty will terminate when through repentance and excipiation the necessary reform has been effected and the uttermost farthing paid.

Even to hell there is an exit as well as an entrance; and when the sentence has been served, commuted perhaps by repentance and its attendant works, the prison doors shall open and the penitent captive be afforded opportunity to comply with the law which he aforetime violated. But the prison remains, and the eternal decree prescribing punishment for the offender stands unrepealed. So it is even with the penal institutions established by man." ("The Vitality of Mormonism," p. 264-265).

J. Reuben Clark, Jr. reasoned: "I am not a strict constructionist, believing that we seal our eternal progress by what we do here. It is my belief that God will save all His children that He can; and while, if we live unrighteously here, we shall not go to the other side in the same status, so to speak, as those who live righteously; nevertheless, the unrighteous will have their chance, and in the eons of the eternities that are to follow, they, too, may climb to the destinies to which they who are righteous and serve God, have climbed." ("Church News," 3/23/1960).

Perhaps God will leave his unrighteous and disobedient children in the Spirit Prison of The Unjust only long enough for them to recognize the error of their ways, and to motivate them to make behavioral changes that are consistent with the teachings of the gospel of Jesus Christ. With a full recognition of their violation of law, such individuals might be required to pay directly for the sins committed in mortality that had fallen outside the merciful sphere of influence of the Atonement of the Savior. Such a punishment would be eternally and endlessly in harmony with the Law of Justice. (See D&C 76:73, 138:8 & 28, Isaiah 61:1, 1 Peter 3:19, & Moses 7:57).

Our Father in Heaven wants us to accept His Firstborn Son and His gospel so that we may avoid the "weeping and gnashing of teeth" that accompany the recognition that our "days of probation are past; (when we) have procrastinated the day of (our) salvation until it is everlastingly too late, and (our) destruction is made sure." (J.S.M. 1:54, see Helaman 13:38).

When we seek "all the days of (our) lives for that which (we) cannot obtain, and ... have sought for happiness in doing iniquity, which thing is contrary to the nature of that righteousness which is in our great and Eternal Head," we must nevertheless ultimately face the consequences. (Helaman 13:38). It is then, in the most difficult circumstances of repentance imaginable, when the uttermost farthing is paid, that the necessary reform can take place.

How much better it would have been to have listened to the prophets. "And in the days of your poverty ye shall cry unto the Lord; and in vain shall ye cry, for your desolation is already come upon you, and your destruction is made sure; and then shall ye weep and howl in that day, saith the Lord of Hosts. And then shall ye lament, and say: O that I had repented, and had not killed the prophets, and stoned them, and cast them out. Yea, in that day ye shall say: O that we had repented in the day that the word of the Lord came unto us." (Helaman 13:32-36).

Such a scenario is in harmony with Brigham Young's belief that "all organized existence is in progress either to an endless advancement in eternal perfections, or back to dissolution. There is no period in all the eternities," he believed, "wherein organized existence will become stationary, that it cannot advance in knowledge, wisdom, power, and glory." (J.D., 1:349).

Joseph Smith declared to an assembly of the Saints: "I could explain a hundred-fold more than I ever have of the glories of the kingdoms manifested to me in vision, were I permitted, and were the people prepared to receive them." (H.C., v. 5, p. 402). After all is said and done, when all the leaders of the church have been quoted and the scriptures cited, the fact remains that we have not been given the revelations that answer the questions relating to progression between kingdoms of glory. But intuitively we want to believe that it is possible.

We all want to
go to the heavenly land,
to enjoy glory in the eternal
world, to enter the Third Heaven to
claim a reward, and to go home to God's
Rest and the Bosom of the Lord. But we don't
want to die first. Too many fear "something after
death, the undiscovered country, from whose bourn
no traveler returns." (Shakespeare, "Hamlet,", Act 3,
Scene 1). They fear an uncertain future and spectre
of a long night of darkness. The shadow of death
conjures up visions of the chains of hell, the
Grim Reaper, the Angel of Death,
and the Fourth Horseman
of the Apocalypse.

Everyone Wants to Go to Heaven

"I pray the Father in the name of
Christ that many of us, if not all,
may be saved in his kingdom at
that great and last day."
(2 Nephi 33:12).

Everyone wants to go to heaven. Everyone wants immortal glory, to go to the heavenly land, the Celestial Kingdom of God, to enjoy glory in the eternal world, to enter the Third Heaven to claim their reward, and to go home to God's Rest and the Bosom of the Lord.

But no one wants to die first. Too many fear "something after death, the undiscovered country, from whose bourn no traveler returns." (Shakespeare, "Hamlet,." Act 3, Scene 1). They fear that uncertain future and the spectre of a long night of darkness. The shadow of death conjures up visions of the chains of hell, the Grim Reaper, the Angel of Death, and the Fourth Horseman of the Apocalypse.

My father died in 1998. He was 86 years old, and it wasn't so disturbing that he died - we'd all been expecting it because of his declining health. it was just that we'd gotten so accustomed to having him around. We still miss him. But one of the best things about his passing was the manner in which he slipped away.

I know he'd been afraid of death, although he wouldn't admit it. Not many things frightened him, but I am sure the process of dying was troubling to his soul. I think he was anxious at the thought of losing his life because he was powerless to change in the least way the inevitable course of events cascading before him. As Isaac Asimov said: "Life is pleasant. Death is peaceful. it's the transition that's troublesome." Then, as it turned out, my dad simply exhaled one last time and was gone. I really think that as he passed through the veil to the other side, he must have exclaimed: "That wasn't so bad after all." Still, I hope he was prepared for what came next.

On a larger stage, I am reminded of the reassuring words of the Lord: "Those that die in me shall not taste of death, for it shall be sweet unto them." (D&C 42:46). The Saints are continually consoled with the promise: "If a man keep my saying, he shall never taste of death." (John 8:52). As Joseph Fielding Smith declared: "They shall never die the second death and feel the torment of the wicked when they come face to face with eternity." ("Church History and Modern Revelation," 1:186).

Everyone wants to go to heaven, but no one wants to die first. But "death hath passed upon all men to fulfil the merciful plan of the Great Creator." (2 Nephi 9:6). "For everything there is a season and a time for every matter under heaven. A time to be born, and a time to die." (Ecclesiastes 3:1). But it all makes sense only if it is viewed in the larger context of the Plan of Salvation, where it was ordained that "as in Adam all die, even so in Christ shall all be made alive." (1 Corinthians 15:22). Sometimes, the inevitable transition is dramatic, as when for Elijah "there appeared a chariot of fire, and horses of fire … and Elijah went up by a whirlwind into heaven." (2 Kings 2:11). Ultimately, however, whether we go out quietly or with fanfare, "neither death nor life … shall be able to separate us from the love of God." (Romans 8:38). Because of that love, "the last enemy that shall be destroyed is death." (1 Corinthians 15:26).

Christ showed us the path we must follow when He said: "I am the way, the truth, and the life: no man cometh unto the Father, but by me." (John 14:6). His Atonement focuses our attention on an empty tomb. "Why seek ye the living among the dead?" asked the angel. "He is not here, but is risen." (Luke 24:5-6).

The two most important days of our lives are the day we were born and the day we find out why. As the scriptures teach: "No man can come unto me, except he doeth the will of my Father who hath sent me." (J.S.T. John 6:44). Helen Keller famously declared: "I believe that no good shall be lost, and that all man has willed or hoped or dreamed of good shall exist forever. I believe in the immortality of the soul because I have within me immortal longings. I believe that the state we enter after death is wrought of our own motives, thoughts, and deeds. I believe that my home there will be beautiful with colour, music, and speech of flowers and faces I love. Without this faith, there would be little meaning in my life. I should be a mere pillar of darkness in the dark. Observers in the full enjoyment of their bodily senses pity me, but it is because they do not see the golden chamber in my life where I dwell delighted; for dark as my path may seem to them, I carry a magic light in my heart. Faith, the spiritual strong searchlight, illuminates the way, and although sinister doubts lurk in the shadow, I walk unafraid towards the Enchanted Wood where the foliage is always green, where joy abides, where nightingales nest and sing, and where life and death are one in the presence of the Lord." ("Midstream"). Such a manifestation of "spirituality," declared David O. McKay, "is the consciousness of victory over self, and of communion with the infinite." (C.R., 10/1969).

How strange it is that physicians monitor "vital signs" only by checking heart rate, blood pressure, and respiration rate; that when they feel for the pulse, they put their finger on the wrist and not on the heart. How presumptuous for them to pompously pronounce patients "dead" when they are only physically inanimate. Physicians "call it," documenting the "time of death" without ever realizing that what they are really doing is documenting the "death of time."

Death is a terminator line and an event horizon beyond which we cannot see. We know nothing of the ebb and flow of life on the far side of our vision. The distinction is absolute, and there are no shades of grey between "life" and "death." As long as we maintain our mortal perspective, we cannot have it both ways; we cannot live both in the world and in eternity.

We cannot easily see the bigger picture. We perceive only Act Two of the Three Act Play, because our Father loves us and created a Plan for us requiring an exercise of free will in an atmosphere in which all possible alternatives are on the table. This necessitated that a veil be placed over our memory. For the time being, as Paul observed, "we see through a glass, darkly." (1 Corinthians 13:12). Now, we know only a part of the bigger picture. Then, we shall face a wider, more vibrant, more animate, and more accurate reality. Paul revealed something about our nature, when he wrote: "When I was a child, I spake as a child, I understood as a child, I thought as a child. But when I became a man, I put away childish things." (1 Corinthians 13:11).

Selfishness might possibly have something to do with our fear of death. If so, it is because we wander and play rather than ponder and pray, because we follow the path of least resistance, and slip into self-induced fogs of carelessness and inattention. Thoughtless stupor dulls our senses, saps our nervous energy, and stilts our tendency to be anxiously engaged. It makes us less likely to feel the chronic pain of a stiff neck, and more likely to accept as natural a limited range of motion, even though it makes us less inclined to look up to the infinite reaches of eternity for comfort and assurance.

When we get caught up in telestial traffic we are less likely to deliberately move toward celestial sureties. Conceptual cul-de-sacs make it less likely that we will find our way out of the maze of mediocrity. Seeking the lowest common denominator, we are less inclined to move to higher ground. If "I" and "Mine" are our favorite pronouns, we will be less likely to expand our vocabulary to include "Thee" and "Thine." If we have gilded tongues, we will be less likely to become fluent in the language of the Spirit. The bottom line is, that if we retreat into our comfort zone, anything that rocks our boat will cause instability, indecisiveness, and insecurity, and we will draw back from the concerted efforts that are required to substantively change.

The familiarity of "here and now" can be a compellingly attractive alternative to the risk associated with breaking camp and moving to greener pastures. "No pain, no gain" is a hard lesson to learn but until we spread our wings, we'll have no idea how far we can walk.

We don't know when our own "deadline" will loom large, but it is certain that filing an extension to buy more time from the grim reaper is not an option. We must take advantage of that which we have, and live purposefully. Sooner or later, we must "pay for the sin of idleness, when the hobnailed boots of indiscretion's marathon dancer have tapped a rowdy two-step across the terracotta of our consciousness; when excess has become our master and reason has been cast into the rumble seat of our libidinous juggernaut. At some point, the piper must be paid!" (Pogo, The Cartoon Philosopher). Better to be anxiously engaged. As Isaac Asimov said: "If my doctor told me I had only six minutes to live, I wouldn't brood. I'd type a little faster." ("Life," 1/1984).

Everyone wants to go to heaven. But if we do not have an inventory of life-sustaining influences to nourish us, we will not be prepared for the birth that we call death. If we pre-play before we re-play, though, our expanding reserve of assets will include prayer, testimony, covenants, temple, family, and a community with the Saints. If we have learned to live and breathe, and have our being in Jesus Christ, our last exhalation on earth will be not an end, but a beginning.

Along the way, some are worn down by life, while others are polished to a high luster and are carried as on the wings of eagles, soaring above the pitfalls, the roadblocks and stumbling blocks, the wily snares of the adversary, the rapids of life, the carnival atmosphere of the world, the vacation homes in Idumea, and the idle talk and loud laughter of aimlessly distracted individuals who mistake the fog of confusion for spa aroma therapy.

The day before his assassination, Martin Luther King, Jr. declared: "I don't know what will happen now. We've got some difficult days ahead, but it doesn't matter with me now because I've been to the mountaintop, and I don't mind. Like anybody, I would like to live a long life. Longevity has its place, but I'm not concerned about that now. I just want to do God's will. He's allowed me to go up to the mountain, and I've looked over and I've seen the Promised Land. I may not get there with you. But I want you to know tonight, that as a people we will get to the Promised Land. And I'm happy tonight. I'm not worried about anything. I'm not fearing any man. Mine eyes have seen the glory of the coming of the Lord." (Memphis, Tennessee, 4/3/1968).

From that elevated vantage point, where the air is a little clearer and there is less atmospheric pollution, we feel as did the aviator who exulted: "Oh, I have slipped the surly bonds of earth and danced the skies on laughter-silvered wings. Sunward I've climbed, and joined the tumbling mirth of sun-split clouds, and done a hundred things you have not dreamed of; Wheeled and soared and swung high in the sunlit silence. Hovering there, I've chased the shouting wind along, and flung my eager craft through footless halls of air. Up, up the long, delirious, burning blue I've topped the windswept heights with easy grace, where never lark, or even eagle flew. And, while with silent, lifting mind I've trod the high untrespassed sanctity of space, I put out my hand, and touched the face of God." (John G. Magee, Jr., "High Flight").

As the Prophet Joseph once said of his personal experience with the Savior: "He enveloped me into his Bosom, and I was carried away in the Spirit." When we surrender ourselves to His influence, our learning process begins in earnest. The scales of darkness fall away, we experience a newfound elasticity as we are healed of our spiritual sclerosis, we develop an immunity to false idolatry, and we are inured to life's misapprehensions. When we sit at the feet of the Master, here on earth, we establish our place at His table in eternity.

No one wants to "die first." But that is exactly what we must do. Our acceptance of His invitation to sup with Him seals our fate. Some "die as to things pertaining to the Spirit" while others are "alive in Christ." All must be "born again" because "the natural man is an enemy to God, and will be unless he yields to the enticings of the Spirit." (Mosiah 3:19). All suffer in this world, but without Christ we suffer not only headaches but also heartaches. These are pains that are avoidable. As Louisa May Alcott wrote of Beth: She "could not reason upon or explain the faith that gave her courage and patience to give up life, and cheerfully wait for death. Like a confiding child, she asked no questions, but left everything to God and nature, Father and Mother of us all, feeling sure that they, and they only, could teach and strengthen heart and spirit for this life and the life to come." ("Little Women").

We have hospital instructions that dictate: "Do Not Resuscitate," because there is no hope of restoration or expectation of a return to a decent quality of life. As care providers, we sometimes say: "Let him go," without knowing his destination. But as Sidney Carton said: "It is a far, far better thing that I do, than I have ever done; it is a far, far better rest that I go to than I have ever known." (Charles Dickens, "A Tale of Two Cities").

"Death is putting out the lamp, because the dawn has come." (T. Ragore). What is "life support" anyway, but an artificial mechanism employed to maintain basic bodily organ system functions? It requires external influences for maintenance. When "life support" is withdrawn, the individual is left on his/her own. The ultimate expression of this principle is in the statement that men are "agents unto themselves" for "the power is in them." (D&C 58:28). If we live large, we can laugh in the very face of death, "for the soul is dead that slumbers, and things are not what they seem. Life is real. Life is earnest. And the grave is not its goal. Dust thou art; to dust returnest was not spoken of the soul." (Henry Wadsworth Longfellow, "A Psalm of Life").

Without life support, we come face to face with the reality that the cost of admission to heaven is death. Some go kicking and screaming, but we have all witnessed those for whom death has had dignity, for whom it seemed to be a sacramental experience. For them, the Lord "is not a God of the dead, but of the living: for all live unto him." (Luke 20:38). For them, the promise is clear: "I am the resurrection, and the life: he that believeth in me, though he were dead, yet shall he live." (John 11:25).

The Eleventh Hymn of the Dead Sea Covenanters declared: "Behold, for mine own part I have reached the intervision, and through the spirit thou has placed within me, come to know Thee, my God." In similar fashion, Moses wrote: "But now mine own eyes have beheld God; but not my natural, but my spiritual eyes, for my natural eyes could not have beheld; for I should have withered and died in his presence; but his glory was upon me; and I beheld his face." (Moses 1:11).

Everyone wants to go to heaven, but no one wants to die first. But "if we advance confidently in the direction of our dreams, and endeavour to live the life which we have imagined, we will meet with a success unexpected in common hours." (Henry David Thoreau). Truly did Socrates reassure us: "All men's souls are immortal, but the souls of the righteous are both immortal and divine."

Evidences of God

"O ye that are bound
down under a foolish and a
vain hope, why do ye yoke yourselves
with such foolish things? Why do ye look
for a Christ? For no man can know of
anything which is to come."
(Alma 30:13).

Albert Einstein is purported to have declared: Everyone who is seriously interested in the pursuit of science becomes convinced that a Spirit is manifest in the law of the Universe. In any event, it seems clear that "earth is crammed with heaven, and every common bush with fire of God. But only those who see take off their shoes. The rest stand around picking blackberries." (Elizabeth Barrett Browning, "Aurora Leigh," Book Seven, 1856). We don't need a burning bush on Sinai, or smoke and thunder emanating from its summit, as physical reminders of God. "The earth rolls upon her wings, and the sun giveth his light by day, and the moon giveth her light by night, and the stars also give their light, as they roll upon their wings in their glory, in the midst of the power of God. Unto what shall I like these kingdoms, that ye may understand? Behold, all these are kingdoms, and any man who hath seen any or the least of these hath seen God moving in his majesty and power." (D&C 88:45-47).

Ralph Waldo Emerson was particularly sensitive to the love letters sent by God to His children. On one occasion he wrote: "Those who have seen the rising moon break out of the clouds at midnight have been present like archangels at the creation of light and of the world." ("Essay - History"). On another occasion, he wrote: "If stars should appear but once in a thousand years, how would men and women believe and adore, and preserve for many generations, the remembrance of the city of God which had been shown." ("Nature," Chapter 1).

From the quiet perspective of his home in Concord, Massachusetts, he mused: "I see the spectacle of morning from the hilltop over against my house, from daybreak to sunrise, with emotions which an angel might share. The long, slender bars of cloud float like fishes in a sea of crimson light. From the earth, as a shore, I look out into that silent sea. I seem to partake its rapid transformations; the active enchantment reaches my dust, and I dilate and conspire with the morning wind. How does nature deify us with a few and cheap elements! Give me health and a day, and I will make the pomp of emperors ridiculous." ("Nature," Chapter 3).

With sensitivity and insight William Wordsworth penned these lines: "Heaven lies about us in our infancy! Shades of the prison house begin to close upon the growing boy. But he beholds the light, and whence it flows; he sees it in his joy. The youth, who daily farther from the east must travel, still is nature's priest, and by the vision splendid, is on his way attended. At length, the man perceives it die away, and fade into the light of common day." ("Ode: Intimations of Immortality"). All too frequently, when we secularize the sacred, profound truths are homogenized into easily digestible forms, ennobling principles are reduced to rational explanation, and expediency replaces undeviating commitment to moral standards of behavior.

Only after we have exerted the effort to squeeze through the strait and narrow gate, will our way open up into broad boulevards lined with fig trees laden with fruit, flooded by sunlight, caressed by soothing breezes, and paved with cobblestones that glint of gold. Only then will there be no billboards to clamor for our attention, no neon lights to distract us, and no cacophony of voices assaulting us from every direction to suppress the serenity of a gospel-centered life. Instead, we will be as the aviator who exulted, "Oh, I have slipped the surly bonds of earth and danced the skies on laughter-silvered wings. Sunward I've climbed, and joined the tumbling mirth of sun-split clouds, and done a hundred things you have not dreamed of; Wheeled and soared and swung high in the sunlit silence. Hovering there, I've chased the shouting wind along, and flung my eager craft through footless halls of air. Up, up the long, delirious, burning blue I've topped the windswept heights with easy grace, where never lark, or even eagle flew. And, while with silent, lifting mind I've trod the high untrespassed sanctity of space, I put out my hand, and touched the face of God." (John G. Magee, Jr., "High Flight").

These emotions are facilitated by our Father in Heaven Who has given something of Himself, that we might grow as we learn to pattern our lives after that of the Great Exemplar. His priesthood "administereth the gospel and holdeth the key of the mysteries of the kingdom, even the key of the knowledge of God. Therefore, in the ordinances thereof, the power of godliness is manifest. And without the ordinance thereof, and the authority of the priesthood, the power of godliness is not manifest unto men in the flesh. For without this no man can see the face of God, even the Father, and live." (D&C 84:19-22).

Faith and Knowledge

*"If ye will enter in by
the way, and receive the Holy
Ghost, it will show unto you all
things what ye should do. Behold,
this is the doctrine of Christ."
(2 Nephi 32:5-6).*

What is the relationship between knowledge and intelligence? Is faith compatible with knowledge? Is perfect faith synonymous with perfect knowledge? The Savior promised: "You shall receive a knowledge of whatsoever things you shall ask in faith." (D&C 8:1). He also explained that "without faith you can do nothing; therefore, ask in faith." Then, He reaffirmed the reason for asking in faith: "Ask," He said, "that you may ... receive knowledge." (D&C 8:10-11).

Knowledge received through an exercise of faith is the foundation of testimony, and is the mortar that binds the building blocks of testimony together. Every worthy thing "you shall receive by faith." (D&C 26:2). A wise Teacher counseled that in our quest for knowledge, "as all have not faith, seek ye diligently and teach one another words of wisdom; yea, seek ye out of the best books words of wisdom; seek learning, even by study and also by faith." (D&C 88:118).

As we build upon a foundation of faith, we are reminded that we "are little children and ... cannot bear all things now; (we) must grow in grace and in the knowledge of the truth." (D&C 50:40). "For the word of the Lord is truth, and whatsoever is truth is light, and whatsoever is light is Spirit, even the Spirit of Jesus Christ." (D&C 84:45). "And the Spirit giveth light to every man that cometh into the world; and the Spirit enlighteneth every man through the world, that hearkeneth to the voice of the Spirit." (D&C 84:46). initially, faith is to believe what we do not see, and the reward of faith is to see what we believe, to see what is real. Some things have to be believed to be seen. Belief is only a mental assent to the truth or actuality of something, without the moral element of responsibility that we call faith.

Ultimately, that light of faith will shine so brightly that it will enlighten our eyes, "which is the same light that quickeneth your understandings; Which light proceedeth forth from the presence of God to fill the immensity of space - The light which is in all things, which giveth life to all things, which is the law by which all things are governed, even the power of God who sitteth upon his throne, who is in the bosom of eternity, who is in the midst of all things." (D&C 88:11-13).

"And if your eye be single to my glory, your whole bodies shall be filled with light, and there shall be no darkness in you; and that body which is filled with light comprehendeth all things." (D&C 88:67). For "that which is of God is light; and he that receiveth light, and continueth in God, receiveth more light; and that light groweth brighter and brighter until the perfect day." (D&C 50:24). As we gain spiritual maturity, "by doing our duty, faith increases until it becomes perfect knowledge." (Heber J. Grant, C.R., 4/1934). "And when the times of the Gentiles is come in, a light shall break forth among them that sit in darkness, and it shall be the fulness of my gospel." (D&C 45:28).

Faith, light, and truth are common denominators, they are irreducible, and establish a baseline for the acquisition of knowledge. Without these qualities, "as far as we degenerate from God we descend to the devil and lose knowledge, and without knowledge we cannot be saved." (Joseph Smith). Without knowledge, there is no faith, there is no light, and there is no recognition of religious truth.

Zarahemla in 30 A.D. provides a classic example, when the people began to be ranked according to their economic or educational opportunities. "Some were ignorant because of their poverty, and others did receive great learning because of their riches." (3 Nephi 6:12). in light of similar circumstances today, this verse demands our thoughtful attention. The gospel teaches that all men and women be given the opportunity to reach their potential. When economic circumstances preclude an education, the lessons of history suggest that individuals, the church, and the state have a moral responsibility to provide assistance, because these individuals and institutions have a vested interest in the national resource represented by the educational development of their members.

Truman Madsen wrote to B.Y.U. alumni in an appeal for contributions, that "The Jews have an ancient saying: 'The world is saved by the breath of students. Even to rebuild the temple, the schools must not be closed.' Today, some of the finest schools are closed, and not just by a padlock on the doors. They are closed to the highest values of our culture, especially religious values; closed by taut admission standards or by exorbitant tuition; closed by an 'openness' that retreats under the clamor for rights without duties, and promotes laxity instead of discipline; closed by the intrusion of federal controls.

Brigham Young University remains open and remarkably unimpeded by these trends. it is one of the most creative undergraduate environments in America. As it extends its reach to hundreds of thousands in the wider world, its geographic location will be less important than its influence. it is already one of the world's leading institutions in adult education. The choice here is not between rebuilding the temple or closing the school. The university is crowned by a temple.

As society disintegrates, the need for a rooted, prepared, expert, spiritually sensitive citizenry is not only clear, but also crucial. it is no mere cliché to say the future of mankind is being made here. If, as someone said, 'the greatest thing in life is to give yourself for something that outlasts you,' this university is one of the bastions of perpetual opportunity. For its product is, in the ultimate perspective, eternal. There could not be a better investment."

Will and Ariel Durant wrote: "If education is the transmission of civilization, then our finest contemporary achievement is our unprecedented expenditure of wealth and toil in the provision of higher education for all. We may not have excelled in the selected geniuses of antiquity, but we have raised the level and average of knowledge beyond any age in history.

The heritage that we can now more fully transmit is richer than ever before. It is richer than that of Pericles, for it includes all the Greek flowering that followed him; richer than Leonardo's, for it includes him and the Italian Renaissance; richer than Voltaire's, for it embraces all the French Enlightenment and its ecumenical dissemination. if progress is real, it is because we are born to a richer heritage, born on a higher level of that pedestal which the accumulation of knowledge and art raises as the ground and support of our being. The heritage rises, and man rises in proportion as he receives it.

What would be the full fruitage of instruction if every child should be schooled till at least his twentieth year, and should find free access to the universities, libraries, and museums that harbor and offer the intellectual and artistic treasures of the race? Consider education as the transmission of our mental, moral, technical, and aesthetic heritage as fully as possible to as many as possible, for the enlargement of man's understanding, control, embellishment, and enjoyment of life." ("The Lessons of History," p. 100-102).

Perhaps the best education, and the best guarantee for the acquisition of knowledge, is to be perpetually thrilled with life. Emerson wrote on one occasion that "the man who has seen the rising moon break out of the clouds at midnight has been present like an archangel at the creation of light and of the world," and on another that "if the stars should appear but one night in a thousand years, how would men believe and adore, and preserve for many generations the remembrance of the city of God which had been shown?" However, the problem with education is that, too often, "one asks for the bread of life, but gets only processed academic factory food served at an automat." (Hugh Nibley, "An Intellectual Autobiography," P. xxiii).

In any event, in the church in Zarahemla in A.D. 30, "there became a great inequality in all the land, insomuch that the church began to be broken up." (3 Nephi 6:14). Perhaps knowledge also enjoys a subtle relationship with liberty. it seems evident that, because the Nephites did not place a high value on providing educational opportunities for all their people, their society as a whole suffered. They ultimately lost their individual and collective freedom, even as they clamored for their personal rights.

James Madison wrote that "knowledge will forever govern ignorance, and a people who mean to be their own governors must arm themselves with the power which knowledge gives." If the Nephites had determined to be a free people in every sense of the word, they ought to have focused their attention on nurturing more diligently their most significant natural resource: themselves. "What spectacle can be more edifying or more seasonable than that of liberty and learning, each leaning on the other for their mutual and surest support?" (James Madison).

Quite clearly, "Satan had great power, unto the stirring up of the people to do all manner of iniquity, and to the puffing them up with pride, tempting them to seek for power, and authority, and riches, and the vain things of the world." (3 Nephi 6:15). But the power of the devil was not overwhelming. These people still had the capacity to exercise their moral agency to decide their own fate. "They did not sin ignorantly, for they knew the will of God concerning them, for it had been taught unto them; therefore, they did willfully rebel against God." (3 Nephi 6:18).

Truly did Edmund Burke declare that "society cannot exist, unless a controlling power upon will and appetite be placed somewhere; and the less of it there is within, the more there must be without. It is ordained in the eternal constitution of things, that men of intemperate minds cannot be free. Their passions forge their fetters." (Letter to a Member of the National Assembly of France, 1791).

These people had sold their birthright for a mess of pottage; they had made a compact with the devil, forgetting that one of his goals is to make all men as miserable as he is, and not realizing that he will not support his followers at the last day. in just three years, those who had revived the secret oaths and covenants of Master Mahan (See Moses 5:30-31) would confront their day of judgment, and they would face it terrifyingly alone.

The fabric of their society was in a process of disintegration. "The people were divided one against another; and they did separate one from another into tribes, every man according to his family and his kindred and friends; and thus, they did destroy the government of the land." (3 Nephi 7:2). As we read the account, we must ask ourselves if it prefigures our own day. The order of government collapsed because the society was degenerate and had decayed from within. "There were no wars as yet among them; and all this iniquity had come upon the people because they did yield themselves unto the power of Satan." (3 Nephi 7:5). "The regulations of the government were destroyed, because of (a) secret combination" that was dedicated to anarchy. (3 Nephi 7:6). Conditions were so disgusting to Mormon that he resorted to figures of speech found in both the Old and the New Testament to describe them. He wrote "the people had turned from their righteousness, like the dog to his vomit, or like the sow to her wallowing in the mire." (3 Nephi 7: 8).

Conditions in our day reflect those found in Zarahemla, and so it is equally important for today's parents to provide for their children the gift of knowledge. Those of the rising generation must be taught how to correctly interpret contemporary events, in order to protect themselves from the worldly influences that encroach on the fortress of their spiritual security. So doing, parents will help their youth to internalize gospel principles and create an impenetrable shield of faith. Armed with knowledge, the youth can then discern between that which is worthwhile and that which is deceiving. With the aid of the Holy Ghost, as knowledge of the gospel increases, Satan's fingerprints, in particular, can be more easily identified.

The sturdiest plants that bear the best fruit are those that have deep roots in good, rich soil. So should it be with our children. They should be provided the best that we are able to offer in music and art, conversation, example, decency, virtue, honor, and spirit. Our children should be allowed to grow freely, but we must be sure to provide rich gospel soil, in order to provide a solid foundation. The spirit of the 13th Article of Faith should be always manifest in our homes, for the very "keys of the kingdom ... consist in the key of knowledge." (D&C 128:14). "If there is anything virtuous, lovely, or of good report or praiseworthy, we seek after these things." To the extent that we do this, we may expect to see our children blossom as creative individuals, and at the same time to stand out as champions for righteousness. If we "train up a child in the way he should go...when he is old, he will not depart from it." (Proverbs 22:6). "Happiness" after all, "is the object and design of our existence, and will be the end thereof, if we pursue the path that leads to it, and this path is virtue, uprightness, faithfulness, holiness, and keeping all the commandments of God." (Joseph Smith, "Teachings," p. 255).

Faith Building

"Be reconciled unto (God)
through the atonement of Christ,
his Only Begotten Son, and ye may
obtain a resurrection, according to the power
of the resurrection which is in Christ, and be
presented as the first-fruits of Christ unto
God, having faith, and obtained a good
hope of glory inn him before he
manifesteth himself in
the flesh." (Jacob
4:11).

God has bestowed his Spirit upon His children, so that they might be able to exercise faith in Christ. He has thus given the "children of men" the power to "become the sons of God" as they "cleave unto every good thing. In reality, Christ has power as their Advocate before the Father, through the Atonement that is the very means of their salvation and exaltation.

Christ utilizes many techniques to build faith among the people. Angels, who are His servants, are often commissioned to the work. "And the office of their ministry is to call men unto repentance, and to fulfil and to do the work of the covenants of the Father, which he hath made unto the children of men, to prepare the way among the children of men, by declaring the word of Christ unto the chosen vessels of the Lord, that they may bear testimony of him." (Moroni 7:31).

The Lord told Joseph Smith: "To some it is given by the Holy Ghost to know that Jesus Christ is the Son of God, and that he was crucified for the sins of the world. To others it is given to believe on their words, that they also might have eternal life if they continue faithful." (D&C 46:13-14). This would apply to all those who listen as the General Authorities of the church bear testimony to the world. "And by doing so, the Lord God prepareth the way that the residue of men may have faith in Christ, that the Holy Ghost may have place in their hearts." (Moroni 7:32).

Today, the Twelve Apostles and other General Authorities of the church declare with boldness their witness of the truth, that faith might be developed in the hearts of all those who hear them. Hence the following sampling from the General Authorities of the church: "I know Him. I testify that He is real. I testify as a witness." (Elder Enzio Busche). "I know that God lives, for as in the words of my predecessor, John Taylor, I have seen Him." (President Spencer W. Kimball). "I know of the divinity of the Lord Jesus Christ, for it has been revealed to me in a most interesting, complete, and beautiful way." (L. Tom Perry). "I leave you with that special witness which is mine to bear, for I have witnessed it with my own eyes, and heard it with my own ears." (L. Tom Perry). "In a coming day I shall feel the nail marks in his hands and in his feet and shall wet his feet with my tears. But I shall not know any better then than I know now that he is God's Almighty Son, that he is our Savior and Redeemer, and that salvation comes in and through his atoning blood and in no other way." (Bruce R. McConkie).

As the spark of faith, struck off the Divine Anvil of God, ignites the flame of resolve in individuals, they develop the "power to do whatsoever thing is expedient" or right to do under the circumstances. That thing is to "repent and be baptized ... in the name of Jesus Christ for the remission of sins, and ... receive the Holy Ghost." (Acts 2:38). This is "the fruits of faith," which is to be saved in the Celestial Kingdom of God. it is the very reason for the ministry of Jesus Christ and His servants among the children of men.

Christ will continue the ministry and work miracles among the children of men, as "long as time shall last, or the earth shall stand, or there shall be one man upon the face thereof to be saved." (Moroni 7:36). But when an individual or a society is fascinated with sorcery, witchcraft, and magic, is mesmerized by telestial trivia, is caught up in conceptual cul de sacs, or is preoccupied with the worship of idols of wood and stone, and thus lacks saving faith, Satan gains the advantage, and the Spirit's capacity to influence life's course wanes.

When the gifts of the Spirit are absent, "then has faith ceased also; and awful is the state of man, for they are as though there had been no redemption made." (Moroni 7:38). if we have procrastinated the day of our repentance, or have waited to develop saving faith to the point that we are spiritually blind to the Light of Christ, then we have become subjected to the spirit of the devil, and he is able to claim us as his own because we can have lost the capacity to distinguish good from evil or light from darkness. When the Spirit of the Lord withdraws, the devil has power over us because we have voluntarily surrendered to him our agency to act independently. This is the final state of the wicked from which there may be no recovery. For such individuals who refuse to repent, it will be as if there had been no redemption made.

Mormon hoped that we would rise to the occasion, when he wrote: "My beloved brethren, I judge better things of you, for I judge that ye have faith in Christ because of your meekness; for if ye have not faith in him they ye are not fit to be numbered among the people of his church." (Moroni 7:39). He was like wise old Tevya, in The Fiddler on The Roof, who told his daughters: "In Anatevka, God knows who you are, and what you may become."

Mormon's judgment that his people were capable of choosing the better part indicates that he believed they still retained a hope in Christ. For "how is it that ye can attain unto faith," he asked, "save ye shall have hope?" (Moroni 7:40). Later, Moroni would voice the same sentiment, declaring: "Wherefore, there must be faith; and if there must be faith, there must also be hope." (Moroni 10:20).

Today, more than ever, we need a hope in Christ and to have the assurance of peace, that the direction of our lives is on course, and that the Lord is pleased with, and approves, our efforts. As Mormon said, hope is born of faith. "Behold, I say unto you that ye shall have hope through the atonement of Christ and the power of his resurrection, to be raised up unto life eternal, and this because of your faith in him according to the promise." (Moroni 7:41).

Hope is not trust in some wildly improbable promise, nor is it a high stakes gamble. it is the inevitable result of well-founded faith, when one is meek and lowly of heart, and in complete control of one's desires and emotions, and when appetites and behavior are within the bounds the Lord has set.

Charity is built upon the foundation of faith and hope, and is the supreme characteristic of the faithful disciple.

Mormon taught "if a man be meek and lowly in heart, and confess by the power of the Holy Ghost that Jesus is the Christ," with a sure hope born of faith, "he must needs have charity." (Moroni 7:44).

"Charity suffereth long" or is the quality of patience from the perspective of God toward people and circumstances, "and is kind" or is characterized by sensitivity toward others, and is empathic, "and envieth not," or is less concerned with telestial trinkets and more focused on celestial sureties, "and is not puffed up," or is humble, "seeketh not her own." or is selfless, "is not easily provoked," but reflects poise under provocation, "thinketh no evil." or has no secret agenda to follow, "and rejoiceth not in iniquity." but is repulsed by sin, "but rejoiceth in the truth," and is spiritually quickened by the resonant realities of well-founded faith, "beareth all things," with patience under provocation, "believeth all things," being naturally drawn to truth, "hopeth all things, endureth all things," or is drawn toward the light, and is continually open to that which is good. (Moroni 7:45).

Without these qualities, we are nothing, because our progression stops. "If ye have not charity, ye are nothing, for charity never faileth. Wherefore, cleave unto charity, which is the greatest of all (the spiritual gifts), for all things must fail (without it)." (Moroni 7:46). it is the greatest of all the qualities of God Himself, Who is the Possessor of all spiritual gifts.

"Charity is the pure love of Christ, and it endureth forever, and whoso is found possessed of it at the last day, it shall be well with him." (Moroni 7:47). Charity can not only motivate us to Christian service, but also prepare us to be like God, so that we will feel comfortable in His Presence. As such, it is a gift of the Spirit that is bestowed upon the faithful by His grace.

"Wherefore, my beloved brethren," urged Mormon, "pray unto the Father with all the energy of heart, that ye may be filled with this love, which he hath bestowed upon all who are true followers of his Son, Jesus Christ; that ye may become the sons of God; that when he shall appear we shall be like him, for we shall see him as he is; that we may have this hope; that we may be purified even as he is pure. Amen." (Moroni 7:48).

The
Spirit gives us
the power to become
the sons and daughters
of God as we cleave unto every
good thing. In addition, Christ has
power as our Advocate before the
Father, through the Atonement
which is the very means of
our salvation and our
exaltation.

Faith is a Principle of Power

"If a man be
meek and lowly in heart,
and confess by the power of
the Holy Ghost that Jesus
is the Christ, he must
needs have charity."
(Moroni 7:44).

As a principle of power, faith motivates us to action. Speaking of Martin Luther, Will Durant said: "By faith, he meant no merely intellectual assent to a proposition, but vital, personal self-committal to a practical belief. He heartily approved of good works; what he denied was their efficacy for salvation. 'Good works,' he said, 'do not make a good man, but a good man does good works.' And what makes a man good? Faith in God, and Christ." ("The Reformation," p. 374-375).

"Faith is the substance (or assurance) of things hoped for, the evidence of things not seen." (Hebrews 11:1-40). In this context, faith is not to receive a sign from heaven. As Alma told the Zoramites, "If a man knoweth a thing he hath no cause to believe, for he knoweth it." (Alma 32:18). No exercise of faith is necessary to receive a sign from heaven. When a sign is given, one might have a sure knowledge of the event, but no expenditure of faith has been necessary to produce it. Under proper circumstances, though, "by doing our duty, faith increases until it becomes perfect knowledge." (Heber J. Grant, C.R., 4/1934). Initially, faith is to believe what we do not see, and the reward of faith is to see what we believe.

Notwithstanding President Grant's definitive declaration, Alma emphasized that at least for the poor Zoramites: "Faith is not to have a perfect knowledge of things; therefore, if ye have faith ye hope for things which are not seen, which are true." (Alma 32:21). Why would he say this? Well, he was correct in the ultimate sense, describing the acquisition of faith when it is in its infancy. In his usage, the verse might more clearly read: "Faith is not to have a perfect knowledge of things gained through our own experiences."

When Alma taught this principle to his Zoramite audience, Korihor had only recently demanded a sign as the condition for his faith, since he trusted only his physical senses. This rational approach, however, is the enemy of faith, since some things need to be believed to be seen. Thus, Saint Augustine taught: "Understanding is the reward of faith. Therefore, seek not to understand that thou mayest believe, but believe that thou mayest understand."

A little girl was out for an evening walk with her dad. She kept looking up at the stars, and finally said: "Daddy, if the bottom of heaven is so pretty, just think how beautiful the top will be." Harold B. Lee taught adults in the Church who might have a bit of corrosive corruption of their child-like faith: "We must learn to walk to the edge of the light, and then a few steps into the darkness; then the light will appear and show the way before us." ("B.Y.U. Today," 3/1991). This is the way faith is developed and strengthened.

Moroni wrote: "Faith is things which are hoped for and not seen; wherefore, dispute not because ye see not, for ye receive no witness until after the trial of your faith." (Ether 12:6). In matters of faith the Lord is not on trial. At the Bar of Justice, He will simply receive the evidence, and our previous acceptance or rejection of that evidence will determine our reward or punishment. The trial following our mortal experience is eminently fair.

The highest pinnacle of our spiritual life will be the unbroken sunshine of absolute and undoubting faith in God's love. In this sense, Helen Keller wrote: "I believe that no good shall be lost, and that all man has willed or hoped or dreamed of good shall exist forever. I believe in the immortality of the soul because I have within me immortal longings. I believe that the state we enter after death is wrought of our own motives, thoughts, and deeds. I believe that my home there will be beautiful with colour, music, and speech of flowers and faces I love. Without this faith, there would be little meaning in my life. I should be a mere pillar of darkness in the dark. Observers in the full enjoyment of their bodily senses pity me, but it is because they do not see the golden chamber in my life where I dwell delighted; for dark as my path may seem to them, I carry a magic light in my heart. Faith, the spiritual strong searchlight, illuminates the way, and although sinister doubts lurk in the shadow, I walk unafraid towards the Enchanted Wood where the foliage is always green, where joy abides, where nightingales nest and sing, and where life and death are one in the presence of the Lord." ("Midstream").

Our conscience awakens us to the truth that "salvation cometh to none ... except it be through repentance and faith on the Lord Jesus Christ." (Mosiah 3:12). We do not take "a leap in the dark," said Truman Madsen. Instead, we "trust in what the spirit learned aeons ago; and religious recognition is just that - re-cognition, a re-knowing, the sum of existence. If we thwart or suppress that instinctive response, we are responsible, and, to a degree, we condemn ourselves. We knew Christ before this life, we know him here, and we will know him hereafter. His sheep do indeed know his voice." ("The Meaning of Christ - The Truth, The Way, The Life: An Analysis of B. H. Roberts' Unpublished Masterwork," B.Y.U. Studies, 1975).

The pathway to exaltation is grounded on the bedrock of faith in Jesus Christ, faith in the divinely inspired mission of Joseph Smith, faith in the witness of Christ contained in The Book of Mormon, and faith in the first principles and ordinances of the gospel that lead us to the ordinances and covenants of the Melchizedek Priesthood. Moroni urged us to "come unto Christ, and be perfected in him." (Moroni 10:32). We do this through the Melchizedek Priesthood that "administereth the gospel and holdeth the key of the mysteries of the kingdom, even the key of the knowledge of God. Therefore, in the ordinances thereof, the power of godliness is manifest." (D&C 84:19-20).

When we dismiss faith promoting experiences, we are "free, and that is a pleasant feeling at first. There are no questions of conscience, no constraints, except the constraints of custom, convention, and the law, and these are flexible enough for most purposes. It is only later that the terror comes. We are free, but free in chaos, in an unexplainable world. We are free in a desert, from which there is no retreat but inward toward our hollow core." (Morris West, "The Devil's Advocate").

Blessings follow the effort it takes to develop faith. The miracles from the scriptures with which we are familiar were only made possible by the exercise of faith, and each of us has the power to develop that same intensity of feeling with the same spectacular results. When we read in the sacred records of these experiences, a way is prepared that we, too, might be "partakers of the heavenly gift." (Ether 12:8). It becomes possible for us to link our feelings with those of the two disciples on the Road to Emmaus, who, after communing with the Resurrected Lord, declared: "Did not our heart burn within us, while he talked with us by the way, and while he opened to us the scriptures?" (Luke 24:32).

Faith is
a principle of power
that motivates us to action.
To Martin Luther, it was more
than an intellectual assent to a
proposition. It was vital, personal
self-commitment to practical belief.
He heartily approved of good works;
what he denied was their efficacy for
salvation. "Good works," he said,
'do not make a good man, but a
good man does good works.
And what makes a man
good? Faith in God,
and Christ."

(The) Fall

"The
way is prepared
from the fall of man,
and salvation is free."
(2 Nephi 2:4).

The world misinterprets the account of the Fall because there have been "taken away from the gospel of the Lamb many parts which are plain and most precious; and also, many covenants of the Lord have they taken away. And all this have they done that they might pervert the right ways of the Lord, that they might blind the eyes and harden the hearts of the children of men." (1 Nephi 13:26-27). The account in Genesis treats the Fall as an event, without delving into its related doctrine. Fortunately, the account in the Pearl of Great Price, the temple endowment, and the inspired commentary by Book of Mormon prophets, help to fill in the gaps.

We know that Satan "sought to beguile Eve, for he knew not the mind of God, wherefore he sought to destroy the world." (Moses 4:6). Eve was pure and without guile and was easily deceived, or taken advantage of. In such situations, the sin is on the one doing the deceiving. Satan told both a truth and a lie. He said that Adam and Eve would have knowledge, but he also said that they should not die. (Genesis 3:4-5). Satan came to Eve with the intent to deceive. He was full of treachery, and he sought to mislead her. He was deceptive, and his offer was a forgery. He was, after all, a liar from the beginning. (D&C 93:15). After God made Adam, he was given the commandment to dress and keep the Garden and to abstain from partaking of the fruit of the tree of knowledge of good and evil. (Moses 3:15 & 17). It is also possible that Eve, having been created at a later time, did not receive the same instructions that had earlier been given to Adam.

After the Fall, God put enmity between Satan and the family of Adam and Eve, for He recognized the danger that would lie in their familiarity with sin. (Genesis 3:15). As Alexander Pope observed: "Vice is a monster of such frightful mien, as to be hated needs but to be seen. Yet seen too oft, familiar with her face, we first pity, then endure, then embrace." ("Essay on Man, Epistle 2").

Genesis tells us that Eve would have "sorrow" in her conception. But as Spencer W. Kimball observed: "I wonder if those who translated the Bible might have used the term distress instead of sorrow. It would mean much the same, except I think there is great gladness in most Latter-day Saint homes when there is to be a child there." ("Ensign," 3/1976).

When Adam and Eve were driven from the Garden, they were "punished" with the very things that would later prove to bring them the greatest happiness. A Savior would be provided for them, but in the meantime, cherubim and a flaming sword were placed to keep the way of the tree of life, to preserve the principle of moral agency that was now in the possession of Adam and Eve. (See Genesis 3:24). Both justice and mercy would allow them and their posterity to experience all of the wonders of mortality, without harming their eternal identity. "For behold, if Adam had put forth his hand immediately, and partaken of the tree of life, he would have lived forever, according to the word of God, having no space for repentance; yea, and also the word of God would have been void, and the great plan of salvation would have been frustrated." (Alma 42:5).

After the Fall, the door to Eden may have swung shut behind Adam and Eve, but there was opened unto them and their posterity another door leading to a knowledge of both good and evil, in the wonderful learning laboratory of life.

Fasting

"Fasting is an instrument
to restore friendship with God."
(Pope Benedict XCVI).

"Now, my beloved brethren ... come
unto Christ, who is the Holy One of Israel,
and partake of his salvation, and the power of
his redemption. Yea, come unto him, and offer
your whole souls as an offering unto him,
and continue in fasting and praying,
and endure to the end; and as the
Lord liveth, ye will be saved.
(Omni 1:26).

In the early days of the Restoration, the Lord told the Saints: "I give unto you a commandment that ye shall continue in prayer and fasting from this time forth." (D&C 88:76). Fasting can unleash the power of God to our behalf, for as we fast, we obtain a spirit that enables us to overcome telestial tendencies and focus on celestial sureties. "A favorite theme of Brigham Young was that the dominion God gives us is designed to test us and enable us to show to ourselves, our fellows, and all the heavens just how we would act if entrusted with God's power." (Hugh Nibley, "Subduing the Earth," p. 89-90). Little wonder, then, that the Lord reintroduced the Law of the Fast in His latter-day church.

When we fast, we go without food and drink. Almost immediately thereafter, a clash arises between the spiritual and temporal sides of our nature. If we focus our energies, this conflict slowly evolves into a harmony where the whole is miraculously greater than the sum of its constituent parts. We develop a toughness that doesn't fold under pressure or fatigue. Our physical desires, held in check by a greater spiritual awareness, actually strengthen our resolve to discipline our nature. We transcend beyond forces pulling us one way or the other, and enter a metaphysical state of euphoria where virtue garnishes our thoughts unceasingly, as the doctrine of the priesthood distills upon our souls as the dews from heaven because our confidence waxes strong in the presence of God. As this process unfolds, the Holy Ghost becomes our constant companion, and our scepter an unchanging scepter of righteousness and truth, and our dominion an everlasting, God-centered, and focused power. Under these conditions, all that is good freely flows in an unending stream. (See D&C 121:45-46). Truly, this transformative spirituality becomes our "consciousness of victory over self, and of communion with the infinite." (David O. McKay, C.R., 10/1969).

Fasting begins and ends with prayer. Without it, we risk failure to focus on spiritual concerns, and we "go hungry." Fasting is of no worth unless it is connected to the Savior through an intimate communion facilitated by prayer.

As Mormon put it, "all things which are good cometh of Christ." (Moroni 7:24). We are teachable when we reach an attitude of humility through fasting and prayer.

Fasting with a purpose helps us to overcome specific flaws, faults, and failings. The Lord said: "If men come unto me I will show unto them their weakness. I give unto men weakness that they may be humble; and my grace is sufficient for all men that humble themselves before me; for if they humble themselves before me, and have faith in me, then will I make weak things become strong unto them." (Ether 12:26-27).

We fast for guidance for others. "And Jehoshaphat feared, and set himself to seek the Lord, and proclaimed a fast throughout all Judah." (2 Chronicles 20:3). Faith is fear that has said its prayers, but sometimes those who need faith the most cannot muster the strength to call upon the Lord for His help. It is then that loved ones must step up to the plate to provide the support group that can carry those who are faltering through their crisis of faith.

We fast to focus spiritual power to help another to gain a testimony or to gain a testimony ourselves. As Alma explained: "I have fasted and prayed many days that I might know these things of myself. And now, I do know of myself that they are true; for the Lord God hath made them manifest unto me by his Holy Spirit." (Alma 5:46). Perhaps it is necessary to fast and pray regularly to gain and retain a testimony of each principle of the gospel. The way of the world is to scrutinize from every rational angle, to form committees charged with the responsibility to analyze data, compile reports, develop hypotheses and paradigms, reach compromise, and finally publish a watered-down conclusion that may be concise but lacks clarity. But "O that cunning plan of the evil one! O the vainness, and the frailties, and the foolishness of men! When they are learned they think they are wise, and they hearken not unto the counsel of God, for they set it aside, supposing they know of themselves, wherefore, their wisdom is foolishness and it profiteth them not. And they shall perish. But to be learned is good if they hearken unto the counsels of God." (2 Nephi 9:29-30).

An appeal to vanity is Satan's way of turning our minds against the Plan of Salvation. "I" and "Mine" are usually accompanied by an unbended knee. Neal A. Maxwell wrote: "To the humble, the simpleness and the easiness of the way are glad realities; to the crowded, ego filled minds of proud men, the sudden burst of light from a spiritual sunrise is irritating rather than awesome, and causes them to blink rather than to stare in reverent awe." ("That My Family Should Partake," p. 82). The principle-centered approach that is necessary to come to knowledge of the truth of all things is founded on meekness, lowliness of heart, and humility.

The prophet Ezra revealed something about his character when he acknowledged: "At the evening sacrifice I arose up from my heaviness; and having rent my garment and my mantle, I fell upon my knees, and spread out my hands unto the Lord my God, and said, O my God, I am ashamed and blush to lift up my face to thee, my God: for our iniquities are increased over our head, and our trespass is grown up unto the heavens." (Ezra 9:5-6). "Then Ezra rose up from before the house of God, and went into the chamber of Johanan the son of Eliashib: and when he came thither, he did eat no bread, nor drink water." (Ezra 10:6).

As long as we are centered on Christ, we can be cheerful when we fast, and not "as the hypocrites, of a sad countenance." (3 Nephi 13:16). We do not publicize our fasting, nor are we like those who "disfigure their faces that they may appear unto men to fast." As the Savior said, "they have their reward. But thou, when thou fastest, anoint thy head, and wash thy face; That thou appear not unto men to fast." (3 Nephi 13:16-18).

When we fast, we petition God in prayer for forgiveness. The psalmist said: "But as for me ... my clothing was sackcloth: I humbled my soul with fasting." (Psalms 35:13). At the same time, we seize the opportunity to forgive others, focusing the spiritual power generated by our fast on our efforts, in a way that is contrary to human nature.

This requires a spiritual sensitivity greater than ourselves. Brigham Young, echoing Confucius, once reminded the Saints: "He who takes offense when none was intended is a fool, and he who takes offense when it was intended is usually a fool." (Cited by Marion D. Hanks, C.R., 10/1973). Fasting is an opportunity that should never be wasted that allows us to bring out the best in ourselves by forgiving others.

One Sunday each month, Latter-day Saints observe a fast day when the faithful neither eat nor drink for two consecutive meals, thus making a fast of 24 hours. In an attitude of fasting, it is natural that the church should meet together to partake of the Sacrament, and to encourage one another by bearing testimony. Everyone who is able to do so fasts on that day. However, "many are subject to weakness, others are delicate in health, and others have nursing babies; of such it should not be required to fast. Neither should parents compel their little children to fast." (Joseph F. Smith, "Gospel Doctrine," p. 244).

When we observe the monthly fast, we are encouraged to help others who are less fortunate than we. To the proper priesthood authority, we give the food, or the money we would have spent on the food for the two meals we have skipped during the fast.

Fasting helps us to develop strength of character. When we exercise a purposeful self-control for just 24 hours each month, we develop the willpower to overcome greater temptations with which we will surely have to grapple. "Who shall ascend into the hill of the Lord?" asked David. "Or who shall stand in his holy place? He that hath clean hands, and a pure heart; who hath not lifted up his soul unto vanity, nor sworn deceitfully. He shall receive the blessing from the Lord, and righteousness from the God of his salvation." (Psalm 24:3-5).

Fasting teaches us how to find God. When we fast, "then shall thy light break forth as the morning, and thine health shall spring forth speedily, and thy righteousness shall go before thee; the glory of the Lord shall be thy reward. Then shalt thou call, and the Lord shall answer; thou shalt cry, and he shall say, Here I am." (Isaiah 58:8-9).

Fasting gives us spiritual understanding. When our lives conform to the prototype established by the Savior, and scales of darkness fall away, the eyes of our spiritual understanding are opened and our hearts swell with the pure love of Christ. Our ears increasingly understand otherwise inarticulate impressions, as fluency is developed, and otherwise inaudible whisperings of the Spirit create soft patterns on our supple souls.

Fasting gives us spiritual power. We can learn much from the experiences of the Sons of Mosiah. It must have seemed altogether remarkable to Alma, when he saw his brethren for the first time after their 14-year mission to the Lamanites, that his highest and best hopes for their welfare had been confirmed. As he learned the details of their experiences during those years, he surely recognized and appreciated their unchangeable formula for success: "They had waxed strong in the knowledge of the truth; for they were men of a sound understanding and they had searched the scriptures diligently, that they might know the word of God. But" Mormon explained, "this is not all. They had given themselves to much prayer, and fasting; therefore, they had the spirit of prophecy, and the spirit of revelation, and when they taught, they taught with the power and authority of God." (Alma 17:2-3). Because they had internalized these qualities of greatness, they had been able to endure and conquer every obstacle on their mission.

The scriptures had become their message and were the tools of their trade. Their confidence, we shall see, was directly related to their knowledge of God's word. "God help all honest men," said Marion G. Romney, "to be born again and come to be of sound understanding and to know the word of God and maintain the spirit thereof by study, fasting, prayer, and work, that we may be blessed with His power and authority!" (C.R., 10/1941).

Fasting is a principle of perfection. It is like a spiritual angioplasty that facilitates the flow of communication between ourselves and God. It is inspired treatment for spiritual sclerosis. Mormon recounted that Ammon, one of the Sons of Mosiah, had "reason to rejoice," for he had been given a second chance to fulfil his life's potential after he had been born again. He must have considered himself very fortunate that God had looked so favorably upon him in the rebellious years of his youth and had been able to see into his heart. His rough exterior had been only a façade reflecting his inappropriate behavior. His true character had only been revealed when, through a spiritual rebirth, he became a new creature in Christ. Fasting on his part, and on the part of his loved ones, had a lot to do with his conversion.

As it aided Ammon, fasting helps us to put off "the natural man," and to instead put on the character of Christ. "All mankind, yea, men and women, all nations, kindreds, tongues and people, must be born again, yea, born of God, changed from their carnal and fallen state, to a state of righteousness, being redeemed of God, becoming his sons and daughters." (Mosiah 27:25). We, like the Sons of Mosiah, are true "Sabra," native-born children of the Covenant. The fruit of the prickly pear cactus, the sabra, has a dry, unappealing skin. But inside, it is sweet and juicy and pleasing to the taste. When God measures us, He puts the tape around our hearts.

Fasting can soften the hearts of others, and it can help them to see into our hearts, as well. "Mormons are like artichokes," began an article in The Boston Globe, in 1967. "At first encounter, you either like them or you don't. But those who have unfavorable first impressions often find that once the outer layers are peeled away, both Mormons and artichokes are most likable. In fact, most people who get to know Mormons become their friends. And a little objective research on Mormon beliefs reveals that, except for a few doctrinal differences, these people who call themselves Latter-day Saints are just like the rest of us - very human beings." (Quoted in Leonard Arrington, "The Mormon Experience," p. 308).

And so, we organize ourselves, and "prepare every needful thing; and establish a house, even a house of prayer, a house of fasting, a house of faith, a house of learning, a house of glory, a house of order, a house of God," because fasting can help us to understand His nature. (D&C 88:119). Joseph Smith wrote: "There are but a very few beings in the world who understand rightly the nature of God (and) if men do not understand the character of God they do not comprehend themselves." ("Teachings," p. 343). Fasting focuses our spiritual and intellectual powers on the principles of perfection that define God's attributes, and that may ultimately describe our own.

Fate

"Wherefore, men are free according to the flesh; and all things are given them which are expedient unto man. And they are free to choose liberty and eternal life, through the great Mediator of all men, or to choose captivity and death, according to the captivity and power of the devil." (2 Nephi 2:27).

There was a merchant in Baghdad who sent his servant to the marketplace to buy provisions. A short while later, the servant came back to the home of his master, white and trembling. He cried out: Master, just now in the marketplace I was jostled by a man in the crowd, and when I turned, I saw that it was Death. He confronted me with a menacing look, and made a threatening gesture. Now, lend me your horse, and I will ride away from this city and thereby avoid my fate. I will go to Samarra, and there, Death will not find me.

The merchant readily lent him his horse, and the servant mounted it, dug his spurs into its flanks, and as fast as the horse could gallop, he was carried away to Samarra.

Then, the merchant went down to the marketplace, and he sought out Death, who was standing in the crowd. He came up to him and asked why he had made a threating gesture to his servant, when he had seen him earlier in the morning. That was not a threatening gesture, said Death. It was only a start of surprise. I was astonished to see him in Baghdad, for I have an appointment with him tonight, in Samarra. (Adapted from W. Somerset Maugham, "An Appointment in Samarra").

"Wherefore, men are free according to the flesh; and all things are given them which are expedient unto man. And they are free to choose liberty and eternal life, through the great Mediator of all men, or to choose captivity and death, according to the captivity and power of the devil."
(2 Nephi 2:27).

Father Forgive Them

"For behold, this is my
church; whosoever is baptized
shall be baptized unto repentance.
And whomsoever ye receive shall
believe in my name; and him
will I freely forgive."
(Mosiah 26:22).

From the Cross at Calvary, the Savior looked down upon the Roman soldiers who had crucified Him, and uttered these remarkable words: "Father, forgive them, for they know not what they do." (Luke 23:34). Incredibly, it was with the same spirit of forgiveness that He regarded His brethren the Jews, who had so recently condemned Him.

Their voices must have stung His ears, however, when He had heard them cry out: "His blood be on us, and on our children. (Matthew 27:5). These were the descendants of those of whom the Lord had spoken through the mouth of His prophet Isaiah: "Fear not, for... with everlasting kindness will I have mercy on thee, saith the Lord thy Redeemer." (3 Nephi 22:4 & 8). Through Isaiah, the Lord of all the earth promised His covenant children: "No weapon that is formed against thee shall prosper; and every tongue that shall revile against thee in judgment thou shalt condemn. This is the heritage of the servants of the Lord, and their righteousness is of me, saith the Lord." (Isaiah 54:17).

These promises notwithstanding, in the courtyard of Pilate, the Jews had betrayed the Bridegroom to whom they had been betrothed. If there were ever justification for the Savior to harbor bitter feelings toward those who had wronged Him, it would be as He staggered under the weight of His cross, as He made His way along the Via Dolorosa, the "Way of Grief, Sorrow, and Suffering," or simply the "Painful Way," knowing that every step would bring Him closer to Calvary, and that the anguish that must have rolled over Him in waves was the result of His betrayal by His brethren.

Long before the Savior's comforting words had illuminated the mind of His prophet Isaiah, and even before the foundation of the world, He had begun to consistently accumulate reserves in His spiritual bank account to be used against the day when He would need them most. He knew from the beginning, even before The Greet and Eternal Plan of Deliverance from Death (see 2 Nephi 11:5) had been explained to the Father's children, that His was to be an infinite and eternal atonement for every sin that would ever be committed by His brothers and sisters. Thus, when the critical hour came in the Garden of Gethsemane, followed by the mockery of his trial before Pilate and His crucifixion on Calvary, He was able to plumb the limitless depths of His mercy and extend His magnificent forgiveness to those who had so grievously offended him. "He was wounded for our transgressions; he was bruised for our iniquities: the chastisement of our peace was upon him; and (yet) with his stripes we are healed." (Isaiah 53:5). Thus, did His prophet Isaiah describe the Atonement of the Savior, over 700 years before His mortal ministry. Truly, the reach of His sacrifice was infinite in both its temporal and eternal scope.

As Alma declared about 125 years before Christ's agony in Gethsemane: "The atonement (was) prepared from the foundation of the world, that thereby salvation might come to him that should put his trust in the Lord, and should be diligent in keeping his commandments, and continue in the faith even unto the end of his life." (Mosiah 4:6). The Atonement to which Alma referred considered every sin that would be individually and collectively committed by the family of man, beginning at the foundation of the world, and only ending after the Lord has come a second time to usher in His millennial reign on earth. The Atonement anticipated the shortcomings, the sins of omission, and the sins of commission that would be frustratingly, repetitively, and painfully exhibited by every generation of the children of men, from the beginning to the end of time. It is all the more remarkable to realize that the Atonement anticipated sins that had not yet been committed. When the Savior stood before the Council and said to His Father: "Here am I, send me," (Abraham 3:27), He knew full well the price that would be required to satisfy Justice in order to obtain mercy. He had the spiritual reserves to make such a statement, but even his maturity as a God in Heaven (see Joseph Fielding Smith, Jr., "Doctrines of Salvation," 1:32), could not take away the pain He must have felt, even then, for the scriptures describe Him as the "lamb slain from the foundation of the world." (Revelation 13:8).

Could His brothers and sisters who were also in attendance at the Council, who so easily and enthusiastically raised their arms to the square to support the Father's proposal (see Job 38:7) have truly felt the import of the moment, that He was not only making history, but that He was also creating a binding foundation and precedent to re-write history? They were eyewitnesses to the vitalization of "the merciful plan of the great Creator." (2 Nephi 9:6). They must have palpably sensed in His condescension the enveloping reach of His love for them. They must have understood His penultimate example of humility, His supreme act of selflessness, and His superlative expression of altruism. He had just become their personal Redeemer, and the power of the Atonement had just been activated in their behalf. We can only wonder how they could comprehend the significance of the events that were unfolding before them; that the exercise of their free will had just been guaranteed, the principles of the Plan certified, the price of their future offenses successfully negotiated, the guarantee of payment made in advance, and the demands of Justice satisfied and equally balanced against Mercy. Cherubim and a flaming sword were even then being prepared, to guard the way, and guarantee the eternal progression of Adam and Eve and their posterity. God's work and glory had been confirmed: To bring to pass the immortality and eternal life of man. (See Moses 1:39).

As Aaron taught King Lamoni's father, around a hundred years before the mortal ministry of the Savior: "Since man had fallen he could not merit anything of himself; but the sufferings and death of Christ atone for their sins, through faith and repentance, (and) he breaketh the bands of death, that the grave shall have no victory … that the sting of death should be swallowed up in the hopes of glory." (Alma 22:14).

With clarity of vision, Alma taught the people of Gideon about the future mission of the Savior. He and other Book of Mormon prophets taught the doctrine of the Atonement in a way that elsewhere in scripture is dealt with incompletely, with uncertainty, and with ambiguity. In Alma Chapter 7, for example, there is little room for confusion. By following Alma's teachings, we can learn from the Atonement and apply its magnificent power to our own capacity for forgiveness.

Alma 7:11 suggests that part of the Atonement was accomplished during the three-year ministry Savior. "And he shall go forth, suffering pains and afflictions and temptations of every kind; and this that the word might be fulfilled which saith he will take upon him the pains and the sicknesses of his people." The description of the suffering of the Savior is particularly poignant in light of Alma's own suffering that came with the recognition of his sins. (See Alma 36:14 & 21). It seems that the work in which the Savior was engaged during His ministry followed a natural progression, and was built "line upon line, and precept upon precept," until His preparation was complete and every necessary detail had been worked out. Early in His ministry, Jesus had said, "My time is not yet come." (John 7:6). But later, when all had been accomplished, He confirmed, "My time is at hand." (Matthew 26:18). So it is with us. We, too, generally develop our capacity for forgiveness over time, as our own schooling in mortality takes us from primary classes, to secondary, and finally to higher education. Sometimes, it is only in the graduate school of hard knocks that we learn how to have charity, and to forgive as the Savior does. It will come naturally.

Alma 7:12 concerns the aspect of the Atonement that was completed upon the Cross. "And he will take upon him death, that he may loose the bands of death which bind his people; and he will take upon him their infirmities, that his bowels may be filled with mercy, according to the flesh, that he may know according to the flesh how to succor his people according to their infirmities." The crucified Christ is the primary focus of Christianity today, but if we fail to understand the Mortal Messiah, we risk receiving only a one-dimensional view that ignores the wonderful harmony that exists between His humanity and His divinity. In the context of this verse, it is well to remember that it is when we have known hardship that we develop empathy, are more likely to overlook the shortcomings of others, and are quicker to forgive them their trespasses. By learning to avoid being judgmental, and by developing benevolent blindness, we are better able to help others to meet their own challenges. The Savior asks us to follow Him to Golgotha, there to experience hardship at the hands of others. If we have embarked upon the journey to Christ, even as we experience adversity due to the influence of others who seek to do us harm, we will not be deterred in our resolve to forgive.

As the Lord explained to Joseph Smith: "If thou art called to pass through tribulation; if thou art in perils among false brethren; if thou art in perils among robbers; if thou art in perils by land or by sea; if thou art accused with all manner of false accusations; if thine enemies fall upon thee; if they tear thee from the society of thy father and mother and brethren and sisters; and if with a drawn sword thine enemies tear thee from the bosom of thy wife, and of thine offspring, and thine elder son, although but six years of age, shall cling to thy garments, and shall say, My father, my father, why can't you stay with us? O, my father, what are the men going to do with you? And if then he shall be thrust from thee by the sword, and thou be dragged to prison, and thine enemies prowl around thee like wolves for the blood of the lamb; and if thou shouldst be cast into the pit, or into the hands of murderers, and the sentence of death passed upon thee; if thou be cast into the deep; if the billowing surge conspire against thee; if fierce winds become thine enemy; if the heavens gather blackness, and all the elements combine to hedge up the way; and above all, if the very jaws of hell shall gape open the mouth wide after thee, know thou, my son, that all these things shall give thee experience, and shall be for thy good. The Son of Man hath descended below them all. Art thou greater than he?" (D&C 122:5-8). The more righteous we are, the better are we able to deal with the suffering that is a part of life, and that is likely not of our own doing. Our blessing may simply be the strength to endure the suffering that is a part of our mortal experience. (See D&C 121:7).

Alma 7:13 focuses on the dimension of the Atonement that was fulfilled in Gethsemane. "Now the Spirit knoweth all things; nevertheless, the Son of God suffereth according to the flesh that he might take upon him the sins of his people, that he might blot out their transgressions according to the power of his deliverance." Latter-day Saints tend to emphasize Gethsemane as the pivotal experience attendant to the Savior's sacrifice, but we can see that it was really a multi-dimensional drama played out on different stages. It began even before the creation of the earth, and will only end when the last repentant sinner has received intercession by the Redeemer, and forgiveness by the Father. In the meantime, our injunction is to develop the Savior's moral stamina, and to become as He is. As we internalize His divine attributes, we become perfected in Him. A key to the process is our capacity to forgive others, because forgiveness is central to the Atonement.

The Atonement's invitation to forgive and to be forgiven stands in counterpoint and is an effective antidote to the inevitable sense of empty despair, despondency, misery, and hopelessness related to the failings that have been and will continue to be an integral part of our schooling in mortality, for it must needs be that there is an opposition in all things. (See 2 Nephi 2:11). In support of Mercy, the power of the Atonement stands independently in the face of an avalanche of wickedness that has been poured out upon the world with increasing vitriol in the Last Days.

The Atonement is the only alternative to an otherwise overwhelmingly negative power overshadowing and influencing the affairs of mankind. Its only stipulation is that we acknowledge our disobedience and go through the process of repentance wherein we recognize our transgression, experience remorse, renounce the self-defeating behavior, resolve to do better, make restitution where possible, and then do our best to establish a reconciliation with the Spirit, and ultimately receive a remission of sin. The Atonement is the only force that has the power to bring about the kind of positive change illustrated in The Book of Mormon, when King Benjamin's people of Zarahemla "cried with one voice, saying: Yea, we believe all the words which thou hast spoken unto us; and also, we know of their surety and truth, because of the Spirit of the Lord Omnipotent, which has wrought a mighty change in us, or in our hearts, that we have no more disposition to do evil, but to do good continually." (Mosiah 5:2). We will have only completed the process of repentance when we, likewise, seek to do good continually, and when our forgiveness of others, painted in bold strokes with a broad brush, is at its foundation. As the Lord said: "I...will forgive whom I will forgive, but of you it is required to forgive all men." (D&C 64:10).

The Atonement allows us to overcome our selfish and morally indefensible desire for justice without mercy. Desperation was really at the foundation of Lucifer's alternative proposal at the Council, when he boasted: "I will redeem all mankind, that one soul shall not be lost." (Moses 4:1). He exhibited his true colors with that revealing assertion. Because he was incapable of forgiveness, the thought of remembering no more the sins of his repentant brethren scared the living daylights out of him. The noble and principled qualities that are expressed in the Atonement stand in contrast to the damning character flaws of the star that fell from heaven. (See Revelation 9:1). Lucifer became Satan because of his unprincipled and unilaterally dogmatic posturing; because he would have had us believe that his counterfeit proposal could grant absolution without apology, adjustment without appreciation, admonishment without adaptation, alteration without affection, amelioration without acquittal, amendment without admiration, castigation without consideration, censure without courtesy, chastisement without charity, clemency without compassion, condemnation without kindness, correction without concern, discipline without deprecation, indebtedness without indemnification, leniency without love, mercifulness without magnanimity, pacification without propitiation, probation without pardon, punishment without penance, reprimand without rectification, rebuke without resolution, reprimand without reassurance, reproof without reconciliation, resolution without reparation, retaliation without regard, retribution without reverence, revenge without respect, tolerance without tenderness, and vengeance without veneration.

The Atonement is the keystone of the Plan of Salvation, that unflinchingly looks directly into the jaws of spiritual death without averting its eyes. It was not the Savior, but the devil who was the first to blink, and who was cast out of heaven. It is he who will not support his children at the last day. (See Alma 30:44).

Our acknowledgement of the necessity of the fundamental principle of opposition within the framework of the Plan does not give us license to act recklessly or to capitulate to the Dark Side, without accountability. Every expression of our exercise of free is simply a confirmation of the trust that our Heavenly Father places in us. He created us with the moral backbone to meet unforgiveness with compassion, intolerance with consideration, prejudice with impartiality, and narrow-mindedness with limitless opportunity for expression.

Opposition serves the useful purpose of allowing us to gauge the success of our internalization of the Plan's provisions. It also gives us a sense of how we are doing in our efforts to participate consciously and energetically, without deviation, in purposeful programs of personal progress that carry us forward on proven paths. Conformity to God's laws has the capacity to provide significant sustainable support and to generate confidence, as we feel ourselves being carried forward as upon the wings of eagles. (See D&C 124:99). Without the comfortable sense of orthodoxy provided by the gospel, life can be nothing more than a cruel joke with a punch line that inevitably pierces our hearts without pity. If we allow ourselves to be left to the wiles of the adversary, we will find ourselves confronted by a sense of utter futility that is the inexorable result of our failure to focus on the innate upward reach that is only generated by the desire, capacity, and discipline to reach out and embrace noble principles. His enticements can leave us gasping for a breath of celestial air, with the feeling that we have been sucker-punched below the belt.

Without the light of the Atonement, we are doomed to suffer in the shadows where we van only experience illusions and caricatures of reality. The discrepancy between marginalized behavior and the ideals of the Plan can become so great that short-lived pleasure in worldly ways evaporates as the morning dew in the full light of day. Sooner or later, when this disparity becomes so great that it reaches "critical mass," a requisite readjustment tears down our façade of corruption and hypocrisy to allow the cultivation of a more nurturing lifestyle made possible by a recommitment to obedience to the foundation principles of the Plan.

Then, for the Plan to have real vitality, we must forgive, even as we are forgiven. Our forgiveness must be anchored to the Atonement, as must every other facet of our lives. We must forsake our carnal nature, for it is nothing more than a shadowy image of Lucifer's rebellion in the Council. If we harbor feelings of revenge, retaliation, or reprisal, and if the basic instincts that were activated by the Fall of Adam are to be conquered, we must fall back on the fire line of the Atonement to contain and conquer the conflagration that is sin.

To illustrate this point, the Great Fire of 1910 was the largest forest fire in U.S. History. It burned about 4,687 square miles in northeast Washington, northern Idaho, and western Montana. It destroyed parts of ten different national forests, and killed 87 people, mostly firefighters. It remained the deadliest event for firefighters in the United States, until September 11, 2001.

By comparison, the Yellowstone National Park fire in 1988 burned about 1,240 square miles. The Yosemite National Park fire in 2013 burned about 384 square miles. Changes in weather often contribute to the control and elimination of wildfires, but what is critical to established firefighting tactics is the strategy of "containment" that is designed to bring the fire within the boundaries of exhaustively and painstakingly constructed fire lines. Only with containment may the blaze be brought under control and ultimately extinguished. The Atonement is like an encircling fire-line that contains with 100% effectiveness the blazing inferno of sin, no matter how much potential fuel has been consumed or what combustible material may yet lie on the forest floor.

This principle of containment, that lies at the heart of Atonement, is so alien to the natural man that Satan, who was the world's original and foremost arsonist, can muster no effective counterproposal. There is nothing within his arsenal to combat the Atonement. The best he can do is keep people from the truth, for the truth will make them free. (See John 8:32). His best strategy is to use the flame thrower of faithlessness to "turn their hearts away from the truth, that they become blinded and understand not the things which are prepared for them." (D&C 78:10). He banks on the fact that "there are many yet on the earth among all sects, parties, and denominations, who are blinded by the subtle craftiness of men, whereby they lie in wait to deceive, and who are only kept from the truth because they know not where to find it." (D&C 123:12). When we understand the power of the Atonement, our capacity for forgiveness, and to be forgiven, will be boundless.

The Atonement was designed to deal with our worst depravities, moral corruption, and degradation, including atrocities such as the Holocaust and World War II, in which over 60 million people, 3% of the world population, lost their lives. The Atonement encompasses the sins of those who took part in the Stalinist purges of the 1940s and 1950s, a period of Soviet history in which nearly 10 million lives were taken. The encircling arms of the Atonement reach as far as the Rwandan genocide in 1994, and the Bosnian ethnic cleansing in 1995. The Atonement also has the capacity to cleanse each of us from our own secret sins and hidden transgressions. The Atonement is the fire retardant that is dumped on the raging inferno of sin.

The Atonement encompasses our every day garden-variety sins, when we are slighted by a waitress, a store clerk, or a civil servant, and respond with anger; when a driver treats us discourteously, and we react in kind; when our spouse is inconsiderate of our feelings, and we counter spitefully; when a work associate treats us with disrespect and our retort drags us down to his lowest common denominator; or when a church leader exercises what we suppose to be unrighteous dominion and our reaction causes us to withdraw from full faith and fellowship. So, too, the Atonement stands ready to save us when we have been, not on the receiving end, but rather on the giving end, of these every-day interpersonal sleights.

If, in any of these situations, we do not beg for our own forgiveness, or ourselves forgive those who have purportedly trespassed against us, we will become vulnerable to a spiritual sickness that mimics the symptoms of those with advanced diabetes whose peripheral circulation has been compromised and who can no longer feel. As we experience the hard lessons of life that the Plan purposely throws our way with frustrating regularity, if we have not learned that the door of forgiveness swings both ways, we will become numb to the better angels of our nature and lose our capacity to touch and be touched by those around us. We will then find ourselves more and more isolated from the sensitivity to our surroundings that is critical to our full participation in the Plan of Happiness. We will find ourselves in a spiritual vacuum, gasping for life-sustaining air.

In beautiful Lancaster County, Pennsylvania, the Amish people have created their own version of the Promised Land. They live simply, without automobiles, electricity, or machinery. They conduct their affairs quietly and without ostentation, in relative isolation from the outside world. They tend their own gardens, sow, and harvest their own crops, prepare their food simply, and fashion their own modest clothing. Their beautiful quilts are prized possessions, and are much coveted by others.

Living among them in 2006 was a 32-year-old "English" milk truck driver. He knew many of his Amish neighbors. On October 2, as evil influences overpowered him, his sanity disintegrated. He felt compelled to enter the simple Amish schoolhouse in Nickel Mines, and shoot and kill five Amish children, while wounding another five. He then turned the gun on himself, and a bullet to the brain ended his own inner torment.

His suicide did nothing to assuage the depth of distress, sense of suffering and gravity of grief among the Amish. But, incredibly, in response to his heinous act, their anguish was not accompanied by anger. There was hurt, but no hate, distress, but no despair, and pain, but no pernicious plotting of payback. There was heartache without hardness of heart. The Amish immediately and without reservation expressed forgiveness for what their neighbor had done. Theirs was not just empty rhetoric, for they put their money where their mouth was. They reached out to his family, and literally wrapped their arms around its members. They attended his funeral, and invited his family to attend their own sorrowful services for their sweet children. Their faith carried them through difficult days and long nights, and blessed them with a remarkable sense of peace.

Some in the media could not understand what was happening within the Amish community. They wondered how they could so freely forgive under such circumstances. But others realized that "Letting go of grudges" is a deeply rooted value in Amish culture. Their willingness to forgo vengeance did not undo the tragedy or pardon the wrong, but rather it constituted the first step toward a more hopeful future.

The Christian Science Monitor very perceptively noted: "For most people, a decision to forgive comes, if ever, at the end of a long emotional journey that may stretch over months, if not years. The Amish invert the process. Their religious tradition predisposes them to forgive even before an injustice occurs." (October 2, 2007). Remarkably, the Amish exhibited the Christ-like forgiveness that we often take for granted as a quality of the Savior, but rarely emulate ourselves.

As the Monitor pointed out, the key was that the Amish had learned to reverse the process of forgiveness. We tend to grapple with forgiveness after the offense. Perhaps the Amish understood the power of the Atonement better than the rest of us, and applied it in literal and personal ways that are hard for the rest of us to imagine, simply because it lies outside of our experience. They seemed to have already reached an epiphany wherein they realized that the Savior is our great Exemplar who forgave us our trespasses even before they had been committed. He took upon Himself the penalty for our sins before we committed them. For the Amish, "the sting of death is swallowed up in Christ." (Mosiah 16:8). His love and compassion, and the depth and breadth of His mercy, know no temporal or spatial bounds. For them, His Atonement was truly infinite in its scope. For them, His arms encircle the vilest of sinners, as well as the worthiest of saints, and His forgiveness is only conditional upon our willingness to repent.

The Monitor continued its observation of the remarkable example of the Amish: "Next to the Bible, the most important book in any Amish household is "der Martyrspeigel" (The Martyr's Mirror) which documents the persecution suffered by the Anabaptists in Europe in the 16 th and 17 th centuries. This book is read aloud to Amish families nearly every day. Among the stories is the tale of one Amishman who was being pursued by a bounty hunter across a frozen lake. The ice cracked, and the bounty hunter fell in. The Amishman stopped and pulled the bounty hunter from what would have surely been an icy death, only to then be taken into custody and later executed for his faith. With such stories told time after time, it is not surprising that there is" within the Amish psyche "such a deep reservoir of forgiveness and grace."

A puckish observation is that revenge is a dish that is best served cold, when we are no longer caught up in the heat of the moment, but can afford to be crafty, cunning, and calculating as we plot our payback. But that stratagem is still like swallowing poison and hoping it will kill the other guy. The word "revenge" is found just thirteen times in the scriptures, but the word "forgive" is found one hundred fifty-five times.

When we ponder the example of the Amish, we remember how Peter came to the Savior and asked Him: "Lord, how oft shall my brother sin against me, and I forgive him? Till seven times? Jesus saith unto him, I say not unto thee, Until seven times: but, Until seventy times seven." (Matthew 18:21-22). We are reminded, as well, of the Lord's injunction to Joseph Smith: "I, the Lord, will forgive whom I will forgive, but of you it is required to forgive all men." (D&C 64:10).

The Lord has commanded that we be perfect, even as our Father in Heaven is perfect. We can be perfect in our home teaching and visiting teaching, in our obedience to the Law of Tithing, and in our observation of the Law of The Fast. We can be perfect in our obedience to the Law of Chastity, and in the sustaining of our leaders. Beyond that, it gets a little tricky, but we can also strive to be perfect in our forgiveness of others, until seventy times seven. The Amish seem to have perfected their forgiveness; which gives us hope that so can we.

With His eternal perspective, the Savior tried to explain to His beloved Apostle Peter that to inherit the Kingdom of God, he would have to change his very nature. He would have to be born again in order to "see the kingdom of God." (John 3:3). He would have to follow the example of "the Lamb slain from the foundation of the world." (Revelation 13:8). He would have to be as a little child, who is "alive in Christ, even from the foundation of the world." (Moroni 8:12). He would have to recognize the power of His ministry, and that He had prepared a way "for all men from the foundation of the world, if it so be that they repent and come unto him." (1 Nephi 10:8). He would have to act upon his understanding that "the plan of redemption" includes the commandment to forgive others without reservation, and that this injunction "was laid from the foundation of the world" through Jesus Christ. (Alma 12:2, see Alma 18:39).

The example of the Amish teaches us a mighty lesson about forgiveness. It puts the Atonement of Jesus Christ in a clearer perspective, and illustrates how mere mortals can develop an eternal point of view to help them to see with greater clarity how they can individually personalize this keystone principle of the gospel. Their model behavior stirs our hearts, and the Spirit quickens us to follow their example. The Lord told the brother of Jared: "Behold, I am he who was prepared from the foundation of the world to redeem my people. Behold, I am Jesus Christ. I am the Father and the Son. In me shall all mankind have life, and that eternally, even they who shall believe on my name; and they shall become my sons and my daughters." (Ether 3:14).

We are reminded of The Lord's Prayer, wherein we are taught: "And forgive us our debts, as we forgive our debtors." (Matthew 6:9-13). Then, in the next two verses, the Savior underscored the quality of forgiveness expressed in His archetypical prayer: "For if ye forgive men their trespasses, your heavenly Father will also forgive you: But if ye forgive not men their trespasses, neither will your Father forgive your trespasses." (Matthew 6:12). It is that simple.

In our society, we too often think that retribution is our right and responsibility. Too many religions in the world wield a sword of vengeance as their God-given duty. In contrast, rather than using religion to bless and legitimize revenge, the Amish believe that God smiles on simple acts of grace that open the door to reconciliation. They believe in allowing God to be the judge of our actions, and that if correction is to be administered, it should be done by His hand. Latter-day Saint doctrine agrees: "Judgment is mine, saith the Lord, and vengeance is mine also." (Mormon 8:12).

If we are ever to successfully deal with the inequalities of life and escape the quicksands of self-pity, we must personalize the lessons of the Atonement. We must change our nature and become new creatures in Christ. If necessary, we must practice in front of a mirror, and recite over and over again until we get it right: "Father forgive them, for they know not what they do." We must become more Amish.

Finding Balance in Our Lives

"See that all … things
are done in wisdom and order;
for it is not requisite that a man should
run faster than he has strength And again,
it is expedient that he should be diligent, that
thereby he might win the prize; therefore,
all things must be done in order."
(Mosiah 4:27).

When we are balanced, we are decided, dogged, determined, indomitable, resolute, untiring, unwavering, and even heroic. Our balance is the contrary of fanaticism, wherein we lose sight of our objectives and redouble our efforts. To be balanced is to be ardent, eager, fervent, enthusiastic, passionate, and zealous, rather than overzealous, wherein we become obsessive and even feverish in our efforts to obtain elusive telestial treasures that are difficult to retain.

In our unstable environment, it takes a great deal of effort to create balance, and very little inattention to allow chaos to reign unchecked. In fact, if we do not consciously focus on structure and stability, and exert efforts to foster a sense of permanency, everything tends to fall apart. For example, a sculpture in marble may be destroyed over millennia by the incessant action of the elements, or in seconds by the careless brush of a coat sleeve. A thousand-year-old redwood tree may be weathered by the storms of centuries, or burn to the ground in hours. The city of Babylon took hundreds of years to build, and its hanging gardens were one of the seven wonders of the ancient world, but it is today only a dusty memory. Even the organization of words into coherent sentences or paragraphs, though etched in stone or sizzling in cyberspace, can be erased with one blow of a hammer, a single keystroke, or one swipe of a magnet over a computer disk.

Balance gives coherence to the behavioral sciences, as well. It explains why friendship can be devastated by an inconsiderate action or word, and how a life of moderation can be forfeit by one thoughtless act of indulgence in a moment of weakness. One glass of liquor can ruin a lifestyle of temperance, and yielding to the passion of the moment can negate the constructive efforts of a lifetime of chaste behavior. Testimony that has taken years to build can be destroyed through carelessness or inattention. The fiery darts of the adversary go hand-in-hand with the law of entropy (that dictates that everything tends to fall apart) that would destroy the balance that is so necessary in our lives.

Even though they may seem to be at odds, however, inasmuch as they come from opposite ends of the behavioral spectrum, the laws of entropy and eternal progression must ultimately be in balance with each other. In fact, it was ordained in heaven, and "must needs be, that there is an opposition in all things." (2 Nephi 2:11). A healthy juxtaposition between opposing points of view is necessary for the Plan of Salvation to work. The perfect understanding by Jesus Christ of the concept of balance allowed Him to create our world and pronounce His efforts "very good." (Genesis 1:31). The Law of Eternal Progression, to which He has bound Himself, rules supreme, but it is as much defined by its opposites in the physical universe as it is by itself. The presence of Satan in the Garden of Eden attests to that fact. (See Moses 4:6).

Since he operates more by subtraction than by addition, the adversary's program that tears down both individuals and relationships, prospers with deceit, deception, and fraud, and thrives on imbalance. He exults in instability. (See Exodus 12:23). We all remember the Hindu scripture, the Bhagavad-Gita, wherein Vishnu in his multi-armed form declares: "Now I am become Death, the destroyer of worlds." Perhaps this is why the natural man is an enemy to God, and has been from the beginning. Nevertheless, when our exercise of agency results in inequality, the disparity may simply be the representation of the manifestation of the natural consequences of imbalance. If this is so, its effects will be inevitable and inexorable unless the Author of Salvation, Who is the Maker and Fashioner of the Universe,. intervenes by utilizing higher laws that trump imbalance. As Paul perceptively explained to the Hebrews: "Ye have in heaven a better and an enduring substance." (Hebrews 10:34).

This may also help to explain the scope of the Savior's injunction: "Be ye, therefore, perfect, even as your Father in Heaven is perfect." (Matthew 5:48). His command may have been as much a statement of fact as it was a plea, an expression of hopeful anticipation, or a commandment. The Plan of Salvation has within its arsenal enough firepower for us to overcome instability in our lives, and then, unencumbered by the wobbly constraints of uncertainty, to move onward and upward along a steady course of eternal progress.

The gate may be strait, and the way narrow, but those who accept Christ as their Guide will find it within their reach to travel a path of progression by threading the eye of the needle and walking a fine line past the seemingly inexorable, unalterable, unavoidable, unrelenting, and unstoppable demands of disproportion. On the other hand, "broad is the gate, and wide the way that leadeth to the deaths, and many there are that go in threat," because they pursue a wavering course of unpredictability. (D&C 132:25). When individuals elect to ignore celestial law, that should be to them as a beacon penetrating the mists of darkness in a telestial world, they have tacitly chosen an alternative course leading to inevitable destruction that is the natural consequence of the operation of the immutable laws of physics that define imbalance, disorder, or entropy.

It is equilibrium in our lives that necessarily sets the stage for the exercise of moral agency and dictates the implementation of other equally important and co-existing laws. Mercy, in particular, exists to mitigate the otherwise inevitable consequences of lives that are out of balance, and through Atonement facilitates our journey of progress in both time and eternity. The principles that make up the Plan of Salvation are the ultimate expression of balance.

Only by incorporating these principles into the conduct of our lives can the disorder and destruction that result from imbalance be recognized, addressed, reversed, and erased with finality. While obedience nurtures the development of personality traits that are consistent with the symmetry of heaven, sin is harmful because it destroys our capacity to develop the steadiness that is representative of the Celestial Kingdom. Disorder takes the disobedient further and further from the influence of the Spirit, whose purpose it is to guide us away from the precipice of destruction to that more secure sanctuary that abides the stability of higher laws. Damnation results from activities that block the channels through which this spiritual power flows. It is the halt in our progression because of imbalance in our lives that is damning.

To counteract the consequences of sin, which is arguably the worst example of imbalance in our lives, our days have been "prolonged, according to the will of God, that (we) might repent while in the flesh; wherefore, (our) state (becomes) a state of probation, and (our) time (is) lengthened, according to the commandments which the Lord God gave unto the children of men. For he gave commandment that all men must repent; for he showed unto all men that they were lost," because of the unsteadiness that naturally followed Adam and Eve's introduction into the telestial world. (2 Nephi 2:21).

Ever since the Fall, Satan has enjoyed a free pass to mingle among the children of men. He is flushed with excitement because he knows how difficult it is for us to resist our natural tendency toward volatility. Many of us love Satan more than we love God, and when we do so, we unavoidably exhibit the behavioral manifestations of that misplaced adoration. Our inattention to celestial signposts carries us onto crooked paths of self-destructive and self-defeating behaviors. We become "carnal, sensual, and devilish." (Moses 5:13). Without the intervention of higher laws, our unbalanced lives point us toward inevitable and ultimate destruction.

The Lord has confidence, though, in our ability to use the blueprint He has provided to set our lives in order, and to bring our behavior into balance with celestial law, and so has He "called upon men by the Holy Ghost everywhere and command(s) them that they should repent." Through the Atonement, repentance becomes a celestial bridge that transports the righteous past the vicissitudes of life to the stability of a world that lies beyond. "And as many as believed in the Son, and repented of their sins, (were) saved" from the effects of slow destruction. (Moses 5:15). Our lives can be like a train wreck in slow motion, but it we follow the counsel of Jehovah, we can fast-forward that newsreel to bring our character into a state of balance and harmony with the Law of Eternal Progression, eventually becoming "heirs of God, and joint heirs with Christ." (Romans 8:17). When we heed the grand design of the Plan, opposition works to our benefit.

When we abide celestial law, the Spirit opens our eyes, "so as to see and understand the things of God, even those things which were from the beginning before the world was." (D&C 76:12-13). We will see things even more clearly when we escape the confining limitations of our mortal clay that now negatively focuses our attention on worldliness, the ultimate negative manifestations of entropy, and on the related unstable nature that denies the power of the Atonement. Too often, we are "like unto a man beholding his natural face in a glass." (James 1:23). We satisfy ourselves with a brief glimpse of salvation, without ever beholding our potential, or without ever breaking free of our enslavement to the upsetting laws of destructive behavior.

When we finally do see things as they really are, and our lives come into a state of equilibrium with a lucidity that comes more from the heart than from the head, perhaps we will better understand how someone like Helen Keller could have had such balance in her life. She wrote not from the shaky vantage point of severe physical impairment and limited sensory stimulation, but rather with steadiness and profound spiritual enlightenment: "I believe that no good shall be lost," she declared, "and that all man has willed or hoped or dreamed of good shall exist forever. I believe in the immortality of the soul because I have within me immortal longings. I believe that the state we enter after death is wrought of our own motives, thoughts, and deeds. I believe that my home there will be beautiful with colour, music, and speech of flowers and faces I love. Without this faith, there would be little meaning in my life. I should be a mere pillar of darkness in the dark. Observers in the full enjoyment of their bodily senses pity me, but it is because they do not see the golden chamber in my life where I dwell delighted; for dark as my path may seem to them, I carry a magic light in my heart. Faith, the spiritual strong searchlight, illuminates the way, and although sinister doubts lurk in the shadow, I walk unafraid towards the Enchanted Wood where the foliage is always green, where joy abides, where nightingales nest and sing, and where life and death are one in the presence of the Lord." ("Midstream").

Imbalance (entropy) in the temporal world that leads us from order to disorder suits the purposes of God as long as we are jarred out of our collective complacency by the created confusion. Remember that when He created the world, He pronounced it "good." When imbalance upsets the stagnation of the status quo, makes us think, gets our juices flowing, prods us to purposefully expend our energy, and constructively puts our agency to work, it will have served its purpose. Brigham Young taught: "The first principle that ought to occupy our attention, and which is the mainspring of all action is the principle of improvement," and this requires us to nurture a sense of balance in our lives, even as we deal with the vagaries of our temporal world, to bring order out of seeming pandemonium. ("Discourses of Brigham Young," p. 87).

Progress becomes the recompense for perseverance, salvation is the reward for surmounting obstacles, and the hope of eternal life is the blessing for enduring opposition. As we delicately balance our experiences, we become more comfortable with the perspective that confirms that gospel principles relating to the eternities can supersede physical laws that pertain only to the temporal world. When we enter into the covenants, something mystical and metaphysical happens. We are figuratively "born of God" and, although our feet are firmly planted on gospel sod, we ascend to dizzying heights without experiencing vertigo. (Mosiah 5:7). In a sense, we have become new creatures in Christ because we have been able to achieve perfect symmetry, oriented more to the laws of the eternal world and the guidance of the Master than to the limitations imposed by the physical world and the destructive effects of disproportion. (See 2 Corinthians 5:17). Our experience is inexplicable, and yet undeniable. "Whatsoever is born of God overcometh the (laws governing the physical) world." (1 John 5:3).

As we think about balance, Spencer W. Kimball's counsel rings with greater urgency. "So much depends upon our willingness to make up our minds, collectively and individually, that present levels of performance are not acceptable, either to ourselves or to the Lord. In saying that, I am not calling for flashy, temporary differences in our performance levels, but for a quiet resolve to lengthen our stride." ("Church News," 3/22/1975). He knew that our equilibrium would be enhanced if we would move forward with purpose.

He knew that the exertion caused by lengthening our stride would cause discomfort, as it stretched the limits of our stability in a violent confrontation that would tear at the very fabric of the natural world. But in doing so, he knew that we would find new spiritual strength. He knew that if we would go the second mile while doubling our stride, we would burst free of the shackles that had limited the expression of our potential, and we would receive "a gift of spiritual independence that would remove the veil of insensitivity from our destiny." (Richard L. Gunn, "A Search for Sensitivity and Spirit," p. 197). This independence would be exhilarating, because it would be accompanied by the recognition of soul-expanding opportunities. It would kindle within us the realization that we are spiritual beings having mortal experiences, and that the powers of heave would countermand the dizzying inequities of life.

Even though we mindlessly toil with blood, sweat, and tears, sacrificing even those things that are near and dear to us in order to obtain telestial treasures, at the end of the day the unevenness of the world can only deliver physical destruction, while steady obedience to the laws of the gospel creates the opportunity to progress eternally. If we nurture a one-dimensional view of the world that focuses on its cares, yielding to the things of the moment, if we lose our balance, we tend to fall into mischief. (See Proverbs 28:14). The gospel allows us to develop poise under provocation, and provides us with a multidimensional view of existence that nurtures an accurate and realistic milieu in which we may gain valuable experience.

Since many of us have not yet completed enough of the curriculum of the gospel to allow ourselves to be the successful architects of our own fate, we are commanded: "Give your language to exhortation continually." (D&C 23:7). "Let us not weary in well doing," wrote Paul. (Galatians 6:9). Because the world goes to such great lengths to throw us off balance, even those who are Born Again require constant and repetitive encouragement in their determination to steady the course and to progress eternally. Truly did Brigham Young believe, that: "All organized existence is in progress either to an endless advancement in eternal perfections, or back to dissolution. There is no period in all the eternities," he declared, "wherein organized existence will become stationary, that it cannot advance in knowledge, wisdom, power, and glory." (J.D. 1:349). When we are at a standstill, we are at risk of toppling over. We must maintain momentum in order to sustain our progress.

We cannot afford to sleep at our posts, to pause to rest on shaky ground, or to allow complacency to sweep us over the precipice of destruction. The gospel stimulates our capacity for affirmative, constructive, and purposeful action, in order to maintain our balance. It is a simple formula: The Lord strengthens and blesses us as we repent and keep the commandments, but not necessarily with telestial toys that might lead us on detours leading away from the steadiness of the strait and narrow path. Nor will He coddle us by making our way easy, lest we be pacified into a false sense of carnal security and lose our forward motion. The constant G-force exerted by the uphill path of progress very subtly counteracts and is in opposition to the downhill and negative effects of complacency that would otherwise result in a free-fall from faith, with disastrous consequences.

Balance is at the very heart of eternal laws that have the capacity to carry us beyond the conventional boundaries of our everyday world. Our five natural senses enable us to relate to our physical surroundings, and act as biological barometers that provide us with reliable measurements to gauge the pervasive and yet inexorable effects of imbalance that almost imperceptibly grind us down.

But gradually, it is our very subtle extrasensory perceptions that bring us to the realization that gospel principles relating to the eternities supersede physical laws governing the temporal universe, and that there may be a reconciliation between the two. When we are "born of God" our orientation is more to the expansive laws of the eternal world than to the restrictive confines of the physical world. When we are in harmony with the eternities, we are in a better state of balance. When we are "born of God (we) overcometh the world" with a freedom from incarceration to the inexorable immutability of the law of entropy. (1 John 5:3). This independence is incalculable, indescribable, and inexplicable, and yet it is undeniable. It is not maturational, but is generational, as we become "new creatures in Christ."

As the process unfolds and we learn to balance our lives, God subtly fortifies us, increasing our capacity to grow with opportunities to be anxiously engaged in good causes. He endows us with the ability to think, so that, on our own initiative, we can generate the power to avoid the conceptual cul-de-sacs and doctrinal roundabouts that would slow or stop our progress and cause us to tip over. He helps us work out our salvation with fear and trembling. He nudges us to move out of our comfort zones into the stimulating environment of service, the cathartic setting of sacrifice, and even onto the painful paths that lead to our own personal Gethsemanes. Socrates said: "Know thyself," Cicero admonished, "Control thyself," and Jesus taught by the greatest example of all, encouraging us to give ourselves completely and without reservation, bringing ourselves into a state of harmony and balance with Him and with the eternities.

The Savior exhorts us to drink copiously and unceasingly from the fountain of truth in order to slake our thirst for principles that gyroscopically orient us toward heaven. He understands the difference between celestial sureties that are represented by eternal progression, and telestial tendencies that are represented by physical laws such as entropy. "Great and marvelous are the works of the Lord," Jacob exclaimed. "How unsearchable are the depths of the mysteries of him; and it is impossible that man should find out all his ways. And no man knoweth of his ways save it be revealed unto him." (Jacob 4:8).

The wise counsel of our prophets of God provides balance in a world that has been confused by weights and measures that have been compromised by the adversary's tampering. Their counsel creates desire in our hearts to negotiate the difficult road to Gethsemane, past the Garden Tomb, and on into Celestial realms. It validates the promises made by our Father that the struggles of mortality would be worth every sacrifice, and that our experiences would be tailored to personal growth and development, as we are obedient to gospel principles. But only if the drama is played out within the context of the Everlasting Covenant, according to the rules established by the Plan of Salvation, can we achieve the balance necessary to receive the anticipated blessings. There has never been another way, nor will there ever be. Only the bedrock of the gospel can provide the footing to restore equilibrium in our lives, provide the stability we so desperately need in an uncertain world, steady the helm as we navigate through treacherous waters, and give us the poise and composure of truly balanced lives.

Today, we must be especially vigilant, and avoid enticements that rivet our attention, consume our energies, and demand our devotion. Sitting with the engine idling while wasting time in telestial traffic jams can damage our capacity and desire to move forward. We must avoid looking beyond the mark or getting sidetracked by doctrinal detours. Our destination is well-defined, and if we only half-heartedly seek truth, it is because our instability causes us to confuse knowledge for intelligence, and think that when we are learned we are wise. We must never fail to understand that to be learned is good, but only if we will hearken unto the counsels of God. The lesson of balance is one that taken to heart kindles faith, protects testimony, and even saves souls.

FOCUS

"If I have ever made any
valuable discoveries, it has been
owing more to patient attention
than to any other talent."
(Sir Isaac Newton).

"We desire to know
the cause of your thoughtless
state. Can you think to sit upon your
thrones in a state of thoughtless stupor?"
(Alma 60:6-7).

While they drew, a kindergarten teacher walked up and down the rows in her classroom of children, observing their work. She stopped at the desk of one little girl and asked what her drawing was. The girl replied, "I'm drawing a picture of God." The teacher paused, and then said, "But no one knows what God looks like." Without missing a beat or looking up from her paper, the girl replied, "They will in a minute." Though tender in years, this child had what we might call "focus."

What is focus? The Savior explained, "the Spirit giveth light to every man that cometh into the world; and the Spirit enlighteneth every man through the world, that hearkeneth to the voice of the Spirit." (D&C 84:46). God has endowed our minds with the ability to resonate with recognition when they encounter truth, and to concentrate on matters of importance, so that ultimately "every one that hearkeneth to the voice of the Spirit (will eventually come) unto God, even the Father." (D&C 84:47). As Helen Keller asked: "Why cannot the soul discard the poor lenses of the body, and peer through the telescope of truth into the infinite reaches of immortality" with an eternal focus? ("My Religion," p. 76).

Focus is the ability to block out the trivial so that every worthy goal is within our reach. When enlightenment by the spirit flows, we experience one of the purest forms of focus. Sensory input from the five natural senses is transformed by the spiritual sixth sense, which then unconsciously orders a hierarchy of value. When we have been conditioned through discipline, diligence, faith, and patience, the most valuable information receives the highest priority and is given immediate attention. We then draw upon all our physical resources to address those concerns of greatest importance. But of those who are preoccupied with telestial trivia, and who squander the enlightenment so freely given and yet so casually and superficially received, the Lord warned: "Wo unto him ... that wasteth the days of his probation, for awful is his state!" (2 Nephi 9:27). Particularly when individuals groan "under darkness and under the bondage of sin," they grope about in a frantic and yet fruitless search for meaning, stability, and focus in their lives. (D&C 84:49).

If we ignore this innate urge to focus, and instead allow ourselves to be habitually distracted by trivial concerns, we sin by omission and risk settling for a life in a "second-class hotel" of our own making. There is, after all, "a tide in the affairs of men, which, taken at the flood, leads on to fortune. Omitted, all the voyage of their life is bound in shallows and in miseries." (Shakespeare, Brutus, in "Julius Caesar," Act 4, Scene 2). "How carefully most men creep into nameless graves, while now and again one or two forget themselves into immortality." (Wendell Phillips, "Speech on Lovejoy").

At a basic level, sin is the inability to focus. it is waste. "It is doing one thing when you should be doing other and better things for which you have the capacity." For example, "why do people feel guilty about T.V.? What is wrong with it? Just this - that it shuts out all the wonderful things of which the mind is capable, leaving it drugged in a state of thoughtless stupor." For the same reasons, "God is not pleased with us for merely sitting in meetings, unfocused on the proceedings. (Hugh Nibley, "Zeal Without Knowledge," p. 264-265). "How vain and trifling have been our spirits, our conferences, our councils, our meetings, our private as well as public conversations," wrote the Prophet Joseph Smith from Liberty Jail. "Too low, too mean, too vulgar, too condescending (too unfocused) for the dignified characters called and chosen of God." (Lucy Mack Smith, "History of Joseph Smith," p. 55).

When Captain Moroni addressed the great neglect of the government officials of his day, he asked: "Can you think to sit upon your thrones in a state of thoughtless stupor, while your enemies are spreading the work of death around you?" (Alma 60:6-7). These bureaucrats had lost their focus, and the temporal and spiritual welfare of the citizens of their society hung in the balance. Heaven seems to hold its breath while waiting upon our initiative.

Society always pays the price for the lack of focus of its policy makers. For example, when spiritual equilibrium is lost, values are often adjusted to bring it back into what is thought to be a state of balance. When gods of wood and stone are worshipped, it is justified as multiculturalism. If perversion is embraced, it is legitimized as an alternative lifestyle. The poor are exploited in the name of government-sponsored lotteries. Unborn children are killed, and the collective conscience is soothed by calling it pro-choice. Power is abused in the name of progressivism. When the media is polluted with obscenities, it is characterized as freedom of expression. The target has been moved so many times that we think we are scoring repetitive bulls-eyes, when in reality the arrows have strayed far from the mark.

Individuals lose their focus gradually, just as they lose their eyesight over time. First they squint, and then they hold the page a little closer or a little farther away. They compensate for their inability to see clearly, whether it is the printed page or their character that they can't read or that is being unconsciously compromised. Church members don't intend to lose their testimonies. Conviction just fades away like a slow leak from an automobile tire, and not as a sudden blowout, and it can all be traced back to a lack of focus that began at a specific point in time.

Focused individuals know that persistence prevails when all else fails. When they hear their team yell "Take the shot!" they move decisively and confidently, visualizing success. They know that they will miss 100% of the shots they don't take, and so they don't hesitate when an opportunity presents itself. Then they mechanically re-play the moves that have aforetime been repeatedly pre-played in their mind's eye. They have envisioned success so many times before the shot is actually taken, that the conclusion is foregone. It is their destiny to succeed, and to believe otherwise would be unthinkable. Those with focus concentrate on what they want to have happen, while the distracted are fixated on what they don't want to have happen. Those with focus work through their problems, instead of working around them. They find mentors to emulate, instead of scapegoats to blame. They look for better solutions, instead of easier ways. When they make mistakes, they readily acknowledge them, instead of shifting the blame to others. In pressure situations, they remember previous victories, instead of past defeats. They realize that while they cannot go back and start a new beginning, they can always redouble their efforts to make a new ending. They have confidence in their ability to create self-fulfilling prophecies. They believe their lives are "fairy tales waiting to be written by the hand of God." (Hans Christian Anderson).

The problem with those who lack focus is not that their expectations are too high, and they fail to attain them. It is that they set their goals too low, and too easily accomplish them. Someone once said that the Lord gave us two ends: one to think with and the other to sit on. Which one we use will determine how well we do in life. in other words, "heads you win, tails you lose."

Good intentions may be noble, but focused achievement is the hallmark of progress. Several of the prophets have been fond of saying: "Work without vision is drudgery, and vision without work is dreamery, but work with vision is destiny!" Spiritual enlightenment gives focused individuals the ability to work with vision. When Paul urged the Philippian Saints to "work out (their) salvation with fear and trembling," he knew that if they put their hearts and souls into the effort, the reward would leave them both physically and spiritually exhausted. (Philippians 2:12). Nevertheless, he told them: "I press toward the mark for the prize of the high calling of God in Christ Jesus." (Philippians 3:14). Sticking to a task often determines our success. It was Dr. George Brimhall who observed that the usefulness of the postage stamp "lies in its ability to stick with something until it reaches its destination."

With eternal perspective, focused individuals push themselves beyond their normal capacity. Spencer W. Kimball said: "So much depends upon our willingness to make up our minds, both individually and collectively, that present levels of performance are not acceptable, either to ourselves or to the Lord. In saying that, I am not calling for flashy, temporary differences in our performance levels, but (for) a quiet resolve to lengthen our stride." ("Church News," 3/22/1975).

At another time, he said: "We have paused on some plateaus long enough. Let us resume our journey forward and upward. Let us quietly end our reluctance to reach out to others, whether in our own families, wards, or neighborhoods. We have been diverted, at times, from fundamentals on which we must now focus in order to move forward." (C.R., 4/1979).

Even after months in Liberty Jail under the most trying circumstances, Joseph Smith maintained his focus. He wrote the Saints that if they would concentrate on charity and if they would be occupied by virtuous thoughts, their confidence would soar in the presence of God, and they would receive personal revelation concerning the doctrine of the priesthood. Their righteous power and authority would be uncontested and unchallenged, their dominion would be everlasting, and by eternal decree it would flow unto them forever. (See D&C 121:45-46)

Those who maintain their focus don't get in the thick of thin things. They have developed an equilibrium that is centered far above the plain of the ego-filled minds of mediocre men, and are thereby insulated from the tumult, confusion, and cares of the world. They have "a firmness unshaken." (Mormon 9:28).

Focused individuals are never led into a false sense of carnal security and complacency. They view their weaknesses in positively constructive ways, and are grateful for their conscious awareness of opportunities for personal improvement. Because they know that weaknesses are part of the tapestry woven into every human condition, they simply maintain an inventory of thread to weave new patterns into the fabric. Joseph Smith acknowledged his youthful weakness, saying: "I was left to all kinds of temptations, and, mingling with all kinds of society, I frequently fell into many foolish errors, and displayed the weakness of youth, and the foibles of human nature; which, I am sorry to say, led me into diverse temptations, offensive in the sight of God ... I was guilty of levity, and sometimes associated with jovial company." (J.S.H. 1:28). in consequence of this lack of focus, he often felt condemned. Concentrating his efforts and attention, however, he sought "Almighty God for forgiveness of all (his) sins and follies, and also for a manifestation," that he might know of his standing before Him. (J.S.H. 1:29). We catch a glimpse of the prophetic mantle that had already fallen upon him when he then declared: "I had full confidence in obtaining a divine manifestation." (J.S.H. 1:29). He had regained his focus. He had seen an island of opportunity in the middle of an ocean of difficulty. He had mustered up an abundance of "will power," unlike those timid souls who operate below their potential and who have plenty of "won't power" that saps whatever energy they may have possessed. Some of us see things as they are, and ask "Why?" Focused individuals dream things that never were, and ask "Why not?"

Brigham Young taught: "The first principle that ought to occupy the attention of all mankind, and which is the mainspring of all action, is the principle of improvement." ("Discourses of Brigham Young," p. 87). Focused individuals constantly strive to do more, to be better, to seek knowledge and wisdom. They emulate the Olympic motto "Citius, Altius, Fortius," or "Faster, Higher, Stronger." They have a firm conviction in the promise of the Lord: "If thou shalt ask, thou shalt receive revelation upon revelation, knowledge upon knowledge that thou mayest know the mysteries and peaceable things - that which bringeth joy, that which bringeth life eternal. (D&C 42:61).

Obstacles are those frightful things we see when we take our minds off our goals. They loom large with an and gratuitous significance. Focus gives us the vision to see beyond potential stumbling blocks and then creativity to turn them into stepping-stones that pave the way to higher achievement. It allows us to see things as they could be, and then to work with all our means to create that reality. "Desire generates power, for a mind once stretched by a new idea never returns to its original dimension." (Oliver Wendell Holmes). Among the greatest virtues we can possess are a well-trained mind, a body to match, and a love of achievement. Without these, we are old before our time.

Focused individuals look in the mirror every morning and say: "This is the beginning of a new day. God has given me this day to use, as I will. I can waste it or use it for good. What I do today is very important, because I am exchanging 24 hours of my life for it. When tomorrow comes, this day will be gone forever, leaving something in its place that I have traded for it. I want it to be gain, not loss; good, not evil; success, not failure, in order that it shall be worth the price I paid for it." (Anonymous). Along the way, focused individuals use what talents they possess, knowing that the woods would be very quiet if no birds sang except those that sang best.

Focused individuals recognize that "religion is more involved in recovery than discovery, (and) that our destiny is not union with Divine realities, but reunion." (B.H. Robert, "The Way, The Truth, and The Life"). "This recognition explains the Prophet's classic statement on religious knowing. Whether written, spoken, or directly presented within, the word of Jehovah has such an influence over the human mind, the logical mind, that it is convincing without other testimony. When it comes as a flow of pure intelligence attended by a burning in the center self, it is of God. Our search for external warrant is really the confirmation and application of what is already, and more certainly, known." (Truman Madsen, "Eternal Man," p. 73, see "Teachings," p. 151).

When individuals have been introduced to noble principles, they are fortunate indeed if their strength of character molds and shapes them in harmony with those ideals. As Spencer W. Kimball once stated: "Every gospel principle carries within it a witness that it is true." ("Ensign," 11/1978, p. 104). In the economy of the gospel, "we often catch a spark from the awakened memories of the immortal soul, which lights up our whole being as with the glory of our former home." (Joseph F. Smith, "Gospel Doctrine," p. 14). This focus allows us to understand that "ideals are like stars. We will not succeed in touching them with our hands. But like the seafaring man in the desert of waters, we choose them as our guides, and following them we will reach our destiny." (Carl Shurz, "B.Y.U. Studies," 16:4, p. 499). Focused individuals are like the child who, when asked what he wanted to be when he grew up, replied in one word: "Obedient." Though tender in years, he had already tasted the sweetness of consistency with his convictions. Some learn while still in their youth, while others are taught through the school of hard knocks about the importance of focus. Sooner or later, though, we all respond to internal promptings and external encouragement. The celestial compass of gospel principles founded on truth is always available to guide disciplined and focused travelers to safe haven at the day of reckoning. It is also there for those who have lost their way, to bring them back to the fold of the Good Shepherd. All will come to understand that the commandments are like the recipe for making a cake. If you want to enjoy the cake, you have to follow the recipe. In heaven, however, there is only one kind of cake served. In the meantime, as Neal A. Maxwell cautioned: "Through ethical relativism, the human race is led into conceptual cul-de-sacs that could entice us to plunge into a freedom which is a bottomless, dark pool of misery."

"Two forces are operating, two voices are calling, one coming out from the swamps of selfishness and force, where success means death, and the other from the hilltops of justice and progress, where even failure brings glory. Two lights are seen on your horizon, one, the last fading marsh light of power, and the other the slowly rising sun of human brotherhood. Two ways lie open for you, one leading to an ever lower and lower plane, where are heard the cries of despair and the curses of the poor, where manhood shrivels and possessions rot down the possessor, and the other leading to the highlands of the morning, where are heard the glad shouts of humanity, and where honest effort is rewarded with immortality." (John P. Altgeld).

Focused individuals trust their instincts. Marvin J. Ashton once said: "A good mission president gets missionaries to trust him. A great mission president gets missionaries to trust themselves." Loren C. Dunn described how his father, a busy stake president, gave his two young sons the responsibility of raising cows on the family farm. He gave the boys wide latitude in what they could do, and they made some mistakes. These were observed by an alert neighbor, who complained to their father. Brother Dunn replied to his concerns, saying: "Jim, you don't understand. You see, I'm raising boys, not cows." ("B.Y.U. Fireside," 5/4/1982).

The best teachers help their students to focus, to get along on their own. They are helped to deepen their own insights and not necessarily to alter their present views. Those who deliver dynamic addresses have learned how to focus, reading themselves full, thinking themselves straight, praying themselves hot, and letting themselves go! B.H. Robert knew how to focus. He advised to "pray, study, think, get prepared, and then let nature caper." He once delivered a sermon in which he "described Christ and the raising of Lazarus. So vivid were his images, and so moving his presence that the audience was carried with him. When, in a loud voice, he repeated the Master's words, 'Lazarus, come forth!' the entire congregation involuntarily came to its feet." (Truman Madsen, "Defender of The Faith," p. 355). These people were focused.

Focused individuals understand and know how to worship and what to worship, for "truth, as well as untruth, may be recognized by its effects. Rendering obedience to its principles of action may test the claims of the gospel. Practicing our religion is the most direct method of gaining a testimony of the truth." (John Widtsoe, "Evidences and Reconciliations"). This is why missionaries since the days of Alma have encouraged those who are seeking truth to focus on "the virtue of the word of God." (Alma 31:5).

Members of the church who are not focused on Jesus Christ will miss the mark. Bruce R. McConkie was, arguably, one of the most focused of the Latter-day Apostles of the Lord. On one occasion, he said: "It is my pattern and custom simply to teach and testify. I do not debate, and I do not argue. If someone wants to contend to the contrary, he is just as welcome as the day is long to do so. But let us understand this. When we deal with God and His laws, when we get in the realm of spiritual things, we are dealing with the things that save souls, and at our peril we are obligated to find the truth. The whole sectarian world sits out there, and they suppose that they have some truth and that they are pursuing a course that will save them. But God has restored the everlasting gospel to us. We have the power of God unto salvation in our hands, as it were. It is our obligation to come to an understanding of what is involved so that we can live in such a manner that the fulness of these blessings and rewards will come to us." ("B.Y.U. Devotional," 1/4/1972). We can do this if we maintain our focus.

If we are to successfully free
outselves from the quicksands
of self-pity and escape the inequalities
of life, we must personalize the lessons of
the Atonement. We must change our nature
and become new creatures in Christ. We must
practice in front of a mirror, if necessary,
and recite over and over again until we
get it right: "Father forgive them,
for they know not what they
do." We must become
more Amish.

Follow the Prophet

"When the Jews heard these things,
they were angry with (Lehi); yea, even
as with the prophets of old, whom they had
cast out, and stoned, and slain; and they also
sought his life, that they might take it away. But
behold, I, Nephi, will show unto you the tender
mercies of the Lord are over all those whom
he hath chosen, because of their faith,
to make them mighty even unto
the power of deliverance."
(1 Nephi 1:20).

The People of Ammon have become a role model for the Saints because after they had established themselves in the Land of Jershon, their trust in the Lord and commitment to their covenants grew to be so powerful that they became the humble recipients of many marvelous blessings. In the Last Days, the prophets of the Lord have made similar promises to every nation that finds itself in circumstances reminiscent of the People of Ammon.

In 1990 and 1991, the world saw the "evil empire" of communism crumble and turn to dust. Perhaps the seeds of its demise were actually sown in the humanitarian acts of its own leaders in the 1970s and 1980s, when they permitted The Church of Jesus Christ of Latter-day Saints to build a temple in East Germany and to allow missionary activity to commence behind the Iron Curtain.

Perhaps too, the inspired counsel of the Prophet to members of the church from Eastern Block countries facilitated change. In 1973, I attended the Second Area Conference of The Church, in Munich, Germany. Seven hundred Saints from the German Democratic Republic (East Germany) had been permitted by their government to cross the Iron Curtain to attend the Conference. Some of these Saints might have seen this trip to the West as an opportunity to escape the tyranny and repression of their native land. Some might have made elaborate plans to defect while attending the Conference. The excitement of Conference might have been heightened by the anticipation of their personal freedom after its close.

But then, in his concluding remarks at the end of the final session on Sunday afternoon, President Harold B. Lee said something like this: "And now we want to caution those Saints from certain countries whose governments have given them special permission to attend this Conference. We want to counsel the Saints to honor their word and to be true to the trust placed in them. Think of the precedent that might be set and the damage done to the spirit of co-operation if you were to betray this trust. Remember the 12th Article of Faith. 'We believe in being subject to kings, presidents, rulers, and magistrates, in obeying, honoring, and sustaining the law.' So, I counsel you to thank the Lord for the privilege of attending this Conference and then return to your homes."

Many in the church find it easy to "Follow the Prophet" on well traveled avenues dotted with conveniently located sidewalk cafes, and on brightly lighted world stages filled with appreciative applause and laudatory comments. But if we were placed in the setting just described, with no- one looking, and no positive peer pressures to sustain correct choices, would you or I have the strength to do so?

"Our lives are but a weaving between ourselves and the Lord. We cannot choose the colors, but He knows what they should be. Oft-times He weaves sorrow, and we in foolish pride, forget that He sees the upper, and we the under side. Not 'til the loom is silent, and the shuttles cease to fly, shall God unroll the canvas and explain the reason why. The dark threads are as needful in the Weaver's skillful hand, as the threads of gold and silver in the pattern He has planned. He knows, He loves, He cares; nothing this truth can dim. He gives the very best to those who leave the choice to Him." (Benjamin Malachi Franklin).

Forgiveness

"If ye forgive men their trespasses, your Heavenly Father will also forgive you." (3 Nephi 13:14).

How can we know if we have received forgiveness of our sins? Mormon identified three key factors in Mosiah 5:2-4.

"And now, it came to pass that when king Benjamin had thus spoken to his people, he sent among them, desiring to know of his people if they believed the words which he had spoken unto them. And they all cried with one voice, saying: Yea, we believe all the words which thou hast spoken unto us; and also, we know of their surety and truth, because of the Spirit of the Lord Omnipotent, which has wrought a mighty change in us, or in our hearts, that we have no more disposition to do evil, but to do good continually. And we, ourselves, also, through the infinite goodness of God, and the manifestations of his Spirit, have great views of that which is to come; and were it expedient, we could prophesy of all things. And it is the faith which we have had on the things which our king has spoken unto us that has brought us to this great knowledge, whereby we do rejoice with such exceedingly great joy." (Mosiah 5:1-4).

First, the Spirit of the Lord comes upon us.

When we have His spirit, our lives are dramatically quickened, and we are as white-hot sparks struck off the divine anvil of God. When His spirit envelops our lives, and they are in harmony with God's purposes, they can become sacramental. "I said to the man who stood at the gate of the year, 'Give me a light, that I may tread safely into the unknown.' And he replied, 'Go out into the darkness, and put your hand in the hand of God. That shall be to you better than a light, and safer than the known way.' (Minnie Haskins, "A Dialogue Between a Man, and the Keeper of The Gate of The Year").

Secondly, we feel a mighty change in our hearts, and we are filled with joy.

The people understood Benjamin when he told them:" "For behold, this day he hath spiritually begotten you; for ye say that your hearts are changed through faith on his name; therefore, ye are born of him and have become his sons and his daughters." (Mosiah 5:7).

Lehi had taught: "Adam fell that men might be, and men are that they might have joy." (2 Nephi 2:25). This is one of the basic messages of the Restoration. When the Fall of Adam is considered in conjunction with the Atonement of Christ, it is clear that both are part of God's Plan of Eternal Progression for man and that its intended goal is our happiness. In fact, Joseph Smith said: "Happiness is the object and design of our existence and will be the end thereof, if we pursue the path that leads to it; and this path is virtue, uprightness, faithfulness, holiness, and keeping all the commandments of God." (Teachings, p. 255). "For man is spirit, the elements are eternal, and spirit and element, inseparably connected" through obedience to the principles of the gospel "receive a fulness of joy." (D&C 93:33).

Lastly, we have no more disposition to do evil, but to do good continually. We have peace of conscience.

The desired result of all gospel-oriented teaching has been achieved when a mighty change had been wrought in the hearts of the disciples of Christ, and their dispositions have changed. They had the spirit of prophecy, the testimony of Jesus, and great knowledge of the mysteries, gained by personal revelation. They have been born again, not by maturation, but by generation. As Paul wrote: "If any man be in Christ, he is a new creature: old things are passed away; behold, all things are become new." (2 Corinthians 5:7). Joseph Smith showed us the way in his last hours of mortality, when he was able to declare: "I have a conscience void of offense towards God, and towards all men." (D&C 135:5).

For Unto Us a Child Is Born

"Unto us a child is born, unto us
a son is given; and the government
shall be upon his shoulder; and his name
shall be called, Wonderful, Counselor,
the Mighty God, the Everlasting
Father, the Prince of Peace."
(2 Nephi 19:6).

These names are all indicative of His service to mankind. Isaiah called the Savior "The Prince of Peace," but His mission was not to bring peace to the earth. "Think not that I am come to send peace on earth," He warned, "I came not to send peace, but a sword." (Matthew 10:34). in fact: "There was a division among the people because of him." (John 7:43). J. Reuben Clark, Jr. taught: "The peace He proclaimed was the peace of everlasting righteousness which is the eternal enemy of sin. Righteousness is peace wherever it abides." (C.R., 4/1939).

One reason Jesus Christ is called the Everlasting Father is because there is no end to the authority of His priesthood. (Isaiah 9:6). He sits upon the throne of David, the prophesied lineage through which the Messiah would come. There, He will establish His kingdom with justice and righteousness. By His determination, "the Lord of Hosts will perform this." (Isaiah 9:7).

Around 600 B.C. Nephi had foreseen the birth of the Savior. Faith precedes the miracle, and signs follow them that believe. He had written that he "was desirous also that (he) might see, and hear, and know of these things, by the power of the Holy Ghost, which is the gift of God unto all those who diligently seek him." (1 Nephi 10:17). Of his companionship with the Holy Ghost, Nephi wrote: "I spake unto him as a man speaketh; for I beheld that he was in the form of a man; yet nevertheless, I knew that it was the Spirit of the Lord; and he spake unto me as a man speaketh with another." (1 Nephi 11:11). The vision that Nephi then beheld concerned the birth of the Savior and compliments the Christmas story found in the New Testament. The Spirit explained to Nephi: "Behold, the virgin whom thou seest is the mother of the Son of God ... And I looked and beheld the virgin again, bearing a child in her arms. And the angel said unto me: Behold the Lamb of God, yea, even the Son of the Eternal Father!" (1 Nephi 11:18-21). When he received this vision, Nephi was commanded that he should afterward stand as a witness of the Savior and "bear record that it is the Son of God." (1 Nephi 11:7).

Little wonder, then, that he later wrote: "We talk of Christ, we rejoice in Christ, we preach of Christ, we prophesy of Christ, and we write according to our prophecies, that our children may know to what source they may look for a remission of their sins." (2 Nephi 25:26). Perhaps recalling the chilly reception his own father had received from the Jews at Jerusalem, Nephi hoped that his own children would "hearken unto the words of the prophets, and destroy them not, but look forward unto Christ with steadfastness for the signs which are given, notwithstanding all persecution - behold, they are they which shall not perish. But the son of righteousness shall appear unto them; and he shall heal them, and they shall have peace with him." (2 Nephi 26:8-9).

Around 30 B.C., Helaman exhorted his own sons Lehi and Nephi: "The Lord surely should come to redeem his people, but ... he should not come to redeem them in their sins, but to redeem them from their sins. And he hath power given unto him from the Father to redeem them from their sins because of repentance." (Helaman 5:10-11). He knew "it is upon the rock of our Redeemer, who is Christ, the Son of God, that (we) must build (our) foundation." (Helaman 5:12). If we follow His counsel, we will not be dragged down to misery and a gulf of endless wo by the enticements of the devil represented by the sectarian philosophies and false theories of men that are continually sweeping over the earth.

Then, the Lord Himself announced His own birth. To the Nephites, He revealed: "On the morrow come I into the world, to show unto the world that I will fulfil all that which I have caused to be spoken by the mouth of my holy prophets." (3 Nephi 1:13). Thirty-three years later, he confirmed: "I came into the world to do the will of my Father, because my Father sent me. And my Father sent me that I might be lifted up upon the cross; and after that I had been lifted up upon the cross, that I might draw all men unto me, that as I have been lifted up by men even so should men be lifted up by the Father, to stand before me, to be judged of their works, whether they be good or whether they be evil." (3 Nephi 27:13-14).

Joseph Smith testified that He "came into the world, even Jesus, to be crucified for the world, and to bear the sins of the world, and to sanctify the world, and to cleanse it from all unrighteousness; That through him all might be saved whom the Father had put into his power and made by him." (D&C 76:40-42). Restored through the instrumentality of Joseph Smith, The Church of Jesus Christ of Latter-day Saints has the most profound tutorial message the world could possibly receive. "For since by man came death, by man came also the resurrection of the dead. For as in Adam all die, even so in Christ shall all be made alive." (1 Corinthians 15:21-22). To those of us who did not see the babe lying in the manger, it matters not that we lived before or following His ministry, for the promise of faith and hope is the same.

(The Importance of) Friends

"My father hath been slain in battle,
and all my kinsfolk, and I have not
friends nor whither to go; and how
long the Lord will suffer that
I may live, I know not."
(Mormon 8:5).

Some of the qualities we look for in friends are charity, honesty, integrity, kindness, and unselfishness. True friends would never think to contribute to our delinquency, hardship, or misery. They would rather leave us better than when they found us.

We read in the Old Testament that after David killed Goliath in the Valley of Elah, he quickly became a hero in Israel. He was on the cover of People Magazine, Muscle Magazine, Outside Magazine, and nearly every tabloid at the newsstand. He made the rounds of all the late-night talk shows, was on The Voice, made book deals with the major publishing houses, entered into negotiations for the rights to a TV Movie, and signed product endorsements with Power Bar, Monster Energy, Muscle Milk, and Red Bull. The exclusive photos of the battle went viral on the Internet, Instagram, and Reels. David had thousands of followers on Twitter, and David Action Figures flew off the shelves at Toys R Us.

Initially, King Saul and all Israel honored him, as well. In particular, it is interesting to read about how Jonathan (King Saul's son) felt about David. Remember, that while David was greatly honored by the people as a war hero, Jonathan received little attention for his own success on the battlefield. Nevertheless, "the soul of Jonathan was knit with the soul of David, and Jonathan loved him as his own soul." (1 Samuel 18:1). Jonathan gave his royal robe and weapons to David: "And Jonathan stripped himself of the robe that was upon him, and gave it to David, and his garments, even to his sword, and to his bow, and to his girdle." (1 Samuel 18:4)

It would have been easy for Jonathan to feel jealous of David. As Saul's son, Jonathan was next in line to be king. However, the prophet Samuel had anointed David to become the next king. "Then Samuel took the horn of oil, anointed him in the midst of his brethren: and the Spirit of the Lord came upon David from that day forward." (1 Samuel 16:13).

After David's slew Goliath, Saul took David into his home and set him over his armies. "And David went out whithersoever Saul sent him, and behaved himself wisely." He was self-deprecating, self-effacing, and spiritually sensitive. "And Saul set him over the men of war, and he was accepted in the sight of all the people, and also in the sight of Saul's servants." (1 Samuel 18:5).

Nevertheless, Saul turned against David. After all, it had been David, and not Saul, who had been invited to appear on Larry King Live, and on The Tonight Show. It had been David who had received the royalties from product endorsements. Professional jealousy became a determining factor in their relationship.

Remember, the magic of Camelot was that King Arthur had a round table constructed for his Royal Court. So too, Ammon's influence in the court of King Lamoni had been his humility. "Where is this man that has such great power?" King Lamoni had asked. "And they said unto him, Behold, he is feeding thy horses." (Alma 18:8-9). So much for self-aggrandizement.

"And it came to pass as they came, when David was returned from the slaughter of the Philistine, that the women came out of all cities of Israel, singing and dancing, to meet king Saul, with tabrets, with joy, and with instruments of musick. And the women answered one another as they played, and said Saul hath slain his thousands, and David his ten thousands. And Saul was very wroth, and the saying displeased him; and he said, They have ascribed unto David ten thousand, and to me they have ascribed but thousands: and what can he have more but the kingdom? And Saul eyed David from that day and forward." (1 Samuel 18:6-9).

Sometimes, it is difficult to be happy about the success of others. We think that if someone else is recognized for their achievements, it will diminish us. Your "A" will overshadow my "B." Your church calling is more significant than mine. Your mission assignment is more glamorous than mine. You seem to have many talents, and I have so few. You're a stud-muffin and I'm such a geek. Your car is way cooler than my beater. Your degree, your education, your job, your experiences, your opportunities, your luck, your house, your kids, your vacations. It will never, ever end, if you have allowed yourself to compose a list.

Jealousy and pride are seductively effective satanic tools designed to negatively influence our spiritual well-being. "When pride has a hold on our hearts, we lose our independence of the world and deliver our freedoms to the bondage of men's judgment." (Ezra Taft Benson). In a shouting contest, or even in a popularity contest, the world will always prevail over the Spirit.

Jonathan was a true friend when his father Saul ultimately sought to kill David. His example forces us to ask ourselves: "What do we do today, when evil influences attack and erode the spiritual independence of our friends, and we see them brought down into the bondage of men's judgments?"

"Jonathan spake good of David unto Saul his father, and said unto him, Let not the king sin against his servant, against David; because he hath not sinned against thee, and because his works have been to thee-ward very good: For he did put his life in his hand, and slew the Philistine, and the Lord wrought a great salvation for all Israel: thou sawest it, and didst rejoice: wherefore then wilt thou sin against innocent blood, to slay David without a cause?" (1 Samuel 19:4-5).

There was a divine principle at the foundation of the friendship between Jonathan and David. "Behold, the Lord be between thee and me for ever," declared Jonathan. (1 Samuel 20:23). Likewise, in The Book of Mormon record, did Alma "rejoice exceedingly to see his brethren, and what added more to his joy, they were still his brethren in the Lord; yea, and they had waxed strong in the knowledge of the truth; for they were men of a sound understanding and they had searched the scriptures diligently, that they might know the word of God." (Alma 17:2).

Joseph Smith reflected the same qualities of friendship that had been exhibited by Jonathan, when he declared: "I salute you in the name of the Lord Jesus Christ, in token or remembrance of the everlasting covenant, in which covenant I receive you to fellowship, in a determination that is fixed, immovable, and unchangeable, to be your friend and brother through the grace of God in the bonds of love, to walk in all the commandments of God blameless, in thanksgiving, forever and ever. Amen." (D&C 88:133).

Joseph Smith reflected the same qualities
of friendship that had been exhibited by Jonathan, when
he declared: "I salute you in the name of the Lord Jesus Christ,
in token or remembrance of the everlasting covenant, in which
covenant I receive you to fellowship, in a determination that is
fixed, immovable, and unchangeable, to be your friend
and brother through the grace of God in the bonds
of love, to walk in all the commandments of
God blameless, in thanksgiving,
forever and ever. Amen."

(D&C 88:133).

Friendship

"They did walk after the commandments
which they had received from their Lord and their God,
continuing in fasting and prayer, and in meeting together
oft both to pray and to hear the word of the Lord. And it came to
pass that there was no contention in the land, because of the love
of God which did dwell in the hearts of the people ... and surely
there could not be a happier people among all the people who
had been created by the hand of God ... neither were there
Lamanites, nor any manner of -ites; but they
were in one, the children of Christ, and
heirs to the kingdom of God.
(4 Nephi 15-17).

"Twas an evening in October, I'll confess I wasn't sober, I was carting home a load with manly pride, when my feet began to stutter, and I fell into the gutter, and a pig came up and lay down by my side. Then I lay there in the gutter and my heart was all a-flutter, 'til a lady, passing by, did chance to say: 'You can tell a man that boozes by the company he chooses.' Then the pig got up and slowly walked away." (Benjamin Burt).

When he was yet "very tender in years, Joseph Smith was "persecuted by those who ought to have been (his) friends and to have treated (him) kindly." Many years later, he recalled "if they supposed me to be deluded (they ought) to have endeavored in a proper and affectionate manner to have reclaimed me." But it was not to be. Alone to face the world, he said "I was left to all kinds of temptations; and mingling with all kinds of society, I frequently fell into many foolish errors, and displayed the weakness of youth, and the foibles of human nature, which I am sorry to say, led me into divers temptations, offensive in the sight of God." (J.S.H. 1:28).

Truer friends should not behave so carelessly. They should make every effort to sustain our strengths, and support us in our efforts to improve ourselves. They should be mirrors on our soul by reflecting our very best qualities. They should strive to bring out the best in us by accentuating our positive qualities and turning a blind eye to our imperfections. They should leave us better than when they found us.

In The Book of Mormon, we are introduced to a man who would have a profound effect upon the fortunes of the Nephite people for hundreds of years, and one who impressed Mormon greatly. "His name was Moroni." (Alma 43:16). He was a man who understood that "the task ahead of us is never as great as the power behind us." (J. Reuben Clark, Jr.). Moroni had a burning zeal to see his friends triumph over their adversaries. He personified he of whom Sir Walter Scott wrote: "Breathed there a man with soul so dead, who never to himself has said 'This is my own, my native land!'

Whose heart hath ne'er within him burned, as home his footsteps he hath turned from wandering on a foreign strand? If such there breathes, go, mark him well. For him no minstrel raptures swell. High though his titles, proud though his name, boundless his wealth, as wish can claim; despite these titles, power, and pelf, the wretch, concentered all in self, living, shall forfeit fair renown, and doubly dying shall go down into the vile depths from whence he sprung, unwept, unhonored, and unsung."

Moroni was a hero in the eyes of Mormon, who learned of his exploits when abridging the records that became The Book of Alma. He stands out in the history of the Nephites as a true friend. Mormon recorded that he "was a strong and a mighty man. He was a man of perfect understanding, yet, a man that did not delight in bloodshed, a man whose soul did joy in the liberty and the freedom of (his friends) and his brethren from bondage and slavery. Yea, a man whose heart did swell with thanksgiving to his God for the many privileges and blessings which he bestowed upon his (friends); a man who did labor exceedingly for the welfare and safety of his (friends). Yea, and he was a man who was firm in the faith of Christ, and he had sworn with an oath to defend his (friends), his rights and his country, and his religion, even to the loss of his blood." (Alma 48:11:13).

In the Old Testament, we read the account of two great friends named David and Jonathan. After he killed Goliath at Elah (see 1 Samuel 17:40), David quickly became a hero in Israel. Today, his picture would have been on the covers of People Magazine and USA Today, he would have made the talk show circuit, and his agent would have nailed down lucrative book deals and rights to a made-for-TV movie. He would have had impressive product endorsements, particularly for Red Bull and Power Bar. Exclusive photos of the battle would have sold for millions to the highest bidder. There would have been David Action Figures, and a David and Goliath video game.

While David was greatly honored by Israel for his exploits in battle, Jonathan received little attention for his own successes. Nevertheless, "the soul of Jonathan was knit with the soul of David, and Jonathan loved him as his own soul." (1 Samuel 18:1). Jonathan went so far as to give his royal robe and weapons to David: "And Jonathan stripped himself of the robe that was upon him, and gave it to David, and his garments, even to his sword, and to his bow, and to his girdle." (1 Samuel 18:4)

It would have been easier for Jonathan to be jealous of David. As Saul's son, Jonathan was next in line to be king. However, the prophet Samuel had anointed David, and not Jonathan, to become the next king. "Then Samuel took the horn of oil, and anointed him in the midst of his brethren: and the Spirit of the Lord came upon David• from that day forward." (1 Samuel 16:13)

After the slaying of Goliath, Saul took David into his home and set him over his armies. "And David went out whithersoever Saul sent him, and behaved himself wisely: and Saul set him over the men of war, and he was accepted in the sight of all the people, and also in the sight of Saul's servants." (1 Samuel 18:5). When we "behave ourselves wisely," we are self-effacing, self-deprecating, and spiritually sensitive.

Eventually, however, Saul turned against David. It was David, and not Saul, who was invited to appear on Larry King Live. It was David who received the adoration of Israel. "And it came to pass as they came, when David was returned from the slaughter of the Philistine, that the women came out of all cities of Israel, singing and dancing, to meet king Saul, with tabrets, with joy, and with instruments of musick. And the women answered one another as they played, and said, Saul hath slain his thousands, and David his ten thousands. And Saul was very wroth, and the saying displeased him; and he said, They have ascribed unto David ten thousands, and to me they have ascribed but thousands: and what can he have more but the kingdom? And Saul eyed David from that day and forward." (1 Samuel 18:6-9).

Sometimes, it is difficult to be happy about the success of others. If you are recognized for your achievements, it will somehow diminish mine. Your "A" will overshadow my "B." Your church calling is more significant than mine. Your mission assignment is more glamorous than mine. You seem to have many talents, and I have so few. You're a studmuffin and I'm such a geek. Your car is way cooler than my beater. Your education, your degree, your house, your kid's achievements, your vacation, your job. The list will never, ever, end if we allow ourselves to mentally compile one in the first place.

Jealousy and pride are the tools Satan designed to influence our spiritual well-being. When they have "a hold on our hearts, we lose our independence and deliver our freedoms to the bondage of men's judgment. The world shouts louder than the whisperings of the Holy Ghost." (Ezra Taft Benson).

When Saul sought to kill David, Jonathan was his true friend and our role-model. Today, when evil influences erode our spiritual independence and we are brought down into bondage, true friends like Jonathan come to our aid. "And Jonathan spake good of David unto Saul his father, and said unto him, Let not the king sin against his servant, against David; because he hath not sinned against thee, and because his works have been to thee-ward very good: For he did put his life in his hand, and slew the Philistine, and the Lord wrought a great salvation for all Israel: thou sawest it, and didst rejoice: wherefore then wilt thou sin against innocent blood, to slay David without a cause?" (1 Samuel 19:4-5).

There was a divine principle at the foundation of the friendship between Jonathan and David: "Behold, the Lord be between thee and me for ever." (1 Samuel 20:23). In the same way, Alma related to his friends, for he "did rejoice exceedingly to see his brethren, and what added more to his joy, they were still his brethren in the Lord; yea, and they had waxed strong in the knowledge of the truth; for they were men of a sound understanding and they had searched the scriptures diligently, that they might know the word of God." (Alma 17:2).

On the other hand, Saul was consumed by hatred for David. Filled with enmity toward both man and God. his thoughts, words, and deeds finally alienated him from the Spirit. David, however, refused to be consumed as was Saul. "Then David arose, and cut off the skirt of Saul's robe privily. And it came to pass afterward, that David's heart smote him, because he had cut off Saul's skirt." (1 Samuel 24:4-5). David had removed the symbol of Saul's authority, but felt absolutely terrible afterwards for having done so.

The story of Jonathan and David reminds us that true friendship and love bring us closer to each other and to God. When Joseph Smith was finally surrounded by the Saints and embraced their fellowship, he was moved to declare: "I salute you in the name of the Lord Jesus Christ, in token or remembrance of the everlasting covenant, in which covenant I receive you to fellowship, in a determination that is fixed, immovable, and unchangeable, to be your friend and brother through the grace of God in the bonds of love, to walk in all the commandments of God blameless, in thanksgiving, forever and ever. Amen." (D&C 88:133).

In the end, "we tell on ourselves by the friends we seek; by the very manner in which we speak; by the way we enjoy our leisure time; by the use we make of dollar and dime. We tell who we are by the things we wear and in the way we wear our hair; by the kinds of things that make us laugh; by the records we play on our phonograph. We tell who we are by the way we walk; by the things in which we delight to talk; by the books we choose from a well-filled shelf. In these ways and more we tell on ourselves." (Anonymous).

If we are ever to
obtain our exaltation and
eternal life, we must do more than
simply acknowledge that Jesus Christ
is our Lord. The Book of Mormon makes
it abundantly clear that the critical point
of conversion, beyond which lie the encircling
flames of fire in the Celestial Kingdom of God,
rests in making a conscious decision to accept
not only Jesus Christ, but also to be obedient
to the commandments. This includes the
covenants we make with God, beginning
with baptism by immersion for
the remission of sins.

(The) Gathering of Israel

*"And I did rehearse unto
them the words of Isaiah, who spake
concerning the restoration of the Jews,
or of the house of Israel; and after they
were restored they should no more be
confounded, neither should they
be scattered again"* (1 Nephi
15:20).

In the Last Days, "as many of the Gentiles as will repent (shall become) the covenant people of the Lord; and as many of the Jews as will not repent shall be cast off; for the Lord covenanteth with none save it be with them that repent and believe in his Son, who is the Holy One of Israel." (2 Nephi 30:2). These are known as God's Covenant People.

As we reflect on the covenant consciousness of the church in the Last Days, we realize that the special relationship that God's people have with Him is really not so self-evident. Even Mormon found it necessary to remind the Nephites that they were "of the house of Israel." (Mormon 7:1). After a thousand years, that remnant had forgotten its noble lineage. Sometimes, members of the church today forget that they are either literally or by adoption of the house of Israel and that they too may claim the covenant blessings promised by God so long ago to Abraham and his descendants.

An angel had asked Nephi: "Rememberest thou the covenants of the Father unto the House of Israel?" (1 Nephi 14:8). He was speaking of the Abrahamic Covenant, preserved in The Pearl of Great Price for those in the Last Days. "My name is Jehovah," the Savior had explained to His servant Abraham, "and I know the end from the beginning; therefore, my hand shall be over thee. And I will make of thee a great nation, and I will bless thee above measure, and make thy name great among all nations, and thou shalt be a blessing unto thy seed after thee, that in their hands they shall bear this ministry and Priesthood unto all nations; And I will bless them through thy name; for as many as receive this gospel shall be called after thy name, and shall be accounted thy seed, and shall rise up and bless thee, as their father; And I will bless them that bless thee, and curse them that curse thee; and in thee (that is, in thy Priesthood) and in thy seed (that is, thy Priesthood), for I give unto thee a promise that this right shall continue in thee, and in thy seed after thee (that is to say, the literal seed, or the seed of the body) shall all the families of the earth be blessed, even with the blessings of the gospel, which are the blessings of salvation, even of life eternal." (Abraham 2:8-11).

Later, Jehovah told Abraham's descendants through Jacob that He would "scatter (them) among all people, from the one end of the earth even unto the other." (Deuteronomy 28:64). This suggests that a very large portion of mankind would ultimately have Israelite blood in order to satisfy the purposes of God.

In Nephi's day, the Ten Tribes had already been lost to the knowledge of the Jews at Jerusalem. (1 Nephi 22:4). About 721 B.C., these tribes of the Kingdom of Israel were led into captivity by the Assyrians. About a year later, according to tradition, they fled toward the north and mysteriously disappeared. Ultimately, after the Babylonian Captivity, all 12 Tribes of Israel would be scattered upon the isles of the sea and among all nations.

Nephi's people were among those who lived "after the manner of happiness" by being partakers of the Abrahamic Covenant. (2 Nephi 5:27). The blessings of that Covenant include the priesthood, eternal marriage, and a land of inheritance. Today, "those portions of the Abrahamic Covenant which pertain to personal exaltation and eternal increase are renewed with each member of the House of Israel who enters the order of celestial marriage. Through that order, the participating parties become inheritors of all the blessings of Abraham, Isaac, and Jacob." (Bruce R. McConkie, "Mormon Doctrine," p. 13-14).

Just as the scattering of Israel was foretold, so too was its latter-day gathering. Jeremiah prophesied: "I will gather the remnant of my flock out of all countries whither I have driven them." (Jeremiah 23:3). God is in control of this Gathering. in fact, on April 3, 1836, in the Kirtland Temple, Moses restored the keys of the gathering of Israel. (See D&C 110:11). One hundred and thirty-nine years later, President Spencer W. Kimball declared: "The brighter day has dawned. The gathering is in progress. May the Lord bless us, as we become nursing fathers and mothers unto our (Israelite) brethren and hasten the fulfillment of the great promises made to them." (C.R. 10/1975). The House of Israel is now being gathered as it accepts the restored gospel and serves the God of Abraham, Isaac, and Jacob. (See Deuteronomy 30:1-5).

There are both physical and spiritual components to the Gathering. First, Israel's spiritual gathering is accomplished as those with the blood of Israel join the church. Converts are Israelites either by blood or by adoption. (See Galatians 3:26-29). Secondly, Israel's physical gathering will occur when she is "gathered home to the lands of (her) inheritance, and (is) established in all (her) lands of promise." (2 Nephi 9:2).

This physical gathering will not be completed until the Second Coming of Christ, but it is already under way, not only among the Jews in Israel, but also among the descendants of Ephraim, who have been gathering since 1830 by virtue of their membership in The Church of Jesus Christ of Latter-day Saints. Zenos prophesied that "when that day cometh" that Israel no longer turns her heart aside from the Master, "then will he remember the covenants which he made to their fathers. Yea, then will he remember the isles of the sea; yea, and all the people who are of the house of Israel." (1 Nephi 19:15-16). in essence, Zenos promised that Israel would be gathered from the four quarters of the earth.

At that day, "all the earth shall see the salvation of the Lord, saith the prophet; every nation, kindred, tongue and people shall be blessed." (1 Nephi 19:17). The members and missionaries of The Church of Jesus Christ of Latter-day Saints bring the message of salvation to a world in desperate need, and by priesthood authority and ordinance will provide the covenant blessings of Abraham to all nations.

The church was restored so that Israel might receive the gospel and enter into the covenants of salvation and exaltation, to teach her how to build temples and to learn how to use them, to clothe her in the garments of the holy priesthood, to give her power and authority among the nations, to prepare her to take the gospel into the world, and to sanctify herself so that she might be holy when she meets the Savior. The Gathering of Israel is taking place to prepare her for a celestial glory.

Today, "every stake on earth is the gathering place for the lost sheep of Israel who live in its area ... Scattered Israel in every nation is called to gather to the fold of Christ, to the stakes of Zion, as such are established in their nations." (Bruce R. McConkie, "Ensign," 5/1977, p. 118). Long ago, Isaiah prophesied that, in the Last Days, the Lord would establish "an ensign for the nations." (2 Nephi 21:12). This "ensign" is The Church of Jesus Christ of Latter-day Saints. As the Lord said to Joseph Smith, "I have sent mine everlasting covenant into the world, to be a light to the world, and to be a standard for my people, and for the Gentiles to seek to it, and to be a messenger before my face to prepare the way before me." (D&C 45:9).

Long ago, Isaiah prophesied
that, in the Last Days, the Lord would
establish "an ensign for the nations." (2
Nephi 21:12). This "ensign" is the Church
of Jesus Christ of Latter-day Saints. As the
Lord said to Joseph Smith: "I have sent mine
everlasting covenant into the world, to be a
light to the world, and to be a standard f
or my people, and for the Gentiles to
seek to it, and to be a messenger
before my face to prepare
the way before me."

General Conference:
The Super Bowl of Spiritual Symposia

"It came to pass that after
Mosiah had done as his father
had commanded him, and had made
a proclamation throughout all the land,
that the people gathered themselves together
throughout all the land, that they might
go up to the temple to hear the words
which king Benjamin should
speak unto them." (Mosiah
2:1).

"My servant, Orson Hyde, (a member of the original Quorum of the Twelve in this dispensation) was called by his ordination to proclaim the everlasting gospel, by the Spirit of the living God, from people to people, and from land to land, in the congregations of the wicked, in their synagogues, reasoning with and expounding all scriptures unto them. And behold, and lo, this is an ensample unto all those who were ordained unto this priesthood, whose mission is appointed unto them to go forth. And this is the ensample unto them, that they shall speak as they are moved upon by the Holy Ghost. And whatsoever they shall speak when moved upon by the Holy Ghost shall be scripture, shall be the will of the Lord, shall be the mind of the Lord, shall be the word of the Lord, shall be the voice of the Lord, and the power of God unto salvation." (D&C 68:1-4).

Following in the footsteps of Orson Hyde, who served for 28 years as President of the Quorum of the Twelve Apostles, officers and members of the church gather at its headquarters in Salt Lake City, Utah, and in stake and ward meetinghouses across the globe, to participate directly or by satellite transmission in the proceedings of the Semi-Annual General Conferences of the church, held each year in April and October. On October 30, 2014, the First Presidency clarified confusion relating to the status of the General Women's Meeting, as well as the General Young Women's Meeting, that since 1994 had been held a week prior to General Conference in April and October respectively, by announcing: "The General Women's Meeting will be designated as the General Women's Session of general conference." A combined meeting is now held semiannually for both women and young women, a week before the general sessions of Conference.

So popular is the Conference, that admission tickets are required to attend sessions in the 21,000 seat Conference Center in Salt Lake City. Members living in the United States and Canada may obtain these free of charge from their local priesthood leaders, although there are generally not nearly enough to go around. Those visiting from outside the United States and Canada may receive tickets under special circumstances. Entrance is limited to those ages eight and older for general sessions and twelve years and older for the priesthood session. Conference attendees are not allowed to bring babies into the Conference Center, for obvious reasons relating to the excellent acoustics of the building.

Those who are invited to speak at General Conference are typically selected from among the General Authorities and General Officers of the church. The General Authorities include the following:

The three members of The First Presidency of the church, the highest governing body of the Church. Its members are special witnesses of the name of Jesus Christ, called to teach and testify of Him throughout the world. Members of the First Presidency travel around the world to speak to members and local leaders. When not traveling, they counsel together and with other general church leaders on matters affecting the worldwide Church, such as missionary work, temple building and spiritual and temporal welfare."2

The twelve members of The Quorum of the Twelve Apostles, "the second-highest presiding body in the government of the church. Its members travel the world as special witnesses of the name of Christ and serve under the direction of the First Presidency."

The seven members of The Presidency of the Seventy, consisting of "seven General Authority Seventies who are called by the First Presidency and given authority to preside over the various Quorums of the Seventy."

The seventy-five members of The General Authority Seventies, who "preach the gospel and serve as special witnesses of Christ to the world. They assist the Quorum of the Twelve Apostles in preaching the gospel of Jesus Christ throughout the world. They serve in the Presidency of the Seventy, in Area Presidencies, and in other headquarters administrative functions. Under the direction of The Quorum of the Twelve Apostles, they travel frequently to meet with and teach church leaders, missionaries, and members of the church in local congregations."

General Authority Seventies "have authority to serve anywhere in the world. The authority of Area Seventies is generally limited to the area where they serve. The Presidency of the Seventy is drawn from the General Authority Seventies, and presides over all quorums of the Seventy."

At the 2015 General Conference of the church, as part of the ongoing evolution of its administration, the General Authorities in the First and Second Quorums of Seventy were combined, reconfigured, and re-designated as General Authority Seventies. Until then, the members of the First Quorum of the Seventy served from the time of their call until approximately seventy years of age. At that time, they transitioned to an emeritus status. Members of the Second Quorum of the Seventy, however, were called for a period of 5 to 7 years, and then were released from their callings. Members of both quorums had been designated General Authorities of the church. The new structure combines the two groups with no separate quorum designation, and its members are now called "General Authority Seventies."

There are three members of a Presiding Bishopric, consisting of "the Presiding Bishop and his two counselors. Each holds the office of bishop, and they serve under the direct supervision of the First Presidency. The Presiding Bishopric is responsible for many of the church's temporal affairs."

Those among the General Officers of the church who may be selected to speak at General Conference include:

Three members of the Relief Society General Presidency, who, "under the direction of the First Presidency, oversee the activities of all Latter-day Saint women ages 18 and over. They help guide and support the women of the church." The Relief Society is one of the oldest and largest women's organizations in the world.

Three members of the Young Men General Presidency, "who provide instruction, encouragement, and support in living the gospel of Jesus Christ for male church members ages 12 through 18. These leaders serve under the direction of the First Presidency and guide and support the young men of the church."

Three members of the Young Women General Presidency, "who provide instruction, encouragement, and support in living the gospel of Jesus Christ for female church members ages 12 through 17. These leaders serve under the direction of the First Presidency and help guide and support the young women of the Church."

Three members of the Primary General Presidency, "who oversee the church's organization that teaches children ages 18 months to 11 years the gospel of Jesus Christ and helps them live its principles. These leaders serve under the direction of the First Presidency and help guide and support the children and their local leaders."

Three members of the Sunday School General Presidency, "who oversee the church's organization that teaches adults the gospel of Jesus Christ and helps them live its principles. These leaders serve under the direction of the First Presidency and help guide and support adult members and their local leaders."

In summary, there are a total of approximately 100 General Authorities, and 15 General Officers of the church. All of them are heavy hitters in the church. These all-stars have extensive experience administering its temporal and spiritual affairs, on the local, regional, hemispherical, and global levels. Many have been honored to be the most valuable players on their stake and ward teams, and some were first-round draft picks at the time they declared their free-agency and emerged from full-time missions into adulthood. A few became rookies of the year. None, however, have received a signing bonus or any other financial incentive to serve. They do not employ talent agents or have personal coaches. Their service is not tied to any church related salary cap; in fact, they receive no salary at all. (Some do receive living stipends). Most of them were not first round draft picks; in fact, many of them were walk-ons who proved their mettle only after they had gotten down into the trenches where they were given the opportunity to show their mettle.

They conduct their lives in quiet contrast to the inflammatory lifestyles of many of the athletes who wear Super Bowl rings. They didn't get where they are thru a series of playoffs and divisional championships. They receive no product endorsements, and sign no lucrative deals with sponsors. They selflessly serve without thought of remuneration or recognition.

On the other hand, there are 53 members of the squad on a Super Bowl football team. It is probably safe to say that each of them dreams of being the star of the show; of taking home the trophy for Most Valuable Player. Each of them, regardless of playing time in the championship game, receives $97,000.00 (for winners) or $49,00.00 (for losers) for their participation. For most of the players, this bonus is chump change, because the average yearly salary per player is around $2.1 million. (The minimum NFL wage is $420,000.00). It should be noted that in the General Conferences of the church, there are no winners or losers. Everyone is treated the same in the Superbowl of Spiritual Symposia.

As noted above, there is no cost of admission to General Conference, and there are no advertising incentives related to the satellite transmission of Conference proceedings to stake centers throughout the world. In contrast, Super Bowl 50 was the most expensive sporting event in U.S. History, with an average ticket resale price of $5,335.00. Interestingly, the most expensive ticket for Super Bowl I was $12.00. (Yes, you read that correctly: Twelve dollars). But then again, fifty years ago, you could typically walk into the Tabernacle on Temple Square to participate in a Conference session, and keep your money in your pocket, to later purchase a "Cinnabon" across the street on South Temple. Now you need that elusive Golden Ticket, but few other things about Conference have changed.

A typical Super Bowl football game lasts three hours and 12 minutes, but the ball is only in play for around 11 minutes. Conference, on the other hand, is composed of four 2-hour general sessions, and a 2-hour Saturday evening session. Every minute is packed with inspiring instruction delivered via music and the spoken word. There is no ostentatious half-time show, and there are no clever advertisements to hold your attention. However, advertisers pony up mega-bucks for exposure on Super Bowl broadcasts. A 30-second commercial for the first Super Bowl in 1967 cost $42,000.00; it hit $1 million in 1995, and C.B.S. is charging $5 million for 30 second ads in 2016, which works out to $166,666.00 per second.

Just for fun, think of the "Super Bowl" value of an invocation or benediction at General Conference. If the average prayer lasted just one minute, its value would be ten million dollars. That said, those who have attended or listened to Conference frequently attest to the fact that they've heard multi-million-dollar prayers, and messages from speakers!

According to the NFL Players Association the average length of the career of a professional football player is about 3.3 years. On the Super Bowl roster of General Authorities (just considering The First Presidency and Quorum of the Twelve) the average length of service is 17.6 years in their current position. Without exception, all of them came from decades of devoted service in other callings. Their average age is 76, and there is no emeritus status. They keep laboring in the vineyard until they are finally released when they are called home to their Heavenly Father.

The Super Bowl is surrounded by extravagant and intense publicity and promotion by the media. Similarly, the April 2016 proceedings of General Conference were translated in real-time into more than 80 languages and were available in 94 languages total via television, radio, satellite, and Internet. But, at the same time, the main-stream media rarely gives General Conference even lip service. Instead, it focuses on worldly matters and debates the merits of the Super Bowl contenders who are going to face off for the Vince Lombardi Trophy on the third Sunday in February. I recall an Area Conference that was held in Spokane, Washington, on May 10-11, 1986. Headlines in the local newspapers that weekend should have declared to a spellbound city: "Largest Priesthood Gathering Ever Held in the Northwest," "Apostles of the Lord Visit Spokane," and "Ten Thousand Saints of The Most High God Assemble." In fact, there was no reference whatsoever to the Conference in either of Spokane's daily newspapers. Instead, the media reported on the health of the economy, the political fortunes of prominent politicians, baseball games, and other telestial trivia.

The media devotes an inordinate amount of attention to the Super Bowl, and sports analysts and commentators discuss every permutation, and dissect every variable relating to the impending contest, ad nauseam, as if the fate of the world hung in the balance. On the other hand, the leaders of the church only go so far as to print the proceedings of the Conference in the Ensign magazine, in the monthly issue that follows the conclusion of Conference. They leave to the members of the church the responsibility to seek spiritual confirmation from the Holy Ghost, and to choose from among the addresses delivered those that are of most relevance to their personal circumstances.

Unlike the conduct of prominent members of The Church of Jesus Christ of Latter-day Saints, the behavior of the members of the National Football League is fraught with controversy. It is almost desirable to be labeled a "bad boy." A good example is the flap surrounding "DeflateGate," that involved the allegation that the New England Patriots had tampered with footballs used in the American Football Conference Championship game (which New England won), by deliberately under-inflating the football so that it would be easier for their quarterback to grip and throw, easier for his receivers to catch, and less likely for him to fumble, especially in the cold and rainy conditions in which the game was played. (Tom Brady, the quarterback, was suspended for four games as a result of the investigation into the scandal, but he remains unrepentant).

Only one General Authority (George P. Lee, a member of the Seventy) has, in recent memory, been disciplined (excommunicated in 1989) by the church for conduct unbecoming a church member. Way back in 1943, Richard R. Lyman, a member of the Quorum of the Twelve, was excommunicated for "a violation of the law of chastity," the last member of the Quorum to be so disciplined.

Many of those who play in the Super Bowl have familiar household names, and are nearly revered by fans and the press, but they possess talents that pale in comparison to those who actively participate in General Conference. Leaders of the church enjoy associations in the rarified atmosphere of a religious society that is unique, reminding us of the introductory remarks made by President John F. Kennedy, who hosted a White House dinner on April 29, 1962, honoring Nobel Prize laureates. He said of them, as could be said of the leaders of the church who gather twice a year to celebrate General Conference, the Super Bowl of Religious Symposia: "I think this is the most extraordinary collection of talent and of human knowledge that has ever been gathered together at the White House, with the possible exception of when Thomas Jefferson dined alone."

Footnotes:

1. Quotations are from LDS.Org

2. As of 2024, prophets, seers, and revelators include:

Russell M. Nelson – year called: 1984. 40 years of service
Dallin H. Oaks – year called: 1984. 40 years of service
Jeffrey R. Holland – year called: 1994. 30 years of service
Henry B. Eyring – year called: 1995. 29 years of service
David A. Bednar – year called: 2004. 20 years of service
Deiter F. Uchtdorf – year called: 2004. 20 years of service
Quentin L. Cook – year called: 2007. 17 years of service
D. Todd Christofferson – year called. 2009. 15 years of service
Neil L. Anderson – year called: 2009. 15 years of service
Ronald A. Rasband – year called: 2016. 8 years of service
Gary E. Stevenson – year called: 2016. 8 years of service
Dale G. Renlund – year called: 2015. 6 years of service
Gerrit W. Gong – year called: 2018. 6 years of service
Ulisses Soares – year called: 2018. 6 years of service
Patrick Kearon – year called: 2024. 0 years of service

If we are to successfully free
outselves from the quicksands
of self-pity and escape the inequalities
of life, we must personalize the lessons of
the Atonement. We must change our nature
and become new creatures in Christ. We must
practice in front of a mirror, if necessary,
and recite over and over again until we
get it right: "Father forgive them,
for they know not what they
do." We must become
more Amish.

(The) Germination of our Faith

"Now, we will compare the
word unto a seed. Now, if ye give place,
the seed may be planted in your heart, behold,
if it be a true seed, or a good seed, if ye do not cast
it out by your unbelief, that ye will resist the Spirit of
the Lord, behold, it will begin to swell within your breasts'
and when you feel these swelling motions, ye will begin to
say within yourselves - It must be a good seed, or that
the word is good, for it beginneth to enlarge my
soul, yea, it beginneth to enlighten my
understanding, yea, it beginneth
to be delicious to me."
(Alma 32:28).

"Whosoever drinketh of the water that I shall give him shall never thirst; but the water that I shall give him shall be in him a well of water springing up into everlasting life." (John 4:14).

Only under these essential conditions, can we be spiritually reborn. "Now I say unto you that ye must repent, and be born again; for the Spirit saith if ye are not born again ye cannot inherit the kingdom of heaven; therefore, come and be baptized unto repentance, that ye may be washed from your sins, that ye may have faith on the Lamb of God, who taketh away the sins of the world, who is mighty to save and to cleanse from all unrighteousness." (Alma 7:14).

"And the Lord said unto me: Marvel not that all mankind, yea, men and women, all nations, kindreds, tongues and people, must be born again; yea, born of God, changed from their carnal and fallen state, to a state of righteousness, being redeemed of God, becoming his sons and daughters." (Mosiah 27:25).

Because of His covenant relationship with the faithful, they may be born again. As Mosiah 5:7 teaches, those who enter into the Covenant become "Born Again Christians." It is not a question of their development or maturation, but rather of generation. One of the most emotional, miraculous, and awe-inspiring events of mortality is birth, and it would be difficult to conceptualize more dramatically, in metaphor, the process of kindling our divine spark, of awakening our eternal potential, or of igniting the spirit lying dormant within each of us as a God in embryo, than to say that we must be born again in order to inherit eternal life.

Latter-day Saints are quintessential Born-Again Christians, for only members of Christ's true church can reach that epiphany through the ministration of His priesthood. (See Mosiah 27:25, Alma 5:14, & 7:14, then Mosiah 15:10-11, Alma 22:15, & 36:24). As the Lord revealed to Joseph Smith, the "greater priesthood administereth the gospel and holdeth the key of the mysteries of the kingdom, even the key of the knowledge of God. Therefore, in the ordinances thereof, the power of godliness is manifest. And without the ordinances thereof, and the authority of the priesthood, the power of godliness is not manifest unto men in the flesh." (D&C 84:19-21).

Without these ordinances, and without the authority of the priesthood, gospel seeds cannot properly germinate. We cannot procrastinate the day of our repentance, and defer our spiritual rebirth until later on when it is more convenient. The example of kernels of grain discovered in Pharaoh's tomb helps to illustrate why this is so.

Thanks to scores of scientific studies, we now have a pretty good idea of how long most seeds are able to germinate. Under normal dry and cool conditions, most seeds will remain viable for only a few years, and anything over 50 to 100 years is quite remarkable. The reason is, of course, that during this time the seed is using up its food supply, albeit very slowly.

In Nineteenth Century England, a mummy was unrolled in London, and in its hand was a small bag of wheat. "Some grains of it were sown and vegetated. Its produce has again been sown and has produced an average of 38 ears or spikes for each grain sown. To be sold in packets of 10 grains each at £1 per packet." In 1843, when The Gardeners' Chronicle ran this ad, the public was already infatuated with ancient Egypt. And nothing was more fascinating than the notion that "mummy wheat," grain discovered in the tombs of kings, would spring to life after thousands of years. At £1 a packet, worth £60 today ($86.00 U.S), people were paying for something more than a few stalks of wheat.

From the start, botanists dismissed the claims of The Gardeners' Chronicle as romantic nonsense. Yet the belief in the astonishing powers of ancient seeds lingered on. "You can blame it on Napoleon. When he invaded Egypt in 1798, he took along 175 scholars. Although his army failed to conquer Egypt, his troop of intellectuals were triumphant. They "discovered" ancient Egypt and so triggered a craze that swept the whole of Europe. Fashionable society was soon in the grip of mummy fever. By the 1840s, the English papers carried regular reports of the amazing regenerative powers of "mummy wheat" - grain discovered in tombs up to 6000 years old." (Source: BrightSurf.com "Pharaoh's Ear," January 23, 2002).

But, alas, just as the living kernels of wheat from Pharaoh's tomb were destined to whither and die without the sustaining influence of light, water, and fertile soil, so our divine potential cannot germinate without the similar influence of the gospel, the priesthood, and the nurturing influence of Jesus Christ.

(The) Gifts of The Spirit

"Deny not the gifts of God, for they
are many; and they come from the same
God. And there are different ways that these
gifts are administered; but it is the same God
who worketh all in all; and they are given
by the manifestations of the Spirit of
God unto men, to profit them."
(Moroni 10:8).

These are the gifts of faith, discernment, wisdom, knowledge, administration, tongues, the interpretation of tongues, faith to be healed, faith to heal, prophecy, the working of miracles, the testimony of Jesus, and believing the testimony of others.

"Now there are diversities of gifts, but the same Spirit ... But the manifestation of the Spirit is given to every man to profit withal. For to one is given by the Spirit the word of wisdom; to another the word of knowledge by the same Spirit; to another faith by the same Spirit; to another the gifts of healing by the same Spirit; to another the working of miracles; to another prophecy; to another discerning of spirits; to another divers kinds of tongues; to another the interpretation of tongues." (1 Corinthians 12:4, 7-10).

"All things must be done in the name of Christ, whatsoever you do in the Spirit." (D&C 46:31). The baptism of water qualifies one for membership in the church but does not assure the total spiritual transformation necessary to regain the presence of God. This comes through the baptism of fire and the Holy Ghost, which is the receipt of the Spirit unto sanctification: "For by the blood ye are sanctified." (Moses 6:60).

Alma asked his brethren, "Have ye spiritually been born of God?" (Alma 5:14). He wanted to know if these baptized members of the church had experienced the pure and unconditional love of Christ and if they had charity for all men. He knew they had been converted to the church; what he really wanted to find out was: Had they also been converted to the Savior and His gospel? Mahatma Gandhi once said, "If a single man achieves the highest kind of love, it will be enough to neutralize the hatred of millions." Alma knew that the pure love of Christ in the hearts of his people would be a dynamic influence for good. With that kind of dedication, the humble disciples of Christ in all ages have performed mighty miracles in His name through the workings of the Spirit.

If the Spirit is dominant, it will guide us unerringly and we may know the truthfulness of all things. Even more importantly, it will mold and shape us into new creatures in Christ. Joseph Smith articulated it best when he said, "By the power of the Spirit our eyes were opened and our understandings were enlightened, so as to see and understand the things of God." (D&C 76:10).

As our powers expand, we experience the glittering facets of the life of the Spirit. "To use the careful preparation and training we receive as a springboard, to be capable of disciplined, controlled procedure and to be receptive to flashes of insight, is what a solid Latter-day Saint should have going for him in his inner life. The gospel sets us free to be creative, and sets us creative to become more free," as we learn to respond to the guidance of the Spirit and enjoy spiritual gifts. ("My Religion & Me," Lesson #9). It is the perfect law of liberty.

Every member of the church "is given a gift by the Spirit of God." (D&C 46:11). When these find expression in the lives of others, they can be positive, motivational, and uplifting for us, as well. Under such circumstances, we are given an opportunity to vividly role-play, for successful experiences must be pre-played before they can be re-played.

Those who have the image of God engraven upon their countenances are they who will recognize their spiritual gifts and give thanks to Him Who has bestowed them. "Who shall ascend into the hill of the Lord," asked the Psalmist, "or who shall stand in his holy place" to partake of the Divine Nature? "He that hath clean hands and a pure heart; who hath not lifted up his soul unto vanity, nor sworn deceitfully." (Psalms 24:4-5).

"To some is given one, and to some is given another, that all may be profited thereby." (D&C 46:12). Sometimes, it is necessary to fast and pray to gain a witness of the Spirit, so that we may then receive a strong, independent testimony of the gospel. Until we have paid the price, however, we cannot comprehend the language of the Spirit, for it is foreign to us. If we have never made the journey to Christ, if we have not traveled the path leading to the tree of life, if we have not worked diligently to harvest the delicious fruit of that tree, we cannot receive "the things of the Spirit of God, for they are foolishness unto (us), neither can (we) know them, because they are spiritually discerned." (1 Corinthians 2:14-15). Faith precedes the miracle of the receipt of spiritual gifts.

Regarding our comprehension of the different manifestations of the Spirit, Marion G. Romney said that "having a testimony and being converted are not necessarily the same thing. A testimony comes when the Holy Ghost gives the earnest seeker a witness of the truth. A moving testimony vitalizes faith, that is, it induces repentance and obedience to the commandments. Conversion, on the other hand, is the fruit or the reward for repentance and obedience." (C.R., 10/1963). Spiritual gifts follow conversion, which is built on the foundation of testimony.

Without interfering with our agency, these gifts are sufficient to guide us to make behavioral choices that are consistent with celestial principles. They bring us into a harmonious orientation with the will of God. His work becomes our passion. He wants each of us to succeed, to pass the individual tests of mortality, and then to move on, having satisfied the entrance requirements for admittance to the Celestial Kingdom. With what greater gifts could our Heavenly Father bless us than those that help us to reach this goal?

"And it shall come to pass that he that asketh in Spirit shall receive in Spirit." (D&C 46:28). It is appropriate to ask for spiritual gifts, that we might grow in the grace of God. As we do so, we become more and more like our Heavenly Father. We grow in spiritual stature. We are able to follow the counsel of the Savior, Who commanded: "I would that ye should be perfect, even as I, or your Father who is in heaven is perfect." (3 Nephi 12:48, see Matthew 5:48). God glories in the possibility that His children who obey Him and endure to the end might develop both His image and His likeness.

"It is a serious thing to live in a society of possible Gods and Goddesses - to remember that the dullest and most uninteresting person you talk to may one day be a creature which, if you saw it now, you would be strongly tempted to worship. it is in the light of these overwhelming possibilities, it is with the awe and the circumspection proper to them, that we should conduct all our dealings with one another ... all friendships, all loves, all play all politics. There are no ordinary people. You have never talked to a mere mortal-- it is immortals whom we joke with, work with, marry, snub and exploit. Our charity must be a real and costly love. Next to the blessed sacrament itself, your neighbor is the holiest object presented to your senses. if he is your Christian neighbor he is holy in almost the same way, for in him also Christ is truly hidden and glorified." (C.S. Lewis).

"If ye by the grace of God are perfect in Christ, and deny not his power, then are ye sanctified in Christ by the grace of God, through the shedding of the blood of Christ, which is in the covenant of the Father unto the remission of your sins, that ye become holy, without spot." (Moroni 10:33). it would be difficult to put more succinctly, yet more powerfully, the essence of the gospel of Jesus Christ, than in this verse. if we open our hearts to the gospel of Jesus Christ, we can become holy, without spot. Even as a lamb without spot, or blemish. (See 1 Peter 1:19, & Hebrews 9:14)

We cannot purchase spiritual gifts with the treasures of the earth. Perhaps this is why in their efforts to obtain the sacred records, Lehi's sons were stripped by Laban of all their gold, silver, and precious things. The task was to be accomplished in the Lord's way, by the power of His mighty arm, which is great in the sight of the faithful, but which has a terrible effect upon the wicked. As Alma asked: "Can ye dispute the power of God?" (Mosiah 27:16). Certainly not, for the arm of flesh is weak in comparison to the power of the Spirit.

The gift of faith is a gift of power that motivates us to action. The miracles from the scriptures with which we are familiar were only made possible by its exercise, and each of us has the capacity to develop that same intensity of faith. When we read in the sacred records of these experiences, a way is prepared that we, too, might be "partakers of the heavenly gift." (Ether 12:8). it becomes possible for us to share the feelings experienced by the two disciples on the Road to Emmaus, who, after communing with the Resurrected Lord, declared: "Did not our heart burn within us, while he talked with us by the way, and while he opened to us the scriptures?" (Luke 24:32).

The gift of discernment is necessary, because there are those in the world, who, as long as they have visible proof, may grudgingly acknowledge the hand of the Lord in their affairs. This class of individual cannot really discern either good or evil; their only reality is that which is received through the five physical senses.

Through the operation of the Spirit, however, Heavenly Father has provided another way to identify the truth. For example, He does not offer up sacred records to be scrutinized, analyzed, criticized, and rationalized by pompous doctors and professors of religion clothed in the robes of the false priesthood and cloistered in the ivory towers of academia. "You cannot prove the genuineness of any document to one who has decided not to accept it," declared Hugh Nibley. "When a man asks for proof we can be pretty sure that proof is the last thing in the world he really wants. His request is thrown out as a challenge, and the chances are that he has no intention of being shown up. After all these years, the Bible itself is still not proven to those who do not choose to accept it. So, The Book of Mormon as an 'unproven' book finds itself in good company." ("An Approach to The Book of Mormon," p. 2).

Nor will the Lord indulge the prurient interest of men who only want theological titillation to satisfy their adulterous curiosity. Again, The Book of Mormon provides a classic example. Critics of that book "often remark sarcastically that it is a great pity that the golden plates have disappeared, since they would conveniently prove Joseph Smith's story. They would do nothing of the sort. The presence of the plates would only prove that there were plates, no more. it would not prove that Nephites wrote them, or that an angel brought them, or that they had been translated by the gift and power of God, and we can be sure that scholars would quarrel about the writing on them for generations without coming to any agreement, exactly as they did about parts of the Bible. The possession of the plates would have a very disruptive effect and it would prove nothing.

On the other hand, a far more impressive claim is put forth when the whole work is given to the world in what is claimed to be a divinely inspired translation. In such a text, any cause or pretext for disagreement and speculation is reduced to an absolute minimum. It is a text which all the world can read and understand, and it is a far more miraculous object than any gold plates would be." (High Nibley, "An Approach to The Book of Mormon," p. 17-18). The only thing that The Book of Mormon does not do is pander to the base instinct of man's fallen and depraved nature.

The gift of wisdom is given to those who press forward with complete dedication, feasting upon the word of Christ and receiving physical and spiritual strength and nourishment. Those who endure to the end with continuing responsibility and accountability are given the promise of hidden treasures of knowledge.

Moroni wrote that "to one is given by the Spirit of God, that he may teach the word of wisdom." (Moroni 10:9). The Lord instructed Joseph Smith to "teach one another the doctrine of the kingdom," to the end that all might be edified in Christ. (D&C 88:77). Perhaps the most dramatic spiritual manifestation that was the result of one seeking wisdom from God, was that received by Joseph Smith in The Sacred Grove. He had read in James 1:5-6: "If any of you lack wisdom, let him ask God, that giveth to all men liberally, and upbraideth not; and it shall be given him. But let him ask in faith, nothing wavering." He learned that wisdom leading to salvation comes from God by revelation.

The Lord said that we should seek not for riches, but for wisdom. To understand spiritual things, one must have discernment or guidance from the Holy Ghost. For example, those who are sincerely investigating the church are taught by the Spirit, and when they are confirmed as members they receive the special gift of the Holy Ghost by ordinance. One of His purposes is to guide the faithful from the covenant waters of baptism, along the strait and narrow path leading to the other ordinances of the priesthood that are necessary if one is to obtain eternal life. This is one reason why members of the church are given the Holy Ghost in an initial priesthood ordinance beside the waters of baptism.

The mysteries of God are those truths that can only be known by revelation from the Holy Ghost. When we "hunger and thirst after righteousness," the doctrine of the priesthood will distill upon our souls as the dews from heaven, and the Holy Ghost will be our constant companion. (See D&C 121:45-46).

To him that will not harden his heart "is given the greater portion of the word, until it is given unto him to know the mysteries of God until he know them in full." (Alma 12:10). All men and women may have access to the spiritual gift of knowledge of the mysteries of God, which are the saving principles of the gospel of Jesus Christ.

When individuals harden their hearts to the truth, however, "to them is given the lesser portion of the word (of wisdom) until they know nothing concerning his mysteries, and then they are taken captive by the devil, and led by his will down to destruction. Now this is what is meant by the chains of hell." (Alma 12:11).

The terrible thing about hardening our hearts is that understanding of "the word" is withheld, which leaves us vulnerable to the devil's influence. The scriptures identify the consequences of sin in very plain language. The effect of sin on those who has been taught the principles of the gospel in plainness is that the guidance of the Spirit is withdrawn, and they are left alone to grope in darkness. Guilt causes them to shrink from church activity, and in the absence of the Spirit, they have no claim on blessings, prosperity, or preservation. Having eyes, they see not, and having ears, they hear not.

Tragically, feeling uncomfortable in proximity to spiritual experiences, they withdraw to lifestyles devoid of such associations. Thus begins a downward spiral that gains momentum as sinful practices, more easily committed, become entrenched. Even worse, those who do this, "the same cometh out in open rebellion against God." (Mosiah 2:37).

"Thus saith the Lord concerning all those who know my power, and have been made partakers thereof, and suffered themselves through the power of the devil to be overcome, and to deny the truth and defy my power. They are they who are the sons of perdition." (D&C 76:31-32). This is spiritual death, or life devoid of light and truth.

When the word and the will of the Lord came to the Saints through President Brigham Young, it was: "Let him that is ignorant learn wisdom by humbling himself and calling upon the Lord his God, that his eyes may be opened that he may see, and his ears opened that he may hear. For my Spirit is sent forth into the world to enlighten the humble and contrite." (D&C 136:32-33).

The gift of knowledge is given to the faithful who seek "line upon line, precept upon precept." (D&C 98:12). Personal revelation is the individual's ultimate source for understanding scripture and knowing God's will. "These currents and many more are part of the flowing fountain of the church. if we do not drink, if we die of thirst while only inches from the fountain, the fault comes down to us. For the free, full, flowing, living water is there." (Truman Madsen, "Christ & The Inner Life," p. 31).

Mormon wrote of Alma's teaching style: "And now, as the preaching of the word had a great tendency to lead the people to do that which was just - yea, it had had more powerful effect upon the minds of the people than the sword, or anything else, which had happened unto them - therefore Alma thought it was expedient that they should try the virtue of the word of God." (Alma 31:5).

Joseph Smith taught the same thing, that "a person can get nearer to God by reading The Book of Mormon than by reading any other book." There is great motivating and sanctifying power in the words of The Book of Mormon, precisely because as a companion to the Bible it is Another Testament of Jesus Christ.

President Ezra Taft Benson counseled: "The Book of Mormon will change your life. it will fortify you against the evils of our day. it will bring a spirituality into your life that no other book will. it will be the most important book you will read in preparation for a mission and for life. A young man who knows and loves The Book of Mormon, who has read it several times, who has an abiding testimony of its truthfulness, and who applies its teachings will be able to stand against the wiles of the devil and will be a mighty tool in the hands of the Lord.

Oh, my brethren and sisters," he continued, "let us not treat lightly the great things we have received from the hand of the Lord. His word is one of the most valuable gifts He has given us. I urge you to recommit yourselves to a study of the scriptures. Read them in your families, and teach your children to love and treasure them. Then, prayerfully and in counsel with others, seek every way possible to encourage the members of the church to follow your example." (C.R., 4/1986).

Moroni wrote "to another (it is given) that he may teach the word of knowledge." (Moroni 10:10). Joseph Smith taught that "it is impossible for a man to be saved in ignorance" of the saving principles of the gospel." (D&C 131:6). We must have knowledge of them and of our Heavenly Father, for Jesus taught, "this is life eternal, that they might know thee the only true God, and Jesus Christ, whom thou hast sent." (John 17:3). Any knowledge that we do have of them is a gift of the Spirit.

The gift of administration is given to those who minister within the priesthood organizations through which the Lord operates His church. These are oriented to bind the promises and blessings of the gospel by means of covenants of action between members and the Lord. Ordinances in particular bridge the gulf between earth and heaven, attest to the nature of God, confirm that His church is founded on unchanging principles, and illustrate that the requirements for obtaining salvation are the same for all mankind.

Churches that operate on borrowed light are sometimes quite popular with people who seek form without substance, and who enjoy the relative ease of putting forth minimal effort in organizations that make no demands for personal sacrifice. But the Spirit powers the Church of Christ, and there is a performance requirement associated with every blessing received.

When we think of the gift of speaking in tongues, the missionaries who serve throughout the world come especially to mind. We also remember the Nephite children whom Jesus blessed. These received an endowment of spiritual power, for the Savior "did loose their tongues, and they did speak unto their fathers great and marvelous things, even greater than he had revealed unto the people." (3 Nephi 26:14). The multitude "both saw and heard these children; yea, even babes did open their mouths and utter marvelous things; and the things which they did utter were forbidden that there should not any man write them." (3 Nephi 26:16).

The gift of the interpretation of tongues may include the ability to hear the words of the scriptures with a clear and unambiguous understanding. For the Lord told Joseph Smith that "these words are not of men nor of man, but of me; wherefore, you shall testify they are of me and not of man. For it is my voice which speaketh them unto you; for they are given by my Spirit unto you, and by my power you can read them one to another; and save it were by my power you could not have them. Wherefore, you can testify that you have heard my voice, and know my words." (D&C 18:34-36).

The gift of faith to be healed was manifest during the Savior's post-mortal ministry when, among the Nephites, He "healed all their sick, and their lame, and opened the eyes of their blind and unstopped the ears of the deaf." (3 Nephi 26:15). Certainly, His efforts to bless the people were enhanced by their great faith in Him. The Savior does not want lukewarm converts; He desires those whose commitment is profound. Then, He can truly bless their lives. After entering the Fold, such devoted disciples may see and hear "unspeakable things, which are not lawful to be written." (3 Nephi 26:18). They remember the counsel of the Master, Who said: "Ye know the things that ye must do in my church; for the works which ye have seen me do that shall ye also do." (3 Nephi 27:21). Without realizing it, these Children of Christ are transformed into a Zion society, "for this is Zion - THE PURE IN HEART." (D&C 97:21). They are called the Church of Christ. What a great example to the Saints in the Last Days are those who have gone before!

We remember the gift of faith to heal when we read in Malachi: "Unto you that fear my name shall the Sun of righteousness arise with healing in his wings." (Malachi 4:2). There is also another dimension of faith to heal. Only six generations after Adam, "Enoch looked upon the earth; and he heard a voice from the bowels thereof, saying: Wo, wo is me, the mother of men; I am pained, I am weary, because of the wickedness of my children. When shall I rest, and be cleansed from the filthiness which is gone forth out of me? When will my Creator sanctify me, that I may rest, and righteousness for a season abide upon my face?" (Moses 7:48). When one comprehends the significance of the terrible pollutions on the face of the earth, and the physical and spiritual cleansing that will be required before the Kingdom of God can return, the concept of "healing" moves to a new level.

At the millennial day, all shall lift up their voice and sing, declaring that "the earth hath travailed and brought forth her strength," as a mother who has borne a new child, "and the heavens have smiled upon her," for she is pure and delightsome. "And she is clothed with the glory of her God," adorned in the strength of His priesthood. "For he stands in the midst of his people (with) glory, and honor, and power, and might. For he is full of mercy, justice, grace and truth, and peace." (D&C 84:101-102).

The Apostle Peter indicated that true Saints "have obtained like precious faith with us through the righteousness of God and our Saviour Jesus Christ. According as his divine power hath given unto us all things that pertain unto life and godliness, through the knowledge of him that hath called us to glory and virtue; whereby are given unto us exceeding great and precious promises: That by these ye might be partakers of the divine nature." (2 Peter 1:1, 3 & 4). These are they who know the power of God, understand His nature, and experience the whisperings of the Spirit.

The gift of prophecy is "the testimony of Jesus." (Revelation 19:10). it follows that any person who has received the spiritual gift of a testimony is a prophet, since a testimony can only be received by revelation from the Holy Ghost, and since prophecy consists of the words holy men speak when they are moved upon by the Spirit.

"Wo unto him that shall deny the revelations of the Lord, and that shall say the Lord no longer worketh by revelation, or by prophecy, or by gifts, or by tongues, or by healings, or by the power of the Holy Ghost!" (3 Nephi 29:6). in contrast, "we testify to the world that revelation continues, and that the vaults and files of the church contain these revelations which come month to month, and day to day." (President Spencer W. Kimball, C.R., 4/1977).

The gift of the working of miracles is a manifestation of the power of God, and so it is incomprehensible to the world. For "the natural man receiveth not the things of the Spirit of God: for they are foolishness unto him: neither can he know them, because they are spiritually discerned." (1 Corinthians 2:14).

"Wo unto him that shall say" in the Last Days, "that there can be no miracle wrought by Jesus Christ; for he that doeth this shall become like unto the son of perdition, for whom there was no mercy, according to the word of Christ!" (3 Nephi 29:7). Those who deny the divinity of Christ cannot be saved on His merits, because they cannot generate the power of saving faith. Therefore, they are damned, because their progression stops until they experience a profound attitude adjustment.

Those who enjoy the gift of a testimony of Jesus Christ unflinchingly bear witness that Jesus Christ was "the Son, the Only Begotten of the Father, full of grace, and mercy, and truth." (Alma 5:48). "Either this man was, and is, the Son of God, or else a madman or something worse. But don't let us come with any patronizing nonsense about His (only) being a great human teacher" as the secular apologists would have us believe. (C.S. Lewis).

The gift to believe the testimony of others includes investigators, little children, and church members in general who listen to the Authorities of the church bear testimony. "And by doing so, the Lord God prepareth the way that the residue of men may have faith in Christ, that the Holy Ghost may have place in their hearts." (Moroni 7:32).

Alma said that preaching the gospel with power and authority is the responsibility of those who bear the priesthood of God. "This is the order after which I am called," he said, "yea, to preach unto my beloved brethren, yea, and every one that dwelleth in the land." (Alma 5:49). He did not make any distinction between member and non-member. Rather, he felt that it was his duty to bring the gift of the gospel to all, for his message was the same, that all must repent and be born again.

Some have all the spiritual gifts. "Unto some it may be given to have all those gifts, that there may be a head, in order that every member may be profited thereby." (D&C 46:29). When the members have faith in the atoning power of Christ, and if they furthermore possess the resolve to do whatever is necessary to activate this energy in their own lives, they will profit by the administration of the gifts of the Spirit. Those who have faith in the power of Christ to save them from their sins will have an abiding motivation to live in accordance with His will. They will look forward with an eye of faith, or with an eternal perspective. They will not only believe in Christ, but they will believe Christ, when He says that they can be celestial material. The manifestation of Spiritual gifts will be a dramatic validation of their continuing efforts to be so. Those who aren't valiant in the testimony of Jesus, who don't stand for something, will fall for anything. if they don't know where they are going, they will end up somewhere else, and probably won't even care that they made the trip.

Beginning in 1830, an unbroken series of prophets has led the church. "Since 1847, these prophets have administered the affairs of the church from Salt Lake City. They have dedicated themselves to their appointed mission of helping the people of the world prepare for eternal life, and for the second coming of Jesus Christ. They have provided leadership for the international missionary program of the church and for the building of temples. The living prophet continues to receive revelations, select and ordain leaders by the spirit of prophecy, and serve as the principal teacher of the church, instructing its members in doctrine and in righteous living." (L.D.S. Infobase). They are aided in these efforts by all of the gifts of the Spirit.

These gifts are given "for the benefit of the children of God." (D&C 46:26). it will be difficult for individuals who have lived a telestial existence to justify their actions before God, in light of the many signs and wonders and gifts He has given so liberally to mankind. "Any man who hath seen any or the least of these hath seen God moving in his majesty and power." (D&C 88:47). "Earth is crammed with heaven, and every common bush with fire of God. But only those who see take off their shoes. The rest stand around picking blackberries." (Elizabeth Barrett Browning, "Aurora Leigh," Book Seven, 1856).

Ours is the Age of Inspiration and of gifts of the Spirit, when the Holy Ghost is being poured out upon men and women in rich abundance. With prophetic foresight, Joseph Smith promised: "God shall give unto you knowledge by His Holy Spirit, yea, by the unspeakable gift of the Holy Ghost, that has not been revealed since the world was until now. (This is a time when) nothing shall be withheld. All thrones and dominions, principalities, and powers, shall be revealed. And also, if there be bounds set to the heavens or to the seas, or to the dry land, or to the sun, moon, or stars, (all this) shall be revealed in the days of the dispensation of the fulness of times." (D&C 121:26-31).

Those to whom the gospel is dispensed "receive the gifts of sensory delight, of fragrance, sound, and form and color. (Theirs) is the realm of human associations, of gratitude, loyalty, and appreciation, of selflessness, helpfulness, and forgiveness, of friendship, love, and compassion. it is the realm of human growth and transcendence and of truth discovered and accepted, of beauty created and enjoyed, of goodness deepened and made manifest in life.

None of us are strangers to these realms of spirit. We have sensed the world about us, smelled its fragrance, heard its sounds, and glimpsed its form and colors. We have warmed our souls in the glow of human associations; have had our moments of selflessness and gratitude, love, and forgiveness. We have felt an upward reach within us when made suddenly aware of a truth, a beauty, a goodness above and beyond our own attainment." (Lael Woodbury, "A Land Unpromised and Unearned," "B.Y.U. Studies," Autumn, 1975).

These whisperings confirm to our hearts that there is more to the gospel than outward observances, obedience, and covenants. Spiritual enlightenment is the key to the discovery of undreamed vistas of otherwise inaccessible experience.

The Apostle Paul testified that "eye hath not seen, nor ear heard, neither have entered into the heart of man, the things which God hath prepared for them that love him." (1 Corinthians 2:9). Nephi declared, "no tongue can speak, neither can there be written by any man, neither can the hearts of men conceive so great and marvelous things as we both saw and heard Jesus speak." (3 Nephi 17:7). President Joseph Fielding Smith, Jr., described the spiritual "impressions on the soul that come from the Holy Ghost (as) far more significant than a vision. it is where spirit speaks to spirit, and the imprint upon the soul is far more difficult to erase."

The scriptures allude to the thin line between the material world and the world of spiritual matters: "And when the servant of the man of God was risen early, and gone forth, behold, an host compassed the city both with horses and chariots. And his servant said unto him, Alas, my master, how shall we do? And he answered, Fear not: for they that be with us are more than they that be with them. And Elisha prayed, and said, Lord, I pray thee, open his eyes, that he may see. And the Lord opened the eyes of the young man; and he saw: and, behold, the mountain was full of horses and chariots of fire round about Elisha." (2 Kings 6:15-17).

"When you lay down this tabernacle, where are you going?" asked Brigham Young. "Into the spirit world," he replied. "Where is the spirit world? It is right here. Do the spirits go beyond the boundaries of this organized earth? No, they do not. They can see us, but we cannot see them, unless our eyes were opened." ("The Vision," p. 55-56).

A reminiscence by a friend and associate of Joseph Smith reflects the gossamer fabric of the veil separating the world we know from the world of spirits. "I am getting tired and would like to go to my rest, said Joseph. His words and tone (both) thrilled and shocked me; like an arrow, (they) pierced my hopes that he would long remain with us, and I said, as with a heart full of tears: Oh Joseph, what could we, as a people, do without you and what would become of the great Latter-day work, if you should leave us? He saw and was touched by my emotions, and in reply he said, Benjamin, I would not be far away from you, and if on the other side of the veil, I would still be working with you, and with a power greatly increased, to roll on this kingdom." ("The Vision," p. 140-141).

It is the challenge of every member of the church to learn to understand the language of the Spirit with fluency. "Twentieth Century Americans (especially), tend to fill space, as if what we have, what we are, is not enough. Being affluent, we strangle ourselves with what we can buy, things whose opacity obstructs our ability to see what is (really) there." (Gretel Erlich, "The Atlantic Magazine"). The bestowal of spiritual gifts is the antidote for poisonous telestial tendencies that choke the expression of celestial sureties.

"And ye must give thanks unto God in the Spirit for whatsoever blessing ye are blessed with. And ye must practice virtue and holiness before me continually." (D&C 46:32-33). The gifts of the Spirit swell one's breast with joy. Spirituality, the kind of life where one may enjoy these gifts, "is the consciousness of victory over self, and of communion with the infinite." (David O. McKay). We are richer today than we were yesterday if we have laughed often, given something, forgiven even more, made a new friend, changed stumbling blocks into steppingstones, if we have thought more in terms of "thyself" than "myself," or if we have managed to be cheerful even when we were weary. We are richer today than we were yesterday if we have used the gifts of the Spirit to bless the lives of others. Such individuals have received the image of Christ in their countenances, and have experienced a mighty change in their hearts. "This changed feeling is indescribable, but it is real. Happy is the person who has truly sensed the uplifting, transforming power that comes from this nearness to the Savior, this kinship to the Living Christ." (David O. McKay).

We must develop our gifts and retain in our minds what these gifts are, remembering that whatsoever is good cometh from God." (Alma 5:40). The gifts of the Spirit are given so that we may have the fortifying influence so necessary to combat evil in the world. "We have no excuse to err in our knowledge and understanding of right and wrong. By inquiring of the Lord and listening to the voice of His Spirit, and having a willingness to be guided thereby, we will always find ourselves on the Lord's side of every issue, and be strengthened to hold fast to that which is good." (Delbert Stapeley, C.R., April 1965).

When we conduct our lives in conformity to the commandments, the windows of heaven will be opened unto us, and the blessings of the Lord will be poured out upon the heads of the Latter-day Saints, to the end "that (we) may not be seduced by evil spirits, or doctrines of devils, or the commandments of men." (D&C 46:7). The mission statement of Moroni and all of the prophets is summarized in the last verses of The Book of Mormon: "Come unto Christ, and lay hold upon every good gift, and touch not the evil gift, nor the unclean thing. Yea, come unto Christ, and be perfected in him, and deny yourselves of all ungodliness." (Moroni 10:30 & 32).

"That ye may not be deceived seek ye earnestly the best gifts, always remembering for what they are given." (D&C 46:8). God will continue the ministry, and work miracles among the children of men, as "long as time shall last, or the earth shall stand, or there shall be one man upon the face thereof to be saved." But "if these things have ceased wo be unto the children of men, for it is because of unbelief, and all is vain." (Words of Mormon 1:36-37). The Last Days mirror those of Mormon, who wrote that "there were sorceries, and witchcrafts, and magics, and the power of the evil one was wrought upon all the face of the land" because of the lack of faith of the people. (Mormon 1:19).

When the gifts of the Spirit are absent, we must declare, as did Mormon, that "faith (has) ceased also; and awful is the state of man, for they are as though there had been no redemption made." (Words of Mormon 1:38). As Alma put it: "For behold, if ye have procrastinated the day of your repentance even until death," or if you have waited to develop saving faith until you were spiritually dead to the Light of Christ, "behold, ye have become subjected to the spirit of the devil, and he doth seal you his," because you can no longer make the vital distinction between good and evil or light and darkness; "therefore, the Spirit of the Lord hath withdrawn from you, and hath no place in you, and the devil hath all power over you," for you have voluntarily surrendered your agency to act independently, "and this is the final state of the wicked," for there is no recovery, and it will be as if there had been no redemption made for such individuals who refuse to repent. (Alma 34:35).

Mormon exhorted his brethren to rise to the occasion. He said: "I judge better things of you, for I judge that ye have faith in Christ because of your meekness; for if ye have not faith in him then ye are not fit to be numbered among the people of his church." (Moroni 7:39).

God is NowHere

"Thus saith
the Lord God: I will give unto the
children of men line upon line; precept
upon precept, here a little and there a little;
and blessed are those who hearken unto my
precepts, and lend an ear unto my counsel,
for they shall learn wisdom; for unto him
that receiveth I will give more; and from
them that shall say, We have enough,
from them shall be taken away
even that which they have."
(2 Nephi 28:30).

If God does not speak to us today, perhaps it is because He cannot. Perhaps He has suffered a massive stroke resulting in aphasia. Maybe He has lost His First Amendment rights, and no longer enjoys freedom of speech. Maybe He has developed xenophobia, and has retreated behind the walls of His kingdom because He feels threatened by those who insist that He does not exist. Maybe He just doesn't care about His children anymore. His silence might be evidence that He has lost interest in us, has other things on His mind, has other priorities, or has become distracted by other, more pressing, concerns. Maybe He has finally realized that we just don't need Him anymore. Maybe He is sitting back and taking a much-needed vacation from His responsibilities because technology has taken His place, science satisfies our needs, and rationalism has assuaged our consciences.

Maybe He is daunted by our advances in the healing arts and feels that His therapeutic powers have become obsolete. Maybe the explosion in information technology has intimidated Him. It might be that He feels overshadowed by our advances in education, that Common Core has finally leveled the playing field, and that there is no longer a need for pointed, and specific, and individual, religious instruction. Maybe He has grown tired of competing against the avalanche of negative press in a media that has its own agenda. Maybe He has been overwhelmed by the mesmerizing wonders of Industrial Light and Magic, and of C.G.I., and feels that His miracles cannot possibly compete with their enchantments. Maybe He has nothing to add to the dialogue, because we've gotten things figured out on our own, and have demonstrated that we are securely in control of our own destiny.

Maybe none of the above is true, however, which begs the question: Does God still speak to His children? Certainly, we must concede that He could, whenever He wished to do so. A second question, then, is: Does God have any interest in or desire to communicate with His children. The scriptures reveal how deeply He has always cared about us, how intensely He has been concerned about our welfare, and how intertwined are our lives with His work and glory. It seems clear that He would no more abandon us to our own devices, than we would leave a toddler unattended in a dark alleyway in the bad part of town. Why would He ever forsake us, or leave us to the whims of a fate beyond His or our control?

Surely, we need His wise counsel now as much as we ever have, because we have the potential to destroy each other and ourselves if we do not carefully follow His Plan. We need Him and His living prophets today, just as we did in times of old, to guide us around telestial traffic jams. We need help to free ourselves from conceptual quicksands. We need inspired guidance to deal with doctrinal dead ends. We desperately need to be shown how to successfully negotiate the minefields of mortality. We need his authorized and ordained priesthood servants to act as our tactical S.W.A.T. team, and as our personal bomb squad, to identify, address, and neutralize, every threat to our spiritual security.

Angelic counsel was given to Joseph Smith almost 200 years ago, when he was told: "Wherever the sound (of the marvelous work) shall go, it shall cause the ears of men to tingle, and wherever it shall be proclaimed, the pure in heart shall rejoice." When we hear the words of living prophets, the Spirit washes over us with a confirmation that is undeniable. But Moroni cautioned: "Those who draw near to God with their mouths, and honor him with their lips, while their hearts are far from him, will seek its overthrow, and the destruction of those by whose hands it is carried." Then, ominously, Joseph was warned: "Therefore, marvel not if your name is made a derision and had as a by-word among such, if you are the instrument in bringing it, by the gift of God, to the knowledge of the people." ("The Messenger & Advocate"). As Jesus taught: "A prophet is not without honour, save in his own country, and in his own house. (Matthew 13:57). Some people just can't handle the glad tidings of joy.

Naysayers notwithstanding, "what do we hear? Glad tidings from Cumorah! Moroni, an angel from heaven, declaring the fulfillment of the prophets - the book to be revealed. A voice of the Lord in the wilderness of Fayette, Seneca County, declaring the three witnesses to bear record of the book! The voice of Michael on the banks of the Susquehanna, detecting the devil when he appeared as an angel of light! The voice of Peter, James, and John in the wilderness between Harmony, Susquehanna County, and Colesville, Broome County, on the Susquehanna River, declaring themselves as possessing the keys of the kingdom, and of the dispensation of the fulness of times!" (D&C 128:20).

Heavenly Father has responded to our needs. Today, we have someone among us who can stand tall, and with a clear vision see the storm clouds before they appear on the horizon. Noah built the ark long before the barometer plummeted, the sky darkened, and the rains fell. The Law of Tithing was introduced as fire insurance to protect our homes while they still stand, before the great and dreadful day of the Lord comes to consume the wicked in its flames. The temple was reintroduced as a preventive measure, that the earth might avoid being utterly wasted at the coming of the Lord. A Proclamation on The Family was made 13 years before the battle lines were drawn over Proposition 8. Pornography was denounced when the Internet was still in its infancy. Self-reliance and self-sufficiency were advocated before the Great Depression brought the world to its economic knees. The Word of Wisdom was given 138 years before the declaration of war on illicit drugs. The Perpetual Education Fund was announced 160 years before Common Core. The watchmen upon the walls see the enemy while he is yet afar off, allowing us to make ready and to keep him from breaking down the hedges of our vineyards. (See D&C 101:54).

Our living prophets teach us how to live in harmony with God's Plan, show us how to prepare the way for the Lord's return, and invite us to participate in the establishment of His kingdom on the earth. "The greatest event that has ever occurred in the world since the resurrection of the Son of God from the tomb and his ascension on high," declared Joseph F. Smith, "was the coming of the Father and of the Son to that boy Joseph Smith, to prepare the way for the laying of the foundation of his kingdom."

Our living prophets show us how to be happy. They have a knack for seeing the eternal principle of agency in a different light. They recognize that the exercise of free will does entail risk, because the element of failure is real and is always just one decision away, but they have confidence that it is the only way that we may justify our claim to unspeakable joy in our Father's kingdom. Without brow beating us, our prophets give us repetitive opportunities to recommit ourselves to our covenants of obedience to tried and true principles. At the same time, they reassure us that the laws pertaining to happiness will qualify us to receive the blessings tied to obedience. They continually find ways to nurture our spiritual well-being, and inner peace with words of encouragement. "Happiness (after all) is the object and design of our existence, and will be the end thereof," said the Prophet Joseph Smith, "if we pursue the path that leads to it, and this path is virtue, uprightness, faithfulness, holiness, and keeping all the commandments of God." ("Teachings," p. 255).

"The most important prophet, as far as we are concerned, is the one who is living in our day and age. Every generation has need of (counsel) from the living prophet. Therefore, the most crucial reading and pondering which you should do, is of the latest inspired words from the Lord's mouthpiece." (Ezra Taft Benson, "New Era," 1975).

Our living prophets share our perspective, but they are also able to see through the clarifying and purifying lens of eternity. They bless our lives in many ways by nurturing our understanding of the Plan of Salvation. The veil that has been drawn over our eyes, preventing us from seeing eternity with an unimpeded view, is nearly transparent to our prophets. Joseph Smith explained as a statement of fact: "Could you gaze into heaven five minutes, you would know more than you would by reading all that has ever been written on the subject." (H.C., 6:50). Asked how he could govern so many people, he replied: "I teach them correct principles, and they govern themselves. His comprehension of the Plan of Salvation allowed him to teach the body of known truth, to clarify truth that had been heretofore hidden from the world, and to reveal new truth to the world that would enrich the quality of our lives. Truly, the Prophet Joseph Smith "was a prism of the Lord Jesus Christ." (Truman Madsen).

Within the Lord's restored Church of Jesus Christ of Latter-day Saints, the Quorum of The First Presidency, and The Quorum of The Twelve, are composed of living prophets, seers, and revelators. The subjects upon which they have recently focused their attention include the call to be Christ-like, how to receive the Holy Ghost, learning by the Spirit, recognizing revelation, the blessings of obedience, sharing the gospel, family history and temple work, priesthood power, education, building strong families, the protective power of prayer, making covenants with God, helping new members, staying out of debt, preparing for The Second Coming, and understanding the scriptures. (See Conference Reports, 10/ 2015).

These prophets, seers, and revelators, who holds the key of the kingdom and who stand next to Jesus Christ at the head of the church, are to be upheld by our confidence, faith, and prayers. (See D&C 107:22). Of the President of the Quorum of The First Presidency, we have been commanded to give "heed unto all his words and commandments which he shall give unto you as he receiveth them, walking in all holiness before me; For his word ye shall receive, as if from mine own mouth, in all patience and faith. For by doing these things the gates of hell shall not prevail against you; yea, and the Lord God will disperse the powers of darkness from before you, and cause the heavens to shake for your good, his name's glory." (D&C 21:4-6).

One such living prophet has taught: "There will be some things that take patience and faith. You may not like what comes from the authority of the church. It may contradict your political views. It may contradict your social views. It may interfere with some of your social life. But if you listen to these things, as if from the mouth of the Lord himself, with patience and faith, the promise is that the gates of hell shall not prevail against you." (President Harold B. Lee, C.R., 10/1970). At the close of a later general conference, President Ezra Taft Benson reiterated: "For the next six months, your conference edition of the Ensign should stand next to your standard works and be referred to frequently." (C.R., 4/1988).

As it was said of Joseph Smith, so could it be said of each of the more than 100 Apostles (as of 2024) who have carried the mantle of prophet, seer, and revelator in the Last Days, that among their greatest contributions has been their knowledge of what is to come after death. They have done much to clarify our understanding of heaven and to make it seem worth working for.

Godly Qualities

(D&C Section 4)

"There are many among us who have many
revelations, for they are not all stiffnecked. And
as many as are not stiffnecked and have faith, have
communion with the Holy Sprit, which maketh
manifest unto the children of men,
according to their faith."
(Jarom 1:4).

"Now behold, a marvelous work is about to come forth among the children of men." (V. 1). Of course, this refers to both the restoration of the gospel of Jesus Christ, and to the publication of The Book of Mormon. These events were critical to the success of the Plan of Salvation, as it relates to the human family in the Last Days. The Lord seldom intervenes directly in our lives; generally, He works through individuals who serve others. Therefore, the Lord cautioned those who would embark on a course of service to God: "See that ye serve him with all your heart, might, mind and strength, that ye may stand blameless before God at the last day." (V. 2). God requires that His servants be totally committed to the work, and have no reservations. (See Matthew 6:24). The Master called His disciples to a higher plane of spirituality, and to a commitment to selfless consecration of effort. He advised them: "Lay up for yourselves treasures in heaven, where neither moth nor rust doth corrupt, and where thieves do not break through nor steal." (3 Nephi 13:19-20). The key is to lose ourselves in service, even as we let our light shine before men. (See 3 Nephi 12:16).

Every member of The Church of Jesus Christ of Latter-day Saints is invited to be a missionary: "Therefore, if ye have desires to serve God ye are called to the work." (V. 3). "My understanding," declared George Albert Smith, "is that the most important mission that I have in this life is first, to keep the commandments of God, and second, to teach them to my Father's children who do not understand them."

As those enlisted in the missionary army of Jesus Christ continue to focus their attention on their less fortunate brethren, they will eventually be brought into complete harmony with the attributes of their Father in Heaven, whose concern is for the eternal welfare of all of His children. "And ye shall be even as I am, and I am even as the Father, and the Father and I are one," said the Savior to the Three Nephites. (3 Nephi 28:10).

"For behold, the field is white already to harvest; and lo, he that thrusteth in his sickle with his might, the same layeth up in store that he perisheth not, but bringeth salvation to his soul." (V. 4). In the Book of Alma, Ammon metaphorically described the harvest to illustrate for his brethren how thousands had been gathered through their missionary efforts. "Behold, the field was ripe," he said, "and blessed are ye, for ye did thrust in the sickle, and did reap with your might, yea, all the day long did ye labor; and behold the number of your sheaves!" (Alma 26:5). His party had come up out of the Land of Zarahemla into the highlands of Nephi to bring a message of love to their brethren the Lamanites. in the absence of that message, they "would still have been racked with hatred (against the Nephites), and they would also have (remained) strangers to God." (Alma 26:9).

"And faith, hope, charity and love, with an eye single to the gory of God, qualify him for the work." (V. 5). The standard of the world is: "Seeing is believing." But seeing is not only irrelevant to the acquisition of faith, it is often the wrong message that is being presented. The example of Madison Avenue testifies that this is all too true. President Harold B. Lee taught: "You must learn to walk to the edge of the light, and then a few steps into the darkness; then the light will appear and show the way before you." This is the way faith is developed and strengthened.

There are probably three classic definitions of faith that are found in the scriptures. The first is that "faith is not to have a perfect knowledge of things; therefore, if ye have faith ye hope for things which are not seen, which are true." (Alma 32:21). This is correct in the ultimate sense. in Alma's usage, the verse might more clearly read: "Faith is not to have a perfect knowledge of things gained through one's own experiences." In the context in which Alma taught this principle to his Zoramite audience, we must remember that Korihor's demand for a sign was the condition for his faith, since he trusted only his physical senses. The rational approach is the enemy of faith. Some things need to be believed to be seen. (See Commentary Reference to Alma Chapter 32).

The second definition is that "faith is the substance of things hoped for, the evidence of things not seen." (Hebrews 11:1). in this context, faith is not to receive a sign from heaven. As Alma told the Zoramites, "If a man knoweth a thing he hath no cause to believe, for he knoweth it." (Alma 32:18). No exercise of faith is necessary to receive a sign from heaven. When the sign is given, one might have a sure knowledge of the event, but no expenditure of faith has been necessary to produce it. Under proper circumstances, though, "by doing our duty, faith increases until it becomes perfect knowledge." (President Heber J. Grant, C.R., 4/1934). initially, faith is to believe what we do not see, and the reward of faith is to see what we believe.

The third definition is that "faith is things which are hoped for and not seen; wherefore, dispute not because ye see not, for ye receive no witness until after the trial of your faith." (Ether 12:6). it is important to remember that in matters of faith the Lord is not on trial. At the Bar of Justice, the Judge will receive the evidence, and our previous acceptance or rejection of that evidence will determine our reward or punishment. The trial that we call the mortal experience is eminently fair.

Our faith leads us to hope in Christ, the assurance of peace, that the direction of our life is on course, and that the Lord is pleased with, and approves, our efforts. As Mormon said, hope is born of faith. "Behold, I say unto you that ye shall have hope through the atonement of Christ and the power of his resurrection, to be raised up unto life eternal, and this because of your faith in him according to the promise." (Moroni 7:41).

Hope is not trust in some wildly improbable promise, nor is it a high stakes gamble. it is the inevitable result of well-founded faith, when one is "meek and lowly of heart," and in complete control of one's desires and emotions. (Moroni 7:43).

Charity naturally follows a foundation of faith and hope, and is the supreme characteristic of a faithful disciple. (Moroni 7:44-48). Mormon taught "if a man be meek and lowly in heart, and confess by the power of the Holy Ghost that Jesus is the Christ," with a sure hope born of faith, "he must needs have charity." (Moroni 7:44, see 2 Nephi 33, & Ether 12:32).

"And charity suffereth long (or is the quality of patience), and is kind (or is characterized by sensitivity toward others, and is empathic), and envieth not (or is less concerned with telestial trinkets and more focused on celestial sureties), and is not puffed up, (or is humble), seeketh not her own (or is selfless), is not easily provoked (but reflects poise under provocation), thinketh no evil (or has no secret agenda to follow), and rejoiceth not in iniquity (but is repulsed by sin), but rejoiceth in the truth, beareth all things, believeth all things, hopeth all things, endureth all things (or is drawn toward the light, and is continually open to that which is good)." (Moroni 7:45).

Without these qualities, man is nothing, because his progression stops. "If ye have not charity, ye are nothing, for charity never faileth. Wherefore, cleave unto charity, which is the greatest of all (the spiritual gifts), for all things must fail (without it)." (Moroni 7:46). It is the greatest of all the qualities of God Himself, Who is the Possessor of all spiritual gifts.

"Charity is the pure love of Christ, and it endureth forever, and whoso is found possessed of it at the last day, it shall be well with him." (Moroni 7:47, See Ether 12:34). Charity motivates us to Christian service, and in doing so it also prepares us to be like God, so that we will feel comfortable in His Presence. As such, it is a gift bestowed upon the faithful by His grace.

"Remember faith, virtue, knowledge, temperance, patience, brotherly kindness, godliness, charity, humility, diligence." (V. 6). We do this, Peter wrote, "that we might be partakers of the divine nature." (2 Peter 1:4). When God said: "Let us make man in our image, after our likeness," He meant not only that man should have the same physical characteristics as his Parents, but the same spiritual characteristics as well. (See Moses 2:26). Like-minded individuals seek each other out, are drawn to each other, and have a natural affinity for each other.

Faith: "For this end was the law given," to prepare mankind to believe in Christ, "and we are made alive in Christ because of our faith." (2 Nephi 25:25).

Virtue: Alma recognized the virtue of the word, or its incredible power to touch the hearts of the people. An example from the life of the Savior teaches this principle. During His earthly ministry, Jesus was filled with the Spirit of God, and so it was natural that the spiritually hungry were drawn to Him. In Him they satisfied their yearnings.

Jesus, in turn, being a wellspring of the Spirit sensed each moment when need drew upon that source: "And a certain woman, which had an issue of blood twelve years ... when she had heard of Jesus, came in the press behind, and touched his garment. For she said, If I may touch but his clothes, I shall be whole. And straightway she felt in her body that she was healed. And Jesus, immediately knowing in himself that virtue had gone out of him, turned him about and said, Who touched my clothes?" (Mark 5:25-30).

This episode from the life of the Savior is meaningful because it gives us assurance that in a wonderfully complete manner God is sensitive to our needs and to our prayers, however small and insignificant they may seem to us. He does hear us, because in conformity to spiritual law, we draw upon the life force, the virtue, that is the Spirit of God. Every time we call upon God, we are, in effect, touching His garment.

Knowledge: "No man knoweth of (God's) ways, save it be revealed unto him." (Jacob 4:8). President John Taylor echoed this verse. He said: "No matter what ability and talent a man may possess, all must come under this rule if they wish to know the Father and the Son. If knowledge of them is not obtained through revelation it cannot be obtained at all." ("The Gospel Kingdom," p. 112). The light and knowledge men receive of God is given by "revelation." This principle is so basic that it almost requires no definition, because it speaks to the very soul of man.

Temperance: Wo unto those who are enslaved by drunkenness, and by selfish indulgence. "Wo unto them that rise up early in the morning, that they may follow strong drink, that continue until night, and wine inflame them!" (2 Nephi 15:11). Such people are blinded to the work of the Lord that is before their very eyes. "They regard not the work of the Lord, neither consider the operation of his hands." (2 Nephi 15:12). They are captive because they have no knowledge of God. "Their honorable men are famished, and their multitude dried up with thirst." (2 Nephi 15:13).

Their condition is contrasted to God's exalted state. "Therefore, hell hath enlarged herself, and opened her mouth without measure; and their glory, and their multitude, and their pomp, and he that rejoiceth, shall descend into it. And the mean (or common) man shall be brought down, and the mighty man shall be humbled, and the eyes of the lofty shall be humbled." (2 Nephi 15:14-15). "But the Lord of Hosts will be exalted in judgment, and God that is holy shall be sanctified in righteousness." (2 Nephi 15:16).

Patience: The Lord is patient and long-suffering, and yet extends His arm of mercy long after the faint-hearted would have given up. When Elijah complained to the Lord that "the children of Israel have forsaken thy covenant, thrown down thine altars, and slain thy prophets with the sword; and I, even I only, am left; and they seek my life to take it away," the Lord responded: "Yet I have left me seven thousand in Israel, all the knees which have not bowed unto Baal, and every mouth which hath not kissed him." (1 Kings 19:14 & 18).

Brotherly Kindness: President Joseph Fielding Smith, Jr. declared: "The greatest crime in all this world is to lead men and women away from the true principles." (C.R., 4/1951). The following story illustrates the level of human decency and concern that is expected of each of us, and particularly of members of the church.

Before Fiorello La Guardia became mayor of New York City, he was a magistrate. One day there appeared before him a man accused of stealing a loaf of bread. Upon questioning, the man explained that he'd committed the crime to feed his family, for they were starving. Whereupon, La Guardia dismissed the case, and sentenced all present in the courtroom to pay a fine for living in a city where a man must steal to feed his family.

The Lord illustrated the gospel principle of concern for the welfare of others, when He said unto them, "I am the bread of life: He that cometh to me shall never hunger; and he that believeth on me shall never thirst." (John 6:35). In the Eternal Court of Justice, what will be the penalty for failure to provide others with the Bread of Life, or for feeding them stale, or moldy, or otherwise unwholesome bread?

Lyman Abbott said: "The brotherhood of man is an integral part of Christianity no less than the Fatherhood of God; and to deny the one is no less infidel than to deny the other." Truly, there is no brotherhood of man without the fatherhood of God. "The mystic bond of brotherhood makes all men one." (Thomas Carlyle). "The universe is but one great city, full of beloved ones, divine and human, by nature endeared to each other." (Epictetus).

Godliness: The covenants we make with God reflect His attributes. God is moral, so He gives us the Covenant of Chastity; He has charity, so He commands us to love Him and each other. God is disciplined, so He gives us the Law of Obedience; because He is a righteous steward, He gives us the Law of Consecration. Because He loves His less fortunate children, He gives us the Law of the Fast. Because His is a perfected, resurrected body, He gives us the Word of Wisdom. Because He is omniscient, He gives us the commandment to seek knowledge. In consequence of the Gift of His Son, He gives us the Law of Sacrifice. Because He rested from His labors on the seventh day, He gives us the Law of the Sabbath.

God is our Father, and He is perfect in every way. He could give us everything He has, but what He is, we must earn for ourselves, as we struggle to overcome adversity and gain self-mastery. The purpose of the covenants we make with Him is to help us to focus our efforts to become as He is. if this were impossible, covenants would be unnecessary.

Charity: The only motive strong enough to encourage men to exercise that self-control required by the gospel of Jesus Christ is love of God and Man. it is no coincidence that these are the two great commandments upon which hang both the law and the prophets.

Humility: There is a contrast between those who are stiff-necked, and those who have faith. Those who suffer from the former condition have difficulty looking up to Heavenly Father for guidance, over to priesthood leaders for counsel, around to seek out those in need, or down in an attitude of humility. The latter enjoy the companionship of the Holy Spirit or Holy Ghost, "which maketh manifest unto the children of men, according to their faith." (Jarom 1:4).

Diligence: President Joseph F. smith declared that "no one needs fear in their heart when they are conscious of having lived up to the principles of truth and righteousness as God has required it at their hands, according to their best knowledge and understanding." When we are diligent in our obedience, our agency enjoys its greatest expression. This is one of the hardest things for the unconverted to understand.

"Ask, and ye shall receive; knock, and it shall be opened unto you." (V. 7). Wo unto those who do not feel the need to receive any more instruction from God. (See 2 Nephi 28:27). The Savior taught: "He that receiveth my law, and doeth it, the same is my disciple." (D&C 41:5). Blessings that follow true discipleship have a performance cost. "Blessed are those which hunger and thirst after righteousness, for they shall be filled. (Matthew 5:6). Receiving the Law of Christ seems to be an ongoing process. Overindulgence is generally to be avoided as a sin of commission, but as the Psalmist wrote of those who diligently pursue a righteous life: "Thou preparest a table before me in the presence of mine enemies; thou anointest my head with oil; my cup runneth over." (Psalms 23:5).

The challenge of individuals and society is not that they receive too much revelation, but that they receive too little. They also look in all the wrong places. Throughout the Bible, the prophets repeatedly warned Israel against dalliances with magicians, sorcerers, witches, familiar spirits, astrologers, exorcists, and in participating in divinations, enchantments, and other activities that solicit the intervention of evil spirits. Isaiah mocked those who relied on such, when he said: "Thou art wearied in the multitude of thy counsels. Let now the astrologers, the stargazers, and the monthly prognosticators, stand up, and save thee from these things that shall come upon thee. Behold, they shall be as stubble; the fire shall burn them; they shall not deliver themselves from the power of the flame; there shall not be a coal to warm at, nor fire to sit before it." (Isaiah 47:13-14).

On one occasion the Prophet Joseph Smith asked: "Does it remain for a people who never had faith enough to call down one scrap of revelation from heaven, and for all they have now are indebted to the faith of another people who lived hundreds and thousands of years before them, does it remain for them to say how much God has spoken and how much he has not spoken?" (H.C., 11:17-18).

Another time, he said: "We shall at last have to come to this conclusion, whatever we may think of revelation, that without it we can neither know nor understand anything of God, or the devil." Revelation is vital to our understanding if we are to successfully negotiate the dangerous passage through mortality.

Joseph Smith said: "I thank God that I have got this old book (as he held up the Bible) but I thank him more for the gift of the Holy Ghost. I have got the oldest book in the world, but I (also) have the oldest book in my heart, even the gift of the Holy Ghost." ("Teachings," p. 349).

The Lord explained the process when He asked: "He that is ordained of me and sent forth to preach the word of truth by the Comforter, in the Spirit of truth, doth he preach it by the Spirit of truth or some other way? And if it be by some other way it is not of God. And again, he that receiveth the word of truth, doth he receive it by the Spirit of truth or some other way? If it be some other way it is not of God." (D&C 50:17-20).

As Paul taught, the key to gospel knowledge is personal revelation, and "let him be accursed who preaches any other gospel." (Galatians 1:8-12). "That which is of God is light; and he that receiveth light, and continueth in God, receiveth more light: and that light groweth brighter and brighter until the perfect day." (D&C 50:24).

God's Tactical Flashlight

"The justice
of God did also divide
the wicked from the righteous;
and the brightness thereof was like
unto the brightness of a flaming fire,
which ascendeth up unto God forever
and ever, and hath no end."
(1 Nephi 15:30).

"How long will ye suffer yourselves to be led by foolish and blind guides? Yea, how long will ye choose darkness rather than light?" (Helaman 13:29).

Sometimes it seems almost as if positive energy comes in discrete packages that are dispensed by especially cheerful individuals who always have a smile on their face and a spring in their step. For example, think of the amazing ability of some to light up the room by their mere presence. Think of charismatic leaders who inspire their followers to defy the odds and attempt the impossible, of those whose compelling charm and magnetic personalities have an almost mystical draw, of those who can so easily captivate others with the sparkle of their rhetoric, of those with the hypnotic ability to mesmerize their listeners with magical word-portraits that are motivational and inspiring, and of the natural appeal and irresistible draw of those whose minds and spirits have been endowed with discernment, inspiration, and revelation, and whose eyes and lips have been touched by the finger of God.

These people have dedicated themselves to worthwhile activities that give their lives meaning and purpose. They are committed to self-improvement and engage with others in ways that are mutually supportive. They do not waste time being defensive, but instead welcome constructive criticism. They share their knowledge and ideas with others and are mentors to those who are on the same path toward self-actualization. They enjoy the journey as much as the destination. They do not allow power and influence to corrupt them or to deter them from focusing their energies on core principles. Even when life throws them a curve, they smile. They realize that happiness is contagious, and as carriers, they infect others with cheerfulness. They are courteous and thoughtful, and speak of others as if their parrot were the town gossip. They are kind and gentle, especially when interacting with the village idiot. When necessity arises, they use diplomacy, celebrating the differences between individuals, because they know that we are all children of God, with unique talents and abilities.

When I visualize these individuals and their capacity to stimulate, encourage, provoke, and persuade others to embrace their positive energy, I compare them to the dramatically illuminating and enlightening power of high intensity tactical flashlights, the kind that are driven by light emitting diodes that are fueled by lithium-ion batteries.

But those who hum with positive energy go even a step further. They not only generate enthusiasm, but they also have learned how to compartmentalize its negative counterparts. They have discovered how to neutralize bad vibrations. In the "Ghostbusters" movie franchise, mischievous ectoplasmic entities captured by the team were transferred to a secure and stable containment field. Our God-given fetters are more subtle, but infinitely more effective, because they do not rely on contraptions that must be plugged in to the wall socket in order to function. Ours consist of powerful spiritual guidance systems that find their expression in the security of obedience to unchanging principles that are then magnified by provident living, and by the solidarity of our repetitive recommitment to covenants through ordinances that are administered by the priesthood.

In "Ghostbusters," the effect of the inadvertent disruption of the electrical power flow to the psycho-kinetic containment unit was catastrophic. In life, the consequences related to ignorance of negative psycho-kinetic energy can be just as calamitous. When we are about to be "slimed" by the seething spiritual gloom that swirls about us like effluent spewing from a broken sewer pipe, we must consciously and deliberately encircle it with a containment boom, channel it into a suitable vessel, and then slam on the lid, securing it tightly. Even if the darkness within the trap is later opened, the discharge that attempts to escape will be dissipated and neutralized, because it will be instantly subjected to the dazzling light emitting diodes that are part of our own customized versions of Dr. Egon Spengler's ingenious portable proton pack.

When we have been quickened by the Holy Ghost, we become His particle accelerators and His tactical flashlights, prominently and strategically set on a hill so that we cannot be hidden. For all the world to see, we confidently publish abroad in the land our noble commission to give "light unto all that are in the house." We let our lights "so shine before men, that they may see (our) good works, and glorify (our) Father which is in heaven." (Matthew 5:14-16). By doing so, the concentrated power that radiates from the Holy Ghost is gathered out from under a bushel, where, left unattended, it could have easily decayed into destructive negative energy. We focus that clean, pure, environmentally friendly light in positive directions. In Ghostbuster terminology, we "cross the streams" when we are faced with inter-dimensional portals that require extreme measures (the "Gozer Gambit") in order to close the door with finality on negative dimensional realities that continually probe our firewalls in an attempt to encroach upon our world.

The darkness that oozes out from those destructive dominions threatens to contaminate our spiritual symmetry, causing a stupor of thought. As Samuel the Lamanite asked: "How long will ye suffer yourselves to be led by foolish and blind guides? Yea, how long will ye choose darkness rather than light?" (Helaman 13:29). If we were to try to teach the world the principles of the gospel by relying upon only the illumination provided by the dim light of the moon, it would be nigh unto impossible. If, for additional illumination, we utilized the glow provided by an inexpensive flashlight, or relied upon the weakened energy reserves of proton packs that lacked a full charge, we might just be able to make out the glimmering facets of the light of the Spirit. These additional lumens of energy are like the faint glow of the microwave background radiation from the Big Bang, and might be likened to the Light of Christ that permeates the universe. At 2.76° Kelvin, it is better than nothing at all, but arguably, since it hovers just above absolute zero, is less than ideal.

Before the introduction of the proton packs or the spiritual tactical flashlights provided by the gift of the Holy Ghost, the real problem in the world was that in their efforts to clarify their consideration of Christ, even earnest seekers of truth were only "multiplying mirrors and studying angles without increasing the light," when what was really needed was a flood of protons "that would not only replace the darkness, but would also illuminate elements and principles that, heretofore, had been only dimly perceived." (See B.H. Roberts, The Truth, The Way, The Life, p. 263). In their attempts to increase the light by playing the angles, they were able to see a bit more clearly, but still, many basic principles remained only dimly perceived. The problem was that these individuals were only spinning their wheels. The number of available lumens of energy had not been increased. What was really needed was more light! Heavenly Father orchestrated the Restoration in order to address the problem of darkness in the world. Hence, the Savior appeared to Joseph Smith in the Sacred Grove as "the light which shineth in darkness." (D&C 11:11).

The Restoration then set in motion a number of protocols that were designed to increase the amount of available light. These measures generously provided more than enough tactical flashlights to go around. Heavenly Father saw to it that every earnest student of the scriptures would be able to read even its fine print with unerring clarity. Its footnotes would snap into sharp focus. Its topical guide would intuitively begin to make more sense. The relevance of the teachings of His prophets, and of additional scriptures, became increasingly apparent. Foundation principles knit together coherently as they were stitched into an understandable pattern, and the power of the word and the witness of truth was conveyed without the need for external warrant.

God decided to change the name of His proton pack to something that would be less trendy but still catch our attention; something that would more dramatically describe the increased illumination. The spiritual tactical flashlight was called "the Gift of the Holy Ghost." Its power would far surpass the output that had heretofore been provided by the Light of Christ. Those who would subsequently enroll in His curriculum would enjoy a many-fold increase in their spiritual visual acuity. Whereas they had been limping along with a few hundred lumens to mark the path of progress, now they would have thousands at their disposal. They would feel that their whole bodies had been filled with light. They would feel the comfort of an increase in their protection from evil influences, and would experience the flush of excitement as they vanquished the adversary with the simple weapons of light and truth. They would savor the indescribable feeling of light penetrating to their nethermost parts. Their souls would resonate with understanding, as when Joseph Smith received "The Vision" known as Section 76 of the Doctrine & Covenants. The prophet is said to have declared: "My whole body was full of light, and I could see even out at the ends of my fingers and toes." (Philo Dibble, Journal record).

This spiritual upgrade of our positron colliders to full-fledged electrostatic accelerators with well-collimated particle beam technology may help to explain the circumstances surrounding the appearance of the Angel Moroni to young Joseph in his bedchamber, in 1821. He later wrote of the experience: "While I was thus in the act of calling upon God, I discovered a light appearing in my room, which continued to increase until the room was lighter than at noonday, when immediately a personage appeared at my bedside, standing in the air, for his feet did not touch the floor. He had on a loose robe of most exquisite whiteness…beyond anything earthly I had ever seen; nor do I believe that any earthly thing could be made to appear so exceedingly white and brilliant. His hands were naked, and his arms also, a little above the wrist; so, also, were his feet naked, as were his legs, a little above the ankles. His head and neck were also bare. I could discover that he had no other clothing on but this robe, as it was open, so that I could see into his bosom. Not only was his robe exceedingly white, but his whole person was glorious beyond description, and his countenance truly like lightning. The room was exceedingly light, but not so very bright as immediately around his person." (J.S.H. 1:30-32).

In the scriptures, light is mentioned 453 times, while light and its contrasting element of darkness are linked together 103 times. One particularly vivid description of darkness is found in The Book of Mormon in the eighth chapter of 3 Nephi. It states that at the time of the crucifixion of Christ, "there was darkness upon the face of the land." (3 Nephi 9:19 See Matthew 27:51). In Book of Mormon lands, so overpowering was the murky blackness, so complete and total and universal, that "those who had not fallen could feel the vapor of darkness." (3 Nephi 8:20, see Exodus 10:21-23). Not only the Holy Ghost, but also the Spirit of Christ had been withdrawn; thus, "there could not be any light at all." (3 Nephi 8: 21, see D&C 84:45-46, & 88:7-13). The survivors of the storm that had swept over the countryside could see neither "the sun, nor the moon, nor the stars, for so great were the mists of darkness which were upon the face of the land." (3 Nephi 8: 22).

Hopefully, this Book of Mormon record is as close as any of us will ever come to understanding just how overwhelming will be the spiritual darkness that will prevail among those who are resurrected to a kingdom without glory, which is as a "lake which burneth with fire and brimstone, which is the second death." (D&C 63:17). For the Sons of Perdition, existence in such a spiritual vacuum will be a living hell.

At the very least, we are reminded of the experience of Joseph in the grove near his home outside of Palmyra, New York: "Thick darkness gathered around me, and it seemed to me for a time as if I were doomed to sudden destruction. But, exerting all my powers to call upon God to deliver me out of the power of this enemy which had seized upon me, and at the very moment when I was ready to sink into despair and abandon myself to destruction - not to an imaginary ruin, but to the power of some actual being from the unseen world, who had such marvelous power as I had never before felt in any being - just at this moment of great alarm, I saw a pillar of light exactly over my head, above the brightness of the sun, which descended gradually until it fell upon me. It no sooner appeared than I found myself delivered from the enemy which held me bound. When the light rested upon me I saw two Personages, whose brightness and glory defy all description, standing above me in the air. One of them spake unto me, calling me by name and said, pointing to the other: This is My Beloved Son. Hear Him!" (J.S.H. 1:15-17). Joseph had walked in darkness, but had seen a great light. He had dwelt in the land of the shadow of death, but upon him the light had shined. (See Isaiah 9:2).

Eighteen hundred years earlier, the Savior had taught the Jews: "If thy whole body, therefore, be full of light, having no part dark, the whole shall be full of light, as when the bright shining of a candle doth give thee light." (Luke 11:36). Joseph had powerfully learned that "light and truth forsake that evil one." (D&C 93:37). The expression of this divine principle was fully realized when he then beheld both the Father and the Son in the Sacred Grove. As Paul had taught the Thessalonian Saints, so had the blessing come to pass: "And then shall that wicked one be revealed, whom the Lord shall consume with the spirit of his mouth, and...destroy with the brightness of his coming." (J.S.T. 2 Thessalonians 2:8).

Just as the Ghostbusters confronted Gozer in its temple on the top of a Manhattan skyscraper at 53 Central Park West, so too, when we face horrifying "Sumerian demons" or giant "Stay Puft Marshmallow Men" in whatever form they choose to masquerade themselves, our training should compel us to turn to our proton packs, "for the Lord is our defence, and the Holy One of Israel is our king." (Psalms 89:18). "And the Lord will create upon every dwelling place of mount Zion, and upon her assemblies, a cloud and smoke by day, and the shining of a flaming fire by night" to resist and overcome the enemy. (Isaiah 4:5).

In the real world, our tactical flashlight versions of proton packs provide powerful bursts of light with the capacity to temporarily stun our adversaries. Spiritual tactical flashlights can do the same thing, but even more efficiently. The power of the ordinances of the gospel and of our related covenants is so great that it can be a shield and a protection to us against evil influences. It can enable us to disorient our foes, so that we might have time to complete our mortal missions and return with honor to our heavenly home.

As Joseph Smith received instruction, the meaning and intent of the scriptures was opened to his understanding, so much so that he could actually comprehend the mind and will of God. (See D&C 76:12). "For the word of the Lord is truth, and whatsoever is truth is light, and whatsoever is light is Spirit, even the Spirit of Jesus Christ." (D&C 84:45).

He may have been the first to explode the myth of using only 10% of our brains. He came to regularly enjoy a many fold increase in the illumination in his mind of difficult to understand principles.

As he matured in the gospel, the unknown possibilities of existence crystallized in his brain. He was transformed to understand in a tangible way that "intelligence cleaveth unto intelligence; wisdom receiveth wisdom; truth embraceth truth; virtue loveth virtue; light cleaveth unto light; mercy...claimeth her own; justice continueth its course, (and) judgment goeth before the face of him who sitteth upon the throne." (D&C 88:40).

As we ponder the scriptures, the Spirit reveals just how breathtaking increasing the light can be. In visions splendid, we are on our way attended by the Holy Ghost, but only if we establish habit patterns to keep our "tactical lights," the spiritual versions of our proton packs, on at all times, locked and loaded with the safety off. We need to keep ourselves worthy and choose wisely, as the Grail Knight warned in the motion picture "Indiana Jones and The Last Crusade." Those of us who bear the vessels of the Lord need to be clean, for "he that keepeth his commandments receiveth truth and light, until he is glorified in truth and knoweth all things." (D&C 93:28).

There are many devices in the world that promote themselves as proton packs, including neutron wands, bozon darts, particle accelerators, and containment lasers. A recent Internet search found over 6 million sites that reference these devices. Most turn out to be inferior imitations offered by less than reputable online retailers. Every one, it seems, endorses itself as the best. But, in our quest to find the Holy Grail of Light, we must never settle for what is really life in a shabby room illuminated by a bare bulb hanging from a frayed cord, in a second-class hotel in the bad part of town. Instead, we must hold out for a positron collider, proton pack, or tactical light powerful enough to illuminate the way to the holy hill of the Lord, and to His tabernacle. (See Psalms 43:3). As Obi Won Kenobe would say: May the Force always be with us!

When we have paid a fair price, and have received our device as advertised, we must handle it with reverence, as if it were a Jedi lightsaber, our own personal Liahona, or even a Urim and Thummim. We must resist the temptation to jump ahead without mastering all of the operating instructions. We must study and practice, and be diligent and consistent in our training. Only then, may we "press forward with a steadfastness in Christ, having a perfect brightness of hope, and a love of God and of all men." (2 Nephi 31:20).

Before initially utilizing the light, we must make sure our batteries are at full capacity, and afterwards, replenish them as frequently as necessary. The dynamo that is the repository of our spiritual strength has a memory like an elephant and likes to be fully charged. However, repeated use will only increase its capacity and make it stronger. The number of cycles available for our use is endless. One helpful feature is the option to leave our light on all the time, so that we may have unbridled confidence that "the sun shall be no more (our) light by day; neither for brightness shall the moon give light unto (us), but the Lord shall be unto (us) an everlasting light, and (our) God (our) glory." (Isaiah 60:19).

If we have been abiding by the Light of Christ, however, we have only been given a glimpse into the limitless power of the intrinsic light that rests within the Godhead. With an awakening comprehension, we begin to understand that our "Father, and the Son, and the Holy Ghost are one," and that they share a palpable divine power and authority. (3 Nephi 11:27). The Holy Ghost, in particular, seems to have the ability to dazzle us with an endless reserve of photons that illuminate every corner of our minds and our spirits. The promises proffered by the combined capacity of the intrinsic light possessed by the Holy Trinity is beyond our comprehension. Particle physics tells us that, at the moment of the Big Bang, there was an incomprehensible number of photons, or units of electromagnetic energy, that were created. The number is 1 followed by 89 zeroes, which is essentially insignificant when compared to the luminosity of God. At the end of the day, "there is no power but of God." The powers that we can define, measure, and quantify as photons, "are ordained of God" for the use of the Trinity, to provide reliable light in a dark and dreary world. (Romans 13:1).

All the members of the Godhead possess the inherent electro-magnetic capacity of a tactical flashlight, calibrated to an infinite scale. Their realm, the Celestial Kingdom, is full of an unfathomable light. In the Kirtland Temple Dedicatory Prayer, Joseph Smith envisioned "bright, shining seraphs" who surrounded the throne of God. (D&C 109:79). Isaiah likewise described seraphim with live coals in their hands. (See Isaiah 6:6). Ezekiel saw the glory of the Lord that "stood over the threshold of the house" of God, and that it "was filled with (a) cloud," and he saw its court, that "was full of the brightness of the Lord's glory." (Ezekiel 10:4).

God has given us clues regarding just how bright His glory really is. He has instilled in us a sense of curiosity that almost compels us to stare in wonder at the night sky, as we attempt to absorb with our minds what seems to be an infinite number of stars. The Milky Way, a glowing smear of light cast from 100 to 400 billion stars, mesmerizes us. Myths from around the world give it its name and explain its origin. The Greeks believed it was created when suckling Heracles dribbled the breast milk of Hera, the wife of Zeus, across the night sky. It was also described as the trail to Mount Olympus, the home of the Gods, and as the path of ruin made by the chariot of the Sun God Helios. In Sanskrit, the Milky Way was called Akash Ganga (Ganges of the Heavens), and was considered sacred. Hindu cosmology explains the galaxy as an ocean of milk churned by the gods for a thousand years in order to release Amrita, the nectar of immortal life. All we know for sure about the Milky Way and our universe is what God told Moses: "The heavens, they are many, and they cannot be numbered unto man; but they are numbered unto me, for they are mine." (Moses 1:37).

But how many stars can we see with just the naked eye, without the aid of a spiritual Hubble telescope or tactical flashlight? The total comes to a paltry 9,000 stars visible across the entire sky, but inasmuch as we can only see half the celestial sphere at any moment, we must necessarily divide that number by two, to arrive at 4,500 stars. We can see about one star per cubic parsec (one second of arc). If we were at the core of the galaxy, we could see 100 times that many, and if we were inside one of the Milky Way's many globular clusters, we could see 1,000 stars per cubic parsec. Both the day and the night sky would be filled with over 4.5 million visible stars! Their light would be so bright that it would fill the entire sky, and we might think that we were near Kolob, which "is set nigh unto the throne of God." (Abraham 3:9).

No wonder that the Lord described Himself as "the light, and the life, and the truth of the world." (Ether 4:12). John said He "is light, and in him is no darkness at all." (1 John 1:15). After Joseph Smith had seen the Savior in vision in the Kirtland Temple, he said: "His eyes were as a flame of fire; the hair of his head was white like the pure snow; his countenance shone above the brightness of the sun; and his voice was as the sound of the rushing of great waters, even the voice of Jehovah." (D&C 110:3). David also described the countenance of the Lord, and wrote that it consisted of "light." (See Psalms 4:6). Jeremiah described the revelatory process as words that were in his heart as a burning fire shut up in his bones, that made him weary with forbearing, so much so that he could not stay. (See Jeremiah 20:9).

Following the long night of apostasy generally characterized as The Dark Ages, light and truth once again illuminate our day, just as they did in ancient times. Isaiah wrote prophetically of latter-day Israel: "Arise, shine; for thy light is come, and the glory of the Lord is risen upon thee. For … the Lord shall arise upon thee, and his glory shall be seen upon thee. And the Gentiles shall come to thy light, and kings to the brightness of thy rising." (Isaiah 60:1-3).

Before time existed, the physical and spiritual properties of light and darkness contributed to a division among the people that culminated in "war in heaven." We can almost hear the clash of words, as "Michael and his angels fought against the dragon, and the dragon and his angels fought against Michael." (J.S.T. Revelation 12:6). Nephi wrote of the eternal consequences of that conflict: "Our father also saw that the justice of God did also divide the wicked from the righteous; and the brightness thereof was like unto the brightness of a flaming fire, which ascendeth up unto God forever and ever, and hath no end." (1 Nephi 15:30).

During His mortal ministry, Christ was "the life and the light of the world (and) the word of truth and righteousness." (Alma 38:9). He declared: "I am come a light into the world, that whosoever believeth on me should not abide in darkness." (John 12:46). Isaiah had prophetically declared that His glory would "kindle a burning like the burning of a fire." (Isaiah 10:16). David expressed the hope we all share, that he would be delivered from the jaws of death, so that he might "walk before God in the light of the living." (Psalms 56:13).

Without the influence of the Savior, and without the comfort of knowing that we have tactical flashlights upon which we can rely, "we wait for light, but behold obscurity; for brightness, but we walk in darkness. We grope for the wall like the blind ... as if we had no eyes: we stumble at noonday as in the night; we are in desolate places as dead men. We roar like bears, and mourn sore like doves: we look for judgment, but there is none; for salvation, but it is far off from us. For our transgressions are multiplied before (God), and our sins testify against us." (Isaiah 59:9-12). In contrast, the light that blazes from our spiritual tactical flashlights shows us the way to dwell within the secure envelope of the word of God. It is "a lamp unto (our) feet, and a light unto (our) path." (Psalms 119:105). His bright and beautiful creations draw us closer to Him. "All things bright and beautiful, all creatures great and small. All things wise and wonderful. The Lord God made them all." (Cecil Francis Alexander).

The Savior taught: "The Comforter, which is the Holy Ghost, whom the Father will send in my name, he shall teach you all things, and bring all things to your remembrance, whatsoever I have said unto you." (John 14:26). When we receive inspiration from heaven, it is as if flash bulbs have gone off in our heads. This may help us to understand why Einstein described the expansion of his understanding of the physical world as "a storm breaking loose" in his mind.

Lightning is a "striking" example of the storm of God, and each time we witness its blinding flash, accompanied by a resounding clap of thunder, we should be reminded of Him. The Savior revealed: "Any man who hath seen any or the least of these hath seen God moving in his majesty and power." (D&C 88:47). That seething energy envelops the earth and turns it into a fiery hot cauldron. There are estimated to be around 2,000 lightning storms raging across the face of the earth at any given time, contributing to over 100 ground strikes per second. The air around these can reach a temperature 3 times hotter than the surface of the sun. The estimated peak power of a single bolt can be 1,000 Giga Watts (one thousand million watts). The total energy pent up and often released in a large thunderstorm is thought to be enough to meet the energy needs of the United States for 20 minutes.

These are impressive statistics, but lightning is just a whisper of the power and influence of God. To provide a constant reminder of Him, ancient Israel kept a fire burning upon the altar in the temple. (See Leviticus 6:13). When Moses was high on the mount, "the angel of the Lord appeared unto him in a flame of fire out of the midst of a bush: and he looked, and, behold, the bush burned with fire, and the bush was not consumed." (Exodus 3:2). Channukah, the Jewish Festival of Light, commemorates the miracle in the temple when the candles of the Menorah burned for eight days, after being filled with only enough oil to last for one. The recurring miracle, however, is not our witness of thunderstorms, or of burning bushes and lamps, but that "truth shineth!" (D&C 88:7). Even the least among us can discern between truth and its dark counterpart, because the former has an intrinsic glow and an enduring quality. It lasts forever, for "intelligence, or the light of truth, was not created or made, neither indeed can be." (D&C 93:29).

The physical manifestations of lightning and thunder from heaven are the equivalents of our spiritual tactical flashlights, and remind us of the power of God, for it is He Who "maketh lightnings." (Psalms 135:7). It is His voice that is the thunder in the heavens, and it is His lightning that streaks across the sky and causes the earth to tremble and shake. (See Psalms 77:18). Lightning may have been created by the hand of God as a type and a shadow, for as it "cometh out of the east, and shineth even unto the west; so shall also the coming of the Son of man be." (Matthew 24:27).

When the angel of the Lord descended from heaven after the death and resurrection of the Savior, "his countenance was like lightning, and his raiment white as snow." (Matthew 28:2-3). As the Psalmist recorded: "His lightnings enlightened the world, (and) the earth saw, and trembled." (Psalms 97:4). Perhaps "thunderings, and lightnings" are the best way to describe how conversation between the Gods in the Celestial Kingdom would sound to mortal ears. (Revelation 8:5). God's testimony, after all, is "the voice of thunderings, and the voice of lightnings." (D&C 88:90).

"And the temple of God was opened in heaven, and there was seen in his temple the ark of his testament: and there were lightnings, and voices, and thunderings." (Revelation 11:19). "And it came to pass" that there was "a thick cloud upon the mount, and the voice of the trumpet exceeding loud; so that all the people that (were) in the camp (of Israel) trembled." (Exodus 19:16). Everyone shared a common experience, as their raw nerve endings were touched by the power and influence of God. "And all the people saw the thunderings, and the lightnings, and the noise of the trumpet, and the mountain smoking." (Exodus 20:18).

"And out of the throne (of God) proceeded lightnings and thunderings and voices." (Revelation 4:5). "When he uttereth his voice, there is a multitude of waters in the heavens, and he causeth the vapours to ascend from the ends of the earth; he maketh lightnings with rain, and bringeth forth the wind." (Jeremiah 10:13). "How oft have I called," He asked, "by the voice of thunderings, and by the voice of lightnings, (D&C 43:25). "And the voice of his word," wrote Daniel, "was like the voice of a multitude. (Daniel 10:6).

At the end of the day, as Rabindranath Tagore mused, there will be eye-kissing, heart-sweetening light that dances at the center of our lives and strikes the chords of our love; and there will be butterflies that spread their sails on a sea of light, with lilies and jasmine that surge up on the wave crests of light that is shattered into gold on every cloud and scattered in profusion as gemstones. This is the familiar light that is the province of all those who have been born again into a newness of life.

This is the light that reminds us that on one special evening two thousand years ago, there was no darkness at all, "but it was as light as though it was mid-day. And it came to pass that the sun did rise in the morning again, according to its proper order; and they knew that it was the day that the Lord should be born." (3 Nephi 1:19).

In the scriptures, the first recorded words of Heavenly Father were: "Let there be light." (Genesis 1:3). His last recorded words were "This is my beloved Son, Hear Him." (J.S.H. 1:17). These two verses are inextricably linked and are bookends to our faith. Our own Sun rises and falls on our desire to be drawn to His light and to be mesmerized by His magic.

(The Appearance of) Gold

Moroni twice referred to the plates,
but only in reference to hiding them in the
earth. (See Ether 15:11, & Mormon 8:4). Likewise,
"Ammaron, being constrained by the Holy Ghost, did
hide up the records which were sacred, yea, even all the
sacred records which had been handed down from
generation to generation, which were sacred."
(4 Nephi 1:48-49). It may simply be that
the custodians of the record were more
focused on the message than
on the material.

Joseph Smith recorded in his History that Moroni told him that the book that was hidden in the Hill Cumorah was "written upon gold plates." (J.S.H. 1:34). But The Book of Mormon record itself does not corroborate Moroni's characterization of the gold composition of the plates. In the church, however, it is commonly accepted that the records, other than the Plates of Brass, were "gold plates." Gold has always denoted value, and at the very least, the precious gift of The Book of Mormon is equivalent to the gifts of gold, frankincense, and myrrh, bestowed by the Wise Men of the East upon the Christ child in Bethlehem.

The first plates that we actually encounter in The Book of Mormon are The Plates of Brass, (see 1 Nephi 3:12) which had "the records of the holy scriptures upon them," including "the genealogy of (Lehi's) forefathers." (Alma 37:3). These plates would yet fulfil prophecy, for they were to be "kept and preserved by the hand of the Lord until they should go forth unto every nation, kindred, tongue, and people, that they shall know of the mysteries contained thereon." (Alma 37:4, see Mosiah 2:9). By these mysteries, Alma meant history and doctrine discerned and understood only by the power of the Spirit.

The Three Witnesses to The Book of Mormon wrote only that they had "seen the plates which contain this record" without reference to the specific composition of the metal, although they went into great detail to describe the engravings themselves and their purpose to benefit humanity. Various Book of Mormon record-keepers referred to "plates of ore." (See 1 Nephi 19:1, Mosiah 21:27, & Mormon 8:5). When the prophets referred to a specific material, it was generally to "brass." (See 1 Nephi 3:3, 3:12, 3:24, 4:16, 4:24, 4:28, 5:10, 5:14, 5:18-19, 13:23, 19:21-22, 22:1, & 22:30, 2 Nephi 4:2, 4:5, & 5:12, Omni 1:14, Mosiah 1:3, 1:16, 10:16, 28:11, & 28:20, Alma 37:3, & 3 Nephi 1:2 & 10:17). "Plates of gold" are mentioned only in Mosiah 8:9 & 28:11, where they specifically refer to the 24 Gold Plates of Ether, which had been found in "a land which was covered with bones of men, and of beasts, and (that) was also covered with ruins of buildings of every kind." (Mosiah 8:8). Mormon, who had access to all the records and who abridged many of them, never referred to plates of gold.

The verse that follows in Alma 37 is interesting because it may give us clues relating to the physical characteristics of the plates themselves. "And now behold, if they are kept, they must retain their brightness; yea, and they will retain their brightness; yea, and also shall all the plates which do contain that which is holy writ." (Alma 37:5, see 1 Nephi 5:19). This might suggest that the plates were subject to tarnishing (something that gold does not do), or the quality of "brightness" might refer to the substance of the messages inscribed on plates of various composition.

The three latter-day Witnesses to The Book of Mormon wrote only that they had "seen the plates which contain this record" without referring to the specific composition of the metal, although they went into great detail to describe the engravings themselves and their purpose to benefit humanity.

We really do not know how many of the plates were actually made of gold. We do know, however, that the plates were heavy. The Eight Witnesses to The Book of Mormon testified that the plates they were shown and "hefted" had "the appearance of gold." The bound plates they handled are estimated to have weighed in the neighborhood of 36 kilograms. The plates from which Joseph translated The Book of Mormon may have been thin sheets of gold, (see "Testimony of Joseph Smith." J.S.H., 1:34) but the text itself suggests that, in general, the Nephite prophets engraved their records on a variety of metals.

Interestingly, not one of The Book of Mormon's authors describe the records upon which they engraved the history of their people as "gold plates," with the prominent exception, noted above, of the Plates of Ether, that are specifically characterized as being of "pure gold." (Mosiah 8:9). Nephi's record was engraven upon "plates of ore." (1 Nephi 19:1). It was the record upon these plates that was pleasing to Mormon and not the plates themselves. (The Words of Mormon 1:4). As a matter of fact, when occasion arose, the various record keepers in The Book of Mormon almost pointedly described only the intrinsic quality of the plates entrusted to their care, while pointedly and characteristically ignoring the temporal value of the metal upon which the records were engraven.

In any case, when Alma told Helaman that the records would "retain their brightness"(see Alma 37:4 noted above), he might have intended a dual meaning. On the one hand, if the plates were to be easily inscribed upon, they might be less tarnish resistant. In the Old Testament, "the word 'nechosheth' is sometimes improperly translated (as) 'brass'. In most places, the correct translation would be 'copper,' although it may sometimes possibly mean 'bronze', which is a compound of copper and tin." ("Smith's Bible Dictionary," p. 97). Oxidation easily clouds the luster of these metals. On the other hand, the clearly understood messages of the records would be preserved for future generations, who would be dazzled by the brightness of their simplicity.

Because gold itself was much more plentiful in the Lands of The Book of Mormon, it many have not mattered to them of what material the plates were crafted. Jacob reported that his people, who still had an "Old World" mindset, had "begun to search for gold, and for silver, and for all manner of precious ores." Note that Jacob qualified as "precious" the ore his people sought. "In the which," or in these precious materials, he continued, "this land … doth abound most plentifully." (Jacob 2:12). In the same vein, Mormon reported: "Both the Lamanites and the Nephites … did have an exceeding plenty of gold, and of silver, and of all manner of precious metals." (Helaman 6:9). As had Jacob before him, Mormon characterized the hoarded materials as "precious metals." Just for context, it is estimated that between 1500 and 1650 A.D., the Spanish alone imported 181 tons of gold, (+/- nine billion dollars worth in 2024) and 16,000 tons of silver from the New World.

Mormon's son Moroni twice referred to the plates, but only in reference to hiding them in the earth. (See Ether 15:11, &

Mormon 8:4). Likewise, "Ammaron, being constrained by the Holy Ghost, did hide up the records which were sacred, yea, even all the sacred records which had been handed down from generation to generation, which were sacred." (4 Nephi 1:48-49). It may simply be that the custodians of the record were more focused on the message than on the material.

Those who have carefully and
prayerfully studied The Book of Mormon and
have grown to appreciate its doctrine will use the
password of "Atonement" to get past Security at the
portal of heaven. As they approach the throne of God,
they will look back to witness the transcendent beauty
of the gate through which they, as heirs of the kingdom,
have entered, which will be "like unto circling flames of
fire; Also the blazing throne of God, wherein" there
shall be "seated the Father and the Son." And the
"beautiful streets of that kingdom," shall have
"the appearance of being paved with gold."
(D&C 137:2-4). Thus, is described in
beautiful imagery, the power of
our covenants that are only
made possible through
the Atonement Of
Christ.

Grace

"We know that it is by
grace that we are saved,
after all we can do."
(2 Nephi 25:23).

Nephi clearly taught that "it is by grace that we are saved, after all we can do." (2 Nephi 25:23). Latter-day Saints, however, tend to emphasize works to the point that it may seem to others that the grace of God takes a back seat to their own efforts to earn salvation. In spite of their focus on accountability, agency, industry, and labor, as they are exhorted to greater dedication, diligence, and duty, the truth is that nothing we can do will ever qualify us to enjoy eternal life. Paul echoed Nephi, writing that it is "by grace ye are saved, through faith, and that not of yourselves. It is the gift of God." (Ephesians 2:8). Luke similarly taught, "We believe that through the grace of the Lord Jesus Christ we shall be saved." (Acts 15:11). Titus affirmed that it is "the grace of God that bringeth salvation." (Titus 2:11).

Grace is one of God's attributes, consisting of the love, mercy, and power by which He may bring us to His stature. Because of His grace, we may enjoy not only what He has, but also what He is. On earth, our lives are days of probation, of testing, or of putting to the proof our declared values. Therefore, as we learn to conform to his lifestyle, we may more fully enjoy His grace.

This process allows us to be raised from physical death by the power of the Resurrection, and from spiritual death by the power of the Atonement. We receive grace proportionately as we conform to the standard of personal righteousness that is required by the gospel Plan. Thus, we are commanded to "grow in grace" until we are sanctified and justified "thru the grace of our Lord and Savior Jesus Christ." (D&C 50:40 & D&C 20:30-32). It is in this sense that Nephi declared that we are saved by grace only "after all we can do," which is primarily to repent of our sins. Because the two are inextricably linked, when the day of repentance is past, so is the day of grace. (Mormon 2:15).

In the scriptures, works are generally associated with obedience to the commandments. Thus, the Savior denounced the Jews, declaring unto them: "If ye were Abraham's children, ye would do the works of Abraham." (John 8:39). In this sense, Paul taught the Romans that "not the hearers of the law are just before God, but the doers of the law shall be justified." (Romans 2:13). Martin Luther correctly understood that faith is "no merely intellectual assent to a proposition, but is vital, personal self-committal to a practical belief. He heartily approved of good works; what he denied was their efficacy for salvation. 'Good works,' he said, 'do not make a good man, but a good man does good works.' And what makes a man good? Faith in God, and Christ." (Will Durant, "The Reformation," p. 374-5). The scriptures clearly teach: "They which have believed in God (should) be careful to maintain good works. These things are good and profitable unto men." (Titus 3:8).

There is always the possibility, however, that we "may fall from grace and depart from the living God." (D&C 20:32). Therefore, James admonished his brethren, as did Paul, to be "doers of the word, and not hearers only, deceiving your own selves." (James 1:22). Without works, it is all too easy to "fall into temptation." (D&C 20:33). When this happens, we lose our focus and wander off in "mists of darkness." (1 Nephi 12:17). In this sense, James taught: "Faith without works is dead." (James 2:26). The grace of God cannot save those who are determined to ignore His entreaties to commit by covenant to an undeviating standard of personal righteousness. To believe that He would do so under these conditions is self-denial.

Faith, on the other hand, is the catalyst that propels us to embrace the saving principles and ordinances of the gospel. If our hearts are right, "then we have confidence toward God. And whatsoever we ask, we receive of him, because we keep his commandments, and do those things that are pleasing in his sight." (1 John 3:21-22). Truly, "we should believe on the name of his Son Jesus Christ, and love one another." (1 James 3:23). But this is not all. We must correctly apply the scriptures to our own behavior, without wresting them, for it is "Satan (who) doth stir up the hearts of the people to contention concerning the points of (His) doctrine. (D&C 10:63). It is the responsibility of the members of Christ's church to teach the true points of His doctrine, in order that the gospel might be established among the nations and that contention might be diminished. Twisting the scriptures that admonish us to good works from their true or proper signification perverts them from their correct application. Such is the case when individuals alter their meaning to justify the damnable doctrine that we are saved by works.

Brigham Young clearly understood his relationship with God, and was totally and utterly dependent upon Him for his personal salvation. He once declared: "There is no man who ever made a sacrifice on the earth for the Kingdom of Heaven, except the Savior. I would not give the ashes of a rye straw for that man who feels that he is making sacrifices for God." (J.D., 16:114). It is through His grace alone and the sacrifice of His Son that we are saved.

Thus, Mormon wrote: "O how great is the nothingness of the children of men; yea, even they are less than the dust of the earth." (Helaman 12:7). Mormon related his nothingness to his debt to God. King Benjamin had urged his people to thank God, and not him, for their peace and prosperity. He said that if they praised Him, and served Him "with all (their) whole souls, yet (they) would be unprofitable servants. (Mosiah 2:20-21). That is because our debt to God is completely beyond our ability to pay. We can do nothing that puts Him in our debt. But God does not ask us to settle our account with Him; He only asks that we keep His commandments. The marvel of God's love is that the more we try to serve Him, the more He blesses us. Therefore, we become even more deeply indebted to Him and remain so forever. When, ultimately, the precious blood of Christ redeems us, it is by grace alone that we enjoy salvation.

We all risk falling into transgression in consequence of a shallow understanding of principles and doctrines. As Alma declared to the inhabitants of Ammonihah, "Behold, the scriptures are before you; if ye will wrest them it shall be to your own destruction." (Alma 13:20). Picking apart the scriptures can distort dogma into meaningless fragments without any coherent connection, or it can redefine doctrine into bizarre and nonsensical definitions. In 1820, the Lord characterized such individuals as those who "draw near to me with their lips, but (whose) hearts are far from me. They teach for doctrines the commandments of men, having a form of godliness, but they deny the power thereof." (J.S.H. 2:19). To rely on our own puny efforts instead of the boundless grace of God for our salvation reduces the Plan of Salvation to a crude caricature without meaning or substance.

The children of men do not easily hearken to counsel. Instead, when things are going reasonably well, they say: "Behold, we are the sons of God; have we not taken unto ourselves the daughters of men? And are we not eating and drinking, and marrying and giving in marriage? And our wives bear unto us children, and the same are mighty men, which are like unto men of old, men of great renown." (Moses 8:21). However, the actions of such self-righteous and self-indulgent individuals are all form and no substance, and the sizzle without the steak. They reveal their true character, when "every man (is) lifted up in the imagination of the thoughts of his heart, being only evil continually." (Moses 8:22).

In contrast, the true doctrine of Christ has been clearly revealed. Anything less than this is evil, because it keeps us from reaching our potential by denying us the benefits of obedience to the laws of the Great Plan of Salvation. (Alma 42:5). The keystone of His doctrine is His grace that is extended to all who claim salvation through faith on His name. The performance requirement expected of His accountable disciples focuses solely on the principles and ordinances of His gospel. "Whosoever repenteth and cometh unto me," said the Lord, "the same is my church. Whosoever declareth more or less than this, the same is not of me, but is against me; therefore, he is not of my church." (D&C 10:67-68). Since the day the church was organized on April 6, 1830, this doctrine has not changed. The Lord's messengers have taught this doctrine without
modification since that time.

Simply stated, this doctrine is that when we have faith in Jesus Christ, truly repent of our sins, and enter into a baptismal covenant with Him, we will receive the Holy Ghost, Who will then direct our development, revealing to us the things we must do to merit salvation. "For the gate by which ye should enter is repentance and baptism by water; and then," in a mystical and incomprehensible way, comes "a remission of your sins by fire and by the Holy Ghost." (2 Nephi 31:17). This puts us on the "strait and narrow path which leads to eternal life" through the grace of God. (2 Nephi 31:18).

As the gates of baptism swing open to reveal a strait and narrow way stretching away to the horizon, the real journey to Christ has only begun. Having been born again, we must continue to press forward with complete dedication and steadfastness, with confidence and a firm determination in Christ, having a perfect brightness of hope, or perfect faith, and a love of God and of all men, which is charity. If we do this, feasting upon the word of Christ, receiving strength and nourishment from the scriptures, and endure to the end in righteousness, we shall receive the grace of God and have eternal life, which is the greatest of all gifts. (See 2 Nephi 31:20). This is the on-going opportunity and responsibility of all who have personally accepted Jesus Christ as their Savior and Redeemer.

Our partnership with God becomes significant to the success of His gospel Plan. In our fallen state, it is our nature to be subject to the influences of Satan. When we have no experience with God, and when we are alienated from Him by spiritual death, we become "carnal, sensual, and devilish" allowing us to be tainted by sin. (Alma 42:10). This is why, from the Fall of Adam, He has provided us with the Plan of Salvation, the Plan of Redemption, or the Plan of Happiness, that mortality might be a preparatory state, where we might develop the behavioral lifestyle and qualities required for redemption from spiritual death.

It is for our benefit that we become acquainted with evil as well as with good, with darkness as well as with light, with error as well as with truth, and with punishment for the infraction of eternal laws, as well as with the blessings that follow obedience. Mortality is really our only opportunity to have these experiences. But without the grace of God, our mortal education would be for naught. As Ralph Waldo Emerson once asked: "What is the use of immortality to one who cannot wisely use half an hour?"

Alma reminded Corianton: "If it were not for the plan of redemption, as soon as they were dead their souls were miserable, being cut off from the presence of the Lord." (Alma 42:11). Justice would demand that they eternally suffer the consequences of their own actions. They would be "in the grasp of justice; yea, the justice of God, which consigned them forever to be cut off from his presence." According to justice, "the plan of redemption could not be brought about" and "mercy could not take effect except it should destroy the work of justice." (Alma 42:12-13). The beauty of the Plan of Redemption, then, is that it meets the demands of perfect justice through the infinite mercy of our Heavenly Father. The Plan allows Him to be both just and merciful at the same time, and to extend His grace to all who approach Him with broken hearts and contrite spirits.

The Plan of Redemption required that "an atonement should be made; therefore, God Himself atoneth for the sins of the world, to bring about the plan of mercy, to appease the demands of justice, that God might be a perfect, just God, and a merciful God also." (Alma 42:15). The Atonement allowed Him to satisfy justice and still mercifully reclaim us from spiritual death. The Savior became the Master of the situation by conquering death. In His sacrifice, the debt would be paid, redemption made, mercy extended, justice satisfied, the covenant fulfilled, and God's will done, all made possible by an extension of His grace. Through all, the power to save souls would remain with the Savior Jesus Christ.

"Each of us lives on a kind of spiritual credit," wrote Boyd K. Packer. "One day the account will be closed, and a settlement demanded. However casually we may view it now, when that day comes and the foreclosure is imminent, we will look around in restless agony for someone, anyone, to help us. And by eternal law, mercy cannot be extended save there be one who is both willing and able to assume our debt, and pay the price, and arrange the terms of our redemption." ("Ensign," 4/1977).

As Alma reminded Corianton, the only payment required for the gift of grace is "the heart and a willing mind." (D&C 64:34). The only things that we must give up are our sins. The father of King Lamoni clearly understood this when he was taught the gospel by Ammon. He said, "If there is a God,...wilt thou make thyself known unto me, and I will give away all my sins to know thee, and that I may be raised from the dead, and be saved at the last day (Alma 22:18). As Alma counseled his son: "Only let your sins trouble you, with that trouble which shall bring you down unto repentance." (Alma 42:29).

The first step in that process is the turning point at which the guilty party consciously recognizes his sin. The second step in the process of repentance is a clear understanding of justice, mercy, and the grace of God, and of the relationship and harmony between them because of the Plan of Redemption. Thus, Alma warned Corianton to cease excusing himself in sin. "O my son, I desire that ye should deny the justice of God no more. Do not endeavor to excuse yourself in the least point because of your sins, by denying the justice of God; but do let the justice of God, and his mercy, and his long-suffering have full sway in your heart; and let it bring you down to the dust in humility." (Alma 42:30).

He was asking his son to allow the grace of God to profoundly transform him as if he were pliant clay in the hands of a Master Potter. Alma knew by his own experience that the children of men can be fashioned into Sons and Daughters of God. Nephi said: "This is the way, and there is none other way nor name given under heaven whereby man can be saved in the kingdom of God. And now, behold, this is the doctrine of Christ, and the only and true doctrine of the Father, and of the Son, and of the Holy Ghost, which is one God, without end." (2 Nephi 31:21). Saving faith, then, is at the foundation of the true doctrine of Christ, and is tied in the scriptures to a specific kind of works that is independent of grace. Perhaps the verse most commonly quoted in this regard by members of the Lord's church is James 2:17: "Faith, if it hath not works, is dead, being alone." The J.S.T. renders this verse: "Faith, if it hath not works, is dead, and cannot save you." The interpretation is both clear and unmistakable. There is no salvation in faith alone. There is no more power in faith without works than there is in food that is not eaten, or in warm clothing that is not worn. Nevertheless, "by works (is) faith made perfect." (James 2:22). The Savior taught: "Every tree is known by his own fruit. For of thorns men do not gather figs, nor of a bramble bush gather they grapes. A good man out of the good treasure of his heart bringeth forth that which is good ... for of the abundance of the heart his mouth speaketh." (Luke 6:44-45).

Ultimately, we are accountable for our own actions, which will either damn us or lift us into the embrace of angels. "Be not deceived," cautioned Paul. "God is not mocked. For whatsoever a man soweth, that shall he also reap." (Galatians 6:7). "For we must all appear before the judgment seat of Christ; that every one may receive the things done in his body, according to that he hath done, whether it be good or bad." (2 Corinthians 5:10). Ultimately, "he which soweth sparingly shall reap also sparingly; and he which soweth bountifully shall reap also bountifully." (2 Corinthians 9:6).

The path of eternal progression is strait and narrow. The gospel standard is undeviating, and there is no room for rationalization or compromise, yet we are all sinners. God put us on the earth with the full knowledge that we would yield to temptation and sin by violating His commandments. Nevertheless, there is no latitude in His declaration, when He said: "I the Lord cannot look upon sin with the least degree of allowance." (D&C 1:31). We must all face that harsh, yet incontrovertible, reality. Fortunately, there is a way out of the moral dilemma created by our inability to comply with all of the requirements of God's law. Faith and repentance lead us to the covenants of the gospel where we receive its ordinances and pass through the strait gate of baptism to obtain a remission of sins, gain membership in the church, and find ourselves on the path leading to personal sanctification through the receipt of the Holy Ghost that urges us on to repetitive repentance in response to recurring transgression. The grace of God will then pluck us out of the gaping jaws of hell, whisk us from harm's way, and lighten our burdens when we find them too heavy to bear.

How fortunate for us that the Lord has promised: "My grace is sufficient for thee: for my strength is made perfect in weakness," (2 Corinthians 12:9), for, as Stephen Robinson has written: "The scriptures clearly teach that God cannot tolerate sin or sinfulness in any degree. He can't wink at it, or ignore it, or turn and look the other way. He won't sweep it under the rug or say, 'Well, it's just a little sin. It'll be all right.' God's standard, the celestial standard, is absolute, and it allows no exceptions. There is no wiggle room. Many people seem to have the idea that the Judgment will somehow involve weighing or balancing, with their good deeds on one side of the scales and their bad deeds on the other. If their good deeds outweigh their bad, or if their hearts are basically good and outweigh their sins, then they can be admitted into the presence of God. This notion is false. God cannot, will not, allow moral or ethical imperfection in any degree whatsoever to dwell in his presence. He cannot tolerate sin 'with the least degree of allowance.' It is not a question of whether our good deeds outweigh our sins. If there is even one sin on our record, we are finished. The celestial standard is complete innocence, pure and simple, and nothing less than complete innocence will be tolerated in the kingdom of God." ("Believing Christ," p. 1-7).

Precisely because of its unyielding standard, however, the gospel is "The Good News" to all those who embrace it, because it encompasses all the principles, covenants, and ordinances that enable us to become sanctified so that we may be worthy to live once again in a state of holiness in the presence of our Heavenly Father. Because of the grace of God, all may "come unto Christ, and lay hold upon every good gift ... and be perfected in him," as they deny themselves "of all ungodliness." (Moroni 10:30 & 32). As Alma did, so should all men "continue in the supplicating of his grace" so that they may stand blameless before Him at His Pleasing Bar. (Alma 7:3).

Sanctification, then, is the process by which we are cleansed from the effects of sin. Thus spiritually renewed, we stand prepared to enter the presence of the Lord. We must submit our will to His, yield our hearts to Him, sustain His servants, preach His gospel, and be obedient to all of the teachings of His church. "Therefore," promised the Lord, "if ye do these things, blessed are ye, for ye shall be lifted up at the last day." (3 Nephi 27:22). His "grace (will be) sufficient for all men that humble themselves before (Him)." (Ether 12:27).

As the Savior taught the Nephites: "This is the gospel which I have given unto you – that I came into the world to do the will of my Father, because my Father sent me. And my Father sent me that I might be lifted up upon the cross; and after that I had been lifted up upon the cross, that I might draw all men unto me … And it shall come to pass, that whoso repenteth and is baptized in my name shall be filled." (3 Nephi 27:13-20).

Thus, Mormon taught that "the first fruits of repentance is baptism; and baptism cometh by faith unto the fulfilling the commandments; and the fulfilling the commandments bringeth remission of sins; and the remission of sins bringeth meekness, and lowliness of heart; and because of meekness and lowliness of heart cometh the visitation of the Holy Ghost, which Comforter filleth with hope and perfect love, which love endureth by diligence unto prayer, until the end shall come, when all the saints shall dwell with God." (Moroni 8:25-26). His people shall "receive of His fulness, and be glorified in Him (and) shall receive grace for grace." (D&C 93:20).

As we grow in grace, we become more and more like our Heavenly Father. We grow in spiritual stature with the power to follow the counsel of the Savior, Who commanded: "I would that ye should be perfect, even as I, or your Father who is in heaven is perfect." (3 Nephi 12:48, see Matthew 5:48). God glories in the possibility that His children who obey Him and endure to the end might become like Him. This may be the ultimate expression of His matchless grace. "If ye by the grace of God are perfect in Christ, and deny not his power, then are ye sanctified in Christ by the grace of God, through the shedding of the blood of Christ, which is in the covenant of the Father unto the remission of your sins, that ye become holy, without spot." (Moroni 10:33). It would be difficult to state more succinctly, yet more powerfully, the essence of the gospel of Jesus Christ. All the teachings of the Savior and His prophets build to this climax. If we will open our hearts to the gospel, we can become holy. Those who are prepared, declared Vaughn Featherstone, "will know Him. They will cry out 'blessed be the name of He that cometh in the name of the Lord; thou art my God and I will bless thee; thou art my God and I will exalt thee.' Our children will bow down at His feet and worship Him as the Lord of Lords, the King of Kings. They will bathe His feet with their tears, and He will weep and bless them … His bowels will be filled with compassion and His heart will swell wide as eternity and He will love them. He will bring peace that will last a thousand years, and they will receive their reward to dwell with Him." (Utah South Stake, 4/1987).

Gratitude

"Gratitude is happiness doubled by wonder."
(G.K. Chesterton).

*"Blessed be the name of our
God; let us sing to his praise,
yea, let us give thanks to his
holy name, for he doth work
righteousness forever."*
(Alma 26:8).

Because God "giveth to all men liberally," one of our greatest challenges is to muster the desire to express real and continuous appreciation. (James 1:5). We who have no resources are forever in His debt, and yet, we may still "buy wine and milk without money and without price."" (Isaiah 55:1).

Someone once said that poverty is never being curious about the world around you, and never wanting to explore it or the people in it. It is untested potential, resulting from self- imposed limitations. It is working a lifetime doing something you don't like. It is having many acquaintances and no friends. It is having so many clothes you haven't got a thing to wear. It is eating so well you have to think about going on a diet. It is having every pill imaginable to cure your body's ills, because you can't afford to be sick. It is being loaded down with toys at birthdays and Christmas, and then being bored silly because there's nothing to do. It is having two degrees and feeling unfulfilled in your job. It is never stopping to see the beauty of the world. It is spending money on make-up, deodorants, colognes, and designer clothes, and still being worried about the image you are projecting. It is never being curious about the world around you and never wanting to explore it or the people in it. It is going from one activity to the next and never stopping to see the beauty in the world outside. It is being white, healthy, middle class and unhappy.

As Dallin Oaks observed: "You can never get enough of what you don't need, because what you don't need won't satisfy you." ("Ensign," 11/1991). Instead, we are commanded to conduct our lives "with prayer and thanksgiving." (D&C 46:7). As we do so, our "righteous desires will add to our spiritual momentum." (Neal A. Maxwell, "Ensign," 11/1996). Our true gratitude is an attitude. It "is not only the greatest of virtues, but the parent of all the others." (Cicero). Gratitude may begin with thanks, consisting of words that are transformed into action.

When we cultivate gratitude, wonderful things happen. Good eclipses evil. Love overpowers jealousy, hate, and prejudice. Light drives away darkness. Knowledge banishes ignorance. Humility overwhelms pride. Courtesy checks rudeness. Appreciation overcomes thanklessness. Abundance overshadows poverty. Well-being replaces weakness. Simplicity supplants perplexity. Harmony displaces discord. Faith controls fear. Hope casts out despair. Charity subdues selfishness. Joy deposes unhappiness, sadness, dejection, and misery. Confidence is substituted for timidity.

Certainty dethrones bewilderment. Assurance dislodges discouragement and even despair. Gratitude is a variation on the Golden Rule: "Fear not to do good, my sons, for whatsoever ye sow, that shall ye also reap; therefore, if ye sow good ye shall also reap good for your reward." (D&C 6:33).

"Those who live in thanksgiving daily have a way of opening their eyes to the wonders and beauties of this world as though seeing them for the first time. Those who live in thanksgiving daily are usually among the happiest people on earth." (Joseph Wirthlin, "B.Y.U. Devotional," 10/31/2000).

The Savior "gave all he had to those in need, for one so meek and small like me. And in return I too will give all that I have, for I will live according to his perfect plan, designed for woman, child, and man. Determined to return someday into his open arms and say: "My life, dear Lord, I lived for you. And through the trials I had, I grew. I served with all my heart and soul. Each day I strived to reach my goal: To become like you in every way, putting faith in you as I knelt and prayed. My love for you cannot be told. As strong as that of prophets old. Oh Lord, my God, to you I gave all that I had, each day I lived." (Anonymous).

Perhaps it is in a multitude of expressions that we best communicate to our Heavenly Father our gratitude for all He has done for us. After all, "we tell on ourselves by the friends we seek, by the very manner in which we speak; by the way we enjoy our leisure time; by the use we make of dollar and dime. We tell who we are by the things we wear, and in the way we wear our hair; by the kinds of things that make us laugh; by the records we play on our phonograph. We tell who we are by the way we walk; by the things in which we delight to talk; by the books we choose from a well-filled shelf. In these ways and more, we tell on ourselves." (Anonymous).

There are at least four-dozen ways that gratitude may be expressed:

We express our gratitude by following the Plan of Salvation.

We maintain a divine perspective even when our own plans go awry. "Behold, the Lord shall come, and his recompense shall be with him, and he shall reward every man, and the poor shall rejoice." (D&C 56:19). Let us be filled with an attitude of gratitude in our journey homeward, but not become too comfortable here, for as C. S. Lewis observed: "Our Father refreshes us on the journey through life with some pleasant inns, but he will not encourage us to mistake them for home." ("The Problem of Pain," Chapter 7).

Perfection is a pathway and not a point. Spencer W. Kimball once told a group of mission presidents: "So much depends upon our willingness to make up our minds, both individually and collectively, that present levels of performance are not acceptable, either to ourselves or to the Lord. In saying that, I am not calling for flashy, temporary differences in our performance levels, but (for) a quiet resolve to lengthen our stride." ("Church News," 3/22/1975). Sir Winston Churchill once said: "Men's and nations' finest hours are those when extraordinary challenge is met with extraordinary effort." The Divine Plan of Salvation was constructed to encourage us to rise to every occasion and to meet the extraordinary challenges of the Last Days.

We express our gratitude by being Defenders of The Faith.

We are as Moroni, who "was a strong and a mighty man; he was a man of a perfect understanding; yea, a man that did not delight in bloodshed; a man whose soul did joy in the liberty and the freedom of his country, and his brethren from bondage and slavery; Yea, a man whose heart did swell with thanksgiving to his God, for the many privileges and blessings which he bestowed upon his people; a man who did labor exceedingly for the welfare and safety of his people. Yea, and he was a man who was firm in the faith of Christ, and he had sworn with an oath to defend his people, his rights, and his country, and his religion, even to the loss of his blood. … Yea, verily, verily I say unto you, if all men had been, and were, and ever would be, like unto Moroni, behold, the very powers of hell would have been shaken forever; yea, the devil would never have power over the hearts of the children of men." (Alma 48:11-13 & 17). Moroni had the spiritual maturity to know that there would be a time to come when "all thrones and dominions, principalities and powers, (would) be revealed and set forth upon all who have endured valiantly for the gospel of Jesus Christ." (D&C 121:29).

As Josiah Gilbert Holland wrote: "God, give us men and women! A time like this demands strong minds, great hearts, truth, faith, and ready hands. Men and women whom the lust of office does not kill. Men and women whom the spoils of office cannot buy. Men and women who possess opinions and a will. Men and women who have honor. Men and women who will not lie! Men and women who can stand before a demagogue and damn his treacherous flatterings without winking! Tall men and women, sun-crowned, who live above the fog in public duty and in private thinking. For while the rabble, with their thumb-worn creeds, their large professions and their little deeds, mingle in selfish strife, lo! Freedom weeps, Wrong rules the land, and Justice sleeps." ("God, Give us Men!"). This kind of courage demands availability. Brigham Young once said something to the effect that he never counted the cost of anything. He just found out what the Lord wanted him to do, and he did it We express our gratitude by developing the habit of sacrifice until we are willing to lay down our lives on its altar.

We should be so committed to the gospel Plan that we are willing to "give up our todays so that others might enjoy their tomorrows." (Inscription at The Military Cemetery of The Pacific, Honolulu, Hawaii). "Greater love hath no man than this," said the Savior, "that a man lay down his life for his friends." (John 15:13). Ever the master of the soft reply, His measured words strengthen our resolve to cultivate a gentle approach to life, to be at peace with ourselves and the world, and to make the Atonement work in our behalf, even as the disobedient "say in their hearts: This is not the work of the Lord." (D&C 58:33).

We express our gratitude by making repentance the focus of our daily attention.

Without repentance, the past would forever hold the future hostage and the Plan of Salvation would be thwarted. "Rejoice, O my heart," sang Nephi, "and give place no more for the enemy of my soul. Do not anger again because of mine enemies. Do not slacken my strength because of mine afflictions. Rejoice, O my heart." (2 Nephi 4:28-30). We express our gratitude by patterning our lives after that of the Savior.

Speaking of those who will inherit eternal life, the Lord said "these are they who are just men made perfect through Jesus the mediator of the new covenant, who wrought out this perfect atonement through the shedding of his own blood. These are they whose bodies are celestial, whose glory is that of the sun, even the glory of God, the highest of all, whose glory the sun of the firmament is written of as being typical." (D&C 76:69-70).

His disciples are "governed by law…preserved by law and perfected and sanctified by the same." (D&C 88:34). The offices and keys of His priesthood, the very types and shadows that are a part of our daily experience, have been given to us "for helps and for governments, for the work of the ministry and the perfecting of (the) saints." (D&C 124:143). We express our gratitude by expressing our thanks in mighty prayer.

We resist the temptation to wander and play, as we resolve instead to ponder and pray. in our prayers, we try to be specific as we articulate why we are thankful, and we acknowledge answers. We understand the relationship between commandments and blessings and "pray always, lest (we) enter into temptation and lose (our) reward." (D&C 31:12). We have learned to rely upon revealed knowledge to gain an appreciation of both the physical world and its spiritual equivalents, "for unto (us) it is given to know the mysteries of the kingdom, but unto the world it is not given to know them." (D&C 42:65).

We express our gratitude by being satisfied when He says "No" in answer to our prayers.

Sometimes, the "no" comes as an answer to the "specifications set forth in our petitions." (Neal A. Maxwell, "Ensign," 7/1982). We swallow our pride as we express thanks for His greater. We prepare to learn from negative responses as much as we do from affirmations, for we know that whom the Lord loves, He also chastens. (See D&C 95:1). When we receive a bouquet of roses, we accept the thorns as well as the buds. Some people grumble that roses have thorns. We try to maintain our perspective, to be thankful that thorns have roses.

"Why is it," asked the poet, "whenever I reach for the sky to climb aboard cloud nine, it evaporates and rains upon my dreams? Is it a matter of science, or simply a matter of fact, that not even a cloud with a silver lining can hold the weight of our dreams without some precipitation? I think I've found the answer to this dilemma. Keep on reaching for the sky, but don't forget your umbrella." (Susan Stephenson).

We don't act like spoiled children in our prayers. We know that our Father will not indulge us with undeserved gifts or yield to our pressure to give us that which we do not need. "For behold, I have prepared a great endowment and blessing to be poured out upon them, (only) inasmuch as they are faithful and continue in humility before me." (D&C 105:112).

Should we, then, ask for yet more blessings? "I was deeply touched one day following our family prayer," said N. Eldon Tanner, "when one of our little daughters said, 'Daddy, I don't think we ought to ask for more blessings. The Lord has been good to us, and I think we should ask him to help us to be worthy of the blessings we already receive." ("Seek Ye First the Kingdom of God," p. 159).

We express our gratitude by hearing His voice and knowing Him when He speaks to us.

For "whoso receiveth not my voice is not acquainted with my voice, and is not of me." (D&C 84:52). He hears us pray for others, in meaningful ways. I am reminded of a pamphlet I received from an evangelist on a street corner many years ago. Its simple message was: "Will you pray for this nameless Communist?" At the time, I thought: "What's the use? Communism will never fall in my lifetime." It seemed to me that it was as well entrenched as the Roman Empire at the time of Christ. But within 20 years, both the Berlin Wall and the Iron Curtain fell. Such is the power of prayer.

In equally powerful ways, our file leaders are "upheld by the confidence, faith, and prayer of the church." (D&C 107:22). Others are helped in less spectacular ways. John Taylor said: "There are some Christian people in this world who, if a man were poor or hungry, would say, let us pray for him. I would suggest a little different regimen for a person in this condition; rather take him a bag of flour and a little beef or pork. A few such comforts will do him more good than your prayers."

We express our gratitude by overlooking the shortcomings of others and focusing instead on the positive.

The fact is, that "there is so much bad in the best of us, and so much good in the worst of us, that it hardly behooves any of us to talk about the rest of us." (Edward Hoch). This is one of the major faults of the "evening news" and of the media, in general.

We express our gratitude by being quick to forgive others.

We know that He is watching with approval as we forgive others who have offended us. We emulate Joseph Smith, who said: "I am calm as a summer's morning; I have a conscience void of offense towards God, and towards all men." (D&C 135:4).

We express our gratitude by keeping the commandments, enduring to the end in righteousness, and recognizing the merits of the principles of righteousness.

Our faith is grounded in bedrock and is a principle of action. "Real righteousness, therefore, cannot be a superficial, ritualistic thing. It must arise out of the deepest convictions of the soul, not out of a desire merely to "go along" simply because that's how things are done! God's power, unlike mortal power, is accessed only by those who have developed, to a requisite degree, God's attributes." (Neal A. Maxwell, "Ensign," 7/1982).

If we "do this thing which (the Lord has) commanded (us, we) shall prosper. Be faithful," He said, "and yield to no temptation." (D&C 9:13). "And, if (we keep His) commandments and endure to the end (we) shall have eternal life, which gift is the greatest of all the gifts of God." (D&C 14:7).

There is a law, after all, irrevocably decreed in heaven before the foundations of this world, upon which all blessings are predicated. When we obtain any blessing from God, it is by obedience to that law upon which it is predicated." (D&C 130:20-21). "For all who will have a blessing at my hands, shall abide the law which was appointed for that blessing, and the conditions thereof, as were instituted from before the foundation of the world." (D&C 132:5). "When obedience ceases to be inconvenient, and becomes our quest, in that moment, God will endow us with power." (Ezra Taft Benson, "Ensign," 5/1998).

We express our gratitude by righteously exercising power or authority.

"The powers of heaven cannot be controlled nor handled only upon the principles of righteousness. That they may be conferred upon us, it is true; but when we undertake to cover our sins, or to gratify our pride, our vain ambition, or to exercise control or dominion or compulsion upon the souls of the children of men, in any degree of unrighteousness, behold, the heavens withdraw themselves; the Spirit of the Lord is grieved; and when it is withdrawn, Amen to the priesthood or the authority of that man." (D&C 121:36-37).

"Since almost all individuals tend to abuse power and authority, how are the relevant lessons about the righteous use of power to be learned except in this laboratory-of-life setting? Could we have truly experienced the risks and opportunities of power merely by attending some pointed lectures or doing some directed reading during our first estate? Was it not necessary to experience, "according to the flesh," what it is like to be on the receiving end of unrighteous dominion? And the necessity of repentance when one has been on the giving end? The general absence, for instance, on the human political scene of attributes such as genuine humility, mercy, and meekness is a grim reminder, again and again, of how essential these qualities are to the governance of self or a nation." (Neal A. Maxwell, "Ensign," 7/1982).

Under specific conditions, we may "tap in to" the power of God. Thus, did Joseph Smith command the irreverent guards at Liberty Jail: "Silence, ye fiends of the infernal pit. In the name of Jesus Christ, I rebuke you, and command you to be still. I will not live another minute and hear such language. Cease such talk, or you or I die this instant." He ceased to speak. He stood erect in terrible majesty, chained, and without a weapon, calm, unruffled, and dignified as an angel. He looked down upon his quailing guards, whose knees smote together, and who, shrinking into a corner, or crouching at his feet, begged his pardon, and [who] remained quiet until an exchange of guards. I have seen ministers of justice clothed in ministerial robes and criminals arraigned before them, while life was suspended upon a breath in the courts of England. I have witnessed a Congress in solemn session to give laws to nations. I have tried to conceive of kings, of royal courts, of thrones and crowns, and of emperors assembled to decide the fate of kingdoms. But dignity and majesty have I seen but once, as it stood in chains, at midnight, in a dungeon, in an obscure village in Missouri." (Parley P. Pratt, "Autobiography" p. 210-211).

"A favorite theme of Brigham Young was that the dominion God gives to us is designed to test us, and enable us to show to ourselves, our fellows, and all the heavens just how we would act if entrusted with God's own power. If we do not act in a Godlike manner, we will never be entrusted with a creation of our own." (Hugh Nibley, "Subduing the Earth," p. 89-90).

We express our gratitude as we acknowledge that He is the sole source of our protection.

The Lord has promised: "There is no weapon that is formed against you shall prosper." (D&C 71:9). "Keep all the commandments and covenants by which ye are bound; and I will cause the heavens to shake for your good, and Satan shall tremble, and Zion shall rejoice upon the hills and flourish." (D&C 35:24). We are called, said the Savior: "to labor in (the) vineyard, and to build up (the) church, and to bring forth Zion." (D&C 39:13).

We express our gratitude by communicating our deep, divine determination to serve Him.

"Therefore, O ye that embark in the service of God, see that ye serve him with all your heart, might, mind and strength, that ye may stand blameless before God at the last day. Therefore, if ye have desires to serve God ye are called to the work ... And faith, hope, charity, and love, with an eye single to the glory of God, qualify (us) for the work. Remember faith, virtue, knowledge, temperance, patience, brotherly kindness, godliness, charity, humility, diligence." (D&C 4:2-6). These are the virtues that accompany discipleship.

We express our gratitude by acknowledging His majesty and power and the authority of His servants.

"The duty of the President of the office of the High Priesthood is to preside over the whole church, and to be like unto Moses ... To be a seer, a revelator, a translator, and a prophet, having all the gifts of God which he bestows upon the head of the church." (D&C 107:91-92). "Let it be fulfilled upon (the faithful members of the church) as upon those on the day of Pentecost; let the gift of tongues be poured out upon thy people, even cloven tongues as of fire, and the interpretation thereof." (D&C 109:36 - Kirtland Temple Dedicatory Prayer).

We express our gratitude by acknowledging the tangible reminders of God's majesty.

"The earth rolls upon her wings, and the sun giveth his light by day, and the moon giveth her light by night, and the stars also give their light, as they roll upon their wings in their glory, in the midst of the power of God. Unto what shall I liken these kingdoms, that ye may understand? Behold, all these are kingdoms, and any man who hath seen any or the least of these hath seen God moving in his majesty and power." (D&C 88:45-47).

We express our gratitude by using our agency wisely to validate the wisdom of His confidence in our self-government.

In some respects, it is easier to govern a whole people than oneself. Of one ancient political leader it is candidly recorded: "And he did do justice unto the people, but not unto himself because of his many whoredoms; wherefore he was cut off from the presence of the Lord." (Ether 10:11). "One can cater to mortal constituencies (it seems) but lose the support of the one who matters!" (Neal A. Maxwell, "Ensign," 7/1982).

In the scriptures there is one definitive definition of discipleship: "He that receiveth my law and doeth it, the same is my disciple." (D&C 41:5). Joseph Smith said of the capacity of the church to govern itself: "I teach people correct principles, and let them govern themselves." (Joseph Smith, "Millennial Star," 13:22, p. 339).

We express our gratitude by demonstrating to Him through our actions that we understand the true value of things and do not covet the profane things of the world.

This applies even to our own goods: "I command thee that thou shalt not covet thine own property, but impart it freely." (D&C 19:26). In so doing so, we "learn that he who doeth the works of righteousness shall receive his reward, even peace in this world, and eternal life in the world to come." (D&C 59:23).

We express our gratitude by understanding the dynamic relationship between commandments and blessings.

"Blessed are they whose feet stand upon the land of Zion, who have obeyed my gospel; for they shall receive for their reward the good things of the earth ... And they shall also be crowned with blessings from above, yea, and with commandments not a few." (D&C 59:4).

We look for the passages of scripture that begin "And for this cause, I have given unto you..." When we recognize the divine causal relationship between commandments and blessings, we will better understand "how to act upon the points of (the) law and commandments," that the Lord has given to us. "And thus (we will) become instructed in the law of (the) church, and be sanctified by that which (we) have received, and (we) shall bind (ourselves) to act in all holiness" before the Lord. (D&C 43:8-9).

We express our gratitude by using God's power to multiply our talents as we turn weaknesses into strengths.

Demosthenes overcame a lisp to become one of the greatest orators of all time. Beethoven composed some of his finest music after he had become deaf. Early in his career, Abraham Lincoln said: "I will prepare myself, and some day my chance will come." Helen Keller triumphed over the silence and darkness in her life to finally write that "faith, the spiritual searchlight, illuminates the way, and although sinister doubts lurk in the shadow, I walk unafraid towards the Enchanted Wood where the foliage is always green, where joy abides, where nightingales nest and sing, and where life and death are one in the presence of the Lord." ("Redbook Magazine"). As a young man, Heber J. Grant couldn't carry a note. Later, he became well known for his singing abilities. Of his experience, he quoted Ralph Waldo Emerson, saying: "That which we persist in doing becomes easier for us to do; not that the nature of the thing is changed, but that our power to do is increased." ("Gospel Standards," p. 355).

We earnestly seek "the best gifts, always remembering for what they are given. For verily I say unto you," said the Lord, "they are given for the benefit of those who love me and keep all my commandments, and him that seeketh so to do; that all may be benefited that seek or that ask of me." (D&C 46:8-9, see v. 10-26). "For what doth it profit a man if a gift is bestowed upon him, and he receive not the gift? Behold, he rejoices not in that which is given unto him, neither rejoices in him who is the giver of the gift." (D&C 88:33).

We express our gratitude by using our means prudently and being wise stewards.

"This is what the Lord requires of every man in his stewardship." (D&C 70:9). "For it is expedient that I, the Lord, should make every man accountable, as a steward over earthly blessings." (D&C 104:13). "And he who receiveth all things with thankfulness shall be made glorious; and the things of this earth shall be added unto him, even an hundred fold, yea, more." (D&C 78:19).

"And inasmuch as ye do these things with … a glad heart and a cheerful countenance … the fulness of the earth is yours, the beasts of the field and the fowls of the air, and that which climbeth upon the trees and walketh upon the earth; Yea, and the herb, and the good things which come of the earth, whether for food or for raiment , or for houses, or for barns, or for orchards, or for gardens, or for vineyards; Yea, all things which come of the earth, in the season thereof, are made for the benefit and the use of man, both to please the eye and to gladden the heart; Yea, for food and for raiment, for taste and for smell, to strengthen the body and to enliven the soul." (D&C 59:15-19). The earth is full and there is enough and to spare, and yet how "could we truly appreciate the supremacy of spiritual things without experiencing the limitations of material things?" (Neal A. Maxwell, "Ensign," 7/1982).

We express our gratitude by carefully managing our time and consecrating it to the service of the Lord.

In gratitude, we make our lives purposeful, recognizing the fleeting nature of time. "Thou shalt not idle away thy time, neither shalt thou bury thy talent that it may not be known." (D&C 60:13). "And when the gossamer veil called time is too much with us, let us recall that, ere long, time will be no more. Time is measured only to man anyway. Meanwhile, let us make allowance for the rapidity with which time seems to pass, especially when we are happy. Jacob found it so: "And Jacob served seven years for Rachel; and they seemed unto him but a few days, for the love he had to her." (Genesis 29:20). On such a scale each of us has but a few days left in mortality!" (Neal A. Maxwell, "Ensign," 7/1982).

"Oh, this world has more of coming and of going than I can bear," mused the poet. "I guess it's eternity I want, where all things are, and always will be. Where I can hold my loves a little looser. Where, finally, we realize Time is the only thing that really dies." (Carol Lynn Pearson, "Time," "New Era," 1/1971).

"Someone once said that time is a predator that stalks us all our lives. I prefer to think of it as a companion that accompanies us on the journey, reminding us to cherish every moment." (Captain Jean Luc Picard). People talk of wasting time, killing time, biding their time, taking their time, and making time. Time flies. "Do you have a minute? Just a second. I'll sleep on it." Robbing a person of time can be just as traumatizing as robbing them of money. In fact, we get "held up at the office" far more frequently than we get "held up at gunpoint." Gratitude is an expression of appreciation to God for the supernal gift of time.

We express our gratitude by ordering our priorities.

When we first seek "the kingdom of God, and his righteousness; (then) all these things shall be added" unto us until ultimately we enjoy eternal life. (Matthew 6:33). When we lose our focus, if we choose mediocrity, rationalization, selfish pleasure, things of the world, the honors of men, or disobedience, we lose power. As long as we remain in this state, we will never partake of the fruit of the tree of life, enjoy its delicious fruit, or feel real gratitude. "Seek not to declare my word," counseled the Lord, "but first seek to obtain my word, and then shall your tongue be loosed; then, if you desire, you shall have my Spirit and my word, yea, the power of God unto the convincing of men." (D&C 11:21).

We express our gratitude by maintaining our concentration, even though we sometimes have purposeless days.

We persevere in our efforts. "The greatest tragedy in life, said Albert Einstein, "is what dies in a man while he is alive." After all: "What doth it profit a man if a gift is bestowed upon him, and he receive not the gift? Behold, he rejoices not in that which is given unto him, neither rejoices in him who is the giver of the gift." (D&C 88:33). Our eternal perspective allows us to deal with change proactively, for it will surely come "like a flash of lightning and a clap of thunder. The people shrink in fear, but after the storm, flowers bloom." ("I Ching, The Chinese Book of Proverbs").

We express our gratitude by experiencing a mighty change through faith on His name.

We've each had a spiritual heart transplant, and now we must take "anti-rejection drugs" for the rest of our lives. After the operation come rehabilitation and physical and spiritual therapy. We had to learn how to eat properly, avoid certain foods and activities, and conduct ourselves in moderate, temperate ways, in order to avoid damaging our new heart. We will be all right, if, as President Hinckley counseled, we have a friend, we have an opportunity for service, and we are nourished by the good word of God. ("Ensign," 5/1999).

We express our gratitude by using our agency wisely and accepting responsibility for our actions.

"For it is expedient that I, the Lord, should make every man accountable, as a steward over earthly blessings, which I have made and prepared for my creatures." (D&C 104:13). We have options and time enough to mend our fences and learn from our mistakes.

We express our gratitude by using our opportunities for failure as learning experiences.

We are "like a bird that, pausing in her flight a while on boughs to light, feels them give way beneath her, and yet sings, knowing that she hath wings!" (Victor Hugo). Our gratitude encompasses our appreciation to God for the learning laboratory of mortality. "Life is a sheet of paper white, where each of us may write a line or two, and then comes night. Greatly begin. If thou hast time but for a line, make that sublime. Not failure, but low aim is crime." (James Russell Lowell).

We express our gratitude in our courage to stand up in the face of those who would destroy the faith they recognize in others, but that is so alien to their own nature.

"It is not the critic who counts, not he who points out where the strong man stumbled or where the doer of deeds could have done them better. The credit belongs to the man who is actually in the arena, whose face is marred by dust and sweat and blood, who tries and comes short again and again, who knows the great enthusiasms, the great devotions and spends himself in a worthy cause; who, at best, if he fails, at least fails while daring greatly, so that his place shall never be with those cold and timid souls who know neither victory nor defeat." (Teddy Roosevelt, "Citizenship in a Republic," Speech at the Sorbonne, Paris, 4/23/1910).

We express our gratitude by bearing adversity well.

Big problems often disguise bigger opportunities, and adversity can be a springboard to greater success. Howard W. Hunter said: "Life has a full share of ups and downs. Indeed, we see many blessings that do not always look or feel like blessings." (C.R., 10/1987). The Chinese word for "crisis" is the same as that for "opportunity." Thus, the Lord counseled: "Be patient in tribulation until I come; and, behold, I come quickly, and my reward is with me, and they who have sought me early shall find rest to their souls." (D&C 54:10). Once we have received the anointing of courage that attends the faithful, as Parley P. Pratt said, we "can never rest until the last enemy is conquered, death destroyed, and truth reigns triumphant." ("Deseret News," 4/30/1853).

"Let all the saints rejoice, therefore, and be exceedingly glad; for Israel's God is their God, and he will mete out a just recompense of reward upon the heads of all their oppressors." (D&C 127:3). "For after much tribulation come the blessings. Wherefore the day cometh that ye shall be crowned with much glory." (D&C 58:4).

Carol Lynn Pearson wrote an insightful poem entitled "Short Roots," with a message that relates to the challenges faced by each of us in our every day experiences that are tailored by a wise Heavenly Father to meet our individual needs: "The tree at the church next door to me turned up its roots and died. They had tried to brace its leaning, but it lowered and lowered, and then there it lay leaves in grass and matted roots in air, like a loafer on a summer day. "Look there," said the gardener. "Short roots - all the growth went up. Big branches - short roots." "How come?" I asked. "Too much water. This tree never had to hunt for drink." Especially in thirsty times, my memory steps outside and looks at the tree at the church next door to me that turned up its roots and died."

We express our gratitude by recognizing the seeming detours and distractions in our lives as opportunities for personal growth.

"How many times, naively, have we vigorously protested while on our way to a blessing?" asked Neal A. Maxwell. "During our schooling in submissiveness, we will see the visible crosses some carry, but others will go unseen. A few individuals may appear to have no trial at all, which, if it were so, would be a trial in itself. Indeed, if our souls had rings, as do trees, to measure the years of greatest personal growth, the wide rings would likely reflect the years of greatest moisture, but from tears, not rainfall. Most of our suffering comes from sin and stupidity; it is, nevertheless, very real, and growth can occur with real repentance. But the highest source of suffering appears to be reserved for the innocent who undergo divine tutorial training." ("Ensign," 7/1982).

We express our gratitude by continuing to express it in times of adversity.

Even in our most difficult times, we can find much for which to be grateful. We need to turn the expression: "Thanks for nothing!" into a positive statement that affirms our faith in God's ultimate wisdom, and we also need to realize that God "maketh his sun to rise on the evil and on the good, and sendeth rain on the just and the unjust." (Matthew 5:45).

We express our gratitude by maintaining a cheerful attitude.

Of all the things we wear, our expressions are the most important. At the end of a letter written by the Prophet Joseph Smith while a prisoner in Liberty Jail, in March 1839, he wrote: "Therefore, dearly beloved brethren, let us cheerfully do all things that lie in our power; and then may we stand still, with the utmost assurance, to see the salvation of God, and for his arm to be revealed." (D&C 123:17). The message from our Father is simple and yet profound in its wisdom: "Be still and know that I am God." (D&C 101:16).

We express our gratitude in the expression of our small sacrifices.

We make a living by what we get but make a life by what we give. "Little people, like you and me, if our prayers are sometimes granted beyond all hope and probability, had better not draw hasty conclusions to our own advantage. If we were stronger, we might be less tenderly treated. If we were braver, we might be sent, with far less help, to defend far more desperate posts in the great battle." (C.S. Lewis, "The World's Last Night, p. 10-11).

"There is no man who ever made a sacrifice on the earth for the kingdom of heaven... except the Savior," declared Brigham Young. "I would not give the ashes of a rye straw for that man who feels that he is making sacrifices for God. We are doing this for our own happiness, welfare, and exaltation, and for nobody else's. What we do, we do for the salvation of the inhabitants of the earth, not for the salvation of the heavens, the angels, or God." (J.D., 16:114).

In the Garden of Gethsemane, the Savior prayed: "Not as I will, but as thou wilt." (Matthew 26:39). "He that asketh in the Spirit asketh according to the will of God; wherefore it is done even as he asketh." (D&C 46:30).

We express our gratitude by walking the walk, and talking the talk.

We should be anxiously engaged in good causes, and do many things on our own, and bring to pass much righteousness. For the power is in us, wherein we are agents unto ourselves. (See D&C 58:27-28). As we emulate God we honor Him with the highest form of praise and adoration. Otherwise, it's all just chaff in the wind.

We express our gratitude by performing acts of Quiet Christianity.

This is service for which there is no recognition, recompense, or reciprocation. "A man filled with the love of God," Joseph Smith said, "is not content with blessing his family alone, but ranges through the whole world, anxious to bless the whole human race." (H.C., 4:227). "There will be times when we applaud and no one notices our pair of happy hands, and no one hears our added decibels – except us and the Lord." (Neal A. Maxwell). An anonymous poet wrote: "I sought to see myself. Myself I could not see. I sought to know the Lord through prayer, but He eluded me. I sought to serve my fellow travelers, and I found all three."

We express our gratitude by opening our arms to those around us.

We are especially kind to "the kids who are different, the kids who don't always get A's; The kids who have ears twice the size of their peers, and noses that go on for days. So, here's to the kids who are different; the kids they call crazy or dumb. The kids who don't fit, with the guts and the grit, who dance to a different drum. Here's to the kids who are different, the kids with the mischievous streak. For when they have grown, as history has shown, it's their difference that makes them unique." (Digby Wolfe).

We express our gratitude by loving our neighbors.

"But you were always a good man of business, Jacob." said Scrooge. "Business!" cried the ghost, wringing its hands again. "Mankind was my business. The common welfare was my business; charity, mercy, forbearance, and benevolence were all my business. The dealings of my trade were but a drop of water in the comprehensive ocean of my business. At this time of the rolling year," the spectre said, "I suffer most. Why did I walk through crowds of fellow-beings with my eyes turned down, and never raise them to that blessed Star which led the Wise Men to a poor abode? Were there no poor homes to which its light would have conducted me?" (Charles Dickens, "A Christmas Carol"). On this sobering note, isn't it interesting that the first five books of the Old Testament speak of keeping the Sabbath day holy just once, but of respecting our neighbors 30 times?

We express our gratitude by doing missionary work and bringing others into the light.

"To sin by silence, when words should be spoken," said Abraham Lincoln, "makes cowards of men." (Original quotation by Ella Wheeler Wilcox). Our missionary zeal "spreads to foreign lands; and this is the beginning of the blessing which shall be poured out upon the heads of my people." (D&C 110:10). "Proclaim my gospel from land to land, and from city to city," urged the Savior. "Bear testimony in every place, unto every people." (D&C 66:5 & 7). For "this gospel shall be preached unto every nation, and kindred, and tongue, and people." (D&C 133:37).
We express our gratitude by acknowledging the qualities of goodness in others.

When we seek to discover the best in others, we somehow bring out the best in ourselves. "The worth of souls," after all, "is great in the sight of God." (D&C 18:10).

We express our gratitude by expressing appreciation to others.

The U.S. Post office dead-letter department receives tens of thousands of letters from children addressed to Santa Claus, asking for toys, but very few after the holidays thanking him for the gifts received.

H. Burke Peterson said of an encounter with President Kimball, "As we were rushing to a meeting, he stopped, took my hand, looked me in the eye, put away all his other cares, and said simply, "I'm sorry we're sometimes so busy. I guess I haven't told you lately how much I love you and appreciate you." (C.R., 4/1977). "Mortal mathematics is forever mistaking who and what counts. We should more quickly express genuine appreciation to others. The arithmetic of appreciation is far less practiced and known than the multiplication tables." (Neal A. Maxwell, "That Ye May Believe," p. 55).

"Let the teacher arise, and, with uplifted hands to heaven, yea, even directly, salute his brother or brethren with these words ... I salute you in the name of the Lord Jesus Christ, in token or remembrance of the everlasting covenant, in which covenant I receive you to fellowship, in a determination that is fixed, immovable, and unchangeable, to be your friend and brother through the grace of God in the bonds of love, to walk in all the commandments of God blameless, in thanksgiving, forever and ever." (D&C 88:132-133).

We express our gratitude by recognizing just how precious are our divine attributes.

When we do so we should seek "the best gifts, always remembering for what they are given ...They are given for the benefit of those who love (the Lord) and keep all (His) commandments, and him that seeketh so to do, that all may be benefited that seek or that ask of (Him)." (D&C 46:8-9).

We express our gratitude by studying the scriptures.

We know that the holy scriptures are "the revelations of God (that) come by the gift and power of the Holy Ghost, the voice of God, or the ministering of angels." (D&C 20:35). We are sobered by the realization that within the scriptures "lies the mystery of mysteries. Happiest is he of human race, to whom our God has given grace, to read, to fear, to hope, to pray; To lift the latch, and force the way. And better had he ne'er been born, who reads to doubt, or reads to scorn." (Sir Walter Scott, notes from the flyleaf of his personal bible).

We pray before beginning to read the scriptures, slow down our minds, and free ourselves from the cares and concerns of the world. As we read, and the solemnities of eternity illuminate our minds, or as we have questions, we continue to pray for understanding. We keep writing materials handy, knowing that ideas or original thoughts that we will want to develop later will germinate within our minds.

We read slowly. For a change, this study is not a race and we do not have to finish a prescribed number of chapters or verses each day. We spend several days pondering principles. We read topically if we want to, and stop to find out what other prophets have said about the same subjects. As we memorize scripture passages, they bloom with hidden meanings we hadn't been aware of, and from time-to-time relevant life experiences pop into our minds, just when we need them the most.

We ask questions as we read and allow the Holy Ghost to illuminate our minds with answers. We take a break from our busy activities to think about the relevance of the passages we are currently studying and pause to let our minds work on their application to our lives' experiences.

We express our gratitude by promoting the cause of Zion.

We prosper her, "that she might "become very glorious, very great, and very terrible." (D&C 97:18).

We express our gratitude by magnifying our callings.

Because we "have desires to serve God (we) are called to the work." (D&C 4:3). "There are many who have been ordained among you, whom I have called," said the Lord, "but few of them are chosen." (D&C 95:5). Nevertheless, those who are faithful in obtaining the priesthood and magnifying their callings "are sanctified by the Spirit unto the renewing of their bodies." (D&C 84:33).

Magnifying a calling means to build it up in dignity and importance, to make it honorable and commendable, to enlarge and strengthen it; simply, to "perform the service that pertains to it." (Thomas S. Monson, C.R., 4/2005). "If you do not magnify your calling," John Taylor taught, "God will hold you responsible for those you might have saved, had you done your duty." ("Deseret News," 8/2/1878). "Therefore, let every man stand in his own office, and labor in his own calling; and let not the head say unto the feet it hath no need of the feet; for without the feet how shall the body be able to stand? Also, the body hath need of every member, that all may be edified together, that the system may be kept perfect." (D&C 84:109-110).

Jacob took his calling so seriously that he declared: "We did magnify our office unto the Lord, taking upon us the responsibility, answering the sins of the people upon our own heads if we did not teach them the word of God with all diligence." (Jacob 1:19). In the Last Days, we are reminded: "There has been a day of calling, but the time has come for a day of choosing; and let those be chosen that are worthy." (D&C 105:35). Members of the church are those who have been called.

"There are many called, but few are chosen. And why are they not chosen? Because their hearts are set so much upon the things of this world, and aspire to the honors of men, that they do not learn this one lesson: That the rights of the priesthood are inseparably connected with the powers of heaven, and that the powers of heaven cannot be controlled nor handled only upon the principles of righteousness. That they may be conferred upon us, it is true; but when we undertake to cover our sins, or to gratify our pride, our vain ambition, or to exercise control or dominion or compulsion upon the souls of the children of men, in any degree of unrighteousness, behold, the heavens withdraw themselves; the Spirit of the Lord is grieved; and when it is withdrawn, Amen to the priesthood or the authority of that man." (D&C 121:34-37).

We express our gratitude by shouting "Hosannas" to the Lord.

"If thou art merry, praise the Lord with singing, with music, with dancing, and with a prayer of praise and thanksgiving." (D&C 136:28). "He that trembleth under my power shall be made strong, and shall bring forth fruits of praise and wisdom." (D&C 52:17).

We express our gratitude by being valiant in our testimony of Jesus.

Those who are valiant "received the testimony of Jesus, and believed on his name and were baptized after the manner of his burial, being buried in the water in his name, and this according to the commandment which he has given. That by keeping the commandments they might be washed and cleansed from all their sins, and receive the Holy Spirit by the laying on of the hands of him who is ordained and sealed unto this power; and who overcome by faith, and are sealed by the Holy Spirit of promise, which the father shed forth upon all those who are just and true." (D&C 76:51-53).

"To be valiant in the testimony of Jesus is to take the Lord's side on every issue. It is to think what he thinks, to believe what he believes, to say what he would say, and do what he would do." (Bruce R. McConkie, C.R., 10/1974).

To be valiant is to be neither ashamed nor confounded nor lukewarm. (See D&C 90:17). "Wherefore, lift up your voice and spare not." (D&C 34:10).

We express our gratitude by worshiping God in the temple, and by honoring our temple covenants.

A temple is built "for a place of thanksgiving for all saints, and for a place of instruction for all those who are called to the work of the ministry in all their several callings and offices." (D&C 97:13). "No form of government, no level of material well-being, will save man," wrote Abba Eban. "He will be redeemed only when towers fall, and Jerusalem triumphs over Babylon. What is at stake, finally, is not only intelligence, but also feeling. Man has to change his heart. Salvation, the prophets tell us, is preconditioned by repentance," which leads the faithful to the temple ordinances. "The redeeming act of God," which is consummated for man at holy altars in the House of The Lord, "waits upon man's initiative." ("My People: The Story of The Jews," p. 59-60).

"Why should it surprise us that life's most demanding tests as well as life's most significant opportunities for growth in life usually occur within marriage and the family?" asked Neal A. Maxwell. ("Ensign," 7/1982). These are relationships best forged at the altars of the temple. "How can revolving-door relationships, by contrast, be a real test of our capacity to love?" he continued. When the ordinances of the temple drive the law into our inward parts, so that it is written upon our hearts, a mighty change takes place. (See Jeremiah 31:33). It is when one is born again that the desired result of all gospel-oriented teaching is achieved. When we are sanctified, holiness erases the disposition to do evil. Our "minds become single to God." (D&C 88:68).

Members of the church who have made covenants with God in the temple are not tormented by confusion, wracked by doubt, or buffeted by bewilderment. They understand the meaning behind the question Paul asked of the Galatian Saints: "Do I now persuade men, or God?" (Galatians 1:10). They are eager to make covenants, for they have personally witnessed the effects of such actions. "Until one is so committed there is hesitancy, the chance to draw back, always ineffectiveness. Concerning all acts of initiative, there is one elementary truth, the ignorance of which kills countless ideas and splendid plans: that the moment one definitely commits oneself, then Providence moves too. All sorts of things occur to help one that would never have otherwise occurred. A whole stream of events issues from the decision, raining in one's favor all manner of unforeseen incidents and material assistance, which no man could have dreamed would have come his way." (Tom Hornbein, "Everest - "The West Ridge," Sierra Club, 1966, p. 100).

We express our gratitude by observing the Word of Wisdom.

When we consciously adopt lifestyles that result in poor physical health, "wisdom cannot reveal itself, culture cannot become manifest, strength cannot fight, wealth becomes useless, and intelligence cannot be applied." (Heraclitus - Philosopher of the Golden Age of Greece). it is critical to the success of the Plan itself that our bodies remain in good condition because they are the mortal tabernacles of our spirits, and our health invites spirituality that leads to joyfulness, the equivalent of eternal life in the Celestial Kingdom of God. "For man is spirit. The elements are eternal, and spirit and element, inseparably connected, receive a fulness of joy." (D&C 93:33). Spirituality invites gratitude. "Spirituality," taught David O. McKay, "is the consciousness of victory over self, and of communion with the infinite." (C.R., 10/1969).

We express our gratitude by being temperate.

Certain things are good for our bodies. Work, cleanliness, rest, and exercise are important and positive components of the Word of Wisdom. Therefore, the Lord commanded: "Cease to be idle; cease to be unclean; cease to find fault one with another; cease to sleep longer than is needful; retire to thy bed early, that ye may not be weary; arise early, that your bodies and your minds may be invigorated" with the capacity to express real gratitude. (D&C 88:124).

We express our gratitude by resisting the provocation to anger.

An angry countenance betrays the physical marks of anger. The Lord's anger is His righteous indignation, but we are talking about something else. Self-defeating anger is troublesome, trying, resentful and irritable. Speaking to Joseph Smith the Lord characterized those who have lost control of their emotions. "Fools shall have thee in derision," He said, "and hell shall rage against thee." (D&C 122:1).

We express our gratitude in our integrity.

Who we are is God's gift to us. Who we become is our gift to God. "Integrity without knowledge is weak and useless," observed Samuel Johnson. "Knowledge without integrity," on the other hand, "is dangerous and dreadful." By entering into covenants, we bind ourselves by own integrity to act in a positive and predictable way. Our covenants engender a sense of responsibility that in turn becomes a powerful reinforcement for affirmative action. By making the commitment known to others, we establish a means of accountability and unify the forces within ourselves that can secure the blessings of heaven.

We express our gratitude by viewing education as a life-long process.

"Knowledge will forever govern ignorance," said James Madison, "and a people who mean to be their own governors must arm themselves with the power which knowledge gives." (Letter to W.T. Barry, 8/4/1822). The problem with many educational programs is that one "asks for the bread of life," explained Hugh Nibley, "but gets only processed academic factory food served at an automat." ("Nibley On the Timely and Timeless"). Perhaps this is why Albert Einstein declared: "Education is that which remains when one has forgotten everything learned in school."

Interestingly, "Utah, of all the states in the last 30 years, has usually had the highest proportion of its population in school, the highest proportion of high school graduates, the highest average number of school years completed, and has usually spent on education the greatest amount in relation to total personal income." (Leonard Arrington, "The Mormon Experience," p. 304). "A recent study of the social origins of American scientists and scholars concludes that, in relation to population, Utah was the most productive of all the states for all fields of learning combined, in all time periods." (Leonard Arrington, "The Mormon Experience," p. 319).

It seems clear that many Utahans believe in the positive aspects of self-improvement, and that "if a person gains more knowledge and intelligence in this life through his diligence and obedience than another, he will have so much the advantage in the world to come." (D&C 130:19). Those who value education have learned by experience that all "who remember to keep (the statutes of God) shall find wisdom and great treasures of knowledge, even hidden treasures." (D&C 88:18-19).

We express our gratitude by knowing how to work.

"I want to bear you my testimony," said Ernest L. Wilkinson, "that if you develop the habit of work, it will be the most invigorating, satisfying, even relaxing and greatest blessing of your life. The opportunity to work is God's greatest blessing to mankind, and this means six days of each week." ("The Banyan," 5/1968). Neal A. Maxwell called work a spiritual necessity, and said that we avoid it at peril to our souls. ("Choose," p. 54). A favorite aphorism of Harold B. Lee was: "Work without vision is drudgery. Vision without work is dreamery. But work with vision is destiny."

Spencer W. Kimball echoed the words of Daniel Burnham, when he said: "Make no small plans for they have no magic to stir men's souls." "Cease to be idle; cease to be unclean; cease to find fault one with another; cease to sleep longer than is needful; retire to thy bed early, that ye may not be weary; arise early, that your bodies and your minds may be invigorated." (D&C 88:124). When we put our minds and our bodies to work, we think big.

We express our gratitude by nurturing family relationships.

Because the gospel gives us direction and our families give us purpose, "no other success can compensate for failure in our own homes." (David O. McKay, C.R., 4/1935). "The most important work we ever do," as a matter of fact, "will be within the walls of our own homes." (Harold B. Lee, "Stand Ye in Holy Places," p. 255).

"I have commanded you to bring up your children in light and truth," (D&C 93:40), "to set in order your families, and see that they are more diligent and concerned at home, and pray always," (D&C 93:50) because "all children have claim upon their parents for their maintenance until they are of age." (D&C 83:4).

"Inasmuch as parents have children in Zion, or in any of her stakes which are organized, that teach them not to understand the doctrine of repentance, faith in Christ the Son of the living God, and of baptism and the gift of the Holy Ghost by the laying on of the hands, when eight years old, the sin be upon the heads of the parents." (D&C 68:25). We know "that righteous parents who strive to develop wholesome influences for their children will be held blameless at the last day, and that they will succeed in saving most of their children, if not all." (Spencer W. Kimball, C.R., 10/1974).

"Every man who is obliged to provide for his own family, let him provide." (D&C 75:28). Therefore, "no true Latter-day Saint, while physically or emotionally able, will voluntarily shift the burden of his own or his family's well-being to someone else, so long as he can, under the inspiration of the Lord and with his own labors, supply himself and his family with the spiritual and temporal necessities of life." (Spencer W. Kimball, C.R., 10/1977).

We express our gratitude by being teachers.

"We save ourselves by our teaching, and we save those who will get in tune with the same Spirit that we have, when we teach those truths. What a glorious and wondrous thing it is not to have to defend them and support them and uphold them. They are true, and they sustain and defend and uphold themselves. And they do it because the work is true." (Bruce R. McConkie, "The Foolishness of Teaching," "Religious Educator," 6:1).

All of us are teachers and all our teaching should be by the Spirit and from the scriptures so that those whom we teach might say, as did the two disciples of Christ on the road to Emmaus, "Did not our heart burn within us, while he talked with us by the way, and while he opened to us the scriptures?" (See Luke 24:32).

We have been commanded to "appoint among (ourselves) a teacher, and let not all be spokesmen at once; but let one speak at a time and let all listen unto his sayings, that when all have spoken ... all may be edified (and) every man may have an equal privilege." (D&C 88:122).

We are to "teach one another the doctrine of the kingdom," and to be diligent in our teaching, so that the grace of God may attend us, so that we "may be instructed more perfectly in theory, in principle, in doctrine, in the law of the gospel, in all things that pertain to the kingdom of God, that are expedient for (us) to understand; Of things both in heaven and in the earth, and under the earth; things which have been, things which are, things which must shortly come to pass; things which are at home, things which are abroad; the wars and the perplexities of the nations, and the judgments which are on the land; and a knowledge also of countries and of kingdoms – that (we) may be prepared in all things" and be ready to complete the mission assignments to which we have been commissioned by the Lord Himself. (D&C 88:77-80).

If we are not accustomed to expressing gratitude, we can start today on this incomplete list and work to live in daily thanksgiving to God. We can follow the Plan of Salvation, defend the faith, lay our lives on the altar of sacrifice, consistently repent, pattern our lives after the Savior, express our thanks in prayer, reconcile ourselves to negative responses to our petitions, gain spiritual fluency, focus on the positive, forgive others, keep the commandments, endure to the end in righteousness, recognize the merits of the principles of righteousness, righteously exercise what power or authority we possess, acknowledge Him as the sole source of our protection, determine to serve Him, acknowledge His majesty and power and that of His servants, see His presence in the earth around us, use our agency wisely to validate the wisdom of our self-government, indicate by our actions that we understand the true value of things and do not covet the profane things of the world, understand the relationship between commandments and blessings, multiply our talents and turn weaknesses into strengths, use our means wisely, manage our time carefully, keep our priorities in order, maintain our perspective even when our days seem purposeless, change our hearts through faith on His name, accept responsibility for our actions and use our agency wisely, use our opportunities for failure as learning experiences, bear adversity well, recognize the seeming detours and distractions in our lives as opportunities for personal growth, continue to express our gratitude in times of adversity, maintain a cheerful attitude, sacrifice (seemingly), be anxiously engaged, perform acts of quiet Christianity, open our arms to those around us, love our neighbors, do missionary work, acknowledge the qualities of goodness in others, express appreciation to others, recognize how precious our divine attributes are, read the scriptures, promote the cause of Zion, magnify our callings, shout Hosannas to the Lord, be valiant in our testimony of Jesus, worship God in the temple and honor our temple covenants, observe the Word of Wisdom, be temperate and not easily provoked to anger, have integrity, view education as a life-long process, know how to work, nurture family relationships, and take our responsibilities as teacher seriously.

What if we haven't yet developed these qualities? "Don't be discouraged if you haven't been an especially grateful person," urged Joseph Wirthlin. "Rejoice and think of what an impression you will make on those who thought they knew you! Think of how delightfully surprised they will be!" ("B.Y.U. Devotional," 10/31/2000).

As we learn to express in thought, word, and deed our gratitude to God, it will come to "include thanksgiving for his tutoring of us to aid our acquisition of needed attributes and experiences while we are in mortality. Our thanksgiving will come because we trust his design of life itself!" (Neal A. Maxwell, "Ensign," 7/1982).

We will be as Ebenezer Scrooge after his transformation, who "lived upon the Total Abstinence Principle, ever afterwards; and it was always said of him, that he knew how to (express gratitude), if any man alive possessed the knowledge. May that be truly said of us, and all of us! As so, as Tiny Tim put it: "God bless us, everyone!" (Charles Dickens, "A Christmas Carol"). And so, we remember the Lord's blessing as we brim with emotion in gratitude for His matchless love: "The Lord bless thee and keep thee. The Lord make his face shine upon thee, and be gracious unto thee. The Lord lift up his countenance upon thee, and give thee peace." (Numbers 6:24-26).

The Lord taught
us all a valuable lesson when
He declared: "I will forgive whom I
will forgive, but of you it is required to
forgive all men." (D&C 64:10). The Sons of
Mosiah knew that their joy and satisfaction
in life, meaning their true freedom, and
also their eternal salvation, depended
on their willingness and capacity
to forgive the Lamanites for the
perceived injustices that they
had committed, that had
supposedly harmed
their people.

Observations

Pointedly
and specifically
to all those whose weak
character has enslaved them in
drunkenness and selfish indulgence,
ancient prophets have spoken a powerful
message. "Wo unto them that rise up early in
the morning, that they may follow strong drink,
that continue until night, and wine inflame them!"
(2 Nephi 15:11). Those whose senses have been dulled
by excess of any kind can be blinded to the pattern of
progress that is before their eyes. "They regard not the
work of the Lord, neither consider the operation of his
hands." (2 Nephi 15:12). They are captive because of
physical addictions and are bound with a stupor of
thought. Because they have become so telestially
traumatized, they have no comprehension of
God. "Their honorable men are famished,
and their multitude (has been) dried
up with thirst." (2 Nephi 15:13).

As the Holy Ghost enlarges our
understanding during Book of Mormon study,
the word of God will bloom with hidden meanings,
and their applications will later pop into our minds at
just the right moments. In a wonderfully whole and
complete way, God will be sensitive to our needs. He
will teach us how to reach out and touch the hem
of the garment of the Savior, to draw upon
His virtue, when our own reserves have
sunk to dangerously low levels.
(See Mark 5:27-34).

No one can
claim that they have
a corner on the Spirit. Each
one of us has been hard-wired to
respond to the invitations by the
Light of Christ and the Holy Ghost
to come and enjoy the fruit of the
Tree of Life. (See 1 Nephi
Chapters 8 & 11).

In these Last
Days, we have sown the wind,
with easy access to divorce, free sex,
and to abortion on demand, and now we
are reaping the whirlwind, as we witness the
destruction of the family, the definition of
marriage, as well as the reconfiguring of
gender orientation. The truth be told,
it is The Book of Mormon, together
with its principles and doctrine,
that is under siege by latter
day revisionists of the
Plan of Salvation.

Civilizations
rise and fall for
complex reasons, but
there may be one single
underlying cause of societal
implosion. Satan has focused his
significant energy and has invested
immense resource on the destruction of
time-honored values, whose expression is
found in the pages of The Book of Mormon.
Those who believe in them may be few, but
they are the warriors who stand to fight
the world alone; to win the battle that
rages in the hearts of men on the
world's last night.

Everything that
comes from the Lord has
been made using the best and
sturdiest materials with foresight,
designed to withstand the tests of both
time and circumstance. But those of us
who are familiar with the scriptures are well
aware of Hosea's terrifying caution that when
the world sows the wind, it can expect to reap the
whirlwind. Thus, knowing the calamity that
would lie ahead, The Book of Mormon was
designed to withstand the worst that the
devil could muster, as he unleashes
destruction upon the world.
(See Hosea 8:7).

The Book of Mormon
always takes a beating from
the enthusiastically ignorant.
For many years, the church was
pilloried for its unconventional
views. Now, it is being ridiculed
for its traditional values. It
may be that our easy
days are over.

We turn to
The Book of Mormon
for guidance, therein to be
sanctified. When we desire to
be immersed in the Spirit, we
discover the process by which
we may be purified from the
effects of sin. This occurs
when the ordinances
drive the law into
our inward
parts.

Those who have the courage
to introduce The Book of Mormon
to their friends and their neighbors are
as "saviors (who) shall come up on mount
Zion." (Obadiah 1:21). They are "set to be a
light unto the world, and to be the saviors
of men" (D&C 103:9), as they share the
gospel message with their brothers
and sisters who are not yet
members of the Church
of Jesus Christ.

The Atonement of Jesus
Christ assures us that every child
of God who has ever lived upon the earth
will be raised to immortality and resurrected
to live forever. But the Lord has revealed that we
have a part to play in His Plan of Salvation, and
The Book of Mormon shows us how we can also be
raised up unto eternal life. We must organize
ourselves to be ready to "prepare every needful
thing; and establish a house, even a house
of prayer, a house of fasting, a house of
faith, a house of learning, a house of
glory, a house of order, (and) a
house of God." (D&C
88:119).

In an
example of
a futile attempt
to sidestep cultural
implosion, and for the
sake of society's collective
expediency, the target has
been moved so many times
to score repetitive bulls-eyes,
that no-one seems to be able to
recognize that it is the arrow of
faith that has strayed from the
mark, which is represented by
our testimony of The Book of
Mormon, manifest as yet
another unimpeachable
witness of Christ.

Some
folks think
that they can
be happy if they
wander and play.
They don't consider
the crucial features of
The Book of Mormon; its
encouragement to ponder
and pray, and to study and
apply doctrine and principles.
Disregarding these elements of
many prophets' counsel, we fall
into old habit patterns that will
increase our vulnerability to
the slippery enticements
of the Adversary.

We have been
foreordained in heaven,
even before the world was,
to have glory added upon our
heads forever, on the condition
of our faithfulness to God as we
support Him in His great work by
our actions, and put into practice
the principles of provident living
that we learn about in The Book
of Mormon. We are better able
to do so if we listen intently,
as we're taught the doctrine
of Christ by the Holy
Ghost.

Lehi made
it perfectly clear to his
family (see 2 Nephi Chapter
2), that their divine right to
exercise their free will in an
atmosphere of opposition
has been intertwined
with creation
itself.

The
temple in the land
of Bountiful helped the
Nephites (see 2 Nephi 5:16),
to imagine what it would be
like coming home from their
mortal missions. It provided
them with the best dress
rehearsals that they
could hope for.

As we are overcome
by the persistent feeling that
The Book of Mormon was written
with us in mind, we tingle with an
awakening realization that we
were called up and chosen
in heaven before we
came to live on
the earth.

In moments
of deep reflection,
we seem to absorb truth
from The Book of Mormon
like a sponge. We discover that
we are the begotten spirit children of
Heavenly parents, and that we lived
in our pre-mortal existence with them
before we began our sojourn on earth.
We experience moments of dejá vu,
when with awakening memories
we realize that we are strangers
on earth who have wandered
from a more exalted
sphere.

Both righteous
Nephites and converted Lamanites
might have seized upon the opportunity to
embrace the powerful influence of the Holy
Ghost that permeated the revelatory walls of
the temple in Bountiful, by internalizing
an attitude that found its expression in
the true order of prayer. Later, when
they returned to their homes, they
might have rehearsed this same
pattern with their children
and grandchildren.

As we mildly and
quietly walk in the light of the
Lord on an errand that brings us to an
appreciation of The Book of Mormon, we
become more comfortable with the truth.
"The wisdom that is from above is first
pure, then peaceable, gentle, and easy
to be entreated, full of mercy and
good fruits, without partiality,
and without hypocrisy."
(James 3:17).

The stellar example that was set by
Nephi, Jacob, Mosiah, Benjamin, Alma, Amulek,
Helaman, Samuel The Lamanite, Mormon, Moroni,
and so many other figures from The Book of Mormon
vigorously illustrates the principle that the power to preach
the gospel comes thru the Spirit. It must reside in both the one
who delivers the word and the one who is receiving it. This is
the magic of gospel instruction. It is a foolproof method for
disseminating information of eternal worth. It cannot be
mishandled or misrepresented. Without the Spirit, we
cannot teach, for the Savior said that "if ye receive
not the Spirit ye shall not teach." (D&C 42:14).
The responsibility is so great, that it is no
wonder that the Savior warned: "Be ye
clean that bear the vessels of the
Lord." (D&C 38:42).

Our intimate
familiarity with the
doctrine of Christ found in
The Book of Mormon catalyzes
a state of innocence and holiness.
The dazzling light of truth exposes
the nature of evil that is abroad in
the land, and the book gives us
"power over that spirit."
(D&C 50:32).

It is in
The Book of
Mormon that
God stands ready
to bestow upon us His
perspective, and He only
waits upon our initiative
before He acts in our
behalf.

Mormon saw our
day, when it is not only
in the media, but also in our
common experience, that we are
assaulted by scribes and Pharisees
with golden tongues who beguile us
with worldly wisdom, politically correct
behavior, and with homogenized values.
They tempt us with subtle sophistry and
words like tolerance, equal opportunity,
and affirmative action. Ever so gently,
they nestle flaxen cords around our
necks. It all seems so reasonable, so
comfortable, so inclusive, and so
open-minded, that we scarcely
notice our surroundings, that
we are being maliciously
led down a terrifying
highway to hell.

The Book of Mormon
inspires us to enjoy the
sweet companionship of the
Holy Ghost, Who stands ready
to guide us through the portal of
revelation to an epiphany where we
might know for ourselves the truth
of all things. Even more, as it molds
and shapes us into new creatures in
Christ, pure intelligence will flow
unto us as the dews of
Carmel.

The
Spirit speaks
"of things as they
really are, and of things
as they really will be," which
are manifest in plainness "for the
salvation of our souls." (Jacob 4:13). In
contrast is intellectual embroidery that is
at times preferred to the whole ensemble of
the gospel; the frills to the fabric, as it were.
Only revelation provides us with absolute
anchors that we so desperately need. If
we give it a chance, we will find that
there is more realism in the word
of God than there could ever
be in a secularism that is
congenitally short
sighted.

If we've never undertaken the
journey that leads to a testimony of
The Book of Mormon, and if we have
not worked diligently to harvest the
delicious fruit of the Tree of Life,
we can't truly receive the things
of the Spirit of God, for they
will seem foolish in
our eyes.

The Book of
Mormon teaches that we
are all the offspring of eternal
beings, and so, deeply rooted within
each of us are the seeds of greatness, for
we have been endowed with the potential to
completely develop the attributes of our Father.
We muster His power by recommitting ourselves
to our covenants with Him. We believe in, and fight
for, the most profound truths and highest standards.
We are set apart to accomplish these tasks because ours
is an eternally significant work that is carried out in
partnership with our Creator. We are set apart by our
convictions, by our righteousness, by our faith,
and by our enthusiasm. We pray that those
who lie within the sphere of our influence
will be blessed and enriched because
of His work that has been given
into our hands.

Our
divine
tutorial
training as
we engage The
Book of Mormon
is a process, and
not a point, and
that is just how
God wants
it to be.

The Book of Mormon is one
of the best things that has happened
to us. As we have read it, we've learned
"how to give and not count the cost, to fight
and not heed the wounds, to toil and not
seek for rest, and to labor and not ask
for reward, save that of knowing
that we do God's will."
(Loyola).

The gospel was the perfect law of liberty for the
Nephites. It set them free to make intelligent choices, to
receive the blessings of the priesthood, to serve others more
meaningfully, and to enjoy unrestrained opportunity
for improvement, as they committed themselves to
the observance of proven principles. With the
gift of freedom to act independently,
they were able to follow a path
of progress, or a pathway
leading to ruin.

Alma
taught the
principles that
relate to the Great
Plan of Happiness.
With no repentance, we
would remain in a wretched
state, and exist forever in our
sins. (See Alma 12:26). Without
baptism, if we were to partake of the
fruit of the tree of life, which is eternal
life, or the highest expression of the grace
of God, it would be impossible to sustain a
celestial existence inasmuch as in our fallen
condition we would be incapable of obedience
to celestial principles. Thus, the Plan would
be frustrated. Mercy and Justice were placed
before Adam and Eve to hedge the way to the
tree of life until they had the opportunity
to participate in the saving ordinances
of the gospel. (See Alma 12:21,
42:2, & Moses 4:31).

When we pattern
our lives after that of the
Savior, we are on solid footing.
He told the Saints in Zarahemla:
"Ye know the things that ye must do in
my church, for the works which ye have
seen me do, that shall ye also do."
(3 Nephi 27:21).

Among the Nephites,
it was their faith that set them
free from the self-defeating behaviors
of confusion, doubt, ignorance, sin, worry,
and guilt, that might have caused them to become
immobilized, and even paralyzed, during their mortal
experience. It was in a garden setting that Adam and Eve
were blessed with freedom to act, but the Nephites sometimes
forfeit that birthright thru the adoption of bad habits. They were
detained by telestial traffic jams, confused by conceptual cul-de-
sacs, and detoured by doctrinal dilemmas of their own making.
When they embarked upon the strait and narrow way, however,
they found a path opening up onto the broad boulevards of
opportunity that led to the perfect law of liberty, and to
an expression of mind, body, and spirit that guided
them toward the surety that is described in the
scriptures as the Rest of the Lord.
(See Alma 7:27).

When our minds
are locked on terrestrial
targets and we even attempt
so-called higher-level thinking
as we study The Book of Mormon,
without the influence of the Spirit, we
risk becoming as sounding brass and
tinkling cymbals. Without the Holy
Ghost's guidance, we will be hollow
on the inside, and the echoes of
silence will be deafening
to our ears.

Jacob addressed
all of those who gun their
engines in telestial traffic jams,
become hoarders of temporal trash,
and who have a fascination with trivial
pursuits: "Wo unto him...that wasteth the
days of his probation, for awful is his state!"
(2 Nephi 9:27). Particularly when individuals
groan "under darkness and under the bondage
of sin," they have no hope, and their lives have
little meaning or stability. (D&C 84:49). They
cannot begin to comprehend that fame is a
vapor, and popularity is an accident, and
those who cheer you today might curse
you tomorrow; that, in the end, the
only thing that endures, the only
thing that you can really count
on, is your character. And
that is something upon
which you cannot
put a price.

For latter-day
apostate Nephites and
Lamanites, the concept of the
Atonement may be hard to grasp
because it was conceived in heaven.
It is not of this world, and if we try
to wrap our finite minds around
it, we will fail to do so. It can
only be spiritually
discerned.

Those who have
become enslaved by
their selfish indulgences
to the point that they "regard
not the work of the Lord, neither
consider the operation of his hands,"
must ultimately drink of the wine of the
wrath of the indignation of God. (2 Nephi
15:12). Without knowledge of heaven, they are
as those who are "famished, and their multitude
dried up with thirst. Therefore, hell hath enlarged
herself, and opened her mouth without measure;
and their glory, and their multitude, and their
pomp, and he that rejoiceth, shall descend
into it (even as) God that is holy (is)
sanctified in righteousness."
(2 Nephi 15:13-16).

We learn from
The Book of Mormon
that following the ministry
of the Savior among the Nephites,
their love for Him, and for each other,
was so great that they were the happiest
people of all those who had ever been
created by the hand of God.
(See 4 Nephi 1:15-16).

The
ignorance
of worldly wisdom
may have contributed to
the problem, but a poor grasp
of eternal principles rested at the
root of apostasy from truth among
the people in the lands of The Book of
Mormon. Even today, the church suffers
from a shallow understanding by some
members of even basic gospel principles.
Consequently, the devil seizes upon their
weaknesses. Satan knows who the Lord's
servants are; each one is a marked man
or woman. Therefore, they all require
for a defense a solid foundation of
doctrinal knowledge, an abiding
testimony of every principle of
the Plan of Salvation, as well
as a witness of the Savior
and Redeemer of the
world.

Because of His concern for
us, God has charged His angels in
heaven with the responsibility to call us to
"repentance, and to fulfil and to do the work of
the covenants of the Father, which he hath made
unto the children of men, to prepare the way by
declaring the word of Christ unto the chosen
vessels of the Lord, that they may
bear testimony of him."
(Moroni 7:31)

Throughout The Book
of Mormon, the Lord gives us
repeated reassurances that it is His
hand that will rule in the Last Days,
and so His people need not fear the vile
threats and dreadful oaths of the wicked.
He has promised: "I will make thy horn
iron, and I will make thy hoofs brass.
And thou shalt beat in pieces many
people; and I will consecrate their
gain unto the Lord, and their
substance unto the Lord of
the whole earth." (3
Nephi 20:19).

Jacob warned his brethren who
had become preoccupied with telestial
trivia: "Wo unto him ..... that wasteth the
days of his probation, for awful is his state!"
(2 Nephi 9:27). Particularly when individuals
groan "under darkness and under the bondage
of sin," they have little meaning or stability
in their lives. (D&C 84:49). They do not
understand that "fame is a vapor, and
popularity is an accident, and that
those who cheer you today may
curse you tomorrow. In the
end, the only thing that
endures is character."
(Horace Greeley).

The
Nephites
endured cycles
of conceit that were
dangerously habitual.
Vanity doggedly tugged
at them, trying to pull them
away from their divine center.
They couldn't seem to remember
that, in order to make their calling
and election sure, they mustn't stray
from their Father's business, but instead
consecrate all that they were, their time
and talents, and everything else with
which the Lord had blessed them,
to promote the gospel of Jesus
Christ and the cause
of Zion.

The thing
about Latter-day Nephites
is that they "are like artichokes.
At first, you either like them or you
don't. But those who have had unfavorable
first impressions quite often find that once
the outer layers have been peeled away, both
(Nephites) and artichokes are most likable. In
fact, most people who get to know (Nephites)
become their friends, while a little objective
research on their beliefs reveals that, except
for a few doctrinal differences, those who
call themselves (the children of Lehi)
are just like the rest of us. They
are very human beings."
(Boston Globe, 1967).

If The Book of Mormon teaches us nothing
else, it leaves us with this impression: Each of us
will find an opportunity to become familiar with the
principles of the Plan of Salvation, because, in the final
analysis, we cannot hope to find lasting happiness, except
we are obedient to the specific rules of behavior with which it is
associated. As Joseph Smith taught: "Happiness is the object and
design of our existence, and will be the end thereof, if we pursue
the path that leads to it, and this path is virtue, uprightness,
faithfulness, holiness, and keeping the commandments."
All else is vanity, and for the those of us who have been
exposed to The Book of Mormon, and who should
thereby know better, it is blasphemous to act
in ways that are incompatible with
celestial principles.

Every time, during the final
stage of their cycles of righteousness,
prosperity, pride, and apostasy, (but for
the glaring example in the 4th century A.D.
in the land round about Cumorah), the Nephites
found it within themselves to cultivate the quality
of contrition, good outweighed evil, love overpowered
jealousy, hate, and prejudice, light drove out darkness,
knowledge banished ignorance, humility displaced pride,
courtesy overwhelmed rudeness, and appreciation overcame
thanklessness. Abundance superseded poverty, well-being
replaced weakness, simplicity overshadowed perplexity, and
harmony supplanted discord. Faith subdued fear, a hope
in Christ cast out despair, charity ousted selfishness,
joy deposed unhappiness, sadness, dejection, and
misery, certainty dethroned bewilderment, and
confidence was substituted for timidity,
while assurance unseated despair
and discouragement.

In these Last Days, the
terrible indictment of those who have
dismissed The Book of Mormon as a thing of
naught mandates that they will have no claim on
mercy because they have willfully chosen to deny
themselves the blessing of baptism by immersion
for the remission of sins. For them, the judgment
will be a very unpleasant experience, as an awful
avalanche of consequences overwhelms them and
smothers their hope of timely deliverance. Given
over to the buffetings of Satan, on their own
initiative they will somehow need to scrape
together their last farthings in order to
personally pay Justice, that they
might meet its demands for
their redemption.

One doesn't need to read
between the lines to see that Book
of Mormon prophets revealed the Lord's
battle plan for the Last Days, when His
invincible missionary army will engage
the forces of Babylon,. Her defenses will
collapse before the bombardment of
love unfeigned, the onslaught
of priesthood principles, and
the overwhelming clout
of covenants.

The fatal flaw of vanity
is that it relies upon misguided
hope, and its strength is built upon
false premises. It is a Ponzi scheme that
can't deliver on its promises. It writes checks
that cannot be cashed because it lacks spiritual
reserves, and it is forever teetering on the brink
of bankruptcy. In contrast, The Book of
Mormon remains as stable and as
secure as the Bank of
England.

The Book
of Mormon is
like a tuning fork
resounding with the
elemental patterns that
are in harmony with truth
on a fundamental level. We
who are as wise as serpents and
as harmless as doves (see Matthew
10:16), have learned how use it as
an instrument that creates perfect
pitch during our quest to
become holy.

If we
feel that we've
been offended, or
we perceive that we've
been wronged by others,
or if we've been wounded
physically, intellectually,
emotionally, professionally,
or even spiritually, we need to
turn to the healing balm of The
Book of Mormon to sooth the
trauma of bruised bodies
or battered egos.

When we feel so
strongly that we are
right that our confidence
obscures our better judgment,
when our standpoint, from our
unimpeachable perspective, appears
to be unassailable, and even when our
supposed invincibility feels like bedrock
beneath the fortress of our self-confidence,
it's the anchor of The Book of Mormon that
will drag us back to earth for a desperately
needed repentance-based reality check
and a generous serving of
humble pie.

The best
thing that The Book
of Mormon has going for
it is that it teaches truth, pure
and simple; and that may be the
only quality that can unerringly
guide us back to the lucidity and
brilliant light radiating from
our eternal Home.

After Alice
had gone down the
rabbit hole, she stumbled
upon The Book of Mormon,
and was curious. And so it was,
that when she met the Cheshire Cat,
she asked him: "Would you please tell
me which way I ought to go from here?"
To which the cat responded: "That depends
a good deal on where you want to go." Alice
acknowledged: "I admit, I don't much care
where." The cat responded: "Then it really
doesn't matter which way you go." Alice
implored: "Just so I go somewhere!"
To which the cat observed: "Oh,
you are sure to do that, if
you only walk far
enough."

Faith is dead without
the accompanying work of
repentance that has been made
possible by Christ's Atonement.
Even the great faith exhibited by
the Nephites lacked the power to
save them from the unalterable
demands of Justice. So that
Mercy might prevail, God
afforded them, and has
provided us, with a
Mediator.

Ultimately,
we are required
to give up only our
sins, (Alma 22:18),
that we might merit
salvation because
of the grace of
God.

If we've
acquired a taste
for the poor imitations
of life that are peddled by the
deceiver, we delude ourselves into
believing they are the genuine articles.
We assuage ourselves with rationalizations
so that we can face ourselves in the mirror, and
sleep better. The irony is, that in other and more
productive circumstances, the forgery might
have been revealed by life lessons learned by
reading The Book of Mormon, prompting
us to course-correct, as if the welfare of
our souls depended on it (which
they most assuredly do).

The
words 'repent'
and 'repentance' are
found in the Bible just
101 times. It seems that
Heavenly Father has chosen
to emphasize the importance
of repentance in our day, and
especially throughout The Book
of Mormon, inasmuch as it is
mentioned 450 times in that
work, in The Pearl of Great
Price, and in the Doctrine
and Covenants.

The stability
of The Book of Mormon
stands in stark contrast to
the exaggerations of the world that
stretch our comprehension and strain
our credulity, causing unbelievers to
stand unsteadily on their spiritual
tippy toes, as they roll the dice
and leave their destiny in
the fickle hands of
fate.

Wo, wo, wo
unto all those who
groan under darkness
and under the bondage of
sin (see 2 Nephi 9:38), who
squander precious resources,
groping about in a frantic but
fruitless search for meaning in
their lives. In short, they fail to
appreciate the stabilizing power
of God's Plan of Salvation that
could have been theirs if they
had only focused on the
soothing influence
of faith.

Book of Mormon
prophets would never ask
us to pay the exorbitant price of
admission to Babylon's amusement
parks. Instead, they urge us to utilize the
principle-based aid stations providentially
positioned in Zion, and that are free to the
public. Faith, repentance, and baptism by
immersion have all been factored into a
performance cost that has been paid in
advance, and that is then disbursed
in a perpetual annuity that takes
the form of the Atonement and
the Sacrament, to perfectly
meet our needs.

The Book of Mormon pointedly teaches us that we "are
free according to the flesh," which is exactly why we need the gospel
in our lives. A wise Father has given us all things "which are expedient
unto (us. Thus, we are liberated, and are) free to choose liberty and eternal
life, through the great Mediator of all men, or to choose captivity and death,
according to the captivity and power of the devil; for he seeketh that all men
might be miserable like unto himself." (2 Nephi 2:27). Thus, Father Lehi
cautioned: Do "not choose eternal death, according to the will of the flesh
and the evil which is therein, which giveth the spirit of the devil power
to captivate, to bring you down to hell, that he may reign over you
in his own kingdom." (2 Nephi 2:29). We have to be constantly
on our guard to identify his hit men, because his agents are
crafty. Of Sherem, Jacob wrote: "And he was learned, that
he had a perfect knowledge of the language of the
people; wherefore, he could use much flattery,
and much power of speech, according
to the power of the devil."
(Jacob 7:4).

We read in The Book
of Mormon that henceforth,
we might never again be tossed
to and fro by the winds of doctrine,
which are those worldly influences
that play mind-games with us,
as they jockey for position in
a fierce competition for
market share.

Those
who demand
that they be shown
outward evidence of the
divine origin of The Book of
Mormon as a prerequisite to their
believing try in vain to circumvent
the processes by which both faith and
knowledge are established. They crave
proof, but do so before having paid the
price. As with adulterers, who selfishly
anticipate instant gratification, they
desire only theological titillation by
thinking that they can somehow
experience the result without
having first accepted the
responsibility.

Those
who endure
to the end eschew
embracing idea-gods
that would otherwise rivet
their attention, consume their
energies, demand their devotion,
divert their direction, obscure their
objectivity, and dilute their God
given capacity to make positive
changes through repentance.
(See Moroni 8:25-26).

The Devil's
enticements lead the
imprudent into conceptual
cul-de-sacs from which there
exist no exits save a stammering
shifting of blame, a frantic flight
from responsibility, rationalized
retreat, confused complacency, a
senseless stupor of thought, and
brazen back-pedaling, that all
lead to unmitigated defeat.
(See 2 Nephi 26:11).

The
world does a
remarkable job
of rationalizing its
naughty behavior, re-
purposing its deviancy,
and re-defining in new-
speak the acceptability of
its conduct, in efforts to
somehow circumvent the
Law of Compensation.
How futile this can be
is illustrated in The
Book of Mormon.

If we've finally determined to put
on "the armor of righteousness" (2 Nephi
1:23, see Ephesians 6:13), we'll be endowed
with the power to obey God's commandments and
the yearning to participate in the ordinances that are
necessary to attain eternal life. But a potential conflict
can arise when there is a discrepancy between priesthood
authority and power. The one comes by the laying on of
hands, and the other thru righteousness. At times, when
those who hold the priesthood are asked to officiate in the
the ordinances, they do so without the supporting power
of Christ. Their acts are validated only because of
their ordination and due to the sustaining faith
of those to whom they minister. We can see
why the Savior would admonish us: "Be
ye clean that bear the vessels of the
Lord." (3 Nephi 20:41).

If we allow
ourselves to sink
into the quicksand of
carnality, and we lose not
only the wide-eyed innocence
of youth, but also our holiness
and our purity, we will forfeit the
happiness that can only accompany
an untroubled soul. This lesson is
taught repeatedly throughout
The Book of Mormon.

Both the Nephites and the
Lamanites knew better than most
that Satan is a dedicated deceiver who
employs every trick of the trade, advocating
evil by making drinking and smoking look
enticing, and by rationalizing cheating, lying,
and stealing. He plays mind games to encourage
drug use, and he clothes the latest fashions in fine
twined linens. Immorality and swearing are woven
into popular music and hit movies. He minimizes
the seriousness of sin by telling us: "Everyone's
doing it." "It doesn't hurt anyone else." "Just
once won't hurt." "I can always repent."
"It's not a big deal." And even, to
our amazement: "The devil
made me do it.

The Book of
Mormon blesses
us with gospel truths
that all might comprehend
in plainness and simplicity. It
bears witness to all of the world of
the divinity of the Savior and teaches
the path to salvation and exaltation in
ways that are easily understood. Since
the Bible today is ambiguous, unclear,
and even contradictory, by contrast, it
must be the result of errors of omission
and commission that were introduced
by uninspired, untutored, and even
maliciously motivated copyists
during the previous three
millennia.

The Three
Nephites who were the
Savior's disciples surely
knew that in the millennial
day, we would live in a state akin
to translation. (See 3 Nephi 28:7).
Our bodies will no longer be subject to
disease or death as we know it, although
we will be changed in the twinkling of
an eye. Isaiah prophesied that during
the thousand years of peace, "there
shall be no more thence an infant
of days, for the child shall die
an hundred years old."
(Isaiah 65:20).

When the
Lord established His
church among the Nephites
in the land of Zarahemla, it was
His purpose to provide for His children, be
they humble or proud, rich or poor, strong or
weak, the chance to associate with their equals in
an uplifting environment that would be infused by
an atmosphere that would nurture a religious basis
upon which they could build relationships. It is to
the extent that we fail to seize these heaven-sent
opportunities that we remain strangers and
foreigners with each other and with
God, starving our souls and
further diminishing
our spirits.

Mormon foresaw that
in the Latter Days one of the
signs of the times would be that the
gospel will be taught with a manifestation
of great power to all people. He knew that, one
day, there would be no need to teach others the first
principles of the gospel because we would all know the
Lord. "Then the heathen that are left round about you shall
know that (it is) I the Lord (who has built) the ruined places,
and (has planted) that that was desolate." (Ezekiel 36:36). The
earth will be renewed to receive paradisiacal glory. "For behold,"
declared the Lord thru His prophet Isaiah, "I create new heavens
and a new earth: and the former shall not be remembered, nor
come to mind." (Isaiah 65:17). "For the Lord shall comfort
Zion; he will comfort all her waste places, and he will
make her wilderness like Eden, and her desert
like the (secret) garden of the Lord."
(Isaiah 51:3, see Mormon
9:11).

Faithful Nephites
could not do everything,
but they could do something to
stem an advancing tide that oozed
from the cesspool of iniquity. First,
they needed to recall that it's always
better to light a candle than curse the
darkness. A thousand points of light,
taken together, will cast a very long
shadow. Abraham Lincoln soberly
reminded us: "To sin by silence,
when words should be spoken,
makes cowards of men." As
Isaiah wrote: "Lift up thy
voice with strength."
(Isaiah 40:9).

Jesus Christ, of whom
Samuel the Lamanite so boldly
testified to the people of Zarahemla,
is the Architect of the cosmos, including
the "Pillars of Creation," elephant trunks of
interstellar gas and dust in the Eagle Nebula,
some 6,500 - 7,000 light years from earth. In a
sermon in 1857 by London pastor Charles Haddon
Spurgeon, entitled "The Condescension of Christ,"
he employed the phrase to describe both the physical
world and the force that binds it all together, that
stems from the Divine Center. "Now wonder, ye
angels," Spurgeon wrote of the birth of Christ,
"the Infinite has become an infant. He, upon
whose shoulders the universe doth hang,
nurses at his mother's breast - He who
created all things, and bears up
the pillars of creation."

Their unshakable testimony
of the Plan of Deliverance governed
the behavior of the righteous Nephites, and
thereby became the catalyst of their purposeful
action. As they sought to gain an understanding
of both the temporal and eternal worlds, they developed
the power to exercise true moral agency. Comprehension
came to them "line upon line and precept upon precept."
(3 Nephi 28:30). It stayed with them, and it will rise
with them in the resurrection, affording tangible
advantages in the eternities. Their life beyond
the veil offers the tantalizing promise of an
exponential expansion of knowledge that
will be accompanied by an awakening
re-acquaintance with heaven.

It was the Nephites' simple faith that
set them free from the self-defeating behaviors
of doubt, indecision, ignorance, sin, worry, guilt,
and confusion, that might have otherwise caused them
to become immobilized, and even paralyzed, in the learning
laboratory of life. In a garden setting, Adam and Eve had been
blessed with freedom to act, but the Nephites could have forfeit that
birthright thru the adoption of bad habits. They might have been
detained by telestial traffic jams, confused by conceptual cul-
de-sacs, and detoured by doctrinal dilemmas of their own
making. But when they followed the strait and narrow
way, they found their path opening up onto broad
boulevards of unlimited opportunity that led
directly to the perfect law of liberty, and to
an expression of mind, body, and spirit
that unerringly guided them to the
surety that is described in The
Book of Mormon as the
Rest of the Lord.

The trials and tribulations that
we are facing today are really not
any more sophisticated than those of our
forbearers. Noah warned his brethren about
a coming deluge. Our prophets warn us about
the rising tide of pornography that is inundating
the world. Moses chronicled the bondage of Israel in
Egypt. Today, we are at risk of the temporal bondage
of financial indebtedness. Elijah rebuked those who
worshipped Baal. Our own prophets warn us of the
spiritual servitude that follows the worship of the
popular idols of the day. Prophets in The Book
of Mormon described the depravations of
Gandianton bands. The D&C warns us
against evil designs of conspiring
men and women in the Last
Days. (See D&C 89:4).

It seems to be
indisputable that
the object and design
of our existence, following
our acceptance of The Book of
Mormon, would be to become the
happiest people who ever dwelt on
the earth. Obedience unleashes a
spiritual cornucopia as we feast
upon the nourishing bread of
life and we drink copiously
from wells of living water.
We ask ourselves how
life could be any
better!

In spite of their best efforts to
gain a foothold and establish traction
on the telestial turf that they called home, it
was sometimes frustrating to the Nephites that
they still seemed to be losing ground. "Now, here,
you see," the Red Queen patiently explained to Alice
in Wonderland, "it takes all the running you can
do, to keep in the same place. If you want to get
somewhere else, you must run at least twice as
fast as that!" (Lewis Carroll). Let us never
forget that one plus the Lord always
constitutes a majority. With His
help, we may run and not be
weary, and walk and
not faint.

The Nephites became successful in
their discipleship only as they struggled
to gain self-mastery, overcame adversity, and
conquered their cankered nature that so often had
suffered them to be disobedient to true principles. As
they moved from dependency to independency, and
finally to the more mature state of inter-dependency,
their obedience to their covenants helped them to focus
their efforts to become as God is. When they regarded
their church membership as a probationary state, or
as a time of testing, of putting to the proof their
professed standard of behavior, and when all
was done within the bounds the Lord had
set, they were less likely to bail out
at the first indication of world
weariness or of tedium.

For Nephites and for the
Lamanites, (as well as for latter-day
Israel), temptation can be a powerful narcotic,
which renders Lucifer a quintessential drug dealer.
He was "a son of the morning," and his influence over
our Father in Heaven's children was truly impressive. His
name means "Light Bearer," and so he was. In the great
Council, he offered to redeem mankind. But even then,
he lacked the faith necessary to allow agency to rule.
He concocted an inoperable counterfeit proposal that
would have denied its participants the power to
utilize free will, that could catalyze positive
change. Because of his passionate, and yet
misguided, promotion of this spurious
proposal, the scriptures refer to him
as Satan, the father of lies, and
as a liar from the beginning,
meaning from before the
foundation of the
world.

Following on the heels
of the betrayal, the trial, and
the crucifixion of our Lord, the word
'Christian' was spat out! " But the Saints
continued to live their lives as He had taught
them, and the world, illuminated by the inspired
ministry of His authorized servants, was suddenly
aflame with faith. The light finally dimmed when
dark mists swirled about, sowing wickedness at
every turn. And so it came to pass, that in the
crucible of that refiner's fire, the humble
followers of the Good Shepherd were
asked, once again, to wear their
title with dignity.

The Nephites
didn't have to deal
with all the temptations
of modern technologies, but
in these Last Days, with only a few
clicks of a mouse, or with nothing more
than a few keystrokes, even those who have
few computer skills can be transported directly
"into enemy territory without having to first pass
thru passport control." (Neal A. Maxwell). Knowledge
can be a dangerous thing if it is not accompanied by
the Spirit of God. "O that cunning plan of the evil one!
O the vainness, and the frailties, and the foolishness
of men! When they are learned they think they are
wise, and they hearken not unto the counsel of
God, for they set it aside, supposing they
know of themselves, wherefore, their
wisdom is foolishness and it
profiteth them not." (2
Nephi 9:29).

Unlike
the submissive,
who approach their
study of The Book of
Mormon in humility,
those who are prideful are
more comfortable with their
own perceptions of truth than
they are with God's omniscience.
pitting their own ability (or should
we say inability) against His power,
their own paltry overtures against His
mighty works, and their stubborn
won't against His gentle will.

Pride is driven
by our selfishness or
self-will, but a spiritual
awakening is encouraged
by a selflessness that leads
us to enlightenment. Pride is
driven by the fear of man, but
a Book of Mormon testimony
is nurtured by our love of our
Father in Heaven. The world's
applause rings loudly in the
ears of the proud, but it is
the accolades of heaven
that warm the cockles
of the faithful.

If
we have
only made
a resolution to
study The Book of
Mormon, it may turn
out to be nothing more
than a promise that is kept
for just a few days or weeks,
before it is abandoned and we
return to former habit pattern.
When the covenant of baptism
fuels our study, however, there's
staying power. Baptism has no
bias, inasmuch as its basis is
belief, nurtured by the culture
medium of faith which feeds
the regeneration of our
spirits.

When we
read The Book
of Mormon, we are
pleasantly surprised
to discover that the Lord
is on our right, and on our
left, and in our hearts. We're
strengthened by a company of
angels thinly disguised as our
family and friends. We recall
the words of Sir Isaac Newton,
who, when he was pressured to
reveal the mystery behind his
accomplishments, quietly
replied that he stood on the
shoulders of giants. We
are familiar with these
as beings from the
unseen world
of spirit.

Reflection,
or introspection, can
be a positive thing, especially
when the Light of Christ is shining
on our countenances. As Alma asked the
Saints in Zarahemla: "Have ye spiritually
been born of God? Have ye received His image
in your countenances? Have ye experienced
this mighty change in your hearts?"
(Alma 5:14).

Our Heavenly Father created the
Plan of Salvation, that is all the more
beautiful because of its simplicity. It was
vaguely established in the Bible, but it has
been clarified in its companion scriptures.
It has been carefully articulated in both
The Book of Mormon and the Doctrine
and Covenants, in order to silence
disputations among the people
concerning vital points
of doctrine.

Our obedience to
the principles and doctrines
of The Book of Mormon needs to be
more than casual. It can save us from our
natural state of carnality, sensuality, and
devilish inclinations. It catalyzes the Law of
Mercy, which mitigates for those who conform
to its requirements the effects of the first Law,
that demands Justice, and it lifts us to a state
of holiness, spirituality, angelic innocence,
and happiness. It grooms us, that we might
one day feel at ease in our heavenly home,
when we find ourselves in the presence
of angels who will serenade us with
celestial lullabies that express
the love of God.

Our Book of
Mormon study involves
the consistent exercise of agency
to clothe ennobling eternal principles
with actions that reflect the right thing to do,
although it may not be easy or convenient. If we
want to have positive outcomes, however, our God
given right to choose must be accompanied by
the strength to exercise moral discipline in
the face of opposition. That's precisely the
behavior that leads faithful inquiry
to testimony, and then to the
waters of baptism.

We are invited to engage in a study
of The Book of Mormon, that we might feel
both the spiritual significance and physical
intensity of the covenants that our Heavenly
Father desires to make with us. When we are
baptized, we feel a palpable promise of peace
that washes over us in concentric waves
influencing everything in their path,
including our testimony of the
truthfulness of The Book
of Mormon.

We may try to carry on
without the comfort of faith in The
Book of Mormon and in the restored
gospel of Jesus Christ. But if we do so, we
must also accept the inevitable negative
consequences tied to hesitant feelings.
This can make our trials much more
difficult than they might have
otherwise needed to be.

Those who
have been card-
carrying members
of The Church of Jesus
Christ long enough to have
experienced a liberal measure
of temporal, spiritual, emotional,
and intellectual symmetry, may
sometimes ask Heavenly Father why
the Plan allows the world to continue to
tug at them? Why has their faith in the
divine origin of The Book of Mormon not
yet been perfected? Perhaps the answer is
that these things have been designed
by divine providence to give them
experience.

287

Righteous
Nephites were generally
asked to take one or two steps
into the dark, so that their faith,
which was their spiritual strong
searchlight, might be activated,
that it might be allowed to do
its job by illuminating and
revealing the stones and
potholes on the road
ahead.

The sometimes
arduous process that
leads to our discovery of the
power that flows out of the Savior's
Atonement and saves us from our sins
hinges upon a deeper and more abiding
faith. It is "the substance of things
hoped for, the evidence of things
not seen." (Hebrews 11:1,
see Alma 32:21).

The Book of
Mormon not only describes
how the disciples of Christ may
inherit eternal life, but it also reveals
that those who travel that path must not
hold anything back. It will be necessary to
invest all that we are and have, including
our assurance, anticipation, confidence,
conviction, expectation, hope, and trust
in the power of the Savior to deliver
on His almost incomprehensible
promise that He can save us
from our sins.

Ultimately, the power
of Mercy to redeem us is
generated in the fiery-hot
crucible of adversity (see
2 Nephi 2:11), for we
receive no witness
until after the
trial of our
faith.

As we adopt
the doctrine in The
Book of Mormon, we are
unabashedly optimistic, and
we are consumed by divine fire.
We are full of faith, as we engage
in our Father's affairs. Idleness, on
the other hand, is the workshop of the
Devil, and our refusal to embrace the
Plan is sin, for it wastes our precious
resources in futile pursuits when we
should have been engaged in other
and more worthwhile activities for
which we have been blessed with
wisdom and understanding,
with the Light of Christ, as
well as with a surfeit of
God-given abilities
thru the Spirit.

Speaking to
those confused
and disillusioned
disciples of Satan who
lie strewn in his wake and
wander the boulevards of the
twin cities of worldliness and
pleasure, Alma said: "Seek not
after riches nor the vain things
of this world; for behold, you
cannot carry them with
you." (Alma 39:14).

The
decision
that was made
by Adam and Eve
in the Garden to choose
the harder right instead of
the easier wrong obviated the
'Progression Paradox' that had
faced them, wherein they would
have remained forever in "a state
of innocence, having no joy, for
they knew no misery; doing no
good, for they knew no sin."
(2 Nephi 2:23). That choice
was anticipated by God,
when He conceived His
"Great Plan of Mercy."
(Alma 42:31).

The
power of The
Book of Mormon
expands our circle of
knowledge as we begin
to comprehend, and put
into practice, the righteous
application of its principles
and its doctrine. So too will
the borders that separate the
kernels of wisdom that we
have grasped, from a yet
undiscovered country.
The more we know, it
seems, the more we
will find there is
to learn.

The awesome
influence of faith that is
illustrated by nearly all the
guardians of the record during
the thousand-year-long history of
the Nephites and Lamanites, creates
bonds of understanding between the
secular and the divine features of our
nature. Mortality, with its twists and
turns, and its permutations and its
combinations, makes more sense to
us when we understand the mind
and will of God in the context of
His marvelous Plan that was
designed to bring to pass
our immortality and
eternal life.

The Great Plan of
Salvation prepares us in
myriad ways to have hands
that are accustomed to lifting
those who need our support, and
feet that take us to those who are
imprisoned by their poor choices,
their bad habits, or by ruinous
circumstances. (See Mosiah
17:8-10). We are ministers
according to the gift of
the grace of God.

We marvel as we discover for
ourselves the plain and precious
parts of The Book of Mormon, whose
inclusion enhances our comprehension
of God's divine design. (See 1 Nephi 13:26
& 19:3). We are certain that, in spite of the tone
of his epistle from Rome, the Apostle Paul had
an equally clear understanding of the Plan.
"O the depth of the riches both of the wisdom
and the knowledge of God!" he lamented.
"How unsearchable are his judgments,
and his ways past finding out! For
who hath known the mind of the
Lord? Or who hath been his
counsellor?" (Romans
11:33-34).

Studying The
Book of Mormon
under the influence
of the Holy Ghost blesses
us to have a more pure form
of focus, transforming our five
natural senses into something that
is wonderful, even a heaven-sent sixth
sense that defies description. Physical
and spiritual resources work in tandem
to compound each other, and to condition
us thru the patience of faith, the miracle
of repentance, the diligence of baptism,
and the Spirit of God, not to mention
the exhilarating renewal that can
be found the ordinance of
the Sacrament.

Our attempts
to comprehend the
universe may help us
to understand ourselves.
If we ask, what is its origin,
or what is its ultimate destiny,
we are really asking where did we
come from, and where are we going.
As we study The Book of Mormon, we
will find the answers to these questions
and more, and we will understand why
we are here on this earth. That should be
more than enough to catalyze the
commencement of our journey
of faith into the future.

The Book of Mormon
teaches us that, in accord
with the requirements of the
Plan, the Lord created the earth as
a testing center and a learning lab.
It was envisioned as a citadel of higher
education; even a place where we would be
given the tools necessary to validate God's
faith in us; to see if we could muster up an
equivalent faith, to be proven worthy of His
trust; and to be provided with the awesome
power and the tactical advantage of our
defensive weapons, such as the gift of
the Holy Ghost, that we would need
to face, and to conquer, our own
wicked Lamanites and apostate
Nephites, and individually
personalized demons.

God's beautiful
Plan of Happiness
exposes us to a constant
flow of insight, intuition,
inspiration, and revelation
that simply streams forth in a
downpour of divine direction. It
also blesses us as we walk along
illuminated pathways and as we
exercise our intellectual and our
spiritual faculties. The Book of
Mormon illustrates how we can
be led as individuals and as a
society to the community of
Christ, so that, together, we
might enjoy the guidance
of the Holy Ghost. The
genius of the Plan is
that it is tailored
to meet every
exigency.

By
permitting
ourselves to become
habitually distracted
by trifling concerns until
they have become our center of
attention and even our obsession,
we learn to ignore innate yearnings
to embrace The Book of Mormon, and
thereby we commit grievous sins
of both omission and
commission.

Wo , wo, wo unto those
insensitive souls who only
casually receive illumination
from The Book of Mormon, that
has been so freely offered. Due to a
misguided obsession with temporal
trivia, they carelessly fritter away
their faith, and waste the days of
their probation rooting through
telestial trash in a fruitless
effort to find meaning
in the dumpsters of
their empty
lives.

Society pays
a heavy price when it
lacks a faithful focus on
The Book of Mormon. When its
spiritual equilibrium is disoriented
and its moral compass is spinning out
of control, its values are quickly adjusted
in a misguided, vain, and sometimes
unconscious attempt to regain a
state of harmony or balance
with the celestial order
of heaven.

An unprincipled
and faithless society
that cannot see the book
that is before its eyes deals
with its spiritual myopia in
a knee-jerk reaction that does
little more than ratchet down
expectations. In the end, those
who lack the fire of faith ask
very little, and receive in
kind. The sad thing is
that they just don't
care, one way or
the other.

Without
the moderating
influence of the Spirit
that is experienced as we
read The Book of Mormon,
we tend to exhibit both hard
hearts and stiff-necks, and
remain overtly and covertly
rebellious. We fail to regain
the flexibility and pliability
that had been cultivated
during our spiritual
therapy before we
cam to earth.

In a
vain attempt
to avoid societal
implosion, as well as
in the name of cultural
expediency, the target has
been moved so many times
to score repetitive bulls-eyes
that no-one will concede that
it is the arrow of faith in the
restoration of the gospel and
in The Book of Mormon
that has strayed far
from the mark.

As
we ponder
and pray, lift
the latch and force
the way, as we study
The Book of Mormon, we
are sanctified. Our minds
"become single to God, and the
days will come that (we) shall see
him; for he will unveil his face" to
us. (D&C 88:68). We'll no longer be
hobbled by limiting beliefs. "Now, we
see through a glass, darkly; but then
face to face; now (we) know in part;
but then shall (we) know even as
also (we are) known." (First
Corinthinans 13:12).

Those who have the courage to act upon
their desire to share their love of The Book of
Mormon and of its witness of the Savior have
therein discovered and important key to their
spiritual revitalization. The more they spread
the joy, the greater is their own happiness,
the more fully does our Heavenly Father
help them to fulfil their own destiny,
and the more does the Holy Ghost
infuse them with a desire to
be valiant in the cause
of Zion.

He who is the
enemy of all that is good
finally betrays his followers
because they can only oppose the
covenant consciousness generated by
The Book of Mormon for so long before his
cunning caresses lead them into conceptual
cul-de-sacs and the doctrinal dead-ends from
which all possible exits lead to doubt, confusion,
uncertainty, ambiguity, hesitation, and retreat,
that precipitously plunge them into a perceived
freedom that is, upon a closer inspection, just
a bottomless pit of melancholy, desolation,
and darkness.

The Book
of Mormon generates a
"Technicolor" backdrop for the
worldwide tapestry that is being
woven by the army of God, who
has been commissioned to seek
out and find the elect, and
draw them into the fold
of Jesus Christ.

Should
we engage in last-
ditch efforts to subvert
the execution of God's Plan
by turning our backs on the
counsel of The Book of Mormon,
our destabilizing but futile efforts
to obtain opportunities that we do not
merit, and to retain blessings we do
not deserve, will reward us with
a pyrrhic victory, at best.

Reading The
Book of Mormon
can help us to break
free of limiting beliefs.
When we brush up against
the stars, we are awakened to
a vision that can, initially, be
blinding, but as our eyes adjust
to the light, we may be surprised
to see the world as it really is
for the first time in our
lives.

The Book of Mormon is our caretaker that
safeguards the stability of our divine center of faith.
As we read it, and its prophets teach us how to draw upon
the power of the Atonement of Jesus Christ, the energy that He
expends to cultivate its sense of permanency prevents our world
from collapsing into disarray or imploding under the dreadful
weight of unresolved sin. He was not only the Lamb slain from
the foundation of the world (see Revelation 13:8), but He was
the Lord God of the Nephites and Lamanites, as well,
(see 2 Nephi 31:13), and He is also our Savior
"yesterday, today, and forever," in
every tense of the word. (See
2 Nephi 27:23).

An
unprincipled
society manages its
spiritual myopia with
knee-jerk reactions that
do nothing but diminish
expectations. Eventually, a
culture that lacks the fire of
faith in the restoration of the
gospel and in the additional
scripture contained in The
The Book of Mormon will
require very little of its
citizens, and will
give back in
kind.

Our Book of Mormon testimonies
sanctify our lives, lending dignity to our
individual efforts, rewarding our timid
achievements, and strengthening
our faltering faith.

We
only gradually
suffer the loss of focus
and faith, just as we lose
the acuity of our vision over
time. Whether it's a testimony
of Book of Mormon doctrine, or
an eye chart that is beyond our
comprehension, we are legally
blind. Although we have eyes,
we can no longer clearly see
what's been placed right
in front of us.

By focusing our
energy on the power of faith,
we are able to harness available
resources to convert our substance
into a life-force, whereby positive,
generous, and significant change
may take place. However, those who
have declined the bounteous offer of
the riches of eternity, that might
have otherwise been unfolded to
their view by embracing The
Book of Mormon, will find
themselves doomed to live
their lives in scarcity
of their spiritual
needs.

If we no
longer believe in
the divine authenticity
of The Book of Mormon, the
compromise of our conversion can
often be attributed to a lack of faithful
focus that initiated the flat spin from which
we could not recover. Blame for the demolition
of our discipleship as well as for the cascade of
unfortunate consequences that follow is often
laid at the doorstep of others, but at the end of
the day, it comes down to us, and to no-one
else. Notwithstanding the guidance of
the Holy Ghost and acting upon its
influence, at the end of the day,
we are the architects of our
own fate.

The
faithful
find mentors
whom they can
emulate, instead
of scapegoats that
are easy to blame.
Instead of looking
for easier answers,
they comb thru The
stories in The Book
of Mormon to find
healthy solutions
to the problems
they face.

They say
that the highway
to hell has been paved
with good intentions. In
regard to the teachings of
The Book of Mormon, if we
have vision, but don't work,
it's dreamery, and even if we
work hard, without vision, we
are doomed to drudgery. If we
focus our faith, however, and
make our study a vital part
of our imagination, it'll be
our destiny to soar among
eagles, rather than walk
with well-intentioned
souls on that fiery
path to Sheol.

In the
city of Philippi, Paul
exhorted the Grecian Saints
to work out their salvation with
fear and trembling. He knew that
if they put their hearts and their souls
into such efforts as an understanding of
The Book of Mormon, it would leave them both
physically and spiritually exhausted. Still,
he invited them to join him, as he pressed on
"toward the mark, for the prize of the high
calling of God in Christ Jesus."
(Philippians 3:14).

The worldly-wise gravely
underestimate the power of well-founded
faith in Jesus Christ, that is encouraged by The
Book of Mormon. When it does its job and convicts us of
our sins, those of us who are on the path of progress take the
matter before the Lord. After we have truly repented and received
forgiveness (a process that may take some time) He will remember our
sins no more in the sense that He will not count them to our detriment.
Life is not akin to a military boot camp, where a hard-boiled drill sergeant
assesses demerits for rules infractions until they have amassed to the point
that harsh punishment is inevitable. Instead, the Atonement wipes the slate
clean, levels the playing field, and resets our pedometer to zero. We begin
our walk anew, brimming over with confidence. We believe Isaiah, who
said: "Though your sins be as scarlet they shall be as white as snow;
though they be red like crimson, they shall be as wool." (Isaiah
1:18). We remember the wise counsel that reminds us that
although we cannot go back to make a new start, we
can begin now to create a brand-new ending.

As we embrace The Book of
Mormon, we have feelings of deja-vu.
When we rejoice in our fellowship with the
community of the Saints and of the household
of God, we sense that we have done so before. (See
Ephesians 2:19). We even vaguely remember a
time in the distant past when "the morning
stars sang together, and all the sons
of God shouted for joy."
(Job 38:7).

We read The
Book of Mormon so
that we might learn to
abide by the laws of heaven,
even as we tarry upon the earth.
We yearn for our hearts to burn
within us, and for the Spirit to
speak to us, so that it might
open up the scriptures to
our understanding.

As we read The
Book of Mormon, we're
blessed with the courage to
stand as "witnesses of God at
at all times and in all things,
and in all places." (Mosiah 18:9).
We join with a chorus of voices that
testifies of His might, majesty, power,
and dominion. (See Alma 5:12). We
dare not shirk our responsibility,
for we are under covenant to do
so. (See Mosiah 18:10 &
24:22).

We
accept The Book of
Mormon because it's our
desire to be redeemed of God
and to be numbered among
those who will participate
in the first resurrection,
that we might enjoy
eternal life.

Every time we pick
up a copy of The Book
of Mormon, it's as if it were
a contemporary declaration to
the world of tidings of great joy.
It carries us on a groundswell of
emotion that lifts us heavenward.
Worship is elevated to something
more dynamic than the simple
mechanical observance of a
multiplicity of ceremonial
rules. Publishing peace is
the daily antidote to
worldly tendencies
that canker our
souls.

In
the Book
of Mormon,
we recognize
that Jesus Christ
is the Son of God,
the Father of heaven
and earth, and is the
Creator of all things.
We honor His name,
and bear it with
reverence and
respect.

In Book
of Mormon doctrine,
the power of godliness is
unmistakable. And without
the authority of the priesthood
that administers the ordinances
that are described within its pages,
that power won't be made manifest
even to those who have professed
to know our Savior Jesus
Christ on multiple
levels.

The
Book of Mormon
was given to the world
so that it might receive the
gospel and enjoy covenants of
salvation and justification, as well
as those of sanctification, and lastly,
of exaltation. It is by the authority of the
holy priesthood of God that ordinances that
relate to those covenants are administered
to everyone who qualifies by worthiness
to receive these blessings.

Every time we read
The Book of Mormon, we are
powerfully strengthened and the
promises of heaven are realized. Its
study invites virtue to garnish our
thoughts. As our confidence builds,
the doctrine of the priesthood distils
upon our heads as the dews from
heaven, the Holy Ghost becomes
our constant companion, and
its guidance flows unto us
without compulsory
means.

When we are
reading The Book
of Mormon, our hearts
swell with gratitude as we
think of the Atonement of the
Lord Jesus Christ. We examine
our lives thru the magnifying
lens of the Spirit to search for
ways to improve. Because of
its teachings, we can fly
higher than eagles and
the Savior becomes the
wind beneath our
wings.

The Holy Ghost
will instill within our hearts a
sound understanding as we study
The Book of Mormon, so that we might
recognize the word of God when we see it.
But this is not all; we also give ourselves
to prayer and to fasting, that we might
enjoy the spirit of revelation and of
prophecy, so that when we are
taught, it is by power and
authority that stems
from heaven.

As we internalize the teachings
that are emphasized throughout the pages
of The Book of Mormon, we become more and
more like our Father in Heaven. The repetition
of its life-lessons nurtures spiritual growth;
its reiteration encourages us to faithful
obedience, and more pointedly, to be
unwavering as we follow the
example of our Savior
and His Son.

Our Heavenly Father has blessed us
with the phenomenon of The Book of Mormon
because He has foreseen the worst circumstances in
which we could ever imagine ourselves. In that book, the
Nephites and Lamanites pre-played, and now we have
the opportunity to re-play, life's great drama. When
He declared: "We will prove them herewith, to see
if they will do all things whatsoever the Lord
their God shall command them," it was
as much a statement of fact as it
was a question of whether or
not we would be obedient.
(Abraham 3:25).

The Book of Mormon can
be our spiritual lightning rod
that helps us to be well-grounded,
as well as a powerful motivator that
shows us how to be positively charged.
We remember Nephi, who described those
who were "pressing forward, and they came
forth and caught hold of the end of the Rod
of Iron; and they did press forward through
the mist of darkness, clinging to the Rod
of Iron, even until they did come forth
and partake of the fruit of the tree."
(1 Nephi 8:24).

To paraphrase
Paul: Thanks be to God
that The Book of Mormon
gives us the opportunity to
lead quiet and peaceful
lives in all godliness
and in all honesty.
(See 1 Timothy
2:2).

In the best
of circumstances,
we begin our mortal
curriculum when we are
of Primary age. The Book of
Mormon then serves as a primer;
it is a tool that helps us to learn the
grammar of the gospel. In this sense,
the book is an exclamation point, or
a punctuation emphasizing the
importance of our journey
to Christ.

"For behold, it is as easy
to give heed to the word of Christ,
which will point to you a straight course to
eternal bliss, as it was for our fathers to give
heed to this compass, which would point unto
them a straight course to the promised land."
(Alma 37: 44). So it is with us. Christ is our
ablest Navigator, our Liahona, and when we
follow the course that He has charted, that
leads us to the waters of baptism, we
will find that no wind can blow
except it fills our sails.

Joseph Smith taught that
it would be to our benefit if we would
pay attention to "the first intimation of the
spirit of revelation. For instance, when we feel
pure intelligence flowing into us, it may give
us sudden strokes of ideas ... By learning the
Spirit of God and understanding it, we may
grow into the principle of revelation." The
Book of Mormon is a schoolmaster that
is designed to bring us, by that same
spirit of revelation, to the doctrine
of our Lord and Savior,
Jesus Christ.

Following on the heels of
our Sabbath day observances,
we read The Book of Mormon at the
start of a week that is sure to have its
ups and downs. In our obedience, there
is consistency. Our study provides us
with a bastion of stability in the midst
of the turmoil of the world. Habitually
reading several pages every day has a
powerful and influential capacity to
center our hearts, might, mind, and
strength upon the foundation that
is our covenant relationship with
Heavenly Father, Jesus Christ,
and the Holy Ghost.

Moses
counseled the
Israelites to build
upon the Rock of their
salvation. He urged them to
"write (their covenants) upon the
posts of (their) houses" and to "not
appear before the Lord empty" handed.
(Deuteronomy 6:9 & 16:16). We would do
well to follow their example by remembering
the covenants that are described in The Book
of Mormon (see Moroni Chapters 2-5), as
we take upon ourselves His name, keep
His commandments, and always
remember Him.

Studying The Book of
Mormon clears our minds
so that we can focus on
eternity against the
backdrop of our
everyday
world.

It is within the pages of The
Book of Mormon that we enjoy a
familiarity with principles that are in
sharp contrast to society's tenets that are
continually morphed by the shifting sands
of cultural expediency. Its doctrine insulates
us from the constantly mutating values of
the world. Left to our own devices, we could
never keep up with its current definition of
morality, because its flavor of the day is
always changing. In contrast, God's
undeviating standard of behavior
defines an unchanging moral
foundation that shapes us
to mature into the full
stature of our
spirits.

If we will exercise
the discipline to step away
from the world of confusion to
follow the difficult path that leads
to our own personal Gethsemane, and
if as we do so we read The Book of Mormon,
we will very quickly recognize that in it, our
Father in Heaven has created a well-established
pattern that will lead to a Christ-centered life. Our
familiarity with it will create an atmosphere where
it is easier to fill our lungs with celestial air, and
where it is more comfortable to recommit ourselves
to internalize every truth relating to our eternal
progression. We'll be endowed with the power to
endure every adversity, that we might see
our lives through to their pre-ordained
end, and do so in righteousness.

When our turn on earth draws
to a close, The Book of Mormon will have
helped us to leave the world a better place than
it was when we found it. It will have prepared us to
pass thru the veil. Because of it, when we finally do so,
we will leave with those we have left behind legacies of
both tangible and intangible remembrances. We will
leave them with our testimonies. We will leave them
with gratitude for the privilege and blessing to
have been knit together in love, as families
that were able to pause in their busy
schedules long enough feast
upon the word of God.

During a busy
week when many of
us will not take the time to
stop and smell the roses, we are
reminded by consistent Book of
Mormon study how reflection can
be uplifting, especially when it is the
Holy Ghost that lights up our features.
As Alma asked the people of Zarahemla:
"Now, behold, I ask of you, my brethren of
the church, have ye spiritually been born
of God? Have ye received His image in
your countenances (and even more
importantly) have you experienced
this mighty change in your
heart?" (Alma 5:14).

As we read The Book of Mormon,
we will receive an indescribable assurance of
peace that will come to us from the Holy Ghost. it
will trigger within our hearts an appreciation of the
intangible evidence of a greater spiritual reality.
When we realize that we are not alone, we will
have begun a journey carrying us to a
higher state of being where we will
find ourselves covered in star
dust as we rub shoulders
with Beings from the
unseen world.

The
Spirit throws
open the windows
of our spirits to let in
more light, so that we might
better understand the principles
and doctrine of The Book of Mormon.
These are mysteries to those who haven't
yet prepared themselves for the consistently
flowing streams of revelation that come from
God. The Lord has assured us, however, that we
"shall know of a surety that these things are
true, for from heaven will (He) declare it"
unto us. (D&C 5:12).

The Sacrament
(see Moroni Chapters
4 & 5), gives our spiritual
muscles pliancy and flexibility,
that there might be enough room for
the companionship of the Holy Ghost,
Who makes Himself "manifest unto
the children of men, according to
their faith" in Jesus Christ.
(Jarom 1:4).

As we
drink copiously
from the words of life
in The Book of Mormon,
we learn to be patient in our
afflictions. Exercising our faith
that the Holy Ghost will be with us
until the end of our days helps us as
we endure our trials and tribulations,
even when they are undeserved, or
when we cannot understand why
they have been given to us.

The principles of the
Plan carry us from baptism to
the covenant of the Sacrament. "For
behold, thus saith the Lord God: I will
give unto the children of men line upon
line, precept upon precept, here a little and
there a little (and) blessed are those who
hearken unto my precepts, and lend
an ear unto my counsel, for they
shall learn wisdom; for unto
him that receiveth, I will
give more." (2 Nephi
28:30).

"The first fruits of
repentance" that is enjoyed by
the repentant faithful, "is baptism;
(for) baptism cometh by faith unto the
fulfilling the commandments; and the
fulfilling the commandments bringeth
remission of sins; and the remission of
sins bringeth meekness, and lowliness
of heart; and because of meekness
and lowliness of heart cometh
the visitation of the Holy
Ghost." (Moroni
8:25-26).

The worth of the
principles of the gospel
is validated through personal
witness or testimony. Our desire
to declare our witness of The Book of
Mormon becomes the outward expression
of our personal dedication to obedience. It
is the public manifestation of our yearning
to enjoy a private covenant relationship with
God. For that to happen, we must voluntarily
surrender our agency to a higher power and
subjugate our ambition to His will.

To
harness
the power
of the Book
of Mormon, we
must be humble
and gentle, and be
easily entreated; be
tolerant, patient, and
long-suffering, and be
temperate in all things.
We must take care to obey
God's laws, and ask only for
the blessings we stand in need
of, always giving Him thanks
for what we have received. We
nurture our faith, our hope,
and our charity, and we
make every effort to
abound in good
works.

The Book
of Mormon speaks
to our spirits, for every
gospel principle carries within
itself a witness that it is true. Its
language is universal, and when the
Holy Ghost illuminates our minds, we
enjoy fluency, familiarity, and ease
with the doctrines, and we take
comfort in the revealed words
of God that open up vistas
of eternal proportion
before our eyes.

With The
Book of Mormon,
the Light of our lives
grows stronger and even
"brighter until the perfect
day." (D&C 50:24). We come
from God, our Home, "trailing
clouds of glory." (William
Wordsworth).

As we read The Book of
Mormon with real intent, we're
easily entreated and determined to
be steadfast in our obedience to every
one of God's commandments. But, for
the conflagration of sin to be initiated,
all that's needed is combustible fuel, an
ignition temperature, and oxygen. We
live in the world, but we don't have to be
of the world. We can't allow the heat of
the moment to get the better of us. The
book will reintroduce us to the strait
and narrow way that detours past
the ammunition dumps that are
the stockpiles of the Devil. The
only light we carry is that
of the Spirit, which poses
no risk of accidental
explosion.

During the process
of an initial reading of The
Book of Mormon, our Heavenly
Father may use the Spirit to show us
our weaknesses, for they can become
a primer on midwifery, facilitating
the arduous course of the growth
and development of our
testimonies.

As we
ponder The Book
of Mormon, we beseech
the aid of the Spirit, that
we might thereafter be "slow
to be led to do iniquity, and
quick to hearken unto the words
of the Lord." (Helaman 7:7). It is
true that there must be opposition,
but without help from above, we can
be easily seduced into partaking of
corrosive cocktails of convenience
that have been cleverly concocted
by a bartender whose familiar
name is Beelzebub.

We strive to
obey the laws that
we'll encounter in The
Book of Mormon, because
we have a strong testimony
that the principles governing
the Fall of Adam, as well as the
Lord's Atonement, were great and
eternal purposes that were prepared
from the foundation of the world.
We can trace that obedience back
to our baptism that testified of
our desire to participate in The
Great and Eternal Plan of
Deliverance from
Death.

The Book of
Mormon reminds us
that the poor, the common
person, the unlearned, and
the native born, may equally
come unto Christ. Its beauty is
that one size fits all. It has
been designed to meet the
needs of every one of
Heavenly Father's
children.

We're here, at this
time, and in this place, by
divine design. What we think
are merely coincidences, when
they are viewed thru the clarifying
lens of eternity, are faith promoting
examples of the Lord patiently working
behind the scenes in our behalf. Nothing
in this life happens by chance. Everything
of significance occurs according to His will.
The Book of Mormon attests that "the works,
and the designs, and the purposes of God
cannot be frustrated, neither can they
come to naught." (D&C 3:1).

When they find themselves
assaulted on all sides by sounding
brass and tinkling cymbals, those who
manifest a prayerful desire to be touched
by the principles, doctrine, and narrative
in The Book of Mormon will find within
themselves the capacity to sift thru the
discordant cacophony of confusing
voices to discover revealed truth,
as they are touched by
the Holy Ghost.

The Book of Mormon
teaches us to suppress the
natural inclinations of the
telestial world that surround
us, continually encroaching
upon our spiritual stability,
threatening to undermine
our faith and testimony
of the principles of
the gospel.

We
approach The
Book of Mormon
that we might come
in the unity of the faith,
and of the knowledge of the
Son of God unto the stature of
the fulness of Christ. As we make
that journey, we retain our distinct
individuality as the spirt born sons
and daughters of God, but we are
unified in every other way.

The Book of
Mormon grounds us
to practical belief, but
its elements commit us
to an upward thrust.
It confirms that
we are known
to God.

Revelation

may be recognized only

if we've allowed ourselves to

fall under the spell of the Spirit.

That will happen only if we live in

a state of harmony with God's Plan.

Our recognition of communication

from the heavens waits upon our

initiative. It is not subject to

amendment, to our private

interpretation, or to the

scrutiny of faithless

sceptics.

The Spirit

teaches us that

darkness can never

abide the illumination

of faith. When we read The

Book of Mormon, we seize the

opportunity to be enveloped in

light, by facing the sunshine of

revelation that is of God. Shadows

may still exist, but they will remain

behind us. Apprehension and timidity

are the traveling companions of gloom,

but they will remain out of sight and

out of mind, and will be powerless

to exert their murky hold on us.

As
we study
the elements
of God's Plan that
are found in The Book
of Mormon, it seems that
our faith should remain fixed
on the revelations the Lord has
given us that relate to our world,
and not on mysteries that have not
been revealed to us, may never be
described, or that just may not
be relevant to our current
circumstances.

It is
only thru the
phenomenon of the
continuing, enduring,
immeasurable, infinite,
uncorrupted, unfathomable,
uninterrupted, and unspoiled
grace that is embodied within
revelation from above, that we
find ourselves "swallowed up
in the joy of ... God, even to
the exhausting of (our)
strength." (Alma
27:17).

One of the
articles of faith of The
Church of Jesus Christ is that
its members believe that the Plan of
God provides us with institutional and
personal continuing revelation that comes
from Heavenly Father thru the medium of the
Holy Ghost. However, if we are "looking for the
spectacular," we might miss out on the "flow
of revealed communication that comes"
from The Book of Mormon. (Spencer
W. Kimball).

The
Book of
Mormon
carries us
to the edges
of eternity, to
the very portals
of heaven, where
"forever" stands
revealed in the
mind bending
panorama
that lies
before
us.

Whenever the white-hot sparks of
revelation have been struck off the Divine
Anvil of God, they ignite an incendiary flame
whose shimmering trail can be traced across the
sky, all the way back to heaven. If we yield to the
natural inclination to suppress the revelation of
The Book of Mormon by dousing it with the
water of worldliness, if we try to contain
it within the fire-line of faithlessness,
or if we bury it under the sand of
skepticism, and especially if we
throw the dirt of doubt on it,
we will never be blessed to
know His mind or will.
(See Alma 19:6).

We know that God remains
sensitive to our needs, because we've
received answers to our effectual and
fervent prayers. As long as we live in
harmony with the laws of heaven that
govern the creation of a testimony of
the Book of Mormon, we'll draw virtue
from its life-force. We'll figuratively
reach out to touch but the hem of the
garment of Jesus Christ, to feel the
spirit of revelation, even when it
seems that, at least outwardly,
we're caught up within the
press of the crowd.

The
Holy Ghost is
both our mentor and
our teacher. If we are good
students, and have done our
homework, He'll reward us with
an illumination of the principles
within The Book of Mormon that
will bathe our minds in a cascade
of insight, intuition, inspiration,
and revelation. Ahead of time, he
will provide us with the answer
key to the exam we will take
following the conclusion
of our curriculum in
mortality.

Oscillations of
familiar and soothing energy
quite naturally resonate from the
Spirit, flowing unto us as the Balm
of Gilead, as we endure the crosses of
world. These are selflessly shared by
the One who has promised to carry us
along on rolling waves of revelation
toward The Book of Mormon, which
is as a shoreline of stability that
nurtures a more sure witness
of the Savior's divinity, no
matter what the tide
might bring in
tomorrow.

Our
vigilant
and prayerful
study of scripture
helps us to acquire an
eternal perspective. Jacob
revealed the formula. He said
"We search the prophets, and we
have many revelations and the
spirit of prophecy; and having
all these witnesses we obtain
a hope, and our faith (in
Christ is) unshaken."
(Jacob 4:6).

We
who have
the faith to
be born again
are set free by the
perfect Law of Liberty
to reach our potential. We
are as the acorns of mighty
oaks, vitalized by The Book of
Mormon as we bask within its
encouraging influence, to
grow to the full stature
of our spirits.

Without
the guidance
of the Holy Spirit,
Whose influence is
revelatory by its very
nature, we risk becoming
more comfortable with our
own perceptions of truth than
we are with God's omniscience.
We pit our marginal capabilities
against the reality of The Book of
Mormon, our own paltry overtures
against His omnipotence, and
our stubborn won't against
His forgiving will.

We are
subjected to a
constant stream of
insight and intuition,
as well as of inspiration
and revelation, that flows
from above in a cascade of
creativity. Divine direction
dictates that we walk along
illuminated pathways as we
implement our faculties of
mind and spirit, that we
might understand the
mysteries within The
Book of Mormon.

Wo
unto those
who groan under
darkness and under
the bondage of sin. They
squander precious resources
groping about in a frantic but
fruitless search for meaning in
their lives. In short, they fail to
appreciate the stabilizing power
that could have been theirs if
they had only focused upon
the nurturing influences
of The Book of Mormon
and the power of the
Atonement.

Sooner
or later, there
will come for each of
us who has undergone a
spiritual heart transplant a
moment in the sun, when the
steady light of understanding
illuminates our minds with the
truth of The Book of Mormon. God
confirms our divine potential as He
quickens the new organs beating in
our chests. It is He Who is responsible
for the unbroken sinus rhythm that
remains in perfect harmony with
the electricity that is in the
air, in heaven.

During our
Book of Mormon
inquiry, there may
come a time when we
"see the light." We may
be dazzled by an A-ha!
moment, when we have an
instant of sudden insight,
intuition, inspiration, and
even revelation, which is
made known to all the
children of God by
the obedience
of faith.

In between
the sights and
sounds, rides and
attractions, and thrills
and spills of our earthly
theme-park experience, it's
The Book of Mormon where we
discover how to utilize spiritual
hygiene practices that remove the
grit and grime that gathers as a
part of life, but still threaten to
foul our inner workings and
curtail our sensitivity to the
impressions that come to
each of us from
heaven.

It's within
the structure
of the principles
and the doctrines
and the ordinances
of The Book of Mormon
that our experiences in the
learning laboratories of life
begin to make sense. Therein
lies the inherent beauty of the
Plan and the key to its success.
Revelatory experiences will teach
us that "the brotherhood of man
is an element of Christianity no
less than is the Fatherhood of
God, and to deny one is no
less infidel than to deny
the other." (Lyman
Abbott).

If we choose not to rely
upon the light-generating
capacity of revelation, we'll be
doomed to dance about in flickering
shadows that illuminate nothing but the
caricatures of reality. The blind will stumble
about in the dark until the discrepancy between
their marginalized behavior and the ideals of
The Book of Mormon becomes so great that
their short-lived pleasure in worldly ways
will evaporate as the morning dew in
the full light of day.

God's great Plan of
Restoration (Alma 41:2), teaches that
Adam fell that we might come to earth in
order to prepare for a resurrection. (See Alma
12:24). Through the Atonement of Christ, we'll
be raised in that "great and last day" clothed
in immortality, in the kinds of bodies we'll
need to dwell in the various degrees of
glory for which we've qualified.
(2 Nephi 33:12).

The Great Plan of Salvation (see
Alma 42:5), hinges upon the ordinance of
baptism. Without it, we're doomed to suffer in
the shadows, where we'll experience only illusions of
reality. Without obedience, the discrepancy between our
marginalized behavior and the ideals of the Plan become
so intense that our short-lived pleasure in worldly ways
must evaporate as the morning dew in the light of day.
When this disparity reaches 'critical mass,' a requisite
readjustment must tear down the façade of corruption
and hypocrisy to allow the cultivation of a more
nurturing lifestyle only made possible by the
Atonement of Jesus Christ and related
obedience to the principles
of God's Plan.

Alma
taught the
principles that
relate to the Great
Plan of Happiness.
With no repentance, we
would remain in a wretched
state, and exist forever in our
sins. (See Alma 12:26). Without
baptism, if we were to partake of the
fruit of the tree of life, which is eternal
life, or the highest expression of the love
of God, it would be impossible to sustain a
celestial existence inasmuch as in our fallen
condition we would be incapable of obedience
to celestial principles. Thus, the Plan would
be frustrated. Mercy and Justice were placed
before Adam and Eve to bar the way to the
tree of life until they had the opportunity
to participate in the saving ordinances
of the gospel. (See Alma 12:21,
42:2, and Moses 4:31).

Alma taught that because of God's
Plan of Mercy, (Alma 42:15), the principle of
agency could be honored, allowing us to encounter
opposition in a mortal setting and to gain experience,
in spite of the fact that Justice would need to be served (in
the absence of repentance and the Atonement) were we to
violate eternal law in the process. When Jesus Christ
stepped forward and offered Himself as the Lamb
Slain From the Foundation of the World, the
Plan swung into action, allowing us to die
without jeopardizing our eternal glory,
subject to our repentance.

Among the Nephites and the
Lamanites in the New World, the great blessing
that stemmed from their regularly recurring repentance
was that by triggering the mechanism of the Atonement that
they might become clean in the sight of God, they were able to get
moving again on the pathway to perfection. After repentance, God
would remember their sins no more. It is true that they might have
recalled them, insofar as they increased their testimonies and
helped them to become more stalwart soldiers in the army of
Christ. But they would no longer be worn down by guilt
or be estranged from the Holy Ghost because of their
filthiness. They had been released from bondage
to sin, which was the most liberating gift
of God that they could receive.

The Nephites were led by their hope
of mercy to repentance and forgiveness because
of the infinite and eternal Atonement of Christ. The
miracle of their spiritual transformation was that, in a
long process of development, they would be privileged to
change their nature until it emulated the character of
the Savior. Because of His grace, they became the
beneficiaries of His implicit promise that all that
He had, He could give us, but what He was,
we could earn for ourselves, "line upon
line, and precept upon precept."
(2 Nephi 28:30).

It was on the very night of the
Savior's birth that the Nephites in the New
World saw how "it came to pass that a new star
did appear." (3 Nephi 1:21). Unwittingly, they became
additional witnesses to His birth. As a result, they began
"to have peace in the land. And there were no contentions." (3
Nephi 1:23-24). The Star shining brightly in the East was
symbolic of their focus on Jesus Christ and the miracle
that had come to pass in far-away Bethlehem. His
gospel became their fortification, and obedience
to their covenants their sanctuary against
the winds of wickedness that were
stirring in the land of
Zarahemla.

Without the intrinsic light
pulsing from nearly every page of The
Book of Mormon, we risk being seduced by a
siren song that is carried on waves of darkness, that
can create an insatiable desire for the world's goods. With
impaired hearing, we may trade life on the straight and narrow
path for what we think is a much-needed vacation in Idumea. If we
follow through on that misguided temptation, and check ourselves in
to "Fantasy Island," we will lose power, purpose, and focus. If we think
that it is better to rely more on our own strength than upon spiritual
preparedness, we will be more inclined in times of crisis to grasp
at the world's goods, rather than to drop to our knees, tightly
hold on to our faith, and with the help of our Father in
Heaven, dig our way out of our problems.

The Book of Mormon answers
questions that we never thought to ask
with spiritual statements from the Holy
Ghost that are undeniable and irrefutable.
He will illuminate our minds with answers,
but only after we have posed good questions.
When the Psalmist wrote: "Be still, and know
that I am God" (Psalms 46:10), he knew that
in quiet moments during our inquiry, we
would experience spiritual symmetry and
intellectual focus that, in response to our
petitions, would allow us to enjoy a
profound comprehension of both
heaven and hell, as well as
everything in between.

If we will not deny His
power, the time will come when we will be
"sanctified in Christ by the grace of God, thru
the shedding of the blood of Christ, which is in the
covenant of the Father unto the remission of our
sins, that we become holy, without spot."
(Moroni 10:33). This is the essence of
many gifts we receive thru the
grace of the Savior.

We know that angels don't really have wings, and yet, we still visualize the angel Moroni, who, John wrote, flew "in the midst of heaven, having the everlasting gospel to preach unto them that dwell on the earth." (Revelation 14:6). Old perceptions die hard, and it does no violence to our faith to dream that we can soar with eagles. After all, Peter Pan told Wendy that as long as we have faith, trust, and pixie dust, we can fly! He reassured her: "So come with me, where dreams are born. Just think of happy things, and your heart will fly on wings, forever, in Never Land!" As he explained: The reason that birds can fly and we can't is that they have perfect faith, for to have faith is to have wings." Who can say if the angels who will come for us to carry us Home will wrap us in their wings and lift us heavenward by taking the second star on the right and continuing straight on 'til morning?

Book of Mormon study should be a time to ponder and pray and move deliberately, rather than wander and play on the monkey jungle of life. For a change, our study is not a race. It is not necessary to plow through a prescribed number of chapters or verses each day. We can spend time focusing on just a single principle, turning it over and over in our minds. We can read ourselves full, think ourselves straight, pray ourselves hot, and let ourselves go. The fresh perspectives that develop should be truly amazing.

Book of Mormon
study may be a time
when we take a break from
our academic endeavors. If
we allow the Spirit to guide
us, it will utilize that time to
turn our attention to divine
tutorial training, that we
might receive the gift
of wisdom that no
textbook could
provide.

When the Nephites and
Lamanites were at their best they
reflected poise under provocation, were
slow to anger, were sensitive to the needs of
others, and were empathetic and humble. They
were less concerned with telestial trinkets and
more focused on celestial sureties. They were
selfless, and had no secret agenda to follow.
They were repulsed by sin, rejoiced in the
truth, were drawn toward the light,
and were continually open to
that which was good.

Whenever
free-will, is exercised, two
conditions quickly become obvious:
the first is the opportunity to make choices
in an atmosphere of opposition, and second is the
necessity of facing consequences that are associated
with those choices. The urgency of reconciliation to heaven's
laws through the Atonement of Jesus Christ is not so apparent,
but it is equally important. The unconverted find it difficult to
understand that when we are diligent in our Book of Mormon study,
our free will enjoys its greatest expression. Unprincipled character is
easily swayed by the siren song so seductively sent by Satan, and
undisciplined minds crumble in the face of telestial temptations
that are so tantalizing and yet so traumatizing, when they
divert our attention from what really matters. The more
we focus on the idols of the day, the less will we
recognize the legitimate rule of heaven
that truly governs our affairs.

As we plumb the depths of The
Book of Mormon, the discipline of faith will
demand that it is "not enjoyment, and not sorrow
that is our destined end or way; but to act, that each
tomorrow (might) find us farther than today. Lives of
great men and women all remind us that we can make our
lives sublime, and departing, leave behind us footprints on
the sands of time. Let us then be up and doing, with a
heart for any fate; still achieving, still pursuing.
Learn to labor, and to wait." (Henry
Wadsworth Longfellow).

We need to make
the most of whatever time we
have left, because 'now' is our turn
on earth. "There is no time like the present,
and no present like time, and life can be over
in the space of a rhyme." (Georgia Bynge). It's
been purported that the last six months of our
mission here will be the best, so begin now
to read The Book of Mormon, if you
haven't already done so!

When we are truly
learned, we are wise (see 2 Nephi
9:28), if we will only allow The Book
of Mormon to work its magic, and take the
form of a recognizable and spiritually coherent
pattern of stability and power that will change
our lives. When we clothe ourselves in that
coat of many colors, we will experience
a spiritual rebirth, not only of
maturation, but also
of generation.

How we have chosen
to engage The Book of Mormon
is a dry run. It is a pop quiz in the
curriculum of life that provides insight
into how we will accept the Savior Himself
at the time of His Second Coming (which is
an event that will be equally surprising, to
many). It will help us to avoid the fate of
those who will ignorantly ask at that
time: "What are these wounds
in Thine hands?" (D&C
45:51).

Our Father in Heaven
has promised Christ's merits
unto all, so that those who repent
are immediately beloved of Him. (See
2 Nephi 31:19). A similar feeling descended
upon the people of Zarahemla, who, after having
been taught by King Benjamin in an address that
has been compared to a General Conference sermon,
"were filled with joy, having received a remission
of their sins, and having peace of conscience,
because of the exceeding faith which
they had in Jesus Christ."
(Mosiah 4:3).

The
Book of Mormon
is like a mathematical
primer. It encourages us to
do more than simply multiply
mirrors or study the angles. If we
pay attention to its principles, our
Father in Heaven will summon the
Holy Ghost to illuminate the way
before us, by permitting us to see
with the eyes of understanding
a heavenly light that envelops
His Son in revelatory
rapture.

The Book of Mormon joins the Bible in
the rarified atmosphere of holy scripture as a
witness of Jesus Christ (see Ezekiel 37:17), but it
also testifies of the restoration of His gospel in these
Last Days. Before we united ourselves with the Saints,
we stood on neutral ground. However, when we entered the
fold through the strait and narrow way of baptism, we could
never again have it both ways. Those who have seen the Light
become His ambassadors who are enthusiastic to stand as
His witnesses "at all times and in all places, (that they
might) be redeemed of God, and be numbered with
those of the first resurrection, that (they might)
have eternal life." (Mosiah 18:9).

Alma provided inspired counsel
when he told his eldest son Helaman
that "it is as easy to give heed to the word of
Christ" Who is our compass, "which will point (us) to
a straight course to eternal bliss, as it was for our fathers
to give heed to this compass," the Liahona," which would point
unto them a straight course to the promised land. Do not let us be
slothful," he urged, or move slowly, "because of the easiness of the
way ... Look to God, and live." (Alma 37:37-38, & 47). The
teachings of prophets like Alma in The Book of Mormon
(see 1 Nephi 18:16, Jacob 3:1, Mosiah 4:3, Mormon
8:33, & Moroni 10:32), bless us with a perfect
opportunity to look up to God. It is our
choice whether we will thereby live,
by doing so.

Without giving it even
a moments' thought, modern-day
Lamanites will seek out a Starbucks
to shell out $8.00 for a cup of hot cocoa,
or $3.50 for a plastic bottle that is likely
filled with tap water. People of affluence
too often "beat my people to pieces, and
grind the faces of the poor, saith the
Lord of Hosts." (2 Nephi
13:15).

Too often, telestially distracted
Nephites amused themselves with games
of Trivial Pursuit, mistaking it for the Game of
Life. The real face of sin, for them and for us, is waste.
It is doing one thing, when something else of far greater
good could be done in its stead. It is settling for mediocrity
when the more challenging road leads to greater heights with
spectacular vistas ahead, just around the next turn in the road.
Sin is a capitulation to spiritual stagnation and a forfeiture
of our eager acceptance of eternal progression's enthusiasm.
It is trading a mess of pottage for our eternal birthright.
It is nothing more than an overnight stay in a
second-class hotel, while God's five star
all-inclusive resort property lies
behind pearly gates, just
down the road.

The nature of the calling of the Three Nephite
disciples was to bear witness to all the world that our
Savior Jesus Christ is the Son of God, Who said, "follow
thou me," and taught the way to salvation and exaltation.
(3 Nephi 31:10, & 3 Nephi Chapter 28). In every age, the Lord's
anointed have been long-suffering, unlike the money lenders
of Babylon who charge usurious interest and who call their
notes mercilessly and with a vengeance. His disciples
consecrate their resources to Him, while the land
grabbers of Babylon plunder the earth and
squander its bounty.

The Book of Mormon teaches that one day, Israel will recognize
Jesus as the Messiah. And so, "by the authority of the Holy Priesthood of
God that has again been restored to the earth, and by the ministration under
the direction of the Prophet of God, Apostles of the Lord Jesus Christ have been to
the Holy Land and have dedicated that country for the return of the Jews; and
we believe that in the due time of the Lord they shall be in the favor of God
again. And let no Latter-day Saint be guilty of taking any part
in any crusade against these people." (Heber J. Grant, C.R.,
10/7/1921 – 27 years before the creation of the State of
Israel, and exactly 103 years before the unprovoked
attack on Israel by the terrorist organization
Hamas, whose stated intention is to kill
every Jew and wipe Israel from the
face of the earth).

For far too long, even though
the majestic clockwork of the Restoration
of the gospel has defined the way to both our
temporal and our spiritual date with destiny, it
has fallen on deaf ears. "Is it not a shame," asked
William Tyndall nearly 500 years ago, "that we
Christians come so oft to church in vain, when
he of four score years old knoweth no more
than he that was born yesterday?" The
restoration of the gospel and The Book
of Mormon have finally redefined
the parameters of eternal
equations.

As we read, and fear, and
hope, and pray, we lift the latch to force the
way" (Sir Walter Scott). We "labor for feeling,
knowledge, and understanding, even as we beware
superstition and the persuasion of worldly wisdom,
philosophy, hypocrisy, and ceremonies." As the Holy
Ghost benevolently enlightens our minds with the
doctrine and principles of The Book of Mormon,
"we walk in the plain and open truth."
(William Tyndall).

At least for the time
being, the truth that is found in The
Book of Mormon blazes brightly, liberated
from the intensity of martyr's fires. We pray
that never again will the church of the devil
"suffer no man to know God's word, but
burn it and make heresy of it."
(William Tyndall).

Elohim (see Exodus
3:18, & "The Father and the Son:
A Doctrinal Exposition by The First
Presidency and the Twelve, 6/30/1916), is
the Father of our spirits as well as of our spiritual
regeneration, Who has imprinted within our sinews
His genetic code. It lies hidden within our DNA sequences,
waiting for our wits to grow sharper so that we may rediscover
our divine lineage. We were born of Him as His spirit children, we
have acquired His qualities and characteristics, and we were raised by
Him to spiritual maturity, until we could progress no more as long as we
remained in our first estate. Therefore, we were added upon, leaving His
presence to fulfill our mortal missions. Even now, as "strangers and
pilgrims on the earth," we are still His spirit sons and daughters
who bear the DNA evidence of His divine nature. (See Hebrews
11:13). The Book of Mormon is our witness that, with the
Restoration of the gospel genome, these truths have
burst forth in a supernal display of
celestial energy.

When we move from the darkness of benighted
thought into the brilliant sunshine and clarity of the
light of truth that shines forth from The Book of Mormon, we
will find ourselves standing shoulder to shoulder with Alma to
"manifest unto the people that (we have) been born of God." (Alma
36:23). We will conquer the self-defeating behaviors and flawed
character traits that had aforetime limited our progression. Our
salvation will consist in our "being placed beyond the power
of our enemies, meaning the enemies of our progression,
such as dishonesty, greediness, lying, immorality,
and other vices." (Joseph Smith).

The Savior's birth remains
the greatest story that has ever been
told. The faithful of every age preserved
and passed on the tale, although, in time,
there were many for whom the Bible had become
a magical book, conveying power and knowledge
without the aid of revelation. Moroni envisioned those
living in the Last Days who had "transfigured the holy
word of God," or who had changed the appearance and
substance of the scriptures. (Mormon 8:33). We
are blessed to have the magic of 3 Nephi to
flesh out the meager narratives of the
four more familiar Gospels of
Matthew, Mark, Luke,
and John.

During the reign of righteous King
Mosiah, most of the Nephites in Zarahemla
hoped to live within sight of a church, while the
Sons of Mosiah wished they could live within a
hundred yards of hell. Sometimes, the Lord will
send His most capable missionaries to His most
wicked children. He arms them with unwavering
faith, a certain knowledge of gospel principles,
firm and abiding testimonies of the doctrines
of the Kingdom, of God's Plan, and of the
Savior, a blessing and setting-apart by
file leaders, the continual prayers of
the faithful, and an endowment
of spiritual power received
in holy precincts.

When we read
The Book of Mormon,
we sometimes can hear the
rustling of the robes of angels
and their voices from the celestial
city as the sound of trumpets speaking
to us, declaring: "Peace on earth, good will
to men." "The heavens declare the glory of God,
and the firmament sheweth his handiwork. (Psalms
19:1). "His voice is heard in the rolling thunder, and His
speech is recorded in the lilac's bloom." (Bruce R. McConkie).
The earth, the sun, the moon, and the stars all "roll upon their
wings in their glory, in the midst of the power of God. All
these things are kingdoms, and any man who hath
seen any or the least of these hath seen God
moving in his majesty and power."
(D&C 84:45-47).

King Benjamin taught: "There is
no other name given whereby salvation
cometh; therefore … take upon you the name
of Christ." (Mosiah 5:8). "Yea, come unto Christ,
and be perfected in him, and deny yourselves of
all ungodliness; and if ye shall deny yourselves
of all ungodliness, and love God with all your
might, mind and strength, then is his grace
sufficient for you, that by his grace ye
may be perfect in Christ."
(Moroni 10:32).

As we read The Book of
Mormon, we lend our voices to the
angelic host to proclaim with them
that our Savior Jesus Christ was born
in Bethlehem. Glory to the newborn
Babe Whose kingdom of heaven is
at hand; yea, He "cometh in his
glory, in his might, majesty,
power, and dominion."
(Alma 5:50).

The memory of the birth of the Savior
could have quietly faded away, but as time passed
and events unfolded, there was instead "no greater drama
in human record than the sight of a few Christians, scorned or
oppressed by a succession of emperors, bearing all trials with a fierce
tenacity, multiplying quietly, building order while their enemies
generated chaos, fighting the sword with the word, brutality with
hope, and at last defeating the strongest state that history had
ever known. Caesar and Christ had met in the arena, and
Christ had won." (Will Durant). Unfortunately, in the
Last Days, the battle lines are once again being
drawn and the conflict is being rekindled
by the enemy of all righteousness.

In The Book
of Mormon, we see our
own passports to perfection. It
invites us to hitch a ride upon the
coat-tails of the Gods, Who will carry
us as upon the wings of eagles with a first
class ticket to our arrival gate in heaven, and
escort us thru baggage claim, port of entry, and
customs control, to the pearly gates, thru which we
will be greeted by angels at our final destination.
Our celestially inspired Book of Mormon travel
brochure suggests that it will be a five-star all
inclusive resort in a room with a garden
view of glory all spread out before us
(and not only housekeeping, but
also daily breakfast is
included).

Alma had been born again, and had
been set free by the perfect Law of Liberty to reach
his potential. (See Mosiah Chapter 27). As Paul taught
the Romans: "We are buried with him by baptism into death:
that like as Christ was raised up from the dead by the glory of
the Father, even so we also should walk in newness of life."
(Romans 6:3). When we are born again, we are as the
acorns of a mighty oak, and we are vitalized by
His nurturing influence to burst forth
to reach the full stature of
our spirits.

When we have become as
our little ones, "submissive, meek,
humble, patient, (and) full of love," the
enticings of the Holy Spirit will help us
to put off our natural inclinations
and become saints through the
Atonement of Jesus Christ.
(Mosiah 3:19).

As we read and study The Book of
Mormon, we realize that its messages were
intended to change our nature, that we might
progress to the point where we reflect God's attributes
in perfection. Our chaste behavior reflects our love of all
of our Heavenly Father's children. Our righteous stewardship
is but a shadow of His omnipotence. As the Spirit expands the
boundaries of our faith, we quietly scratch the surface of our
comprehension of omniscience. We begin to appreciate the
significance of Christ's mortal ministry, and we
determine to inaugurate our own journey to
Bethlehem, Gethsemane, the Garden
Tomb, and the Silver City.

The fine line between
"want" and "need" was often blurred by
the Nephites, who focused on telestial trinkets
and temporal trash. Spiritual stagnation made it
hard to recognize the differences between poverty and
wealth. But when they were at their best, they were
more comfortable seeking spiritual gifts rather
than the profane baubles of the world and
the ornaments of the ungodly.

"Be still, and know that I am God,"
counseled the Lord. (D&C 101:16). With that
quiet confirmation comes the admonition to see
that we serve Him with all our heart, might, mind,
and strength. (See D&C 4:2). All that He asks of us
is that we focus our affections, will-power, reasoning
faculties, and physical efforts on our worship. To help
us do that, God gave us not only the Greatest Story
Ever Told, but also The Book of Mormon, and as
icing on the cake, He gave us the Holy Ghost,
as well, to bear witness of all that He
had done. (See John 14:6).

The Book of Mormon teaches us
that there are no "God forsaken" souls, for
all have access to the Light of Christ, and to the
intimate comfort of prayer. The only reason we may
not feel close to Him is because it is we who have moved,
and not He. The story is told of two friends at Auschwitz
Concentration Camp during World War II. One felt completely
alone and forgotten, his situation hopeless. The other knelt down
each morning to pray, and his companion finally berated him
for it. "For what could you possibly thank God, given our
terrible circumstances?" he asked. His friend simply
replied, "I thank God every day that He didn't
make me like them."

When we read and study The
Book of Mormon, we need to lower our
defensive shields and believe in a book that
might seem incredulous to us if we were to think
about it rationally. All of us have "limiting beliefs,"
which are those stories we tell ourselves that cause us to
sabotage our own best intentions and efforts. They haunt us
as they diminish our abilities and obscure our goals. Most people
don't realize it's possible to change them, and for that matter, may
not even realize that they have them. Breaking free from limiting
beliefs can unleash the power of our potential. In fact, The
Book of Mormon is full of magic patiently waiting
for our wits to grow sharper so that
we can appreciate it.

The Book of Mormon
quotes Isaiah as it alludes to
Mary, and to the birth of Jesus in
Bethlehem. (See 2 Nephi 17:45). She
was a young woman who had obviously
accepted her special calling with profound
sobriety, and who was prepared to sacrifice other
opportunities for self-fulfillment to instead nurture
her Newborn Son. As a writer once asked: "Are women
who enjoy motherhood intellectual dropouts? What
would have become of the human race had Eve
rejected motherhood in favor of pursuing a
more gratifying career in the already
promising apple industry?"
("Time Magazine").

The book of Nephi, who was
the son of Nephi, who was the son of
Helaman reads like a fifth Gospel in The
Book of Mormon. It illustrates how the Lord
came into the world to generate enthusiasm in
His disciples, create confidence in their hearts, and
show them how He could fix their mistakes rather than
assigning blame. He was certain of His authority, but He
still delegated responsibility. He knew how, but more often
showed how. He never reduced work to drudgery, but rather
elevated it to excitement. Instead of concentrating power,
he generated co-operation. He never drove His disciples
forward, but was always out in front of them
leading them to green pastures
and still waters.

As we read and study The Book of
Mormon, we give thanks for our bishops,
fathers, mothers, teachers, ministers, friends, and
neighbors, who have selflessly and even unconsciously
strengthened our testimonies and nurtured our struggling
spirits so that we might have a more sure witness of the Savior.
Sir Isaac Newton, whose accomplishments included defining the
theory of gravity and the laws of motion, inventing calculus, and
writing his Philosophiae Naturalis Principia Mathematica, (or
Principia), one of the most important works in the history
of science. Asked how he was able to do it all, he simply
replied: "I stood on the shoulders of giants."

The Book of Mormon
is a primer on gratitude. But what
if, when we attempt to master that trait, we
think it's almost too late? "Don't be discouraged
if you haven't been an especially grateful person,"
counseled Joseph Wirthlin. "Rejoice, and think of what
an impression you will make on those who thought they
knew you! Think of how delightfully surprised they
will be when they realize how much you have
changed!" (See Mosiah 5:2-5).

When we make our first forays into
The Book of Mormon, we remember that if we
always do what we always did, we'll always get what we
always got. Even if we are on the right road, we're going to
get run over if we just sit there. Those who seek improvement
have high ideals that "are like stars. We will not succeed in
touching them with our hands. But, like the seafaring
man in the desert of waters, we choose them as our
guides, and following them, we will reach
our destiny." (Carl Shurz).

The Book of Mormon helps us to yield
to the Savior that with which it is most difficult
for us to part: our former selves. We are free to choose,
but we cannot choose to escape the consequences of our poor
decisions. In the novel "The Picture of Dorian Grey," by Oscar
Wilde, a particularly handsome young man's portrait degenerates
over time in response to his moral depravity and self-indulgence, while
at the same time his face retains its alabaster innocence. He adheres to the
philosophy that the only way to eliminate a temptation is to yield to it. After
many years of decadence have taken a mighty toll on his character, he loses his
mind, grabs a knife and attacks the picture that with such stark realism and
accuracy has reflected his mounting debauchery. The servants of the house
awaken to a cry from his locked room and break down the door. There
lies the body of an unrecognizable old man, stabbed in the heart,
his face withered and decrepit. By the ring on his finger,
they identify the disfigured corpse as their master.
Beside the emaciated figure is the picture
of Dorian Gray that has reverted
to its original loveliness.

Commentary, Compendia, & Observations Index

Moroni taught:
Those who believe "in
Christ, doubting nothing,
whatsoever he shall ask the
Father in the name of Christ
it shall be granted him; and
this promise is unto all" who
have faith in the power of
God to reveal His will.
(Mormon 9:21).

Commentary
Volume One
Born in The Wilderness

- 1 Nephi
- 2 Nephi
- Jacob
- Enos
- Jarom
- Omni
- Words of Mormon
- Observations
- Author's Note
- Addendum – A Sampling of Scriptures

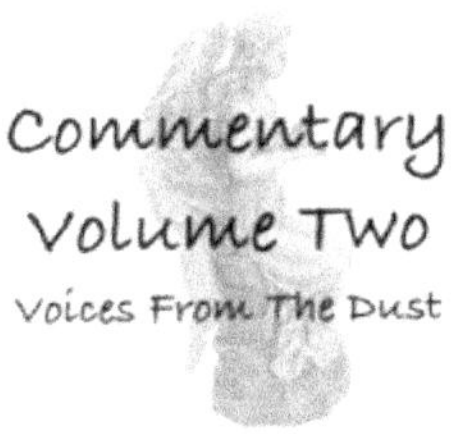

Commentary
Volume Two
Voices From The Dust

- Mosiah
- Alma
- Observations
- Author's Note
- Addendum – A Sampling of Scriptures

Commentary
Volume Three
Journey to Cumorah

- Helaman
- 3 Nephi
- 4 Nephi
- Mormon
- Ether
- Moroni
- Observations
- Author's Note
- Addendum – A Sampling of Scriptures

When
situational
ethics guide our
behavior, and when
every man walketh in
his own way, and after
the image of his own god,
the erosion of our capacity to
accept Latter-day scripture will
be met by the chaotic collision
of cultural disintegration
with the stability of
the gospel.

Compendium
Volume One

- Introduction
- Questions Answered by The Book of Mormon
- Topical Index
- Observations
- A few of my favorite things
- Familiar Scriptures
- Commentary & Compendium Index

Compendium
Volume Two

- Introduction
- Questions Answered by The Book of Mormon
- Topical Index
- Without The Book of Mormon
- Observations
- Introduction to the Isaiah Chapters
- "And it came to pass in The Book of Mormon
- "Ad thus we see" in The Book of Mormon
- "Behold" in The Book of Mormon
- "Wherefore" and "Therefore in The Book of Mormon
- The Appearance of Gold
- The Use of The Name of Christ
- Pragmatism in The Book of Mormon
- Dry Humor in The Book of Mormon
- A Book of Mormon Timeline
- Commentary and Compendium Index

Compendium
Volume Three

- Compendia Index
- Essays That Relate to Teachings in The Book of Mormon
- Observations
- Commentary, Compendium, & Observations Index

Compendium
Volume Four

- Compendia Index
- Essays That Relate to Teachings in The Book of Mormon
- Observations
- Commentary, Compendium, & Observations Index

Compendium
Volume Five

- Compendia Index
- Essays That Relate to Teachings in The Book of Mormon
- Observations
- Commentary, Compendium, & Observations Index

Do we really think it is
easier to yield to temptation,
and more difficult to resist sin?
Is rebellion easier because it is more
difficult to acknowledge and then to
act upon the revelations of God that are
found in The Book of Mormon? Can it be
easier to live in disorienting and swirling
fog of conflicting values, and harder to
be guided by what He has written
with His finger on the fleshy
tables of our hearts?

Compendium
Volume Six

- Compendia Index
- Essays That Relate to Teachings
  in The Book of Mormon
- Observations
- Commentary, Compendium, & Observations Index

Compendium
Volume Seven

- Compendia Index
- Essays That Relate to Teachings
  in The Book of Mormon
- Observations
- Commentary, Compendium, & Observation Index

Compendium
Volume Eight

- Introduction
- Hebrew Poetry in The Book of Mormon
- Synonymous Parallelism
- Antithetical Parallelism
- Synthetic Parallelism
- Climactic Parallelism
- Chiasmus
- Book of Mormon Scriptures Illustrating

Observations
Volume One

- 550 Observations

Observations
Volume Two

- 550 Observations

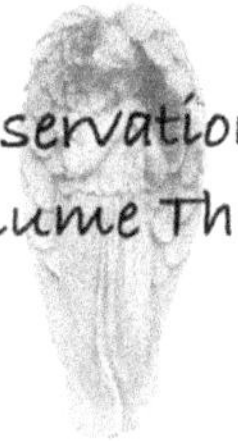

Observations
Volume Three

- 550 Observations

Observations
Volume Four

- 550 Observations

Often, it
is only when
we have enrolled
in the graduate school
of hard knocks, and have
pre-paid the required tuition,
that we obtain the credits that
are earned by our obedience to
the promptings of the Spirit that
are the form and the substance of
revelation. If we will take the time to
read The Book of Mormon, we will be
at our best. W\We will find ourselves
particularly sensitive to the comfort
that can come thru the revelatory
whisperings of the Spirit.

Observations
Volume 5

- 550 Observations
- Commentary, Compendium, & Observations Index

Observations
Volume 6

- 550 Observations
- Commentary, Compendium, & Observations Index

Heavenly Father
tenders the currency of
revelation to purchase the
golden tickets for our passage
back Home. We reimburse Him with
soul-sweat, as it works on our sense
of duty, on our conscience, and on our
scruples, to nurture our faith to believe.
We no longer see things as they are and
wonder: 'Why?' Instead, we dream about
things that never were, and ask: 'Why
not?' The Book of Mormon helps us
to work thru our problems rather
than working around
them.

A Book of Mormon Commentary
Volumes One -Three

Compendia
Volumes One - Eight

Observations
Volumes One - Six